the ALLERGY self-help cookbook

the ALLERGY self-help cookbook

Over 325 natural foods recipes, free of wheat, milk, eggs, corn, yeast, sugar and other common food allergens

by Marjorie Hurt Jones, R.N.

Rodale Press, Emmaus, Pa.

Printed in the United States of America on recycled paper
containing a high percentage of de-inked fiber.

Library of Congress Cataloging in Publication Data

Jones, Marjorie Hurt.
    The allergy self-help cookbook.

    Includes indexes.
    1. Food allergy—Diet therapy—Recipes. I. Title.
RC588.D53J65 1984   641.5′631   84-8419
ISBN 0-87857-505-7   hardcover

2   4   6   8   10   9   7   5   3   1   hardcover

Address all inquiries to: Rodale Books
                            Rodale Press, Inc.
                            33 East Minor Street
                            Emmaus, Pennsylvania 18049

Notice

While self-help is vital to effective relief of allergies, many readers will also need medical guidance. In infants and children, for instance, food allergy may be hard to distinguish from a serious infection without medical help.

The information in this book can help you to control your food allergies; however, it is not meant to replace medical diagnosis or treatment. If you are under the care of a physician for your allergies, be sure to inform him or her of any major changes you make in your diet or environment. In some cases, your medication may need to be adjusted.

Dedicated to the memory of my parents,
Helen Talbert
Earl L. Hurt

Contents

List of Tables, Charts and Graphs

Preface

I've been coping with allergies all my life. As an adolescent, I sneezed my way through every hay fever season. My skin itched if I wore wool and burned when I used soap. But I didn't develop food allergies until just a few years ago. Then my life got a real jolt. When anyone reacts adversely to milk, wheat or other basic foods in a normal diet, eating becomes an obstacle course. Trying to cook, dine out or share meals with others is a mind-boggling challenge.

I searched libraries and bookstores for a cookbook that would help me. I found a number of allergy cookbooks—all practically useless. One book was touted as being wheat free, yet nearly all of the recipes contained milk and dairy products, eggs and corn—equally common food allergens. Another cookbook claimed to omit wheat, corn, milk, eggs and yeast, but it was divided into a separate section for each category. So it was of little help to anyone who had to avoid all five, or who cooked for a family in which people were allergic to different foods.

Still other so-called allergy cookbooks used questionable ingredients such as coffee, cocoa, chocolate chips, flavored gelatin, imitation maple flavoring, marshmallows, nondairy creamers, hickory-smoked barbecue sauce, maraschino cherries and soft drinks—to name just a few. Those items are chock full of artificial flavors and colors, additives that can trigger or aggravate allergies in asthmatics and other allergic people.

To make matters worse, most recipes I found called for salt, sugar and saturated fats, ingredients that contribute to a number of chronic diseases, whether you have food allergies or not.

So I set to work adapting my own recipes. Of necessity, I began to keep a notebook of my work. For example, to find an alternative to wheat, I experimented with rice flour, amaranth and other flours. I learned that each performed differently. In the same way, I began to explore new foods to fill other gaps—new fruits and vegetables, less allergenic meats, and other wholesome, but little used, foods.

While developing these recipes, I got a lot of feedback from other people with food allergies. I taught adult education classes on Coping with Allergies sponsored by the Nutrition for Optimal Health Association (NOHA), an educational organization in the Chicago area. People in those classes helped me to understand what they considered to be their greatest needs. I heard pleas like, "I need a recipe for a grain-free cake for my child's birthday party next week." Or, "We miss cookies at our house!" Or, "I'd be so happy if I could only eat bread again."

I met other people in the waiting room of Thomas Stone, M.D., a clinical ecologist in Rolling Meadows, Illinois. Many of them shared invaluable tips with me. Others raised problems they faced. And Dr. Stone himself offered some helpful recommendations.

The result of my work and experience is a cookbook geared toward every allergic person who's ever stood in front of an open refrigerator and wondered, "What can I eat?" You'll be able to confidently plan menus for every mealtime need—breakfast, lunch, dinner, dessert, snacks, beverages, picnics and holidays.

Cooking at my house has gotten a lot simpler since I figured out how to sidestep food allergies yet still prepare delicious meals. This book will show you how to do the same.

Acknowledgments

I want to thank the following people who have shared their expertise and time with me. It is no exaggeration to acknowledge that without the help of these valued friends and professionals this book would not have happened. Their input is most appreciated.

William G. Crook, M.D., of Jackson, Tennessee, clinical ecologist, who explained to me how *Candida albicans* may be the culprit when allergies fail to respond to dietary adjustments alone.

Susan Dart, of Lake Forest, Illinois, whose natural foods column helped shape my thinking.

Sharon Faelten, of Bethlehem, Pennsylvania, my editor, who literally shaped this book from my copious manuscripts.

Marjorie Fisher, of Evanston, Illinois, president of the Chicago Chapter of the Human Ecology Action League (HEAL), and resource for food families and game meat.

Stanley Jones, of Deerfield, Illinois, my husband, whose patience and support became legendary through a rough year.

Jane Kinderlehrer, of Allentown, Pennsylvania, who learned of my work and recommended me as an author.

Kenneth Patchen, of Mundelein, Illinois, grower and supplier of amaranth, who kept me supplied and supported my work.

Barbara Peter, of Lake Forest, Illinois, professional home economist and resource for information on soy food.

Theron Randolph, M.D., of Chicago, Illinois, clinical ecologist, who returned my calls to answer questions along the way.

Barbara Sachsel, of Highland Park, Illinois, my nutritional mentor, who was always available to discuss issues.

Thomas Stone, M.D., of Rolling Meadows, Illinois, clinical ecologist, who opened his office to me and answered questions.

Introduction

Some of the best-loved dishes of the world are the result of the necessity to improvise with foods a cook had on hand. Bouillabaisse, the French stew of assorted fish, was first thrown together by fishermen on the docks at Marseilles. Minestrone, the versatile Italian soup, is a catchall for the bounty of ingredients available at harvest. Chili, borscht, cornbread and countless other dietary staples all grew out of the need to make do with limited ingredients.

Food allergy is just another limitation that can be turned to the cook's advantage. This book will help you eliminate common allergens by giving you alternatives to standard ingredients and teaching you how to prepare good-tasting meals that the whole family will enjoy. It picks up where the doctor's diagnosis leaves off— when you come home and say to yourself, "What do I do now? How will I ever manage without milk? Or eggs? How can I make food the kids will eat?"

This book will show you how, step-by-step. If there's one "catch," it's that all your cooking will have to be done from scratch. But as you chop, measure, stir and blend, you'll feel confident in knowing *exactly* what goes into the meals you eat. And you'll once again be able to enjoy dishes you thought were out of the question.

Remember sandwiches? They're possible again. And you'll find recipes for breads, rolls, muffins, crackers and flatbreads.

You'll be able to make desserts that are tasty enough to serve to company, including cakes, ice cream and cookies for holiday festivities and children's birthday parties. You'll learn to prepare creamy soups without milk, cream or wheat flour for thickener.

And you'll be able to make beverages that have no milk or sugar, to drink as is or pour on cereal. With homemade sauces and condiments, you control the ingredients. And you can enjoy wheat-free, egg-free pasta. (That's right, you can have "spaghetti" and meatballs again!)

You'll find recipes for dips, spreads, meats, fish, poultry, game and snack foods for camping, traveling and picnics—in short, enough to make any family with food allergies completely self-reliant.

And well nourished. My nursing experience and background in biology led me to take management of food allergies one step further, into nutrition. Anyone whose diet is restricted in any way has special nutritional needs. For example, people who can't drink milk or eat cheese are sacrificing nature's most concentrated sources of calcium and usually need to take a supplement to make up the deficit. People who are allergic to citrus fruits often need a supplemental source of vitamin C. Yet they also may be allergic to vitamin C supplements made with cornstarch. So nutrition, too, is addressed.

Only wholesome, health-building ingredients are used. You won't find any refined sugar, salt, hydrogenated fat (or excessive use of other fats). Those foods contribute to high blood pressure and heart disease, among other health problems, and compound the problems of people with food allergies. And because the recipes use brown rice, buckwheat and a wide variety of legumes, nuts, seeds, fruits and vegetables, they're high in fiber. That helps to prevent diverticular disease, colo-rectal cancer and other lower gastrointestinal problems. So these recipes help you eat the best diet you can in terms of both allergies *and* overall health.

Another important aspect of a successful food allergy diet is food rotation. By avoiding a specific food allergen for several months and then spacing consumption of that food once every four days or longer, many people may eventually tolerate allergenic foods more easily and eat a less restricted diet. (See the section, Planning a Diversified Rotary Diet.)

Because the kitchen is the center of food preparation, I've offered several tips on how to minimize exposure to molds, household cleaners and other potential allergy triggers in the kitchen. And because you may want to dine out occasionally, I've also shared tips on how to select food in restaurants.

You'll soon find that this is not just a collection of recipes, but an allergy cookbook in the truest sense—a how-to manual for people with food allergies to live by. To help you further, the Appendix lists purchasing sources for a number of less allergenic foods and useful cooking aids—sort of a "yellow pages" for allergic cooks.

All this planning does take commitment, but it's worth it, because you'll feel better and you can look forward to eating "normal" delicious food. My favorite comment came from a man who came to fix one of my kitchen appliances and sampled Cookies on Parade, which I happened to be baking that day. He munched a few and said, "What do you mean, they're for a special diet? They taste like real food to me!"

That's what's so special about this cookbook. It's all real food.

PART I
Getting Started

Exploring
New Ingredients

Once you know which foods you're allergic to, the next step is to learn to make the most of what you *can* eat. In developing recipes for this book, I've concentrated on finding alternatives to common allergens—milk, wheat and other common grains, sugar and corn sweeteners, butter and fruits and vegetables such as citrus and green beans. I've also tried not to overemphasize eggs or soy—or any other common food, for that matter—since anyone can be allergic to any food. And I've introduced recipes for little-used but less allergenic foods such as lamb, rabbit, spaghetti squash and amaranth flour, to name just a few.

In exploring new ingredients, it pays to be an optimist. Is the glass half empty or half full? Are you going to mourn the foods you can't have or focus on what you *can* eat? You'll find that cooking and eating are more enjoyable if you approach your diet with a positive sense of adventure.

Milk Alternatives

Milk is difficult to avoid when buying commercially prepared foods, but it's one of the easier foods to sidestep when cooking from scratch.

Second to breastfeeding, most allergy doctors suggest soy milk for infants and toddlers who are allergic to cow's milk. Many older children and adults can use soy milk, too, more so with cereal or in cooking and baking than as a drink. Prepared soy milk is available in health food stores everywhere, although flavor and palatability vary from product to product. Or you can make your own soy milk, using the tried-and-true Cornell University method given in this book (see Index). Demand for soy milk also has led to the development of soy ice cream and other soy-based dairy substitutes.

If you can eat soy freely, that's fine. However, soy is an increasingly common food allergen in its own right. And many milk-allergic people complain that they've been "soyed-out"—they're just plain tired of soy—and now they react to it. So if you use soy milk, try to ration it in intervals of four days or longer.

In cooking and baking you can often substitute Zucchini Milk for cow's milk (see Index). Zucchini Milk is somewhat thicker than cow's milk, so you may need to cut back on the flour in baked goods in which it's used.

Allergy doctors and patients alike have discovered that many infants and children who can't tolerate cow's milk thrive on goat's milk. Although both cows and goats belong to the Bovine family, evidently their milk differs enough from each other so that goat's milk can be tolerated by many who can't drink cow's milk. Part of the reason may be that fat globules in goat's milk are smaller, making it easier to digest. Consequently, goat's milk—and goat's-milk products—are worth a try. Canned or powdered goat's milk is available in many health food stores. In some areas, you can buy fresh goat's milk.

Chevre, or goat's-milk cheese, is a welcome alternative for people who are allergic to many regular cheeses. (Watch out for blends of cow's milk and goat's milk, called mi-chevres, or blends mislabeled as "100 percent goat cheese." Call the distributor if you have to.) Depending on its age, goat's-milk cheese may be creamy and smooth, crumbly and dry, soft or hard. And flavor intensifies with age. I have found some chevres that resemble cheddar cheese and others that are much like cream cheese. I suggest that you start with mild, "young" goat's-milk cheese at first, until you get accustomed to its distinct flavor and texture.

As the dairy industry experiments further, you can expect to find still other goat's-milk products available—ricotta, yogurt, cottage cheese and Camembert, for example. Until then, I've developed recipes for goat's-milk cheese and yogurt that I think you'll enjoy, if regular cheeses are off-limits (see Index).

Sometimes, you can substitute unsweetened juice or water for milk—which is what I've done in many recipes. To make up for omission of milk solids, use ¾ cup juice or water for each cup of

3

milk in a recipe. I have also developed a number of beverages from nuts, fruit and herb teas, among other foods.

I do not recommend that people with food allergies use non-dairy creamers or toppings. Some of those milk substitutes actually contain whey, lactose or caseinate—all milk derivatives. In addition, non-dairy substitutes are usually made from corn, soy or coconut and contain flavor additives and petroleum-based chemicals—all of which are potential allergens. So chances are, you're better off with the milk substitutes suggested earlier.

With the exception of goat's milk, none of these milk substitutes matches the nutritional makeup of milk. Many people will need to take a calcium supplement to help make up the difference. (For more information, be sure to read the sections, Nutrition Basics in Brief and Goat's Milk and Cheese Dishes.)

Alternatives to Wheat and Grains

Wheat intolerance—and grain allergy in general—is probably one of the most perplexing of all food allergies. Our diet relies so heavily on wheat-based bread and baked goods that other flours are practically unheard of (or, like rye, usually used only in combination with wheat flour). Rye, barley, oats and millet are not necessarily the answer. Many people who are allergic to wheat are also allergic to related grains. Of the four, only oats seems to be relatively non-allergenic.

To overcome that problem, I've borrowed from Middle Eastern, Indian and Oriental cuisines. A number of cereals and legumes—rice, chick-peas, lentils, potatoes, tapioca and arrowroot, among others—are ground or mashed to produce flours, meals or starchy bases of wonderfully diverse flavor and texture.

Amaranth is a newly available grainlike food that's of special value to people who are allergic to grains. Amaranth flour shares many of wheat's excellent cooking properties and because it has not been widely used, can be tolerated by almost everyone. Buckwheat is somewhat less allergenic than grain and may be tolerated easily. You can buy these alternative flours in ethnic food stores or health food stores, or from the distributors listed in the Appendix.

Because I am allergic to wheat, I've had a strong personal interest in developing recipes using alternative flours. I quickly discovered that each flour has its own set of cooking properties which I describe in the accompanying table. This information will save you hours of experimentation and frustrating results when you want to make grain-free versions of your family's favorite baked goods. And it will help you to understand the various options given in my recipes. For example, oat flour and chick-pea flour are both excellent thickeners, but oat flour gives milk-free sauces a grayish tinge . . . making chick-pea flour the better choice. And so it goes.

TABLE 1

Cooking and Baking with Alternative Flours

If you're allergic to wheat, you can substitute other starches and flours to make breadings, sauces or baked goods. Each flour has certain strengths and weaknesses, so this information will help you choose alternatives that will work best in each case.

Amaranth

Flavor and Color	Color varies from off-white to nearly black. Most common varieties are the color of mild honey. Flavor is grainlike, mild and almost nutty. If flour gets old, the flavor may get stronger. Flavor mixes well with other foods, especially spices, carob and nuts (see Comments).
Breading	Excellent, especially when puffed. Browns quickly. Use medium or medium-low heat. If breaded food browns before it is cooked through, place it in a 350° oven for 10–20 minutes or until food is done. Herbs may be added to complement food: tarragon or Italian Seasoning for chicken, and dill or Pizzazz Seasoning for fish (see Index). Try others, too.
Thickening	Each variety differs in its thickening ability. To test your flour: Combine 1 cup of cool water with 2 tablespoons amaranth flour; bring to boil, stirring. Should thicken within 15 minutes.
Baking	Excellent. Substitute for 25 percent of total flour, and use brown rice or oat flour for remainder. For grain-free baked goods, substitute amaranth for 75 percent of the total flour and use arrowroot, tapioca-starch flour or potato starch or flour for the remainder (see Potato Flour and Potato Starch).

continued

5

TABLE 1—*Continued*

Comments	Amaranth is not related to wheat or other grains. Used in the proportions suggested, amaranth produces baked goods that are moist, with excellent flavor and texture. Availability is still spotty and inconsistent. Some health stores carry it, and it is available by mail. See Appendix for addresses. Cost is still relatively high. As more people discover it, request it and buy it, expect supply to increase and prices to drop. Refrigerate or freeze to protect the flavor and quality of the flour. If your health food store stocks amaranth flour on the open shelf, suggest that it be kept in a cooler. Home grinding is difficult. Whole-seed amaranth is about the size of a poppy seed, so it slips right through many grinders. Small nut and seed grinders usually work well for small quantities. Grind about 2 tablespoons at a time. Or buy the flour and keep it cool. Rich in nutrients and higher in protein and fiber than any grain. Contains B vitamins and a good showing of minerals, including calcium.

Arrowroot

Flavor and Color	Snow white. Flavorless. Can be used "anonymously" in baked goods. Add herbs or spices for flavor.
Breading	Browns quickly and well. Produces golden, crispy coating.
Thickening	Excellent. Substitute for equal amount of cornstarch. Or dissolve 1 tablespoon per cup of cool liquid for medium-thick sauce, more for thicker sauce. Bring to boil and allow to bubble for 3 minutes only; prolonged cooking will thin sauce. To thicken stew: Add arrowroot dissolved in liquid to boiling stew during last 5 minutes of cooking; stir until thick and clear. Leftovers may need to be rethickened.
Baking	Substitute for 25 to 50 percent of total flour. Combine with other wheat alternatives. Will lighten wheatless baked goods.
Comments	Silky powder, much like cornstarch. Buy in bulk—by the pound—in health food stores. Store in tightly sealed jar and refrigerate to prevent absorption of moisture.

6

Brown Rice Flour

Flavor and Color
Mild flavor influenced by spices, herbs and ingredients such as honey, cinnamon or maple syrup. Produces light, off-white sauces and baked goods.

Breading
Not good. Gets mushy instead of crisp. Instead use crumbs of Rice-Flour Pancakes, Rice Tortillas or Caraway-Rice Crackers, finely ground in blender (see Index).

Thickening
Satisfactory. Use 25 percent more than wheat flour (2½ tablespoons for each 2 tablespoons).
Texture is somewhat grainy, but not offensive.
For smoother sauces, let flour stand in the liquid for a few hours to soften.

Baking
Excellent for cookies and pie crust.
Cakes tend to be dry unless mixed with other flours or ground nuts. Substitute ground nuts for 25 percent of the flour.
⅞ of a cup (1 level cup less 2 tablespoons) = 1 cup wheat flour.
Use rice flour in equal portions with oat flour. For example, for 1 cup wheat flour use ½ cup rice flour plus ½ cup oat flour.

Comments
Contains no gluten; considered the least allergenic of the grains.
To avoid dryness in baked goods: Add moist dates or other dried fruits that have been plumped. Puree fresh, unsweetened canned or dried fruit (stewed) and use for all or part of the liquid. Add grated vegetables, such as carrots or zucchini. Increase oil content. (No need to increase oil with nuts.)

Buckwheat Flour, Dark (ground from roasted groats)

Flavor and Color
Strong and characteristic. Often blended with a milder flour or starch to moderate the flavor.

Breading
Very good. Crisp, dark brown coating.

Thickening
Not good. It thickens only as it cools. Not practical for sauces.

Baking
Satisfactory but less desirable than the white flour (see below).

continued

TABLE 1—*Continued*

Comments	*Note:* Commercial buckwheat flour may contain a small amount of wheat flour. Look for "100 percent pure buckwheat flour" on label. Buckwheat contains gluten, a problem for people with gluten intolerance. Strong flavor not appealing to everyone. Suggest you try white (unroasted) buckwheat flour, below.

Buckwheat Flour, White (ground from unroasted whole groats)

Flavor and Color	Mild and mellow. Seems totally different from dark flour. Easily made at home (see Comments).
Breading	Excellent. Crisp, dark brown coating, with milder flavor.
Thickening	Same as above.
Baking	Excellent. Very similar to brown rice flour: light with a tendency to be dry. To overcome dryness, see Comment #2 under Brown Rice Flour.
Comments	Mild flavor appeals to most people. Many of my taste-testers who didn't care for dark buckwheat flour proceeded to gobble baked goods made with home-ground, *white* buckwheat flour. One of the cheapest and easiest alternatives to wheat flour. To grind your own: Buy white, unroasted whole groats. Grind ½ cup at a time in a blender, for 1 or 2 minutes. Pour into sifter or sieve and shake. Repeat, adding any that didn't sift through. Repeat process until you have as much flour as you need. (It takes 7 minutes to grind and sift 2 cups of flour.) Store whole groats at room temperature.

Chick-pea (Garbanzo) Flour

Flavor and Color	Mild. Blends well with other flour (not "beany"). Produces a yellow, rich-looking sauce.
Breading	Only fair. Doesn't get crisp. Better when mixed with ground seeds.
Thickening	Excellent. Approximates wheat for this function. Good choice to thicken soups or stews.
Baking	Excellent. Use 25 percent with other flours for high-protein baked goods. Use 50–50 with ground nuts. Experiment (has much potential).

Comments	Sometimes packaged as "gram" flour—not to be confused with graham flour, which is a wheat flour. Read labels carefully.
	Use commercial flour only. Dry chick-peas are so hard they break the average nut and seed grinder, and dull the blades of a blender.
	As with any legume there may be a problem with digestibility. Start with 1½ tablespoons per cup and fill it with rice or other flour (this is approximately 10 percent).
	Found in Indian and Middle Eastern groceries.

Legume Flour (other than chick-pea)

Flavor and Color	Mild flavor. Color varies with bean used.
Breading	Same as for chick-pea flour.
Thickening	Not suitable.
Baking	Same as for chick-pea flour.
Comments	Except for soy, legumes may be ground in a blender. Run blender for about 5 minutes for each ½ cup of beans ground. Sift or put through a seive to catch large particles. I especially recommend "red" lentils—actually peach-colored—and yellow split peas. They make attractive and appetizing baked goods. Consider flour from white, red or pink beans, too, depending on the appearance you prefer.

Nut, Peanut and Seed Flours

Flavor and Color	Excellent. Grinding tends to release the flavor.
Breading	Not suitable, unless mixed with a flour.
Thickening	Not suitable.
Baking	Excellent. Use for 25 percent of flour, or to taste. For example, sesame seed flour may be fine in small amounts but overpowering in large amounts. Reduce oil in recipe to compensate for high oil content of flour. Good replacement for wheat germ.
Comments	May use raw nuts and seeds or use toasted, which provide richer flavor. Buy the freshest nuts and seeds you can find, unsalted.

continued

TABLE 1—Continued

To grind walnuts, pecans or other soft and oily nuts, add 1 or 2 tablespoons of a starch to prevent excessive clumping. (Use the starch from the measured amount in recipe.)

To grind nuts: Small nut and seed grinders do about 2 tablespoons at a time. While food processors do a fine job making finely chopped nuts, they do not make them fine enough to consider them a flour. A blender is preferred. Using a blender, grind ¼ cup at a time. Blend briefly using on/off turns. Strain or sift. Return any chunks to blender, add next ¼ cup and repeat. Particles should be fine enough to pass through the strainer. Do not overprocess. Grind only what you will use; do not store.

Above procedure suitable for cakes or other recipes where texture is critical. For pancakes, muffins or cookies, just grind and add to the flour or add liquids to ground nuts or seeds to make a nut milk, depending on the recipe.

If you are allergic to nuts, replace the amount of nut flour in a recipe with an equal amount of another flour or starch called for.

Ideally, nuts should be kept in a cool place—an unheated pantry or a refrigerator.

Note: Apparently most sesame seeds are hulled chemically. There is one source of nonchemically hulled sesame seeds available that I know of; it is Protein-Aide by International Protein Industries, Inc. Address in Appendix; available by mail order.

Oat Flour

Flavor and Color
Flavor is acceptable and does not dominate.
Color of baked goods is brown and appetizing.
Color of sauce is gray, unless curry, paprika or other high-color seasoning is added.

Breading
Good.
Browns nicely.

Thickening
Very good. Use same amount as wheat flour (2 tablespoons to 1 cup liquid).
Stone-ground oat flour makes a slightly smoother sauce than ground rolled oats, but either is satisfactory.

Baking
Excels in cookies and pancakes—may be used for 80 to 100 percent of flour called for.

Too heavy for cakes—use 50–50 with rice flour, arrowroot or tapioca-starch flour or white buckwheat.

Comments Stone-ground oat flour is now available commercially and can be used in equal measure for wheat flour.
To grind your own: Blend 1¼ cups rolled oats into fine powder; makes 1 cup flour.

Potato Flour

Flavor and Color White. Bland.

Breading Not suitable.

Thickening Can be used to make some sauces. Contributes potato flavor to sauces, so not always desirable.

Baking Substitute ½ to ⅝ cup potato flour for each cup of wheat flour.
Combines well with brown rice flour to add body to cookie dough. Let batter stand a few minutes before baking to allow flour to absorb liquid.

Comments Made from cooked potatoes. Do not confuse with potato starch.

Potato Starch

Flavor and Color White. Bland.
Add herbs or seasoning.

Breading Browns quickly. Crisps well.

Thickening Poor—turns to glue.

Baking Suitable for cakes but not breads. Needs eggs, baking powder or other leavening.

Comments Made from raw potatoes. Do not confuse with potato flour. Looks and feels like cornstarch.

Soya Powder

Flavor and Color Bland.
Only slightly "beany." Flavor easily camouflaged by other flavors. When mixed with fruit, spices, carob or nuts, the other taste dominates.
Makes golden soy milk.

continued

TABLE 1—*Continued*

Breading	Good. Makes a crispy coating. Add herbs for flavor.
Thickening	Does not thicken liquids.
Baking	Use for 25 percent of total flour. In this combination with grain flour, it produces high, good quality protein. Mixes successfully with amaranth, buckwheat, ground nuts and starches. Baked goods have a good texture and retain moisture.
Comments	Commercial processing of soybeans for flour isn't standardized. Soy must be cooked to be digested. When and how this is done greatly influences the flavor and quality of the flour. Least satisfactory is grinding the dry beans (as is done with grain) and dry roasting the flour. Some flour is even marketed raw. Fearn Soya Powder is finer than other flours and usually tastes better. Fearn's Soya Powder contains all the natural oil of the soybean. Oil content of a recipe you are converting may be reduced by 1 teaspoon for each ¼ cup used. *Because soy is a common allergen, use it no more than once every four days, if you can tolerate it.*

Tapioca-Starch Flour

Flavor and Color	Same as for arrowroot.
Breading	Same as for arrowroot.
Thickening	Excellent. Substitute for equal amount of cornstarch. Or use 1½ as much as wheat flour to thicken a sauce. As with arrowroot, add during last 5 minutes of cooking, or it will get rubbery.
Baking	Same as for arrowroot.
Comments	Do not confuse with tapioca or tapioca granules. If tapioca-starch flour is not available at health food stores near you, purchase from mail-order source (see Appendix). Storage is the same as for arrowroot.

Sweeteners

Sugar is usually made from cane (a grass related to wheat), corn (a common allergen) or beets—or a blend of those. And you can't necessarily tell which sugar is which from the label. So most allergic people are better off using honey, maple syrup, date sugar or dried fruits. These alternative sweeteners don't behave like white sugar, though, so cooks need to understand a few things before substituting them wholesale.

Honey is about twice as sweet as sugar, so you can use half as much. Also, honey changes the proportion of liquid-to-dry ingredients—a critical factor in producing light, finely textured baked goods. To adapt your own recipes, you will need to either add more flour or decrease the total amount of liquid called for. To further insure lightness in baked goods, add an additional ½ teaspoon baking soda per cup of honey used. Bake 25 degrees lower to prevent overbrowning. (My recipes have already taken these factors into account; no adjustment is necessary.)

Some other helpful tips for cooking with honey:

- To measure honey, use the same cup you used to measure any oil in a recipe. The honey will slip out easily.
- If you are using a recipe that calls for eggs, gradually pour the honey into well-beaten eggs in a thin stream, beating continuously. That dramatically increases the volume of baked goods, so you won't end up with a heavy, dense product.
- Do not overheat honey—its flavor and color may change. There's nothing wrong with granulated honey. But if you want to reliquify it, place the jar in a bowl of warm (not hot) water. It may take an hour or longer, depending on the size of the jar.
- Store honey in a tightly covered container, preferably in a cool, dark place. Freezing or refrigeration is not harmful but will thicken or granulate honey.

Pure maple syrup has a very distinct flavor, so you can't substitute it in just any recipe. It's best used in breakfast breads and certain desserts. Be sure to avoid maple-*flavored* syrups—they're usually made of corn syrup, and many contain sodium benzoate, a common allergen for asthmatics.

Maple syrup is not quite as sweet as honey and may be substituted in equal measure for sugar—or perhaps 75 to 80 percent,

13

depending on your taste for sweets. When baking with maple syrup, I find I need to decrease the total amount of liquid ingredients in a recipe by nearly the full amount of syrup used. In other words, for each cup of maple syrup used, omit at least ⅔ to ¾ cup of the other liquids (usually water, juice and oil).

Maple sugar granules are simply dehydrated maple syrup. Maple sugar is available in health food stores or by mail order (see Appendix) and can be used like brown sugar, but it is expensive. So is date sugar, which looks like brown sugar but doesn't dissolve as well. These both come in handy for a child's birthday cake or other special treats that need to look and "feel" as much like regular fare as possible.

Some of my recipes are sweetened with dried fruit or fruit juice (or both) and I'm quite pleased with the results (for example, see Index for Spicy Fruit Drops and Elegant and Easy Fruitcake). The recipes for Two-Step Carrot Cake, Rice-Flour Carrot Cake and Apricot-Rice Pudding contain honey and dried fruit. Buy dried fruits from stores that keep them refrigerated, especially if you are allergic to molds and other fungi. In the course of being dried, fruits pick up minuscule spores of otherwise harmless yeasts and molds. To minimize growth and reproduction of molds, always store dried fruit in the refrigerator at home. Rinse before using. Incidentally, fresh fruits make good sweeteners, too, and I've used them liberally as the basis for various shakes and desserts.

Molasses, sorghum and barley malt originate from grains, so they may trigger allergies in grain-sensitive people. I include molasses in just a few recipes, with honey listed as an alternative. Rice syrup is a *tentative* possibility as a sweetener—the only brand I could find contains a little barley, so read labels closely.

Citrus

Avoiding citrus in cooking isn't much of a problem, except when lemon juice or some other acid is needed to help leaven baked goods or to give tang to certain dishes. Sometimes you can substitute vinegar—if you're not sensitive to fermented foods (which often contain yeast). For people who are allergic to both citrus and yeasts, I offer pure vitamin C crystals as yet a third alternative. Use crystals made from sago palm rather than corn, available at either health food stores or from the distributor listed in the Appendix. To convert your own recipes, substitute ¼ teaspoon vitamin C crystals for each tablespoon of lemon juice.

14

Oils and Fats

Margarine is a potential problem for allergic people because it may contain either milk solids or soy oil as well as artificial additives. And butter is out for people who are allergic to milk. So in baked goods, your best bet is to use various bottled vegetable, nut and seed oils. Unless a particular type of oil is listed in a recipe, choose from olive, sunflower, sesame, almond, walnut and peanut oil (depending on what you're not allergic to). Always read labels to be sure that the oil is not combined with lesser amounts of other types of vegetable oil.

Meats

There are more than 25 different families of mammals, so if you're allergic to beef or pork, you still have plenty to choose from— lamb, rabbit, venison, and so forth. Similarly, people who are allergic to chicken and turkey are likely to be able to eat pheasant, quail or duck with no problem. Fish offer more than 30 commonly eaten families to choose from. With all those options, you should be able to cook and tolerate some forms of meat, fish or fowl. (Diversifying your choice of foods is discussed more fully in the section, Planning a Diversified Rotary Diet.) I've developed a number of recipes for lamb, venison and rabbit (see Index). To incorporate other, more exotic game and wild fowl in your menu, keep in mind that undomesticated game and birds need to be braised or stewed rather than broiled or baked, because their meat is leaner and less tender. Marinating the meat before cooking also helps.

Even if you can eat pork, you may not be able to eat ham or bacon because of a possible reaction to nitrites or other preservatives, or unspecified curing agents or seasonings. On the other hand, additive-free pork sausage is okay, as long as it's cooked well and drained of fat.

Unusual Fruits and Vegetables

If you're allergic to citrus fruits, bananas, berries, melon or other commonly eaten fruit, a whole world of exciting options awaits you: Turn to kiwi, mangoes, currants, figs and a number of other choices to satisfy your cravings for sweet, juicy fruit. If you're allergic to peas, tomatoes, green beans or celery, introduce yourself to artichokes, Chinese cabbage (bok choy) or Japanese radishes (daikon), for example. Unusual fruits and vegetables are available in many stores—you may have simply overlooked them until now. I've given brief "personality profiles" of several in the accompanying table to help you make their acquaintance.

The recipes in this book are in no way restricted to odd or exotic produce; rather, I give enough options to accommodate individual tastes and tolerances, so you can still eat everyday produce

TABLE 2

Unusual Fruits and Vegetables

To make a clean break with allergies to common fruits and vegetables, try these alternatives.

Food	Description
Fruits	
Cherimoya	Size of a grapefruit. Irregular brown surface looks like handhewn wood. Flesh is creamy white with seeds dispersed throughout the fruit (as in watermelon).
Currants	Small red or black fruit in tiny grapelike clusters. Shriveled like miniature raisins.
Kiwi fruit	Approximate size and shape of a lemon. Skin is greenish brown and fuzzy. Flesh is green with tiny black edible seeds.
Mango	Green, gold or rosy. Oval, about the size of small cantaloupe, but irregularly shaped. May have streaks of pink. Flesh is golden.

if it's no problem for you. Nevertheless, variety helps to prevent new allergies from developing.

Incidentally, some people think they're allergic to pineapple because it burns their mouth or tongue. That irritation is caused by an enzyme that can be destroyed by boiling the pineapple or pineapple juice for two minutes.

Purchase and Storage Information	Comments
Shipped and sold underripe. Ripen at room temperature until it yields to gentle pressure. Store in refrigerator up to 1 week. Remove from the cold about 1 hour before eating.	Fruit is not sprayed or dusted. Cut halves or wedges, like a melon. Very sweet and juicy—cross between a very sweet pear and a pineapple or papaya. Discard seeds. Available in specialty shops in spring.
Dried currants more common than fresh.	Terrific alternative to raisins. Work well in baked goods, with less tendency to sink than raisins. May be plumped by soaking in liquid.
Usually purchased when firm. Ripen at room temperature. When soft to touch, eat or refrigerate until needed. For best flavor, let stand at room temperature for 1 hour before eating.	When ripe and soft, flavor is both tangy and sweet. If eaten too soon it's less sweet. Cut in half crosswise and eat with a spoon, like a miniature melon. Or peel and cut crosswise into 1/4" slices.
Buy green, ripen at room temperature. Ripe fruit yields to gentle pressure and will have a pink blush.	When ripe and soft, it is very sweet and juicy. Flesh adheres tightly to large stone. To eat, cut away from stone and gently pull the skin off, working over a dish to catch the juices. Cube or slice into thin wedges. One mango may serve 2 or more people.

continued

TABLE 2—*Continued*

Food	Description
Papaya	Pear-shaped, but larger than a pear. Skin is green, sometimes with streaks of yellow. Flesh is golden. Center contains a clump of black seeds, easily removed.
Persimmon	Size and shape vary. Skin is flame orange and very smooth. Flesh is also orange.
Pomegranate	Size of an orange. Skin is mottled, wine and white. Interior is full of seeds, each surrounded by a bit of bright red flesh. Like citrus fruit, sections are divided by a membrane, which is not eaten.

Vegetables

Food	Description
Bean sprouts	Slender shoots. Pale off-white in color.
Bok choy (Also called Chinese celery or Chinese chard)	Resembles Swiss chard, only longer. Stalks are pale, almost white, while leaves are dark green.

Purchase and Storage Information	Comments
Usually purchased when firm. Softens and turns yellow as it ripens at room temperature.	Available in many supermarkets as well as specialty shops. When soft and ripe, flavor is mildly sweet. Cut in half lengthwise and eat with a spoon. Contains an enzyme that aids digestion and tenderizes meat, especially game (see Tender-Meat Marinade, Index). Seeds are edible (see Peppy, Index).
Firm or partially soft when purchased. Ripen at room temperature until very soft and sweet.	Flavor is sweet but with a "bite." When ripe, causes the mouth to pucker. Eat peeled or unpeeled.
Purchase when firm. Ripen at room temperature until fruit yields to gentle pressure, but is not soft.	To eat, cut through the skin surface only and pull apart with your hands. Seeds should be bright red; discard any that are dark. Because the seeds are difficult to separate from the flesh, many people prefer to eat the flesh, seeds and all. Otherwise, you can suck the flesh from the seeds. (Pomegranates take patience to eat.)
Choose fresh-looking sprouts. The tips should not be dry or brown. Short sprouts are younger and more tender. Commercial sprouts may be bleached. Sprout your own for more color. Store in refrigerator in vegetable crisper or in a glass jar.	Crisp and delicate in flavor, these have been around for centuries in the Orient and are associated with Oriental food, stir-fries and multivegetable salads. Cook briefly, if at all: Blanch for 2 minutes, steam for 3–5 minutes, or stir-fry during last 2 minutes of cooking.
Look for crisp, fresh-looking leaves and firm stalks.	May be used like Swiss chard. Slice stalks as you would celery, and use in stir-fry dishes. Or tear greens and toss into a stir-fry for last 2 minutes.

continued

TABLE 2—Continued

Food	Description
Celeriac (Also called celery root or parsley root)	This strain of celery is cultivated for the root, not the top.
Chayote (sha-yo-te) squash	Green, about the size of summer squash. Flesh is pale green like honeydew. Single seed.
Chili peppers	Many varieties. Come in many sizes, shapes and colors—green, yellow and red. Flesh is usually the same color as the skin.
Collard greens	Large, broad-leaved greens.

Purchase and Storage Information	Comments
The smaller roots are more desirable; they may become woody as they mature. A sprouted root also denotes age. Press firmly to detect soft spots of decay. Trim roots and tops and store in vegetable crisper of refrigerator.	Primarily used in soups and stews. Can also be braised, steamed or used in salads. Peel before cooking and cut into bite-size pieces. (Discolors when exposed to air, so plunge into water with vinegar, lemon juice or vitamin C crystals immediately after cutting.)
May be eaten when young and tender or when dark green and hard. Refrigerate like zucchini.	This is a staple food of many countries in North Africa, South and Central America and the West Indies and is growing in popularity in this country. Use tender squash in salads and firmer ones cooked in soups, main dishes, as a vegetable or in desserts. To steam, wash well and cook whole until tender. Peel while still hot. Split, remove seed and serve. Allow 1 per person, if small.
Look for bright, shiny skins; avoid any that are shriveled. Store in refrigerator (unless drying them intentionally).	Range from mildly hot to very hot. Skin is thin but tough. Traditional method of removal is to spear with a fork and char the skin over a burner of the stove. Rotate until the skin is black and blistered. Enclose in a paper bag for 15 minutes, then slip skin off. Or char under a broiler, turning until they are completely charred, and proceed as above. Handle with great care. Wear gloves. *Do not touch the face or eyes with chili on your hands.* The juice irritates and burns, causing great discomfort.
Should be fresh and crisp, not limp or wilted.	A traditional vegetable in the South, but regarded as unusual north of the Mason-Dixon line. See Swiss chard for preparation.

continued

TABLE 2—*Continued*

Food	Description
Daikon (Also called Japanese radish or winter radish)	Large, white radish. Usually several inches in length, perhaps over 1 foot. (Some markets cut them into pieces.)
Fennel (Florence fennel)	Resembles celery, with fernlike tops.
Globe artichokes	Pear-shaped, but larger. Rough exterior with "leaves" or petals. Green in color, sometimes with a few brown spots (due to frost), which seem to enhance flavor.
Jerusalem artichokes (Also called sunchokes)	Knotty brown tubers. Size of new potatoes, but irregular in shape.

Purchase and Storage Information	Comments
Choose a firm root, free of nicks and with no signs of decay. Store in refrigerator in vegetable crisper until ready to use.	Grate, slice or julienne (cut into matchsticks). Add to salads or a stir-fry. Eat raw or cook briefly— perhaps 3–5 minutes, depending on the size of the pieces. Flavor is radishlike.
Look for crisp stalks and fresh leaves. Store in vegetable crisper of refrigerator.	Labeling can be confusing. Fennel is often marked "sweet anise" because of the licorice flavor. Trim, wash and slice as you would prepare celery. Eat stem raw, like celery, or cook as a hot vegetable.
Select artichokes that are plump and heavy. Avoid those with signs of decay or leaves that have begun to spread.	Flavor is delicate, so usually served with tangy sauces or fillings. Cut the top third off, exposing the heart. Snap leaves back and remove (reserve, if you like them). Boil or steam until tender, about 20–40 minutes, depending on size. Remove hard fuzzy "choke" with a spoon. Allow 1 per person. Leaves may be steamed separately, dipped in a sauce and pulled between the teeth. Makes an interesting and light appetizer.
Should be firm with no soft spots. Store in a cool place or refrigerate.	Scrub well with a vegetable brush. Discolor rapidly if not used quickly. Eat raw or cook in water for 20 minutes or until tender. For a special treat, slice either raw or cooked chokes and spread thinly with Sunflower Seed Butter (see Index for Nut or Seed Butter).

continued

TABLE 2—*Continued*

Food	Description
Jicama (hick-a-ma)	Brown, round, flat tubers. Can grow very large. A "small" one is between 1 and 2 pounds. Larger ones may be woody.
Kale	Green or purplish-green; deeply frilled, curly leaves. Doesn't form head.
Kohlrabi	Small globes with leaves. Color is white, pale green or purple.
Lamb's-quarters	Grow as a weed. Pick fresh. Not in most markets.

Purchase and Storage Information	Comments
Select as you would potatoes, looking for firmness. If they are too large, ask for halves or quarters. (Many markets oblige). When stored in a cool, dry place, jicama keeps well for 10 days or more.	Mild, slightly sweet flavor and super-crisp texture are their greatest assets. Remain snow white long after cutting. Thin slices are excellent for dips and spreads, in place of crackers. Shred into salads. To use in place of water chestnuts and bamboo in stir-fry: Add during last 2 minutes of cooking time so they heat through. They retain their crunch when cooked briefly.
Look for thin ribs and stems and crisp, healthy-looking leaves. Wash well. Trim stems and strip leaves from center ribs. Pat dry, roll in towel, and store in vegetable crisper of refrigerator.	Tear up and steam briefly to use in place of spinach in casseroles. Or drain, chop and season to steam as a vegetable.
Should be very firm with fresh-looking leaves. Globes 3 inches or smaller are most desirable.	Young leaves may be cooked like spinach, but primary use is for globes. If vegetable is very fresh, steam without peeling, and peel after cooking. If more mature, peel thick fibrous covering, quarter or slice, and boil in a little water until tender. Or peel, slice thinly, and add to stir-fry in place of water chestnuts and bamboo for last 3–5 minutes of cooking, depending on their thickness. They add terrific "crunch."
Ideally, cook the same day. However, may be washed, dried, rolled in a towel and stored in the crisper for 1 or 2 days.	Steam briefly, like spinach. Flavor is also similar to spinach, though more delicate. A little lemon juice adds a pleasing touch.

continued

TABLE 2—*Continued*

Food	Description
Leeks	Look like huge, green scallions.
Nappa cabbage (Also called Chinese cabbage)	Pale white-green, shaped like romaine lettuce. Averaging 10–12 inches long.
New Zealand spinach	Looks like spinach growing from a short stalk.
Parsnips	Size and shape of carrots, but cream colored.
Rutabaga	Large as a Spanish onion. Often waxed. Outer skin color may be pale yellow to orange.
Shiitake (shi-tah́ke) mushrooms	Larger and flatter than regular mushrooms. Creamy color with hints of brown.

Purchase and Storage Information	Comments
Choose small leeks with fresh-looking green ends.	Related to onions, but more delicately flavored. Tricky to clean because dirt is caught in the inner layers: Split them lengthwise and run water through. Very versatile—bake, broil, braise, puree, stew or add to soups, salads, appetizers or stews.
Look for fresh-looking outer leaves; avoid browning edges. Store in vegetable crisper of refrigerator. Smaller bunches tend to have more delicate flavor.	Very versatile; sweet and crisp. Outstanding in salads, stir-fries and as a vegetable by itself. Available year 'round. No cooking odor.
Look for fresh leaves. Best cooked the day of purchase, or wash, dry, wrap in towel, and store in vegetable crisper of refrigerator.	New Zealand spinach is not in the same food family as "regular" spinach. Leaves are thicker, less suitable for salads. To cook, steam briefly. Stalks may be chopped into bits and cooked like peas.
Should be firm with no sprouting. Store in refrigerator.	The carrot's less-well-known cousin has a distinctive flavor of its own. Scrub well and steam. When tender, skin slips off easily. To add to soup or stew, peel and slice.
Avoid those with many sprouts. Waxing seems harmless. Firm vegetables retain freshness best.	Peel heavy outer coating with potato peeler. Dice and steam, or boil in ½ cup of water in a heavy pot with a tight lid. Mash like potatoes, moistened with cooking water.
A little browner than regular mushrooms. Avoid signs of decay. Store in a brown paper bag, refrigerated.	Discard tough stems. Julienne broad head (slice into matchsticks).

continued

TABLE 2—*Continued*

Food	Description
Snow peas	4- or 5-inch flat pods. Eaten for the crisp pods (which contain only token, underdeveloped peas). Light green in color.
Sugar snap peas	Fuller, rounder, heavier than snow peas.
Swiss chard	Large green leaves on tall stalks.

Other Helpful Options

I've found the following foods to be of additional help in diversifying my diet and adding interest and flavor to my meals.

Carob powder. This is made by grinding pods of carob (also called St. John's bread), a subfamily of the Legume family. Carob is usually available in health food stores as roasted or toasted dry powder. Carob tastes much like chocolate, minus the fat and bitterness of chocolate. It's naturally sweet and high in fiber.

I don't use carob chips in this book because the ingredients

Purchase and Storage Information	Comments
Available frozen, but fresh are best. Avoid droopy or wilted pods. Should look fresh and free of blemishes. Refrigerate until ready to use.	Wash. Remove stem and string from 1 side. Pat dry for a stir-fry, where they require only 2 or 3 minutes to cook and change from light green to bright green. Do not overcook (or color fades again). Add to stews or mixed-vegetable dishes for last few minutes of cooking.
Same as snow peas.	Remove stem and string. May eat pod and all, raw or cooked briefly. Steam 4–5 minutes or stir-fry, as snow peas.
Look for fresh-looking greens and white, firm ribs. Avoid chard with spongy ribs. Wash well, shake out water, pat dry, and store rolled in a dry towel in vegetable crisper of refrigerator.	Wash leaves thoroughly to remove sand and soil. Delicious lightly steamed. Use as you would spinach. Leaves and stems may be cooked together for interesting contrast, or strip greens from stems; steam the greens and chop the stems to add to salad. Either or both may be torn or chopped to add to a stir-fry in last 2 minutes of cooking. If serving steamed chard as a side dish, add a little lemon juice or vinegar (or sprinkle with vitamin C crystals) to enhance flavor.

are not standardized: Different manufacturers combine carob with any of a variety of ingredients, often including soy lecithin and corn sweeteners. And it's not always easy to find out what's in carob chips. That makes them a potential problem for people with food allergies.

Kombu (kelp). A sea vegetable with a naturally salty flavor, kombu can be used as a salt substitute. It's high in trace minerals, especially iodine. About 3 percent of the population is allergic to high concentrations of iodine, so beware. However, kombu is no problem for most people when used in moderation as a condiment.

Miso. This is a fermented soy food paste, varying in flavor and degrees of saltiness. Use miso the same way you would use bouillon cubes: Dissolve a small amount in boiling water to make a flavorful broth or soup. You can reheat miso soup, but it is best not to boil it.

The Book of Miso (Autumn Press, 1976) lists 29 varieties of miso, with hundreds of subtypes, so shop around and try different kinds of miso from different sources. Some miso contains barley or rice, so check labels if you are allergic to grains. Salt content of miso ranges from 6 percent for sweet, light-colored varieties to 14 percent for dark red and brown miso. The midrange is usually labeled "mellow" and contains 8 to 10 percent salt.

Wheat-free tamari. Tamari soy sauce is also a fermented soy food. In the process of fermentation, tamari develops a deep, rich flavor that tastes saltier than it is. Each teaspoon contains 267 milligrams of sodium, compared to 2,132 milligrams of sodium in a teaspoon of salt. However, you can use much less tamari—about ¼ teaspoon—to get the same degree of salty flavor and flavor enhancement imparted by a whole teaspoon of salt.

When buying tamari, read labels. Ordinary fermented tamari soy sauce (or shoyu) is a mixture of soybeans and wheat and may also contain caramel coloring, corn syrup, MSG and preservatives. Several companies now offer a purer, wheat-free tamari, available in most health food stores, or from the distributors listed in the Appendix.

Planning
a Diversified
Rotary Diet

People with food allergies are most likely to be allergic to foods they eat every day, in one form or another: milk, wheat, eggs, corn, yeast and citrus fruits, among others. By avoiding allergy-producing foods for a while and then spacing consumption of each of those foods by four days or longer, your body may once again be able to tolerate allergenic foods. And rotating *all* the foods you eat prevents new allergies from developing. (How long you initially need to avoid foods depends on the severity of your symptoms.)

Food rotation is an approach to allergy developed in 1934 by Herbert J. Rinkel, M.D., which for the most part went ignored. Over the past few years the Diversified Rotary Diet has been resurrected by a small number of allergists both in the United States and abroad, with excellent results. It can be used to diagnose, treat and prevent food allergies. The diet works well for what are known as "cyclic" allergies—reactions that tend to fade if you avoid the food for a period of time. For example, following a Diversified Rotary Diet has taught me that I can eat wheat only once a week. If I eat it more often than that, I become groggy and lethargic, to the point where I feel as though I've been drugged.

For me, wheat is a "cyclic" allergy. In contrast, my skin itches and I break out in hives each and every time I eat shrimp or crab, no matter how infrequently. Those are "fixed" allergies, and I've accepted the fact that they are not going to disappear. So I avoid shrimp and crab.

Because most food allergies are cyclic allergies, food rotation is a tremendous help to many people. Used along with a diary of symptoms, a Diversified Rotary Diet can also help to detect unsuspected food allergies. As a bonus, food rotation may help you to better tolerate any inhalant allergies you may suffer, such as allergies to pollen or dust. That's because food and inhalant allergies produce a cumulative effect, called the "allergic load." The fewer allergens of *all* types that you're exposed to, the better you'll feel.

In addition to recommending that you rotate each food every four days, doctors who've used the Diversified Rotary Diet have established five other basic guidelines to follow.

Eat only foods to which you are not allergic. That may seem obvious, but there's no sense including a food that you know makes you itch, sneeze or experience other discomfort until you have time to build up your tolerance.

Rotate food families. This is an interesting concept that requires us to familiarize ourselves with the biologic classification of foods, presented in Table 3, Food Families, later in this section. We have already spoken of the need to allow a four-day interval between ingestions of each food, but we haven't considered the role of "first cousins" in the same family. It works like this: Say you eat oranges for breakfast Monday morning, and plan to do the same on Friday. On Wednesday you may eat another type of citrus fruit. Perhaps you'll choose grapefruit, or maybe lemon squeezed over plain, broiled fish. At any rate, related foods in the same family may be eaten on the second day. Usually. Unless you're dealing with a major offender. If wheat is your nemesis, you may be instructed to abstain from it, *plus* its first cousins rye, barley (and malt) and oats. Other cousins don't seem as similar to the body, so perhaps you can have rice or sorghum. Maybe. You'd have to be tested to see how you tolerate them. You can see why Diversified Rotary Diets are so individual.

Learning about food families is fascinating—and full of surprises. For example, almonds, walnuts, cashews and peanuts are members of different food families, even though we usually refer to them collectively as "nuts." So following a Diversified Rotary Diet, you can eat almonds on Monday, walnuts on Tuesday, cashews on Wednesday and peanuts on Thursday without repeating a food family (provided you're not allergic to any one of those foods). You may be equally surprised to learn that foods bearing little or no resemblance to each other are "siblings under the skin." For example, tomatoes, eggplants, potatoes and peppers are all members of the Nightshade family. Certain other foods, such as amaranth, pineapple and sesame seeds are "loners," unrelated to other foods that we customarily eat, so you can rotate them without concern for their relationship to other foods.

To set up a Diversified Rotary Diet of your own, first choose 28 foods that you know you can eat without experiencing symptoms. Arrange those foods into a menu of three meals a day, plus snacks, for four days. For the first four days, your diet will be very simple. To get started, refer to the Sample Diversified Rotary Diet for One Week (at the end of this section). Because choices are somewhat limited at first, you can eat as much as you want of each food, to fill up. During the second four days, add one additional food or ingredient to each meal, being careful to rotate all beverages, oils, garnishes and ingredients.

To help further, I suggest you order *The Rotation Game: A Diversified Rotation Diet* from Diet Design, P.O. Box 15181, Seattle, Washington 98115. Designed by Sally J. Rockwell, a nutritionist, it's the most complete method I've seen for rotating foods easily, and is especially useful for teaching children to follow the diet.

As you work with the Diversified Rotary Diet, you'll learn how to rotate cooking oils, spices, sweeteners—in short, anything you include in a dish. For example, soy oil, safflower oil, sunflower oil and corn oil are each products of different plants. To help you rotate ingredients, most of the recipes in this book have a number of alternative ingredients—choices between two or three different flours, oils, sweeteners or herbs. And a number of recipes consist of foods from only two or three food families, to help you prepare stews, salads and desserts, yet remain on a Diversified Rotary Diet (see Index to Recipes for a Diversified Rotary Diet).

Keep a diet diary. Write down every food you eat and note any symptoms you experience. Should a specific symptom recur a few times, you can then look back over your notes to find out what foods may have triggered the reaction. If you get headaches every so often, for instance, you may discover by checking your diary that your headaches always follow meals that contain green beans or some other specific food. If that happens, drop the food in question from your Diversified Rotary Diet for about two months, then try it again. If the symptom does not reappear, you can reintroduce that food into your diet. Thus a diary helps you to detect foods to which you may be allergic *and* to plan your next few meals.

Diversify your diet. Eating the same few foods day in and day out causes and reinforces food allergies. Conversely, eating a variety of foods decreases exposure to common allergens and prevents new food allergies from developing. To diversify your diet, rethink traditional meals. People who are allergic to milk, eggs and grains may have to get used to breakfasts of, say, honeydew melon and walnuts or salmon and cantaloupe. Also, try foods from families you're not accustomed to eating, and choose less commonly eaten members in each food family. For example, the raw material for a salad may consist of spinach or chard (greens that are not related to lettuce), beets instead of tomatoes, and avocado instead of cucumbers. When choosing protein sources, use less common members of the poultry, meat and fish families. Many people who are allergic to chicken find they can tolerate pheasant and quail, which are eaten far less frequently. Many people who are allergic to beef can eat lamb, mutton or venison with no trouble whatsoever. Because there are so many different families of fish, allergic people usually find that they can eat fish every day as long as they choose a different kind.

Luckily, less common produce and meats are more readily available than ever in this country. To help you locate game and other foods, purchasing sources are listed in the Appendix.

Eat whole, uncomplicated foods. Single ingredient foods are much easier to rotate than combination foods, which may contain an array of ingredients and additives to which you may be allergic. For example, a potato may be fine, but potato chips are not. Steak may be okay, but hot dogs are not. Orange juice may be fine, but orange drink is not.

In addition to those guidelines, I'd like to share a few tips and shortcuts that have helped me to follow a Diversified Rotary Diet.

Label everything. Nothing is more frustrating than not being able to recognize a food. But labeling is especially important for people on a Diversified Rotary Diet. It isn't enough to know a muffin is a muffin—you need to know what kind of flour, nuts and oil it contains.

Prepare enough of a dish for more than one meal and freeze what you don't use. That saves precious time and works especially well for people who are rotating chicken, turkey, lamb, patties, burgers and so forth. You get two or three times as much food for your efforts.

Group frozen foods together by category in wire bins or cardboard boxes in the freezer. Label each one—chicken, turkey, lamb, burgers, stock, stews, casseroles, and so forth. That makes it a cinch to rotate meals. And you can quickly tell which staples are in short supply, without burrowing through a mountain of loose packages.

Remember to rotate snacks. Nuts, seeds and fruits are popular snack foods that are easy to rotate. In addition, you can make snacks from recipes in this book.

To help children rotate snacks, make a game of it. Number each day of the calendar one through four, repeating the sequence for the whole month. Number all snacks accordingly. That way, children can tell at a glance which snacks they're allowed to eat each day. For children too young to read, color code the calendar and corresponding snacks with adhesive-backed, colored dots, sold in stationery stores.

Your Personal Diversified Rotary Diet

Because no two people have exactly the same set of food allergies, there is no one Diversified Rotary Diet to suit everyone. To establish your own Diversified Rotary Diet plan, exclude any foods to which you are allergic. Allow an interval of four days or more before repeating a specific food. When you are free of symptoms, you can then begin to reintroduce marginally allergenic foods— foods to which you think you may have been allergic but aren't sure about, or foods which you can tolerate sometimes but not others. Test only one food at a time.

Ideally, anyone with food allergies should adopt a Diversified Rotary Diet for life. If you return to repetitious, monotonous eating patterns, your food allergies will probably recur and you'll have to start all over. However, food rotation is demanding, so many doctors concede that people with moderate food allergies need only follow a strict Diversified Rotary Diet—rotating *all* their food—periodically, to reestablish their tolerance to certain foods or to help weather allergic "bad times." I personally rotate my diet during hay fever season only, from mid-August to the first killing frost. That's when all my allergies seem to be their worst. If you're allergic to tree pollen, you may find that following a Diversified Rotary Diet in spring helps to relieve both your food allergies and your pollen allergies. Or you may choose to rotate your foods after the winter holidays. During the rest of the year, you may be able to choose foods more freely, perhaps rotating only major food allergens rather than all your food.

Because food rotation can limit consumption of major sources of important nutrients, certain deficiencies are not uncommon. Be sure to read the section, Nutrition Basics in Brief. Also, be aware that allergic reactions are not limited to itching, sneezing, wheezing and gastrointestinal complaints. Allergy can produce headaches, depression, fatigue, irritability and other mental and emotional symptoms, as well.

"But I'm Not Better . . ."

If followed conscientiously, a Diversified Rotary Diet usually leads to fewer allergic symptoms and an increase in energy levels. *Usually.* But some people experience little if any change in their symptoms, lack a sense of well-being, and find themselves still dragging through life no matter how carefully they stick to the diet. If you don't improve, review your diet with your allergy doctor. You may be overlooking something. Or you may be one of the few people whom doctors call "universal reactors"—people who are allergic to virtually all foods commonly eaten in the typical American diet. If that's the case, you can take the Diversified Rotary Diet one step further and try a "rare foods" diet. By eating unusual meats, vegetables, fruits and grains—such as rabbit, parsnips, kiwi fruit and amaranth—for three to six months, you may be able to clear your system of food allergies. Then gradually reintroduce more familiar foods one at a time, in rotation.

Other rare foods include pheasant, venison, duck, beaver or other wild game, rutabaga, turnips, jicama, artichokes, Brazil nuts and macadamia nuts, to name a few. To incorporate these new foods in your diet, read about alternative flours and unusual fruits and vegetables in the section, Exploring New Ingredients. Also, the Appendix lists purchasing sources for wild game and other unusual foods should you have trouble locating them in specialty stores in your area.

Consider the possibility that the common yeast germ *Candida albicans* may be contributing to your health problems. Yeast-connected symptoms include chronic and overwhelming fatigue, depression, headache and complaints related to the reproductive and digestive systems. Doctors have only recently recognized the importance of candida in allergic disorders. Avoiding yeast-containing foods is part of the answer. So is cutting out sugar and honey, because the candida organism thrives on simple carbohydrates. In fact, some people need to restrict consumption of all carbohydrates (especially fruits) until they improve.

36

William G. Crook, M.D., author of *The Yeast Connection* (Professional Books, 1983), says that when candida is brought under control—by diet, medication, or both—allergies diminish. The immune system has a chance to heal, and severe allergies may diminish into minor annoyances. They may even fade away entirely.

And finally, don't overlook the possibility that you may be allergic to dust, pollen, chemicals or other inhalants. Some of your symptoms may be triggered by fumes from your gas stove or furnace, formaldehyde in building materials, seasonal weeds, grasses or trees. If you are breathing something to which you are allergic, you may require further testing to help sort out these environmental factors.

Controlling food allergy is not a cure-all. It is one very big step on the road back to robust health.

TABLE 3

Food Families

To prevent reactions to foods to which you are allergic, you may also need to avoid foods to which they are closely related. This chart can also help you to plan a Diversified Rotary Diet. (Botanical family names of plants appear in parentheses, following common names.)

Family	Plant Foods
Algae *(Algae)*	Agar-agar, carrageen, kelp (kombu)
Amaranth *(Amaranthaceae)*	Amaranth
Apple (subfamily of *Rosaceae)*	Apple, crab apple, pear, quince
Arrowroot *(Marantaceae)*	Arrowroot
Banana *(Musaceae)*	Banana and plantain
Beech *(Fagaceae)*	Beechnut and chestnut
Berry (subfamily of *Rosaceae)*	Blackberry, boysenberry, dewberry, loganberry, raspberry, rose hips, strawberry
Birch *(Betulaceae)*	Filbert, hazelnut, oil of birch (wintergreen)
Brazil Nut *(Lecythidaceae)*	Brazil nut
Buckwheat *(Polygonaceae)*	Buckwheat, garden sorrel, rhubarb

continued

TABLE 3—Continued

Family	Plant Foods—Continued
Caper (Capparidaceae)	Caper
Cashew (Anacardiaceae)	Cashew, mango, pistachio
Chicle (Sapotaceae)	Chicle (chief ingredient of chewing gum)
Chocolate (Sterculiaceae)	Chocolate (cocoa), cola, gum karaya
Citrus or Rue (Rutaceae)	Citron, grapefruit, kumquat, lemon, lime, orange, pomelo, tangelo, tangerine
Coffee (Rubiaceae)	Coffee
Composite (Compositae)	Artichoke[1], chamomile, chicory, dandelion, endive, escarole, lettuce, safflower, sunflower seeds, tarragon
Conifer (Coniferae)	Juniper berry (gin) and pine nuts
Custard-Apple (Annonaceae)	Pawpaw and cherimoya
Ebony (Ebonaceae)	Persimmon
Flax (Linaceae)	Flaxseed
Fungus[2] (Fungi)	Mold in certain cheeses, mushroom, truffle, yeast
Ginger (Zingiberaceae)	Cardamom, ginger, turmeric
Gooseberry (Saxifragaceae)	Currant and gooseberry
Goosefoot or Beet (Chenopodiaceae)	Beet, chard, lamb's-quarters, spinach, sugar beet
Grain (cereal or grass) (Gramineae)	Bamboo shoots, barley, corn, lemongrass, millet, oats, rice, rye, sorghum, sugarcane, wheat, wild rice
Grape (Vitaceae)	Grape
Heath (Ericaceae)	Blueberry, cranberry, huckleberry
Honeysuckle (Caprifoliaceae)	Elderberry

1. Theron Randolph, M.D., a leading proponent of the Diversified Rotary Diet, tells me that while sunflowers and Jerusalem artichokes are members of the Composite family, they are so unlike lettuce and other members of that family that they may be rotated separately, as though they were a family in themselves.

2. Fungi are technically a plant division, not a single family, but doctors using the Diversified Rotary Diet regard them as one family for purposes of dietary planning.

Family	Plant Foods—Continued
Iris (Iridaceae)	Saffron
Kiwi (Actinidiaceae)	Kiwiberry (kiwi fruit)
Laurel (Lauraceae)	Avocado, bay leaf, cinnamon, sassafras
Legume (Leguminosae)	Alfalfa, bean (kidney, lentil, lima, mung, navy, pinto, soy, string), carob, guar gum, gum acacia, kudzu, licorice, pea (black-eyed, chickpea, green), peanut
Lily (Liliaceae)	Asparagus, chive, garlic, leek, onion, sarsaparilla, shallot
Macadamia (Protea)	Macadamia nuts
Mallow (Malvaceae)	Cottonseed, hibiscus, okra
Maple (Aceraceae)	Maple syrup
Melon or Gourd (Cucurbitaceae)	Cantaloupe, cucumber, gherkin, honeydew, muskmelon, pumpkin, squash, watermelon
Mint (Labiatae)	Basil, catnip, horehound, lemon balm (melissa), marjoram, mint, oregano, peppermint, rosemary, sage, savory, spearmint, thyme
Morning-Glory (Convolvulaceae)	Jicama[3] and sweet potato
Mulberry (Moraceae)	Breadfruit, fig, mulberry
Mustard (Cruciferae)	Horseradish, mustard, radish, rutabaga, turnip, watercress and varieties of cabbage: broccoli, brussels sprouts, cabbage kraut, cauliflower, Chinese cabbage, collards, kale, kohlrabi
Myrtle (Myrtaceae)	Allspice, clove, guava
New Zealand Spinach (Tetragoniaceae)	New Zealand spinach
Nightshade or Potato (Solanaceae)	Eggplant, potato, tobacco, tomato. This family includes all foods called "pepper" (except black and white pepper), such as cayenne, chili pepper, green pepper, hot pepper sauce, paprika, pimiento, red pepper

continued

3. *Botanists differ in their classification of jicama. Some consider it a legume, others relate it to the sweet potato. Doctors using the Diversified Rotary Diet prefer to relate jicama to the sweet potato, or the Morning-Glory family.*

39

TABLE 3—*Continued*

Family	Plant Foods—*Continued*
Nutmeg (*Myristicaceae*)	Nutmeg and mace
Olive (*Oleaceae*)	Olive
Orchid (*Orchidaceae*)	Vanilla
Palm (*Palmaceae*)	Coconut, date, sago palm starch
Papaya (*Caricaceae*)	Papaya
Parsley (*Umbelliferae*)	Carrot, celeriac, celery, lovage, parsley, parsnip. Also these spices: angelica, anise, caraway, celery seed, coriander, cumin, dill, fennel
Pepper (*Piperaceae*)	Peppercorns
Pineapple (*Bromeliaceae*)	Pineapple
Plum (subfamily of *Rosaceae*)	Almond, apricot, cherry, nectarine, peach, plum, prune, wild cherry
Pomegranate (*Punicaceae*)	Pomegranate (also, grenadine syrup)
Poppy (*Papaveraceae*)	Poppyseed
Purslane (*Portulacaceae*)	Purslane
Sedge (*Cyperaceae*)	Chinese water chestnuts
Sesame (*Pedaliaceae*)	Sesame seed
Soapberry (*Sapindaceae*)	Litchi nuts
Spurge (*Euphorbiaceae*)	Tapioca
Tea (*Theaceae*)	Tea
Walnut (*Juglandaceae*)	Black walnut, butternut, English walnut, hickory nut, pecan
Yam (*Dioscoreaceae*)	Chinese potato and yam

Family	Mammals
Bear	Bear
Beaver	Beaver
Bovine	Beef cattle (including veal), buffalo, goat, sheep (lamb and mutton) and their milk and milk products

40

Family	Mammals—Continued
Camel	Camel and llama
Cat	Mountain lion
Deer	Caribou, deer (venison), elk, moose, reindeer
Hare	Hare and rabbit
Hippopotamus	Hippopotamus
Horse	Horse
Opossum	Opossum
Pronghorn	Antelope
Squirrel	Squirrel
Swine	Hog (pork)

Family	Birds
Dove	Dove and pigeon (squab)
Duck	Duck, goose and their eggs
Grouse	Ruffed grouse (partridge)
Guinea Fowl	Guinea fowl
Pheasant	Chicken, cornish hen, seafowl, pheasant, quail and their eggs
Turkey	Turkey and their eggs

Family	Fish
Anchovy	Anchovy
Anglerfish	Monkfish
Bass	White perch and yellow bass
Bluefish	Bluefish
Catfish	Catfish
Codfish	Cod (scrod), cusk, haddock, hake, pollack, whiting
Croaker (freshwater)	Freshwater drum
Croaker (saltwater)	Croaker, drum, sea trout, silver perch, spot, weakfish (spotted sea trout)
Eel	American eel
Flounder	Dab, flounder, halibut, plaice, sole, turbot
Harvestfish	Butterfish and harvestfish
Herring (freshwater)	Shad (roe)
Herring (saltwater)	Pilchard (sardine) and sea herring

continued

TABLE 3—*Continued*

Family	Fish—*Continued*
Jack	Amberjack, pompano, yellow jack
Mackerel	Albacore, bonito, mackerel, skipjack, tuna
Marlin	Marlin and sailfish
Minnow	Carp and chub
Mullet	Mullet
Perch	Sauger, walleye, yellow perch
Pike	Muskellunge, pickerel, pike
Porgy	Northern scup (porgy)
Salmon	All salmon species and all trout species
Scorpionfish	Rosefish (ocean perch)
Sea Bass	Grouper and sea bass
Sea Catfish	Ocean catfish
Silverside	Silverside (whitebait)
Smelt	Smelt
Sturgeon	Sturgeon (caviar)
Sucker	Buffalofish and sucker
Sunfish	Black bass, crappie, sunfish
Swordfish	Swordfish
Tilefish	Tilefish
Whitefish	Whitefish

Family	Shellfish
Abalone	Abalone
Clam	Clam and quahog
Cockle	Cockle
Crab	Crab
Lobster	Crayfish, langostinos, lobster
Oyster	Oyster
Scallop	Scallop
Shrimp	Prawn and shrimp
Snail	Snail
Squid	Squid

Family	Amphibians
Frog	Frog

SOURCES: *Clinical Ecology*, by Lawrence Dickey (Springfield, Ill.: Charles C Thomas, 1976).

Dictionary of Flowering Plants, by J. C. Willis (Cambridge: Cambridge University Press, 1973).

Gray's Manual of Botany, Eighth Centennial Edition, compiled by Merritt Lyndon Fernald (New York: D. Van Nostrand Co., 1950).

Hortus Third: A Concise Dictionary of Plants Cultivated in the United States and Canada, compiled by Liberty Hyde Bailey and Ethel Zoe Bailey (New York: Macmillan Publishing Co., 1976).

The New York Botanical Garden Illustrated Encyclopedia of Horticulture, by Thomas H. Everett (New York: Garland Publishing, Inc., 1981).

How to Set Up a Diversified Rotary Diet

The one-week menu plan shown in the Sample Diversified Rotary Diet is an example of how to plan a nourishing diet while rotating foods. I'll explain the reasons for my choices and show you how to plan a diet of your own, based on the same principles.

To begin, make a list of 12 foods to which you are not allergic. Then arrange them into a basic "skeleton" diet of 1 food per meal for four days. For Days 1 through 4 on the Sample Diversified Rotary Diet, I've chosen honeydew melon, carrots, lamb, peaches, broccoli, turkey, apples, zucchini, salmon, strawberries, cabbage and chicken, shown in capital letters. You may substitute other fruits, vegetables and protein sources. Be sure that foods from the same food family are no closer than two days apart. (Refer to Table 3: Food Families in this section for that information.) Honeydew melon and zucchini, for example, are both members of the Gourd family and appear on Days 1 and 3 in the Sample Diversified Rotary Diet. Dr. Theron Randolph and others who have treated thousands of people with a Diversified Rotary Diet say that members of the same food family must be rotated every two days to avoid daily exposure to similar foods. That controls symptoms and prevents new food allergies from developing.

Whatever foods you choose, you can eat them at any time of the day. Eating fruit in the morning, vegetables at lunch and meat, fish or fowl at dinner is purely arbitrary, based on custom and convenience. Also, you can eat as much of each food as you want, to fill up.

Because most people plan and shop for a week's worth of meals at a time, I've carried this diet plan over to Days 5, 6 and 7. I've chosen cantaloupe, parsnips, scrod, nectarines, cauliflower, duck, apples, butternut squash and whitefish, shown in capital letters. That shows that the menu for Day 5 doesn't have to be a carbon copy of Day 1. In fact, they *shouldn't* be identical. Doctors who prescribe

continued

Sample Diversified Rotary Diet for One Week

This is an example of how to plan a Diversified Rotary Diet, in which no food is eaten more frequently than every fourth day. In this case, beef, citrus, shellfish, egg, grains, milk, yeast and members of the Composite

	Day 1	**Day 2**	**Day 3**
Breakfast	HONEYDEW MELON walnuts (amaranth)	PEACHES almonds (arrowroot)	APPLES pecans (buckwheat)
Sweetener	honey	pureed peaches	unsweetened apple juice
Lunch	CARROTS sole (pears)	BROCCOLI butterfish (persimmon)	ZUCCHINI flounder (grapes)
Oil	sunflower seeds and sunflower oil	olive oil	sesame seeds and sesame oil
Dinner	LAMB tomato or onion (or both) (papaya)	TURKEY sweet potato (figs)	SALMON celery and parsley (kiwi)
Snack	cashews	macadamia nuts	pine nuts

How to Set Up a Diversified Rotary Diet—*Continued*

this diet encourage people to eat as wide a variety of foods as possible, both to prevent new allergies from developing and to help insure intake of essential nutrients. And, of course, the cardinal rule of food rotation, as explained earlier in this section, is that you do not repeat any one *food* more often than every fourth day. In the Sample Diversified Rotary Diet, for instance, apples appear on Days 3 and 7, four days apart.

family (ragweed and its relatives) are omitted. To set up a Diversified Rotary Diet based on your own food allergies, see the accompanying instructions.

Day 4	Day 5	Day 6	Day 7
STRAW-BERRIES filberts (tapioca-starch flour)	CANTALOUPE walnuts (amaranth)	NECTARINES (OR APRICOTS) almonds (arrowroot)	APPLES pecans (buckwheat)
maple syrup	honey	pureed nectarines	unsweetened apple juice
CABBAGE grouper (plums)	PARSNIPS goat's-milk cheese (pears)	CAULI-FLOWER tuna (pineapple)	BUTTERNUT SQUASH pork (grapes)
avocado and avocado oil	sunflower seeds and sunflower oil	olive oil	sesame seeds and sesame oil
CHICKEN potato and cayenne (banana)	SCROD asparagus (mango)	DUCK sweet potato (raspberries or grapes)	WHITEFISH celery, tomato and/or onion (watermelon or blue-berries)
Brazil nuts	pistachio nuts	macadamia nuts	pine nuts

At this point, the "skeleton" diet—foods shown in capital letters only—can serve either of two purposes. A few people have so many food allergies that they need to stick to a minimum number of foods, at least until they feel better. Or you can use this plan to test for food allergies, first adding one new food and then another to determine what foods may be causing problems. (Because the diet is very limited at this point and doctors often prohibit nutritional supplements

continued

How to Set Up a Diversified Rotary Diet—*Continued*

during testing, try to insure intake of at least modest amounts of calcium, vitamin C and other essential nutrients. And as you are finished testing, you may wish to add the purest forms of nutritional supplements you can find. For more information, read the section, Nutrition Basics in Brief and see the Appendix for purchasing sources.)

If your food allergies are not very severe and you can eat a wider range of foods, you can add 1 more food per meal. For Days 1 through 4, I've chosen walnuts, sole, tomatoes or onions, almonds, butterfish, sweet potato, pecans, flounder, celery, parsley, filberts, grouper and potato and cayenne, shown in lowercase letters. If you then add a sweetener, a cooking oil and another food for snacks each day, you build up to 36 different foods for four days. I've added honey, sunflower oil, cashews, pureed peaches, olive oil, macadamia nuts, unsweetened apple juice (or apple-juice concentrate), sesame oil, pine nuts, maple syrup, avocado oil and Brazil nuts. I've chosen nuts for snacks because they're easily carried to school or office, but there's no reason you can't choose other foods such as dried fruit or raw vegetables. Again, be sure that foods belonging to one food family are eaten two days apart.

Eventually, you can add still more foods to your menu, as illustrated by foods listed in parentheses in the Sample Diversified Rotary Diet, giving you a grand total of 48 food choices within any four-day period. I've omitted grains, but if you can eat wheat, rice, oats, barley, rye and other grains, your options will be wider yet.

You need more than just a list of foods to plan meals, though— you need recipes.

To get the most variety possible out of your food choices, combine related foods together into a single dish. Peach-Almond Ice Cream, for example, combines almond with a fruit in the Plum family, to which it's related. It would make a perfect dessert for Day 2 of the Sample Diversified Rotary Diet. Similarly, you can prepare delicious stews and chowders by combining foods from one or two families. Basic Beet Borscht, for example, is made primarily from foods in the Goosefoot family. For dozens of other recipes that can help you to make tasty, satisfying meals out of a few foods, see the Index to Recipes for a Diversified Rotary Diet at the end of this book. Once you get the hang of it, I think you'll find it surprisingly easy to follow your personal Diversified Rotary Diet.

Nutrition
Basics in Brief

Allergy doctors have just begun to realize that people with food allergies have special nutritional needs. That's no surprise, really. If you have to avoid one or more fundamental foods such as milk, bread or citrus for long periods of time, you run some risk of a deficiency, because those foods are major sources of one or more essential nutrients. And you need to make up the difference to stay healthy. In other words, you don't want to solve one problem food allergy—and at the same time set yourself up for another—nutritional deficiency. Yet getting your quota of certain nutrients on a restricted diet can be tricky, depending on what you're allergic to.

Beef, poultry and other protein sources. Animal foods such as beef, poultry, fish, game, milk, eggs and cheese each contain a full complement of 20 amino acids approximating the protein makeup of our own bodies. So those foods are the protein sources we can use most efficiently. However, if you're allergic to any of those foods, or if you are rotating them at four-day intervals, you can match the protein efficiency of animal foods with vegetable sources of protein. Simply mix legumes—beans, peas or peanuts—with grains or nuts. Legumes supply the amino acids that grains and nuts need for the body to fully utilize available protein. These protein components are utilized more efficiently when those foods are eaten together than when they are eaten separately at consecutive meals. Combining foods in this way is called protein complementation. For people who are allergic to legumes, amaranth and buckwheat also complement grains and nuts.

47

"Mixing and matching" vegetable sources of protein pays an added nutritional dividend: It fits in perfectly with advice to cut down on saturated fat, most of which comes from red meat and other animal sources. That recommendation comes from the United States Senate Select Committee on Nutrition and Human Needs report of 1977 and is intended to reduce the incidence of heart disease among Americans. Many of the recipes in this book combine complementary sources of vegetable protein, to help you in meal planning.

Milk. Anyone who avoids milk, cheese, yogurt and other dairy products is likely to be low in calcium and possibly low in vitamin D, which we need to utilize calcium properly. Non-dairy sources don't quite measure up: Three-and-a-half ounces of granular amaranth contains approximately 250 milligrams of calcium—about as much as 6 ounces of low-fat milk or 1 ounce of Swiss cheese. Some beans, greens and other vegetable sources contain between 50 and 125 milligrams of calcium per half-cup serving. However, we need between 800 and 1,200 milligrams of calcium a day to prevent brittle bones and other health problems. That's hard to achieve by diet alone, even if you can drink milk and eat cheese. If you can't, getting enough calcium is nearly impossible. Supplements of calcium gluconate or calcium carbonate can help to insure against a deficiency, especially for growing children and pregnant, nursing or postmenopausal women, whose calcium needs are greatest of all. (Calcium lactate may be a problem for people with milk allergy, because it contains lactose, a milk product.)

Fortified milk also happens to be our main source of vitamin D, other than sunlight. In the northern hemisphere, the probability of getting enough vitamin D from natural sunlight is very slim during the coldest six months of the year. Other than milk, possible food sources of vitamin D are fatty fish (such as mackerel), eggs, liver and butter. If those foods are off-limits to you, or if you eat them infrequently, vitamin D supplements can take up the slack. No need to take more than an average of 400 International Units a day, though.

As is the case with many supplements, some vitamin D capsules contain artificial colors, flavors or preservatives to prevent rancidity. Your best bet may be preservative-free cod liver oil (provided you're not allergic to it) and vitamin D from safflower oil. (See Appendix for purchasing source.) Since vitamin D is fat-soluble and is stored by the body, either of these may be taken every fourth day in a quantity that *averages* 400 International Units per day.

Citrus fruits. Fresh orange juice and grapefruit juice provide plentiful amounts of vitamin C. Tomatoes, peppers and strawberries are also rich sources. If you are allergic to any of those foods, try to eat cantaloupe, potatoes, sweet potatoes, cabbage, broccoli, brussels sprouts, spinach and other green, leafy vegetables to be sure you get enough. Vitamin C builds good health in a number of ways— it helps to fight infections, speeds wound healing and improves absorption of iron and folate (a B vitamin), to name just a few. But for people with allergies, getting enough vitamin C is of special importance: It counteracts the release of histamine, a major factor in allergic reactions such as itching, runny nose, sneezing and hives. In their book *The Vitamin C Connection* (Harper and Row, 1983), Drs. Emanuel Cheraskin, Marshall Ringsdorf and Emily Sisley say, "[Vitamin C] counteracts food allergies. The antihistaminic action of vitamin C can enable people to tolerate foods they otherwise could not eat." But it may be hard to get vitamin C on a diet limited by allergies to citrus, in which case supplements are important.

Because many vitamin C supplements are based on corn or citrus fruit, people who are allergic to those foods may be better off buying pure vitamin C crystals made from sago palm. (Purchasing sources are listed in the Appendix.) Whether you're relying on food or supplements for vitamin C, it's best to space consumption throughout the day rather than try to get your day's allotment in one meal. That's because vitamin C is water soluble—the body does not store it. You need to replenish the supply every few hours.

Wheat and other grains. Wheat germ and wheat-germ oil are two of the most concentrated sources of vitamin E. Whole-grain cereals and bread are fairly good sources of both vitamin E and B vitamins, along with fiber and other nutrients. So people who cannot eat wheat and other grains—or those who eat them only once every four days or longer—can miss those nutrients if they're not careful. You can probably meet your minimum requirement for vitamin E by eating nuts, seeds and vegetable oils such as safflower, sunflower, peanut and soybean oils, among others. However, many health professionals feel strongly that the Recommended Dietary Allowance for vitamin E for adults—12 to 15 International Units— is far too low, and that 100 to 400 International Units is much closer to a truly healthful level. Among other functions, vitamin E acts as an antioxidant. That is, vitamin E protects against cancer

TABLE 4

Food Sources of B Vitamins

Many of the richest sources of B vitamins happen to be common food allergens. Choose food sources carefully to avoid a deficiency. (See Appendix for names of manufacturers who sell nonallergenic nutritional supplements.)

Vitamin	Food Sources	Comments
Thiamine (B_1)	**Brewer's yeast, brown rice, chicken livers, oats, pork, rice bran, rice polish, whole wheat flour,** blackstrap molasses, fish, legumes, meat, nuts, poultry	Without grains, may be hard to get an adequate supply. Thiamine may also be in short supply if you don't eat meat and legumes fairly frequently.
Riboflavin (B_2)	**Brewer's yeast, liver, tongue and other organ meats, milk and dairy products,** almonds, eggs, green leafy vegetables	If you're allergic to milk, other dairy foods or brewer's yeast, you may be at risk of deficiency. If you are allergic and vegetarian too, the risk increases.
Niacin (B_3)	**Brewer's yeast, fish, lean meats, organ meat, peanuts, poultry, rice bran,** avocados, dates, eggs, milk	Niacin supplements come in two forms: niacinamide and nicotinic acid. Both forms can be used to treat pellagra. Nicotinic acid can help lower cholesterol but may cause flushing. And niacinamide can help depression. Discuss with your doctor which is best for you.
Pyridoxine (B_6)	**Bananas, chicken (white meat), fish, meats (especially organ meats),** brewer's yeast, peanuts, soybeans, walnuts, whole wheat flour	Omitting meat would also eliminate a lot of B_6 from your diet.

NOTE: Boldface type indicates major sources of vitamins; regular type indicates modest sources.

Vitamin	Food Sources	Comments
Cobalamin (B_{12})	**Meat (especially organ meats),** dairy products, eggs, fish, oysters	If your diet excludes meat, fish, eggs and dairy products, you may need supplements. Some people may not absorb B_{12} properly and may require injections.
Pantothenic Acid	**Brewer's yeast, organ meats,** egg yolk, milk, mushrooms, salmon, whole wheat flour	Essential to a healthy immune system and possibly helpful to people with allergies.
Folate or Folic Acid	**Brewer's yeast, liver,** avocado, banana, beets, broccoli, brussels sprouts, cantaloupe, oranges, romaine, spinach, whole wheat flour	Requirements are small and sources diverse. Try to include some food sources of folate in your daily diet.
Biotin	**Kidney, liver,** egg yolk, fish, legumes, milk, nuts, whole wheat flour	Although the best sources of biotin are common allergens, requirements are small and it can be synthesized by intestinal bacteria.

by preventing polyunsaturated fats we eat from turning into peroxides, substances that can damage cells or promote tumors. Vitamin E also shields cells against the effects of pollution. (One word of caution: Since vitamin E enhances the tone of the heart muscle, people with high blood pressure or heart disease should check with their doctor before taking this supplement. Even then, it's usually best to begin at a low dose, and increase or decrease the amount gradually.)

For people who want to consume protective amounts of vitamin E but are allergic to wheat germ oil, soy-based supplements are available from at least one source I know of—Carlson's, listed in the Appendix. Some of those supplements are purified to the point where little soy remains, minimizing the chances of causing a reaction. (Synthetic forms of vitamins A and E are derived from

51

petroleum and may cause reactions in people who are allergic to petroleum products of all kinds.)

As for B vitamins, if you can eat brown rice, you're in luck— it can contribute fair amounts of these important vitamins. If you're allergic to all grains, try to eat beans, seeds, eggs, pork, organ meats, buckwheat and amaranth to get your supply of Bs (see Table 4, Food Sources of B Vitamins).

Yeast. Nutritional yeasts, such as brewer's yeast, are excellent sources of the trace minerals chromium and selenium, plus B vitamins. If you're allergic to yeast, be sure to include other sources of those nutrients in your daily diet. Chromium is found in liver, beef, cheese, chicken and whole grains. Selenium is found in fish and whole grains. For sources of B vitamins other than grains and yeast, see Table 4. And yeast-free supplements of those trace minerals are available (see Appendix).

Soy. Soybeans and soy products are the richest, least-expensive sources of vegetable protein. Lecithin is a soy product that is a concentrated source of choline, a little-known nutrient that is essential to the brain and nervous system and helps to sharpen memory. For people who are allergic to soy, alternative sources of choline are beef liver, eggs and fish.

Other Essential Nutrients

Here are a few other essentials to look for:

Vitamin A. This fat-soluble vitamin helps to fight infection and maintains the health of our eyes, skin and tissues that line the body. Most yellow and orange food and deep green, leafy vegetables are respectable sources of vitamin A. That includes apricots, broccoli, cantaloupe, carrots, nectarines, peaches, pumpkin, spinach, squash, sweet potatoes and Swiss chard. If you can eat those foods and do so regularly, you can meet your basic requirement for vitamin A quite easily.

Many nutrition-oriented doctors recommend larger amounts of vitamin A—up to 25,000 International Units for adults—to help prevent cancer and other diseases. Fish liver oil is the most common source of concentrated vitamin A, a problem for people who are allergic to fish. Fish oil perles also contain preservatives to retard spoilage. The capsules themselves may be made of either beef or pork gelatin, may contain preservatives, and may contain artificial colors or flavors. If you're allergic to any of those, look for liquid cod liver oil or for supplements of beta-carotene, named for carrots, one of the most plentiful vegetable sources of vitamin A. (Beta-carotene derived completely from carrot oil may be better than that derived from petroleum, from the standpoint of allergies.) Of course, the only way to be absolutely sure the product you are considering contains nothing to which you're allergic is to write to the manufacturer for a list of specific ingredients.

Zinc. The Recommended Dietary Allowance for this mineral is 15 milligrams for adults. Zinc is considered helpful to clear up eczema and other skin problems, sharpen night vision, heal wounds, fight infection and perform other functions. Three ounces of lean beef or calf's liver supplies a little over 5 milligrams of zinc. Toasted wheat germ contains almost 1 milligram per tablespoon. Whole wheat flour also contributes some zinc. If you're allergic to beef or wheat, other good sources of zinc include Brazil nuts, cashews, chick-peas, peas, pumpkin seeds and soybeans. Supplements of zinc gluconate can also help assure adequate intake.

Iron. Meat is by far the richest source of iron. If you can't eat meat of any kind—or if you eat meat sparingly for one reason or another—it's very tough to get the 10 to 18 milligrams of iron needed for rich, red blood, strong immunity and peak energy levels. If you need supplements to insure your supply of this mineral, look for "ferrous" forms—they're absorbed better than "ferric" compounds. Consuming plenty of vitamin C, too, boosts iron absorption.

This basic guide should help you cover the essentials of good nutrition on a limited diet. If you decide to consult a doctor for more detailed information about the nutritional needs of you and your family, keep two things in mind: Don't assume that what he or she recommends for one member of the family applies to all. Especially with small children, avoid guesswork. And don't assume that if a little is good, more is better. (That applies to medicines as well as to supplements.)

The field of nutrition in general is relatively new. The study of nutrition as it applies to food allergy is even newer. Research has proven that nutritional needs increase under any form of stress or illness, and allergy certainly qualifies as a stress, and at times, as an illness, too. Whatever symptoms you're trying to relieve, it's probably safe to say that a well-nourished body is better able to cope than one that is chronically deficient in essential nutrients. Hopefully, as more health professionals investigate this area, we can look forward to even more information to manage food allergy successfully.

What's for Lunch?

When lunch time rolls around, people with food allergies can't just go to the refrigerator and pull out whatever happens to be on the shelves, or open a can of soup from the pantry. At work or school, it's even more difficult: The cafeteria may not serve anything that fits their diet. Yet with some advance planning, lunch doesn't have to be a big dilemma. While the tips and suggestions offered here make great lunches either at home or away, they're especially useful for people who carry their lunch. (Restaurant lunches are covered in the section, Dining Out.)

Sandwiches. If allergy to yeast or grains (or both) prevents you from eating commercially baked bread, take heart: A number of breads in this book make excellent sandwiches. In fact, I specifically devised Steamed Savory Sandwich Loaf with the lunch-carrying crowd in mind. People who can eat yeast but not wheat will find Yeast-Raised Rice-Flour Bread a close second to any wheat loaf. Tortillas and Flatbreads can also pinch-hit for sliced bread. Wrap them around the filling of your choice.

Sliced home-cooked meats and poultry are often the best choice of sandwich filling for people limited to very simple foods. For more elaborate fillings, make poultry and fish salads with the mayonnaise alternatives given in the section on Salad Dressings, Sauces and Condiments. Baked Chicken Salad, Tofu Salad, Better Burgers, Hot Tuna Patties and Peanut Burgers all do well as sandwich fillings. So do bean spreads of all types, including South-of-the-Border Sandwich Spread.

If you love peanut-butter-and-jelly sandwiches but are allergic to peanuts or sugar (or both), try Nut or Seed Butter with Simple-Simon Jam or Old-Fashioned Fruit Butter.

Soups. Nothing revives you on a cold, damp day like a steaming bowl of soup, stew or chowder. Minestrone, Potato Soup and Kidney-Bean Stew are so substantial, they're meals in themselves. Double the recipes and freeze in single-serving-size containers to use as needed.

If a soup is too chunky for your thermos bottle, blend it to a puree. Serve with crackers, muffins or a salad.

Salads. Salads can make lunch time a feast. Choose from Eclectic Potato Salad, Three-Bean Salad, Cauliflower-Dill Salad, Jicama "Hot Stuff" Slaw, Hold-the-Lettuce Salad and Confetti Rice Salad. Pack in a wide-mouth jar with a tight-fitting lid.

To make tossed salads, think beyond lettuce, tomato and cucumber. (If you have food allergies, you may have to!) By adding leftover cooked beans, peas, meat, fowl or fish, you can build a simple salad into a hearty and satisfying meal. Pack dressing separately so the salad doesn't get soggy. Supplement your salad with a Muffin, Flatbread, Crackers or Oat Scones.

Fruit, nuts and seeds. These frequently show up as lunch-box treats whether people have allergies or not because everyone enjoys a change of pace now and then. But together, fresh, cooked or dried fruit, nuts and seeds can serve as a simple meal. Fruit-nut-seed combinations are particularly helpful to people who are following a Diversified Rotary Diet and need to make a meal from foods from only one or two food families. For example, almonds, apricots, cherries, nectarines, peaches, plums and prunes all belong to the same family. Combining almonds with any of those fruits makes a simple yet interesting meal which is also high in fiber, vitamins and minerals. For people who are allergic to nuts, seeds from pumpkin, squash and sunflowers make excellent companions for fruit.

Although nuts and seeds are best stored in a cool place, you don't necessarily need to refrigerate them for a short time. So they are convenient to carry for a midday snack while shopping or doing other errands. I often carry Brazil nuts and dried pineapple or papaya for just such emergency meals.

Leftovers. For the ultimate in creative lunches, be on the lookout for dinner foods that have lunch-box potential, especially if there's a stove or hot plate to reheat food where you work. In fact, I often cook a surplus of a meal for just such purposes. I call these "planovers." For example, if you bake a whole chicken for dinner,

55

save the legs for a future lunch, freezing them until needed, if necessary. Pack along with a Muffin and some fruit. Leftover Vegetarian Chili, Versatile Meatballs and Zesty Supper Loaf are other examples of dinner foods that add variety to lunches.

Desserts. If you can afford the calories, many of the baked goods in this cookbook make easily portable desserts to round out your lunch. Many are high in protein and can be used to augment a meatless or dairy-free lunch. For starters, try a piece of Banana Bread, Gingerbread, Two-Step Carrot Cake, Rice-Flour Carrot Cake or Pineapple-Prune Cake. Any of the Steamed Breads also travel well. Or tuck a handful of Cookies on Parade, Dream Cookies or Hidden Treasures in your lunch-to-go.

Beverages. The simplest hot beverage is a cup of herb tea, made with tea brought from home. Or pack a thermos of Tea and Berry Punch, Nice Tea, Melon Cooler, Nut Milk, Nut-Fruit Shake or No-Milk Shake.

Aside from the individual recipes highlighted here, many of the Snacks and most of the Picnic, Camping and Outdoor Foods travel well and add additional variety to brown-bag lunches.

Other helpful tips. Remember to keep foods cold until you are ready to eat them, or until you reheat them. If you pack your lunch the night before, refrigerate overnight, and refrigerate again at work or school, if you can. If not, pack food in an insulated lunch box with a jar of ice. (See the section, The Allergy-Free Kitchen for more information about less allergenic materials for packing food.)

Plan each week's worth of lunches in advance. That prevents the need for last-minute decisions and helps to assure you of lunches that are free of troublesome foods. If you're well prepared, you won't have to "make do" and risk an allergic reaction.

The Allergy-Free Kitchen

Anyone with food allergies faces two concerns when stepping into the kitchen. Above all, you have to stock food you can eat. But you also need to take a close look at how you store and prepare food and clean up. For even if you pay careful attention to what you eat, you won't feel completely well if something else in the room, such as molds or gas fumes, is making you ill.

Few of us realize that the kitchen can be one of the densest pockets of pollution we encounter, indoors or out, city or country— even if it's always scrupulously clean. To illustrate my point: A government worker in Washington, D.C., wore a portable pollution monitor throughout a typical day as part of a study on environmental health. (See graph of Kitchen Air Pollution: Higher Than You Think.) In the course of the day, he commuted to his office, trailing behind a smoky diesel truck, and sat among smokers in the cafeteria. Yet he was exposed to the most pollution at 9:00 P.M., *while cooking dinner in his kitchen.*

What makes the kitchen such an allergy trap? Cooking odors, for one thing, which can trigger reactions in highly allergic people. Fish, eggs, and onions are the common offenders, but any food can do it.

"Anyone who reacts to a food when they eat it can react just as readily to its fumes, because they get into the bloodstream," said one doctor I spoke to.

Another primary allergy trigger in the kitchen is a gas-burning appliance, which gives off nitrogen dioxide, a major irritant and pollutant. Gas stoves are the primary offenders, although gas hot-

(continued on page 60)

Kitchen Air Pollution:

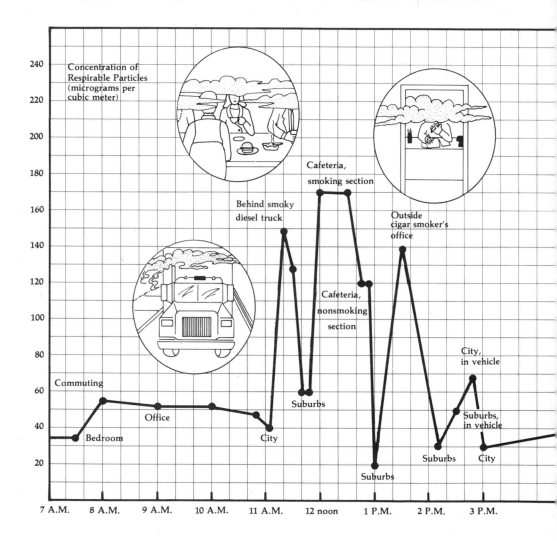

This graph charts the amount of pollution breathed by one individual during the course of a typical day of commuting to and from work and relaxing at home at night. He was exposed to the highest concentration of air particles — including potential allergy triggers — while preparing dinner in his kitchen.

Higher Than You Think

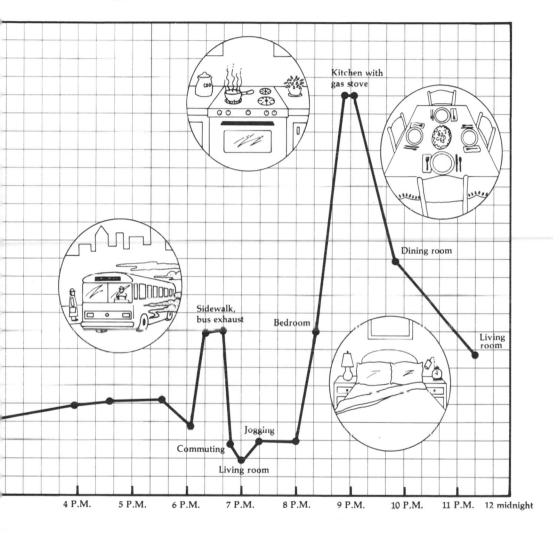

Kitchen with gas stove

Dining room

Sidewalk, bus exhaust

Bedroom

Living room

Jogging

Commuting

Living room

4 P.M.   5 P.M.   6 P.M.   7 P.M.   8 P.M.   9 P.M.   10 P.M.   11 P.M.   12 midnight

SOURCE: *Reprinted by permission from "The In's and Out's of Air Pollution," by John D. Spengler and Steven D. Colome,* Technology Review, *August/September, 1982, p. 32.*

Chart illustrations by Diane Ness Shaw.

water heaters, gas dryers and unventilated gas and kerosene space heaters give off offending fumes, too.

Aside from cooking odors and gas fumes, kitchens often harbor molds, dust, formaldehyde, plastics and other petroleum products—all common allergy triggers. You may be surprised to see formaldehyde among those allergy triggers, but the National Academy of Sciences estimates that 10 to 12 percent of the people in the United States may be supersensitive to formaldehyde, even when exposed to minuscule amounts of the substance. If you're one of those people, you can suffer headaches, eye-ear-nose-and-throat symptoms or other respiratory reactions, including attacks of hay fever and asthma.

No allergy cookbook would be complete, then, without a cook's tour of the kitchen to examine potential problem areas. Chances are you won't need to make all of the changes discussed—that will largely depend on what you or your family is allergic to.

An Allergy Inventory

Kitchen cabinets. One of the biggest sources of formaldehyde, especially in new or remodeled kitchens, is particle board cabinets, constructed with formaldehyde-containing glues. Sherry Rogers, M.D., an allergist in Syracuse, New York, says that there are two things you can do about them. One is to paint the cabinets with a coat or two of latex paint, to seal in the formaldehyde. (The paint fumes take a few weeks to die down, though, so it's best to paint before you leave on vacation.) Or you can install one of the few air filters that are capable of dealing with formaldehyde fumes, one being the High Country Air Filter listed in the Appendix.

If you plan to build a new home or have your kitchen remodeled, ask the cabinetmaker to use real wood, not particle board, and formaldehyde-free glue. Metal cabinets are okay, too. If you've been in your present kitchen for several years or longer, chances are formaldehyde is no longer a problem.

The stove. If you have a gas stove, replacing it with an electric range is a major stride toward making your kitchen less allergenic—particularly if you're sensitive to petroleum products and gas fumes. In a study of 137 homes in one Wisconsin community, levels of nitrogen dioxide—a major by-product of gas combustion and a primary trigger of allergy—averaged five times that of outdoor levels in kitchens with gas stoves. Kitchens with electric stoves had nitrogen dioxide levels below outdoor levels. If for some reason you can't get rid of your gas stove, vent the fumes outdoors by having an adequate exhaust system installed. (Gas furnaces should also be vented.)

Very rarely, an individual may be allergic to fumes of heated metal coils on an electric range. I know one woman who overcame that by buying a ceramic range, formerly manufactured by Corning and now offered by Amana (see Appendix).

Cookware. The best cookware for people with food allergies are pots and pans (and bowls, pie plates and casseroles) made of either enamel, enamel-coated iron, lined copper, glass, glazed ceramic (such as Corningware), stainless steel, or aluminum bonded to stainless steel. None of those materials seem to migrate into food. Iron migrates, but that's good for you, so iron cookware is fine, too.

Uncoated aluminum presents a potential problem: Traces of aluminum can leach into food, especially into acid foods like citrus, cherries, tomatoes and rhubarb. The same goes for aluminum pie plates. The symptoms of aluminum toxicity mimic senility. Just how big a threat this may be is highly controversial. Nevertheless, the fact remains that some people may be more vulnerable to aluminum exposure than others because of the individual differences in the way our bodies break down and absorb or excrete the metal. While not an allergic problem per se, the last thing a person with allergies needs is aluminum poisoning. However, aluminum is an excellent heat distributor. Aluminum pots bonded to an inner surface of stainless steel are the perfect answer, combining aluminum's excellent heat-conducting properties with an impervious, noncorrosive finish. If you already own uncoated cookware and don't care to switch, be sure to use it to cook nonacid foods only. That applies to aluminum pie plates, as well.

Non-stick coatings—namely Teflon II and Silverstone—are a boon to people who are allergic to dairy products because they help you to cook without butter. And they seem to be safe, according to scientific reports. I personally enjoy the convenience and easy cleaning of non-stick cookware with no ill effects. In fact, one scientist states that there has never been a case reported in which a person became ill from normal cooking with non-stick cookware. But everyone—allergic or not—needs to bear two things in mind: When using this cookware, don't use scrapers or steel wool on non-stick coatings—the coating will scratch and leach into food, which is an aesthetic problem if not an allergic one. Because many people with allergies react to plastic utensils, I recommend using a flexible metal spatula, sliding it under the food carefully. When the pan eventually gets scratched and nicked, replace it. And don't broil food in a pan with a non-stick coating or overheat empty stove-top pans. Although the plastics used for non-stick coatings are among the most heat-stable substances known, they can break down when superheated. Short of accidentally leaving an empty pan on high heat, though, that's highly unlikely.

Clay cookers are a bit expensive, but they're a wonderful replacement for plastic roasting bags for cooking roasts, poultry and potatoes. Enamel roasting pans also work well—and sometimes cost less.

Individual-serving-size ceramic au gratin casseroles (such as Corningware's) to "freeze, heat and eat" food are convenient for "TV dinner" type meals. They usually have a plastic lid, but you can get around that by placing a layer of cellophane on top of the food between the food and the lid, to block any plastic from leaching into the food during storage.

Food storage. I can't discuss food storage without talking about plastic. Because it's so versatile, it's everywhere. But people who are sensitive to plastics and other petroleum derivatives need to think twice about this miracle material. Food scientists at Rutgers University have found that plasticizers in the polyvinyl chloride (PVC) film used to wrap meat migrate into the meat. That's also true of "clingy" plastic food wraps. And a report in the *Journal of Environmental Health* found that vinyl chloride in PVC can leach into vegetable oils and vinegar, as well. Fortunately, there are safe alternatives to plastic.

● Buy meat from a butcher who will use cellophane or butcher's paper to wrap your meat, and use the same materials to store meat at home. Of the two, butcher's paper is thicker and better for wrapping frozen food. For long-term freezing, place paper-wrapped food in a plastic food storage bag, to prevent loss of moisture.

● Cellophane comes in sheets and bags of various sizes. You can buy it at specialty stores, some health food stores and mail-order firms listed in the Appendix. It tears and isn't impervious to air, so cellophane is best for wrapping sandwiches and other short-term storage of foods.

- Buy spring water, oils and nut butters that come in glass bottles, not plastic.
- Store leftovers in glass—either wide-mouth mayonnaise-type jars or canning jars. They're a safe, no-waste way to hold not only soups and sauces but solid foods like carrots and celery sticks.
- If you wrap food in aluminum, be sure to place the shiny side against food—the dull side contains a plastic coating. While we're on the subject, china, stoneware or glass dishware is better than plastic.

Even if it takes you a year or two to completely phase plastic out of your kitchen, it's worth it. One doctor tells of a women who had a stubborn nagging cough for 20 years. She went to a number of specialists and underwent several tests, yet no one could help her. After a 45-minute investigation of the woman's home environment, the doctor concluded that the woman was allergic to plastics. She says that after the woman got rid of all the plastic in her kitchen, her cough disappeared.

So many paper products, including lunch bags and paper towels, contain formaldehyde that these articles can be a problem for formaldehyde-sensitive people. If that's the case in your family, carry lunches in cellophane bags, cloth tote bags, or insulated lunch "boxes." Use a clean, absorbent cotton towel instead of paper towels to pat dry salad greens, fish, meat or poultry.

Cooking and drinking water. If you or someone in your family is allergic to chlorine, formaldehyde or something else in your household water supply, you may have to choose an alternative source of water for cooking and drinking. If you buy bottled water, be sure it's sold in glass, not plastic bottles. Even then, glass-bottled water is sometimes transported in plastic-lined trucks or stored in plastic vessels before it's bottled. That may explain why you may be able to tolerate one brand of bottled water but not another. It's a very individual matter.

If you can't find suitable bottled water, you may need to install a water filter. As far as I can tell, the best home water purification method is a double-cannistered activated carbon filter installed below the sink and attached to a separate faucet, bypassing the regular tap. Studies show that this technique effectively removes chlorine, industrial chemicals, disagreeable taste and bad odors (see Appendix for purchasing sources).

Well water may be the best, least expensive solution. If you know someone who has well water of good quality, try it to see if it agrees with you. I am comfortable drinking water from our well and strongly prefer it to "city" water.

Picnic baskets and brown bags. While we may prepare all of our food in the kitchen, we don't always eat it there. Picnicking and brown-bagging are an American way of life. Once you decide what to pack, you want to choose vessels and utensils that are just as safe as your food. Thermos bottles are practically *made* for allergic people, who often need to carry their own beverages rather than chance soda machines or other roadside supplies. Look for glass-lined, stainless steel bottles, not plastic. (You're most likely to find them in camping supply departments and well-equipped hardware stores.)

If you work in an office where styrofoam cups are standard issue at the coffee station, use a china or earthenware mug from home instead. A University of Connecticut chemist claims that lemon oil in tea has a special knack for dissolving polystyrene materials. Then again, other researchers feel hot liquid is what corrodes the cup. Either way, allergic people are better off with a more trustworthy drinking cup.

If you like to camp or picnic, buy an inexpensive set of stainless steel flatware just for that purpose, rather than using plastic flatware. As far as I can tell, plastic handles pose no problem.

Cleaning Up

Cleaning up is an unavoidable part of cooking—and equally fraught with allergy pitfalls.

Oven cleaners. Of all the offensive cleaning compounds that allergic people find in their kitchen, oven cleaners are by far the worst. Any chemicals that dissolve baked-on grease and grime are potent stuff and highly irritating to asthmatics and other people with sensitive airways or skin. Instead of commercial cleaners, use the following method—it's harder on your elbows, but easier on your lungs: Following a spill, sprinkle with salt. After the oven cools down, scrape off burned food and wipe with a damp sponge. And use a scouring soap pad on wire racks. Self-cleaning ovens may or may not be safe for you—that will depend on your own sensitivity to fumes.

Mold. Mold is ruining Leonardo da Vinci's *The Last Supper*.

And mold can ruin your meals, too, if you're allergic to it. I don't necessarily mean molds on forgotten leftovers. Molds that grow surreptitiously in the refrigerator drip-pan and garbage pail, especially in warmer, humid months of the year, can trigger respiratory allergies such as hay fever or asthma. And a microbiologist at Indiana-Purdue University found that the drip pans in self-defrosting (frost-free) refrigerators harbor a certain type of bacteria that can easily slip past the sweeping action of bronchial cilia in the airways and lodge in the lungs, also triggering respiratory allergy. Here are some ways to eradicate kitchen mold.

- Clean the drip pan at least once a month and the garbage pail weekly.
- If you grow herbs or ornamental plants in wicker baskets in your kitchen, check for mold growth that can proliferate in moisture-laden wood.
- Wipe down every square inch of your kitchen twice a year with a solution of either Clorox, borax, vinegar or baking soda diluted in water (depending on which of those you can tolerate).
- If your kitchen sits partially below ground level or adjoins the basement, a dehumidifier will help to check mold growth.
- Compost heaps can harbor mold. So if you're allergic to mold, wear a face mask to carry vegetable trimmings out to the pile. Or ask someone else to do it for you.

Wooden cutting boards (and wooden countertops, for that matter) are a potential hideout for molds and bacteria, a health hazard regardless of allergy. From that standpoint, plastic cutting boards are safer and more sanitary. If you're allergic to plastics, be sure to buy the hardest plastic cutting board you can find. One doctor told us that harder boards are less likely to bother sensitive people. And I find that harder boards are easy to keep clean—free of stains and odors—by running them through the dishwasher.

The kitchen sink. If you have sensitive skin, wash dishes with a hypoallergenic all-purpose cleaner such as Amway's L.O.C. or Bio-Pure's All-Purpose Cleaner, listed in the Appendix. Better yet, wear either cotton-lined rubber gloves, or cotton Dermal Gloves under an unlined pair, whenever you put your hands in water—to scrub walls, woodwork, floors, countertops and appliances. Dry, chapped skin is easily irritated and vulnerable to allergic reactions. That's why it's good to use a moisturizing lotion in winter, when dry air contributes to redness and chapping. Always keep a bottle of moisturizer by the kitchen sink, and be sure it's a fragrance-free, lanolin-free hypoallergenic brand such as Ar-Ex (see Appendix).

Dish towels, like many other fabrics, are steeped in formaldehyde and can trigger dermatitis, because formaldehyde reacts readily with skin protein. (That's why it's used as embalming fluid). Formaldehyde can also trigger various other reactions in sensitive people. Wash new towels several times to get rid of any formaldehyde. And buy all-cotton or Irish linen towels.

Alternative cleaners. Ammonia and ammonia-based cleaners are great for sponging off fingerprints and smudges but ammonia fumes can trigger violent reactions in asthmatics and other people with sensitive airways. Borax and water is an alternative, nontoxic solution. Here are some other cleaning tips.

- Shine appliances with club soda, rubbing alcohol or vinegar and water instead of commercial, petroleum-containing waxes. (In fact, hospitals routinely use rubbing alcohol to clean stainless steel equipment.)
- Clean windows and shine the toaster with a solution of vinegar in water or a nonaerosol, pump-style window cleaner.
- Floor wax has been known to give some people headaches or trigger other unpleasant reactions as it's applied. If you have a no-wax floor in your kitchen, you're in luck. Just mop it with borax and water. If you must wax the floor, choose a warm day so that you can open the windows. Afterwards, leave the house for a few hours while the fumes die down.

Air fresheners. Air fresheners—both the aerosol and "stick-up" types—usually contain formaldehyde, which doesn't freshen the air at all but numbs your sense of smell—permanently, in some cases. And aerosol products often contain hydrocarbons, a petroleum derivative. So if you're allergic to formaldehyde or petroleum products, "air fresheners" don't belong in your kitchen. Here are some better, safer alternatives.

- Eliminate the source of odors—pets, trash, old food, and so forth.
- Sprinkle good old-fashioned odor-absorbing baking soda in cat litter and trash pails. Leave an open box of baking soda in the refrigerator.
- Open a window or turn on the fan. Ventilation is the only true source of fresh air.

To get rid of common cooking odors, smoke and other airborne offenders, you have to have a good kitchen exhaust fan. Aside from a fan, an air filter of some type can further help to purify the air you breathe while you cook and eat, and it prevents cooking odors and other fumes from traveling to other areas of the house, too.

Air-conditioning acts like an air filter, since air is whisked out of the house and replaced with outdoor air, which is presumably less contaminated. If you don't have central air-conditioning, you'll need an extra-large size room unit for the kitchen to deal with heat generated by cooking.

If your home is located near traffic, industry or fields that are sprayed heavily with pesticide, your air conditioner must have a charcoal filter or other means to purify incoming air. Also, be sure the air intake is not located near a garage, chimney or other source of fuel exhaust.

Air filters themselves come in different types and don't all work equally well. Electronic air cleaners rid the air of numerous larger particles, but many give off ozone, which can aggravate asthma, especially when they're new. A number of allergy doctors recommend HEPA (High Efficiency Particulate Air) filters, which are more efficient but may possess paper filters containing formaldehyde. Formaldehyde is tough to get out of the air, one doctor explains, because the particles are so small. For people sensitive to chemicals, the best unit is High Country Air Filter, listed in the Appendix.

Kitchen Decor

Not everything in a kitchen is purely utilitarian. We each add our personal touches. Many decorative items may be fine for most people but can be troublesome if you have certain allergies.

For instance, if you're thinking of carpeting your kitchen, think again. Carpeting complicates life for people with allergies because it's harder to keep clean, it harbors molds when wet and it's usually installed with petroleum-based glues. All-cotton, washable scatter rugs are a better alternative. So is ceramic tile, although it's expensive and hard on the feet—and plummeting dishware.

Plastic flowers or other ornaments collect dust, the nemesis of many allergic people. And the plastic itself can trigger subtle reactions. Crockery and wrought iron trivets are among the safer alternatives, on both counts. (Practical, frequently used items collect less dust than idle ornaments.)

Use cotton or linen tablecloths or placemats, not plastic. For easy maintenance, you can choose either cotton terry or permanent-press cloth—wash either several times to remove any formaldehyde.

Candles make dinnertime special or romantic. For people allergic to fragrances or petroleum products, beeswax candles are safer than regular petroleum-based candles. So are "floating candles"—special wicks that float in vegetable oil ponded in attractive glass vessels.

At the risk of sounding like a broken record, I want to emphasize that any changes you make in your kitchen will depend on what you're allergic to and how bad your symptoms are. But many of these suggestions not only rid the kitchen of common allergy triggers; they also help keep it clean and organized. And that makes meal planning and cooking easier.

Dining Out

Dining out can be a pleasure even if you have food allergies—whether you're sitting in a sidewalk cafe in New Orleans, taking a business client out to lunch or sharing a candlelight dinner with someone special. All it takes is confidence and a game plan. I've learned, for instance, to ask questions about how food is prepared. Sometimes I order food that's not on the menu. And I've developed a backup plan for those rare occasions when I'm allergic to everything on the menu.

But before I discuss specific tactics, I'd like to share a few general guidelines that help me dine well on restaurant cuisine.

The better the restaurant, the more choices you'll have. I've found that in order to avoid major food allergens—corn, wheat, milk, soy, eggs, yeast and so on—I have to eat in fairly good restaurants that prepare food to order, rather than fast-food restaurants.

Call ahead. Find out what's offered, how it's prepared, and whether the chef can adapt a dish for you. And ask if they have a no-smoking section. Again, the better the restaurant, the more likely they'll be able to accommodate you. If calling ahead isn't feasible, request the same information when you arrive. If an airline meal is on your agenda, calling ahead for a special meal is a must.

The safest policy is to order plain, unadorned food—preferably baked, broiled or steamed. Sauces, toppings, marinade and casseroles multiply the number of hidden ingredients you're likely to encounter.

Be flexible. If you're rotating foods once every four days, your menu choices may be limited even further. In that case, it's wiser to break rotation and eat something you had yesterday than to eat something you shouldn't and risk an allergic reaction. For example, if turkey's the only meat listed that you can eat, but you had turkey the day before, it's better to eat turkey two days in a row than to eat a meat that would make you ill. But resume your Diversified Rotary Diet as soon as possible.

Carry Alka-Seltzer Gold or other alkaline salts with you. They help to neutralize an allergic reaction if you happen to eat something that doesn't agree with you. That's an emergency out, but it works.

Breakfast

I've noticed that in most restaurants, if you can't eat eggs, toast, milk or cereal, your breakfast choices boil down to fruit, fruit juice or oatmeal. As for fruit, you'll usually find grapefruit or melon (when it's in season), and if you're really lucky, fresh strawberries, bananas or peaches. Most places don't keep a lot of fruit on hand, however, because they worry about it spoiling, so it's not unusual to find they're out of fresh fruit even if it's on the menu. That may leave only fruit juice and oatmeal (assuming you can eat oats). You could combine the two—a great taste, and a great idea if you can't drink milk. Honey is another way to perk up a bowl of oatmeal. (If it's not on the table, ask for it). Ask if it's pure honey, though. I've seen some that's extended with corn syrup. The same is true for maple syrup. It's a rare restaurant that carries the more expensive, pure maple syrup.

Pancakes, as you probably know, are little more than wheat, milk and eggs. If you're allergic to any of those foods, pancakes are off-limits. Be careful if you're considering buckwheat pancakes—they usually contain no more than 30 to 50 percent buckwheat. The rest is wheat flour.

If you like hash-brown potatoes, ask if they're cooked in butter or oil. And has anything else been added? To be safe, you might consider ordering a baked or steamed potato.

Which brings us to another way to get around the limitations of breakfast menus: Think beyond traditional breakfast fare. If you can eat beef, order a small steak or hamburger patty. Or ask the waiter or waitress if the kitchen has any turkey or other plain, roasted meat left over from the night before. (Even if plain turkey

70

or other meat is not on the menu, the restaurant may have some on hand to use in turkey salad, for example. So ask.)

If you'd like a hot beverage but can't have coffee or tea, the easiest thing to do is carry your own herbal tea bags and order a pot of boiling water. It may even be necessary to order and pay for a cup of tea, even though you'll use your tea bag instead of theirs.

Sometimes the only breakfast place for miles around is a dough-nut shop or fast-food restaurant, in which case your choices may be limited even more. So it's always a good idea to carry dried fruit, nuts, flatbread or some other portable food from home. No one should have to eat food they know will make them ill. A back-up plan prevents you from finding yourself with nothing to eat for the most important meal of the day.

Lunch

In this country "lunch" seems to be synonymous with "sand-wich," and if you can't eat wheat, that's a problem. Here are some alternatives I've devised.

- Order sandwich "fixin's" without the bread and eat them with knife and fork. Or carry flatbread from home and make your own sandwich with whatever you order.
- Take advantage of luncheon specials that feature plain broiled fish, chicken or beef with a cooked vegetable on the side. These are often quite good.
- In a pinch, you may want to order a steaming bowl of oatmeal and supplement it with a cooked vegetable.
- Fresh fruit from the appetizer list makes a good dessert. If you order something such as fresh strawberries, peaches or banana, be sure to tell them, "No cream."

The Salad Bar

The best thing about salad bars is that most of the foods are offered separately, so you can choose what you want and pass up what you're allergic to. But salads can be booby traps if you don't know how to recognize and avoid the trouble spots.

If you can't eat lettuce, take spinach. Or make a hearty, re-spectable salad with no greens whatsoever. In fact, skipping greens

71

might be a good idea even if you're not allergic to lettuce: You may be allergic to sulfur dioxide or any one of a number of related sulfur compounds widely used to keep greens crisp and fresh. Because sulfites are powerful antioxidants and antimicrobials, they keep lettuce and other fruits and vegetables from wilting and turning brown. That's great for the restaurant but bad news for people who are allergic to sulfites. Asthmatics, in particular, have been known to suffer anaphylactic shock (sudden unconsciousness, with little or no blood pressure) when exposed to sulfites.

(It's easy to mistake that reaction for a heart attack or choking episode, unless a fellow diner realizes that the problem started with the salad. If someone collapses at dinner, summon paramedics promptly or rush the victim to the closest hospital emergency room, and be sure to mention the possibility of allergy, so the person gets the right treatment. If you have severe food allergies, it's a good idea to wear a Medic Alert tag saying so. The address is in the Appendix.)

Reactions to sulfites aren't always so severe, of course. But if you have any reason to suspect that sulfites are a problem for you, you can save yourself a lot of trouble by asking the restaurant manager if any of the fruits or vegetables have been treated. And that goes for "house salads" as well as make-it-yourself salads.

If the only salad available is the house salad, ask the waiter or waitress to list all the fixings, including garnishes such as croutons. Ask them to omit anything you can't eat. If they don't, send your salad back for another.

Other potential trouble spots in the salad arena are combination foods—potato salad, cole slaw, apple salad, and so forth. For example, plain garbanzo beans (chick-peas) would probably be a good choice, whereas a three-bean salad may not be.

Salad dressings are the final hurdle. They may contain any of a number of ingredients—egg, cornstarch, milk, stabilizers or flavor enhancers. You're better off if you choose the oil and vinegar or a squeeze of fresh lemon juice. When I'm dining close to home, I usually carry homemade salad dressing in a small, tightly sealed bottle, secured with a plastic bag. Otherwise, I choose lemon juice.

Dinner

Many of the tactics that get you through lunch will also get you through dinner, with a few added tricks.

Some restaurant menus are detailed; others consist of a few

scrawled phrases on a chalkboard. Either way, you have to ask questions. For example, if you are considering broiled chicken or broiled fish, here are some questions you should ask.

- Has the chicken been marinating in anything? If so, what?
- Is the chicken rubbed with butter or oil? If so, has it already been done or can this step be omitted?
- Is paprika or any other seasoning used? This may or may not be acceptable to you. (Don't argue with them about the skin on the chicken. It prevents excessive drying, and you can remove it yourself.)
- Is the fish brushed with butter or oil? If you're allergic to milk, butter should be omitted. If oil is used, what kind is it? If your server seems uncertain, order "dry broil."
- Are any crumbs or herbs added to the fish?
- Is lemon juice used in preparation?

Any of those ingredients may be okay for you, but you need to know what you're eating, so you have to ask. And they're just a few examples of the *kinds* of questions you'll need to ask, depending on what foods you are allergic to.

If you order beef, find out if it's been tenderized with MSG (monosodium glutamate). Even in tiny amounts, MSG has been known to trigger migraine headaches and other allergic-type symptoms in many people.

When it comes to potatoes, your best bet by far is a whole, uncut baked potato. I find that if you don't specify "uncut," the cook may slit it open and dress it up with either sour cream or butter, a problem if you're allergic to milk products. Similarly, ordering a potato baked in the half shell won't guarantee that the cook won't scoop out the center and mash it with milk. Of course, if you can have milk products, stuffed potatoes are fine. Scalloped potatoes have flour and milk, and french fries and hash browns have cooking oil, so they're not safe for everyone. Parsleyed potatoes are usually dipped in butter or margarine ahead of time. Find out what the restaurant uses, then decide.

Speaking of margarine, I don't recommend it for potatoes—or anything else. Most brands contain milk solids, and all contain various color, flavor and texture additives. If any of those ingredients bother you, margarine is going to be a problem. If an unadorned potato doesn't appeal to you, bring enough salad dressing from home to moisten it.

73

For many people, wine, candles and flowers make a dinner very special. But for some, those niceties can put a real damper on the meal. Many wines contain sulfites and other additives. If you're allergic to chemicals, you could end up with a headache or other discomfort from the wine and think it was something you ate. Most candles are made of petroleum, so if you know for a fact that you're allergic to petroleum products, ask the server not to light the candle on your table. Flowers are rarely a problem, unless they're a very pungent type such as lilacs or marigolds. But if they bother you, feel free to ask that they be removed.

Other Helpful Tips

If you make clear, specific requests, yet receive the wrong food despite your efforts, don't hesitate to send it back. You need not be rude, merely firm. After all, restaurants are in business to please diners. By the same token, be sure to reward excellent service and cooperation at tip time.

If speaking up makes you uneasy, consider taking a class in assertiveness training. Once you get past the "I'm dying of embarrassment stage," you'll enjoy meals away from home as much as everyone else does. It's important to be able to take control and still feel good about yourself.

Sometimes you head for a restaurant because you're simply too tired to cook, or you don't have time for a home-cooked meal. Perhaps you have to chauffeur the children to ball practice or music lessons or have to rush off to night school or an early evening meeting. Things like that happen to everyone sooner or later.

To cut down the need to fall back on restaurant food, I prepare a few entrees to freeze in reserve, which I call "planovers." It really doesn't take any extra effort: If I'm cooking a dinner that freezes well, such as Grain-Free Stuffed Peppers or Chickburgers, I double the amount and freeze half. Soups and stews are also likely candidates. I also try to maintain a good supply of frozen Stocks and Italian and Tomato-Free Spaghetti Sauces as starter ingredients for quick, easy meals.

Parties and Other Social Occasions

Not all meals away from home are eaten in restaurants. Dinner at the homes of friends or relatives, business buffets, church banquets, birthday parties and even an outing at the ball park all qualify as dining out. For those occasions, too, planning ahead can save the day.

For family get-togethers and visits with close friends, your best bet is to explain your situation to the hostess ahead of time and bring your own special food. A host or hostess who sincerely cares about you will not be insulted or try to force you to "just try a little" of some deleterious food. He or she may even offer to prepare something that you can eat. Children may ask why Aunt Marge is eating different food, or a newcomer to the group may stare, but by and large you're in a comfortable and accepting environment. Focus on the pleasure of being with family and friends and exchanging ideas in lively discussions. Remember, you can enjoy these occasions and the company of others so much more when you're feeling well.

A more difficult social situation occurs when you are called upon to dine with strangers, perhaps in a business setting, at a banquet or when a friend wants you to meet his or her family. Those situations are often stressful even without food allergies to cope with. To bring your own food invites attention and only makes things more complicated. If you can bring your own food easily and comfortably, fine—it's never improper when your health is at stake. But if that's inconvenient or awkward, simply eat before you go, then bring an herbal tea bag and sip tea slowly through the meal. If pressed for an explanation, simply say you have special food allergies or give some other brief explanation. You don't have to go into elaborate detail. Sometimes, you can politely sidestep the situation altogether by asking, "May I join you after dinner?" when you're invited for a meal.

Children's social lives pose similar problems. Your child's own birthday party is simple to handle compared to invitations to others' parties, because you can make the party food yourself. Yet even when your child is a party guest, you may have more options than you realize. One Mom I know always offers to bake the birthday cake as her child's gift to the birthday child. The host parents are usually delighted. If that doesn't work out, she sends a special goodie with her child to eat while the others have birthday cake. That takes a fair amount of self control and confidence on the part of the child, and may not work for everyone. But it's worth a try.

The only other options that I see are either declining the invitation and planning a special activity in its place, or accepting the invitation, food and all, and hoping for the best. How you feel about this may depend on how a lapse in dietary restrictions affects the youngster and how well the child can accept his or her dietary limitations.

The post-party behavior of one little girl I know was so consistent that it helped her family and her allergist detect a severe sensitivity to both beet and cane sugars—prime ingredients of birthday party fare. The child would leave for afternoon parties a sunny, happy child and return tired and grumpy. The grumpiness soon gave way to uncontrolled tears. She would then cry herself to sleep with no dinner, spend a fitful night and wake up gaunt and exhausted. When she didn't eat sugar, she was fine. Needless to say, the girl now takes sugar-free treats from home to birthday parties. She remembers all too clearly how terrible she felt, and handles her situation very well.

Kids *can* handle more than we give them credit for. If the child is tested for food allergies and sees a direct connection between the offending foods and the symptoms they trigger, the battle is half won. Helping the child develop a strong sense of responsibility for his or her own health is one of the greatest gifts parents can give. The worst way to handle the problem is to declare that the youngster must comply "Because I (or the doctor) said so." Parents become enforcement officers and are too often viewed as adversaries. Then as soon as they aren't looking, the child cheats. Allergies last a long time, so dealing with them positively is worth the whole family's efforts.

Packing Your Own Food

As I mentioned earlier, there are going to be occasions when carrying food from home is the most reliable answer. "Brown-bagging" needn't be limited to toting your lunch to the office. If you can't eat franks, popcorn or soda, for example, you can take your own snacks to the ball park. I even pack food and water for an occasional day of shopping and errands. A pint jar full of ice cubes and water serves as both a beverage and "refrigeration" for food packed with it. If you pack a juicy snack, like fresh peaches, plums or pears, pack a damp washcloth in a plastic bag so you can wipe your fingers when they get sticky. When I first started this routine, I sometimes packed an elaborate lunch and then drove off without it. So put your lunch in the car as soon as you make it.

In many ways, it has never been easier to carry food safely. Insulated lunch boxes are available in many supermarkets and department stores. Larger coolers are available for weekend trips. I've carried breakfast (including flatbread) for two people on four-day trips by replenishing the ice morning and evening. (At least two battery-operated car refrigerators are available that I know of. They're listed in the Appendix.) I supplement the chilled food in my cooler with purchases of fresh fruit, vegetables, nuts and rice crackers for when I run out of flatbread. (More than anything else, trying to find bread away from home is one of the most frustrating tasks of all, so you're better off planning ahead and carrying your own.) If you happen to find plenty of options available in restaurants, just save the food to use later.

All that might seem like a lot of trouble, especially at first. The reward for all this "bother" is that you'll be able to feel good, even when you're away from home.

The flip side of dining out is entertaining. So right now, while your courage is high, start planning an outing with the family or invite a few friends in. Armed with the recipes in this book, you can serve an allergy-free meal everyone can enjoy. (For more tips on entertaining, see the section, Holiday Foods.)

PART II
Recipes

Breakfasts

Breakfast no longer has to be the toughest meal of the day to plan, even if you're allergic to eggs, milk, or wheat cereal. Here you'll find pancakes and waffles made of rice and oats—and others of amaranth, buckwheat, pumpkin seeds, coconut and carob for those who must avoid or rotate grains. Adding to the variety are granolas, muesli, breakfast cakes and puddings. You'll also want to see the section on Breads for muffins, flatbreads and other baked goods that can be served at breakfast.

Don't stop with breads and cereals, though. One of the things that helps allergic people most is to break out of the rut of eating the same types of foods, day after day. Once you realize that breakfast doesn't have to consist of toast and eggs or cereal and milk, the possibilities are nearly endless. For example, consider having a lamb pattie or chicken leg, left over from dinner and reheated. I relish soup in the morning, and another one of my favorites is fresh baked or broiled fish, for which recipes appear elsewhere in this book.

For those mornings when time is going to be short, cook ahead or double recipes. Then refrigerate or freeze for reheating later. Pancakes and waffles, for instance, reheat especially well in a toaster oven. You can easily prepare Oatmeal Patty Cakes, Stove Top Breakfast Rice Pudding and Instant Rice Pudding the night before and reheat them in the morning.

With all those options, breakfast will be as nutritious, satisfying and easy to plan as the rest of the day's meals.

80

Breakfast Buckwheat and Oats _____

Serves 6.

A hearty hot cereal, satisfying with or without milk.

⅔ cup white or
     roasted
     buckwheat groats
⅔ cup rolled oats
⅓ cup soya powder (or
     soy grits, for
     chewier texture)
½ cup raisins
     (optional)
4 cups water
     maple syrup

Combine the buckwheat, oats, soya powder or soy grits and raisins in a 3-quart saucepan. Stir in the water. Simmer gently for about 12 minutes, or until thick. Serve with maple syrup.

Grain-Free Granola _____

Makes 7 to 8 cups.

1½ cups amaranth
     flour
  1 cup chopped
     walnuts or other
     nuts
½ cup potato starch
½ cup peanuts
½ cup sunflower
     seeds or sesame
     seeds
½ cup grated
     unsweetened
     coconut
1½ teaspoons ground
     cinnamon
¾ cup mashed
     bananas or
     pureed fruit
⅓ cup oil or walnut
     oil
¼ cup maple syrup
     or honey
  1 tablespoon lemon
     juice
1½ teaspoons pure
     vanilla extract
⅔ cup raisins

Mix the flour, walnuts or other nuts, potato starch, peanuts, sunflower seeds or sesame seeds, coconut and cinnamon in a large bowl.

Mix the bananas or fruit puree, oil, maple syrup or honey, lemon juice and vanilla in a small bowl. If honey is very thick, heat mixture briefly to liquefy.

Pour the liquid over the dry mixture. Stir well to coat dry ingredients. If mixture seems too dry, add a few tablespoons water.

Spread mixture in a lightly oiled jelly-roll pan. Bake at 300° for 45 to 60 minutes, stirring every 15 minutes. Remove from the oven and cool. Stir in the raisins.

Variation: Omit lemon juice and add ¼ teaspoon vitamin C crystals to dry ingredients.

NOTE: This is a chunkier granola than you may be used to. Eat it out of hand as a snack or top it with fruit juice for a quick breakfast.

High-Protein Granola _____

Makes 7 cups.

Combining a grain with a legume, seeds, nuts and amaranth gives you a high-protein breakfast dish. That's a plus if you can't drink milk. Serve with Pineapple Milk.

2½ cups rolled oats
  ¾ cup amaranth flour
    or oat flour
  ½ cup chopped
    walnuts
  ½ cup shredded
    unsweetened
    coconut (optional)
  ⅓ cup sunflower seeds
  ⅓ cup peanuts
  1 teaspoon ground
    cinnamon
  ½ cup sunflower oil
  ½ cup honey
  1 teaspoon pure
    vanilla extract
    (optional)
  ¾ cup raisins or other
    dried fruit
    (optional)

In a large bowl, combine the oats, flour, walnuts, coconut, sunflower seeds, peanuts and cinnamon.

Combine the oil and honey in a small saucepan. Heat briefly to liquefy the honey. Stir in the vanilla. Pour over the oat mixture. Mix well.

Spread mixture in a thin layer in a jelly-roll pan. Bake at 350° for 20 to 30 minutes, stirring mixture every 10 minutes. Granola is done when it is golden brown.

Allow to cool, stir in raisins or other dried fruit, then store in the refrigerator in tightly capped jars.

Instant Rice Pudding _____

Serves 1.

This quick breakfast-in-a-bowl is amazingly satisfying and supplies lots of vitamins, minerals and fiber. It's a great alternative to ready-to-eat cereals and milk. Adding peanuts, nuts or seeds boosts the protein content.

  ¼ cup unsweetened
    fruit juice
  6 pitted dates
  ¾ cup cold cooked
    basmati or brown
    rice (see
    Appendix)
  peanuts, nuts or
    seeds (optional)

Combine the fruit juice and dates in a blender. Process on high speed for 20 seconds, until dates are chopped but not necessarily smooth. Pour mixture over rice in a cereal bowl. Top with peanuts, nuts or seeds.

Stove Top Breakfast Rice Pudding ⎯⎯⎯⎯⎯⎯⎯⎯⎯⎯

Serves 4.

Try this in place of hot cereal. You'll never miss the milk.

1 pound tofu
1 cup raw basmati
    rice (see
    Appendix)
2⅓ cups unsweetened
    apple juice
¾ cup chopped dried
    apricots
½ cup raisins or
    chopped dried
    apples
¼ teaspoon
    powdered ginger
    (optional)
½ cup maple syrup
    or unsweetened
    apple-juice
    concentrate
2 tablespoons lemon
    juice or ½
    teaspoon vitamin
    C crystals
2 tablespoons
    almond oil (or
    other oil)
½ cup chopped
    toasted almonds

Drain the tofu for 20 to 30 minutes by pressing between cotton towels to extract as much moisture as possible. Crumble it with a fork.

Wash the rice in several changes of cold water to clean and remove excess surface starch.

Place the rice, apple juice, apricots, raisins or apples and ginger in a large frying pan. Bring to a boil, then reduce the heat, and simmer for 10 minutes. Stir once, remove from the heat, and set aside for 10 minutes.

Place the tofu, maple syrup or juice concentrate, lemon juice or vitamin C crystals and oil in a blender or food processor. Process until smooth. Pour over rice mixture and toss lightly to mix. (If desired, add a little hot water for a creamier consistency.) Sprinkle with almonds.

Variation: Substitute brown rice for the basmati. Because brown rice takes so much longer to cook, you should plan on at least 45 minutes' cooking time.

NOTE: If you'd like a quicker breakfast, use cold cooked rice. Simmer the dried fruit in about 1 cup of liquid until soft, then add the cooked rice and allow to heat.

Fried Rice ⎯⎯⎯⎯⎯⎯⎯⎯⎯⎯⎯⎯⎯⎯⎯⎯⎯⎯⎯⎯

Serves 2.

An Oriental favorite that gives breakfast a new twist.

¾ cup cooked brown
    rice
2 teaspoons oil
1 egg
1 tablespoon water
1 teaspoon wheat-free
    tamari sauce
  dash of cayenne
    pepper

In a large saucepan, sauté the rice in the oil for 5 to 7 minutes.

In a cup, lightly beat the egg, water, tamari and cayenne with a fork. Pour over the rice, and cook, stirring, just until the egg is set.

Muesli

Serves 1.

A Swiss-style breakfast in a bowl that's enormously satisfying. My favorite apples for this dish are Yellow Delicious, McIntoshes and Jonathans. Top with more apple juice to taste.

¼ cup rolled oats
1 unsprayed apple, diced
¼ cup chopped peanuts or walnuts
2 tablespoons sunflower seeds
2–4 tablespoons chopped raisins
1–2 tablespoons unsweetened apple-juice concentrate
1–2 teaspoons lemon juice or a pinch of vitamin C crystals

Toast the oats in a dry frying pan over medium heat for 5 minutes, until they darken slightly and have a toasty fragrance. Transfer to a large bowl, and toss with the apple, peanuts or walnuts, sunflower seeds and raisins. Moisten with juice concentrate and lemon juice or vitamin C crystals.

NOTE: If you like, you can combine the oats with a coarsely chopped apple and unchopped nuts and sunflower seeds in a food processor. Grind to the desired consistency. Stir in the raisins.

Creamy Breakfast Cereal

Serves 1 to 2.

This creamy cereal is ideal for infants, toddlers and convalescents. Soaking the grain overnight and then whisking the cereal as it cooks produces a very smooth porridge. And the variations that follow give you a wide choice for rotating foods.

3 tablespoons brown rice flour
1 cup water
1 tablespoon maple syrup
⅛ teaspoon ground cinnamon (optional)
1–2 teaspoons oil
Real Applesauce or Old-Fashioned Fruit

Sift the flour into a small saucepan. (Save any fibrous particles remaining in the sifter for use in muffins or pancakes.) Whisk in the water, cover, and allow to stand overnight.
In the morning, bring the mixture to a boil. Add the maple syrup and cinnamon. Whisk constantly for about 10 minutes, or until cereal is thickened to whatever consistency you desire. Stir in the oil. Serve hot with Real Applesauce or Old-Fashioned Fruit Butter made of pears.

Butter made of pears (see Index)

Variations: Replace the brown rice flour with either 3 tablespoons oat flour, ¼ cup white buckwheat flour or 3 to 4 tablespoons amaranth flour. (For directions on making white buckwheat flour, see Table 1, Cooking and Baking with Alternative Flours, in the section, Exploring New Ingredients.)

NOTES: Digestion of gluten-containing foods requires the presence of certain enzymes that infants may lack. For that reason, be sure to check with your pediatrician before offering your child foods containing oat, buckwheat, wheat or rye.

If you're an allergic mother, you may decide to preventively rotate your child's foods. In that case, you may also want to rotate wheat, rye, barley and millet cereals.

Grated-Apple Delight

Serves 1.

A muesli-like concoction that makes a satisfying breakfast or even an interesting side dish with dinner. For variety, use a different fruit each time you make it. I especially like fresh peaches.

½ cup cold cooked brown rice
2–4 tablespoons chopped nuts or seeds
2–4 tablespoons raisins, currants or dried fruit
1 unsprayed apple, shredded
¼ cup unsweetened fruit-juice concentrate, pureed fruit or Apricot Topping (see Index)

Combine the rice, nuts or seeds and raisins, currants or dried fruit with the apple in a bowl. Stir in the juice concentrate, fruit puree or Apricot Topping to moisten.

NOTE: You can use a blender or food processor to shred the apple and chop the nuts. Just add them with the juice concentrate, fruit puree or Apricot Topping; chop with on/off turns.

Sweet-Potato Delight

Serves 1.

Since this has become my favorite grain-free breakfast or lunch fare, I always bake an extra sweet potato for this dish. It's a big help for people who follow a Diversified Rotary Diet because it's a meal in itself.

2–4 tablespoons chopped nuts or pine nuts
1 ripe banana
1 medium sweet potato, cooked
1 teaspoon oil
1 tablespoon maple syrup (optional)

In a large frying pan, dry-roast the nuts over medium heat for a few minutes. Shake the pan often.

Cut the banana in half lengthwise. Cut the sweet potato into ½″ slices.

Add the oil to the pan. Push the nuts to the outer edges. Place the banana pieces, flat sides down, in the pan. Add the sweet potatoes. Cover, and cook for 2 minutes. Uncover, and cook for 5 minutes, until everything is heated through and browned on one side. Drizzle with syrup before serving.

Buckwheat Breakfast Cake

Makes 1 cake.

A grain-free coffeecake with a brownie-like texture.

1⅔ cups water
½ cup raisins
½ pound pitted dates, chopped
⅓ cup oil
2 tablespoons lemon juice or vinegar or ½ teaspoon vitamin C crystals
1 cup buckwheat flour
1 cup arrowroot
1 teaspoon baking soda
1 teaspoon ground cinnamon
½ cup chopped walnuts

Combine water, raisins and dates in a 3-quart saucepan. Boil for 10 minutes, then set aside to cool. Stir in the oil and lemon juice or vinegar or vitamin C crystals.

Into a medium bowl, sift the flour, arrowroot, baking soda and cinnamon.

Stir the flour mixture into the saucepan. Mix well. Stir in the walnuts.

Spread batter into an oiled 8″- or 9″-square baking pan. Bake at 400 for 20 minutes, or until the top is firm when touched.

NOTES: You'll find the dates easier to chop if you dip your knife into hot water periodically.

For milder flavor, use white buckwheat flour. (See Table 1, Cooking and Baking with Alternative Flours, in the section, Exploring New Ingredients.)

Oatmeal Patty Cakes ─────────────────────

Serves 2 to 4.

We served this to a teenager who's allergic to milk, and he was delighted to be able to enjoy breakfast cereal again after struggling for so long with dry cereals moistened with juice.

1¼ cups water
⅔ cup rolled oats
¼ cup raisins
1 tablespoon soy grits (optional)
¼ teaspoon ground cinnamon
2 teaspoons oil
2 tablespoons Apple Butter (see Index)
2 tablespoons chopped pecans

Combine the water, oats, raisins, soy grits and cinnamon in a saucepan. Bring to a boil, then reduce heat, and simmer for 5 minutes. Stir frequently. Stir in oil, and let stand, covered, for 5 minutes.

Divide the mixture into 2 large or 4 small mounds on small plates. With the back of a spoon, flatten each mound into a patty. Spread the top of each with Apple Butter, and sprinkle with nuts. Eat with a fork.

Variations: Substitute ½ cup steel-cut oats and 3 tablespoons oat bran, rolled oats or oat flour for the rolled oats. Combine in a small saucepan. Bring to a boil, then reduce heat. Cook and stir for 15 minutes until mixture is very thick. Add oil. Turn off heat, cover tightly and leave pot on burner. (Don't lift lid to peek.) After 15 minutes, remove lid and stir. Test to see if oats are soft enough to enjoy. If not, cover and let stand an additional 5 minutes. Serve as above.

NOTE: For a speedy breakfast, cook oat mixture the night before and spread in lightly oiled flat soup bowl. Cover and chill. (A double batch fits in a pie plate.) To serve, cut in pie-shaped wedges and cook for a few minutes on each side in a non-stick pan. (Or cook in a little oil in a regular frying pan.) They'll be ready to eat in 5 to 8 minutes. Serve as above.

Banana-Buckwheat Breakfast Cake _____

Makes 1 cake.

Yet another good way to introduce buckwheat to newcomers—the mild flavor is enhanced by banana and maple. Serve it plain or shortcake-style, with Banana Topping.

1¼ cup white
    buckwheat flour
    (see Note)
⅔ cup arrowroot
1½ teaspoons kombu
    powder
    (optional)
  1 teaspoon baking
    soda
¼ teaspoon vitamin C
    crystals
½ teaspoon grated
    nutmeg
½ teaspoon ground
    cinnamon,
    optional
½ cup chopped
    walnuts
1¼ cups mashed ripe
    bananas
⅓ cup walnut oil
½ cup maple syrup
    Banana Topping
    (optional; see
    Index)

In a large mixing bowl, combine the flour, arrowroot, kombu, baking soda, vitamin C crystals, nutmeg and cinnamon. Stir in the walnuts.

In another bowl, mix the bananas, oil and maple syrup.

Pour the liquid ingredients into the flour mixture. Stir to combine; do not overmix. Turn into an oiled 8"- or 9"-square baking dish. Bake at 400 for 22 to 25 minutes, until top is brown and cake tester inserted in the center comes out clean.

Split squares of warm cake and top with generous dollops of Banana Topping.

NOTE: For directions on making white buckwheat flour, see Table 1, Cooking and Baking with Alternative Flours, in the section, Exploring New Ingredients.

Coconut-Carob Griddle Cakes _____

Serves 1 or 2.

These unusual breakfast treats contain no flour, nuts or seeds. And if you bake them on a non-stick griddle, they require no oil.

½ cup grated
    unsweetened
    coconut
¾ cup water
¼ cup cool water
  2 tablespoons
    arrowroot

Place the coconut in a blender, and grind to a fine powder. Transfer to a small saucepan. Add the ¾ cup water. Boil for 10 minutes, until most of liquid has been absorbed and mixture is the consistency of a paste.

Meanwhile, combine cool water, arrowroot, carob powder and baking soda in the

2 tablespoons carob powder
½ teaspoon baking soda
2 teaspoons pure vanilla extract (optional)
¼ teaspoon vitamin C crystals
   maple syrup, Fruit-Solo Sauce or Goat's-Milk Yogurt (optional; see Index)

blender. Process briefly. Add hot coconut mixture and blend on high setting for 2 minutes. Pour batter into a small bowl. Just before cooking, stir in the vanilla and vitamin C crystals.

Drop 1 tablespoon of batter at a time onto a heated non-stick griddle. Cook until browned on bottom. Turn and cook other side until browned. Serve with maple syrup, Fruit-Solo Sauce or Goat's-Milk Yogurt.

Buckwheat Pancakes

Makes about 20 to 24.

People who love the flavor of buckwheat will enjoy these at breakfast, topped with maple syrup or Fruit-Solo Sauce.

½ cup buckwheat flour, white or dark (see Note)
½ cup soy or amaranth flour
½ cup arrowroot
½ cup ground nuts
1½ teaspoons baking soda
1½ teaspoons ground cinnamon
1½ cups warm water
3 tablespoons oil
2 tablespoons maple syrup or honey
2 tablespoons lemon juice
¼ teaspoon pure almond extract (optional)

In a large bowl, combine the buckwheat flour, soy or amaranth flour, arrowroot, nuts, baking soda and cinnamon.

In a small bowl, combine the water, oil, maple syrup or honey, lemon juice and almond extract. Stir into the flour mixture. If necessary, add more water to make thin pancakes.

Drop spoonfuls of batter onto a preheated, ungreased non-stick griddle or frying pan. Cook about 5 minutes on each side, until brown.

Variation: For a citrus-free version, substitute ½ teaspoon vitamin C crystals and 2 tablespoons of water for the lemon juice.

NOTE: For directions on making white buckwheat flour, see Table 1, Cooking and Baking with Alternative Flours, in the section, Exploring New Ingredients.

Rice-Flour Pancakes _____

Makes 20.

Rice flour produces soft, tender baked goods and lovely pancakes. Just don't make the pancakes too thin. (Unlike Amaranth Pancakes, though, these don't make sturdy sandwiches.)

¼ cup nuts
½ cup boiling water
½ cup water
2 tablespoons honey or maple syrup
1 tablespoon lemon juice
1 egg
1 tablespoon oil
⅔ cup cooked brown rice
¼ cup amaranth flour
¼ cup rice flour or rice bran
1 teaspoon baking soda

Grind the nuts to a fine powder in a blender. Add the boiling water, and process for 20 seconds. Add enough additional water to raise the level to 1 cup. Blend in the honey or maple syrup, lemon juice, egg and oil.

In a large bowl, mix the rice, amaranth flour and rice flour or rice bran.

Preheat an ungreased non-stick griddle or frying pan until a drop of water sputters across when dropped on it. Then add the baking soda to the liquid mixture, and quickly stir it into the flour mixture.

Spoon batter onto the griddle or pan. Turn the pancakes when bottoms are browned. Lightly cook the other sides.

Variations: For a citrus-free recipe, add ¼ teaspoon vitamin C crystals to the dry ingredients and omit the lemon juice. You can replace the amaranth flour with ¼ cup brown rice flour. For richer pancakes, use ½ cup nuts. And for egg-free pancakes, replace the egg with 2 tablespoons water.

To make Blueberry Pancakes, stir ¾ cup berries into the basic batter just before cooking.

Pumpkin-Seed Pancakes _____

Serves 1.

These simple milk-free, wheat-free, egg-free pancakes are a big help to people on a Diversified Rotary Diet. Make the pancakes very small so they will be thin and crisp. Eat them out of hand or top with Old-Fashioned Fruit Butter, Fruit-Solo Sauce or mashed bananas.

⅓ cup pumpkin seeds
⅓ cup boiling water

Grind the seeds to a fine powder in a blender. Add the water, and blend for 30 seconds. Allow the batter to rest for 5 minutes.

Drop 1 tablespoon of batter at a time onto a heated non-stick griddle. Cook until bubbly on top and browned underneath. Turn and cook other side until brown and crisp.

Variations: For spicy pancakes, add ¼ teaspoon ground cinnamon to the blender. Or use ¼ teaspoon of either powdered ginger, grated nutmeg, ground cloves or ground allspice.

Amaranth Pancakes

Makes about 18 4″ pancakes.

Delicious and grain free, these pancakes are sturdy enough to toast (in an oven or toaster oven) and make into sandwiches for lunch. For a real treat, try them with peanut butter or Peanut-Butter Spread.

1 cup amaranth
    flour
½ cup arrowroot
½ cup ground nuts
1 teaspoon baking
    soda
1 teaspoon ground
    cinnamon
1¼ cups water
2 tablespoons lemon
    juice
2 tablespoons oil
1–2 tablespoons maple
    syrup or honey

In a medium mixing bowl, combine the flour, arrowroot, nuts, baking soda and cinnamon.

In a small bowl, mix the water, lemon juice, oil and maple syrup or honey. Stir liquid into flour mixture to combine well. The batter will be thin.

Drop spoonfuls of the mixture onto a preheated, ungreased non-stick griddle or frying pan. (The pancakes will be very thin.) When pancakes are bubbly on top and browned on bottom, turn and cook other side. As the batter stands, it may thicken; thin it with a little water.

Variations: You can replace the lemon juice with ½ teaspoon vitamin C crystals or 2 teaspoons cream of tartar. Mix it with the flour.

NOTE: If you want to use these pancakes as flatbreads, cool them on wire racks, then stack, wrap and refrigerate until needed. Warm in a toaster oven or on wire racks placed on cookie sheets in a moderate oven for a few minutes. Use to make mini-sandwiches.

Oat-Rice Waffles ⎯⎯⎯⎯⎯⎯⎯⎯⎯⎯⎯⎯⎯⎯

Makes 4.

These waffles are crisper than those made with rice flour and soy. They're nice with Real Applesauce or Old-Fashioned Fruit Butter or just eaten out of hand.

½ cup nuts
¾ cup boiling water
¼ cup molasses
2 cups rolled oats
½ cup brown rice flour
1 teaspoon Corn-Free Baking Powder (see Index)
½ teaspoon baking soda
⅓ cup oil
2 eggs

Grind the nuts to a fine powder in a blender. Slowly add enough water to bring the level up to 1 cup. With the machine running, add the molasses.

Place the oats in a mixing bowl. Pour the nut mixture over them, and set them aside to soak for several minutes.

In another bowl, combine the flour, Corn-Free Baking Powder and baking soda.

Add the oil and eggs to the oat mixture. Stir in the flour mixture.

Bake according to the directions included with your waffle iron, using about 1 cup of batter per waffle.

Rice Waffles ⎯⎯⎯⎯⎯⎯⎯⎯⎯⎯⎯⎯⎯⎯⎯⎯

Makes 3.

Rice flour makes soft, rather delicate waffles. Top with your favorite sauce or fresh fruit.

¼ cup Brazil nuts
¾ cup boiling water
2 tablespoons oil
2 tablespoons honey, molasses or maple syrup
2 eggs
1 teaspoon pure vanilla extract
1 cup cooked brown rice
⅔ cup brown rice flour
⅓ cup amaranth flour or soy flour
¾ teaspoon baking soda
½ teaspoon grated nutmeg (optional)

Grind the nuts to a fine powder in the blender. Add enough water to bring the level up to 1 cup. Blend 30 seconds. Add the oil and honey, molasses or maple syrup. Blend to mix. Allow to cool to lukewarm, then blend in the eggs and vanilla.

In a large bowl, mix the rice, rice flour, amaranth flour or soy flour, baking soda and nutmeg. Pour in the liquid mixture, and stir to mix.

Bake according to the directions included with your waffle iron, using 1 cup of batter per waffle.

Variations: Use ½ cup nuts for richer waffles; decrease boiling water accordingly. You can also replace the amaranth flour or soy flour with rice bran or more rice flour.

For brownie-like Dessert Waffles, replace the amaranth flour or soy flour with ¼ cup carob powder and 4½ teaspoons rice flour. If desired, use pecans instead of the Brazil nuts, and fold an additional ½ cup chopped pecans into the batter.

For Banana-Rice Waffles, use only ¼ cup boiling water with the nuts. When liquids have cooled, add 1½ cups banana chunks to blender.

For Spicy Rice Waffles, add 1 teaspoon ground cinnamon and ½ teaspoon powdered ginger to flour mixture.

NOTE: If you're serving the waffles with a sweet sauce, such as Peachy Topping, use the amount of sweetener given. If topping is to be diced fresh fruit, add 2 tablespoons more sweetener.

Amaranth-Spice Waffles

Makes 3 to 4.

At our house we enjoy these grain-free waffles for leisurely weekend brunches. Serve along with fresh fruit.

½ cup Brazil nuts or cashews
¾ cup boiling water
¼ cup maple syrup or honey
2 eggs
1 cup amaranth flour
⅓ cup arrowroot
2 teaspoons Corn-Free Baking Powder (see Index)
1 teaspoon ground cinnamon
1 teaspoon powdered ginger
½ teaspoon grated nutmeg (optional)

Grind the Brazil nuts or cashews to a fine powder in a blender. Add enough water to bring the level up to 1 cup. Blend 30 seconds. Add the maple syrup or honey; blend again and set aside to cool to lukewarm. Then add the eggs.

In a large bowl, mix the flour, arrowroot, Corn-Free Baking Powder, cinnamon, ginger and nutmeg. Pour in the liquid mixture, and stir to mix.

Bake according to the directions included with your waffle iron, using about 1 cup of batter per waffle.

Variations: Use 3 eggs for waffles that are just a little lighter in texture. Maple syrup gives a crisper texture than honey does. For extra-light and crispy waffles, separate the eggs. Add the yolks to the liquid in the blender. Beat the whites until stiff. Fold them into the batter just before baking.

Carob-Buckwheat Waffles _____

Makes 4 to 5.

Crisp, delicious and brownie-like, these grain-free waffles make a fine brunch, luncheon or late-evening treat. The buckwheat flavor is very subtle.

⅓ cup pecans
1 cup boiling water
¼ cup walnut oil
¼ cup honey
1 cup white
    buckwheat flour
    (see Note)
⅓ cup carob powder
½ cup coarsely
    chopped pecans
2 teaspoons Corn-Free
    Baking Powder
    (see Index)
¾ teaspoon ground
    cinnamon
    (optional)
¼ teaspoon baking
    soda
2 eggs
1 tablespoon pure
    vanilla extract
    (optional)

Grind the pecans to a fine powder in a blender. Add the water, and blend for 30 seconds. Add the oil and honey; blend again. Leaving mixture in the blender container, allow it to cool to lukewarm.

Meanwhile, combine the flour, carob, chopped pecans, Corn-Free Baking Powder, cinnamon and baking soda in a large bowl. Mix well.

When the liquid mixture has cooled to lukewarm, blend in the eggs and vanilla. Pour liquid mixture into the flour bowl. Mix to moisten all dry ingredients.

Bake according to the directions included with your waffle iron, using about ½ cup of batter per waffle.

Variations: Use 3 eggs for waffles that are just a little lighter in texture. For extra-light and crispy waffles, separate the eggs. Add the yolks to the liquid in the blender. Beat the whites until stiff. Fold them into the batter just before baking.

NOTE: For directions on making white buckwheat flour, see Table 1, Cooking and Baking with Alternative Flours, in the section, Exploring New Ingredients.

Spanish Eggs in Vegetable Nests _____

Serves 4.

Another option for people who can eat eggs but not toast. For a totally grain-free breakfast, you can omit the rice layer and serve the eggs with crisply toasted Amaranth Pancakes.

2 cups cooked short-
    grain brown rice

Preheat the oven to 300°. Divide the rice into 4 portions. Press each portion into a flat

⅓ cup chopped
    onions
⅓ cup chopped green
    peppers
⅓ cup chopped
    celery
1½ teaspoons olive oil
1 garlic clove,
    minced or
    pressed
2 cups Tomato
    Sauce (see
    Index)
1 tablespoon lemon
    juice
½ teaspoon dried
    basil
¼ teaspoon dried
    oregano
    dash of cayenne
    pepper
    (optional)
4 small zucchini,
    shredded
4 eggs
    chopped black
    olives (garnish;
    optional)

pancake about 6″ across on an ovenproof salad plate. Place the plates in the oven, and turn off the heat. Let stand to warm until eggs are done.

Sauté the onions, peppers and celery in the oil until crisp-tender, about 5 to 7 minutes. Add garlic, and sauté 1 minute. Pour the Tomato Sauce into the pan; add lemon juice, basil, oregano and cayenne. Cover the pan, and simmer for 5 minutes.

Steam the zucchini for 5 minutes.

Break the eggs, 1 at a time, into a small saucer. Slip each into the Tomato Sauce. Cover the pan, and poach the eggs for 4 minutes, or until done to your taste.

Remove rice dishes from the oven. Divide the zucchini among them, and shape each portion into a nest. Slip an egg into each nest, and top with Tomato Sauce. Garnish with olives.

Eggs Florentine

Serves 4.

A tasty breakfast or brunch dish for people who can have eggs but not toast. (To save time, make the Creamed Spinach the night before.)

Creamed Spinach
    (see Index)
4–8 eggs

Divide the Creamed Spinach among 4 oiled ramekins or individual casseroles. With the back of a spoon, make 1 or 2 depressions in spinach. Break an egg into each depression. Bake at 375° for 10 minutes, or until whites are firm.

Variation: You can place the spinach in a large non-stick frying pan. Using the back of a spoon, make 4 to 8 depressions in the spinach. Bake as above. Use a spatula to serve.

Breads

Bread is the greatest single area of concern for people with wheat and yeast allergies. Your quest for suitable bread may be what prompted you to buy this book. You made the right decision—many wheat-free and yeast-free breads *are* possible if we think beyond the pre-sliced, airy loaves sold in grocery stores. After all, people met their bread needs very well for thousands of years by simply combining whatever flour was available with water, patting the dough into a flat, round shape and cooking it quickly on hot rocks at a fire's edge. The various Tortillas and the Fruited Flatbread given here use that same method. (Crackers are simply a variation of Flatbreads and are found in the Snacks section.)

Skillet bread, too, is a very simple yet satisfying alternative to sliced bread. Quick Skillet Bread, given here, can be made with any one of five different flours. Surely there's one version there for you!

The 9 muffin recipes that begin this section and the variations that follow are so light and good-tasting, it's hard to believe they're made without wheat, milk or eggs. At our house, where sweet desserts are the exception rather than the rule, muffins often take the place of cake, cookies or pie. Or we eat them as a snack, with a cup of herb tea. And I always feel ahead of the game when I have several muffins stored in the freezer.

I was not very successful at making quick breads without eggs and sugar until it occurred to me to steam them. Batter takes more time to steam than to bake, but steamed breads aren't any more work to mix than a traditional nut bread. And they've turned out to be another milestone in my quest for breads. Steamed bread slices well without crumbling, and holds together well enough to go brown-bagging.

When you break out of the sliced-bread-in-a-wrapper rut and start experimenting, the sky's the limit! You can reheat leftover Pancakes or Waffles in a toaster oven and use them in place of toast or even as a sandwich bread. (Recipes appear in the Breakfasts section.) Some of those same pancakes can be broken up into Handy Crumbs and used just as you would breadcrumbs.

Apple-Walnut Muffins

Makes 12.

These muffins—and the eight versions that follow—save the day for people who can't eat wheat, corn, sugar or milk but yearn for piping hot breakfast bread. They can even be made without egg.

1¾ cups sifted
    amaranth flour
¼ cup sifted
    arrowroot
2 teaspoons baking
    soda
1½ teaspoons ground
    cinnamon
½ teaspoon vitamin C
    crystals
1 cup chopped
    apples
½ cup chopped
    walnuts
¼ cup ground
    walnuts
¾ cup unsweetened
    apple juice,
    cider or
    applesauce
¼ cup walnut oil
¼ cup honey
1 egg (optional)
1 teaspoon pure
    vanilla extract

Sift the flour, arrowroot, baking soda, cinnamon and vitamin C crystals into a large bowl. Stir in the apples, chopped walnuts and ground walnuts.

Whisk the apple juice, cider or applesauce with the oil, honey, egg and vanilla in a small bowl. Pour into the flour bowl. Mix with a few swift strokes. Do not overmix.

Divide among 12 muffin cups. Bake at 375° for 18 to 20 minutes, or until center of muffin feels firm.

NOTE: You can replace the vitamin C crystals with 2 tablespoons lemon juice or vinegar; reduce apple juice, cider or applesauce by 2 tablespoons.

Banana-Nut Muffins

Makes 12.

1¾ cups sifted
    amaranth flour
¼ cup sifted
    arrowroot
2 teaspoons baking
    soda
½ teaspoon vitamin C
    crystals
½ teaspoon grated
    nutmeg
½ cup raisins or
    chopped nuts
¼ cup ground nuts
1 cup mashed ripe
    bananas
⅓ cup water
¼ cup oil
¼ cup honey
1 egg (optional)
1 teaspoon pure
    vanilla extract

Sift the flour, arrowroot, baking soda, vitamin C crystals and nutmeg into a large bowl. Stir in the raisins or chopped nuts and ground nuts.

Whisk the bananas, water, oil, honey, egg and vanilla together in a small bowl. Pour into the flour bowl. Mix with a few swift strokes. Do not overmix.

Divide batter among 12 muffin cups. Bake at 375° for 18 to 20 minutes, or until center of muffin feels firm.

Variation: Replace the nutmeg with 1 teaspoon cinnamon.

NOTE: You can replace the vitamin C crystals with 2 tablespoons lemon juice or vinegar; use only ¼ cup water.

Cranberry-Nut Muffins

Makes 12.

¾ cup cranberries
2 tablespoons honey
1¾ cups sifted
    amaranth flour
¼ cup sifted
    arrowroot
2 teaspoons baking
    soda
1 teaspoon ground
    cinnamon
½ teaspoon vitamin C
    crystals
½ cup chopped nuts
¼ cup ground nuts
1 teaspoon grated
    orange rind
    (optional)
¾ cup water or

Coarsely chop the cranberries. Place in a small bowl, and mix with 2 tablespoons honey.

Sift the flour, arrowroot, baking soda, cinnamon and vitamin C crystals into a large bowl. Stir in the chopped nuts, ground nuts and orange rind.

Whisk the water, orange juice or apple juice with the oil, ¼ cup honey, egg and vanilla in a small bowl. Pour into the flour bowl. Mix with a few swift strokes. Do not overmix. Gently fold the cranberries into the batter.

Divide batter among 12 muffin cups. Bake at 375° for 18 to 20 minutes, or until center of muffin feels firm.

NOTES: If desired, use up to 1 tablespoon grated orange rind. You can replace the vitamin C crystals with 2 tablespoons lemon juice or vinegar;

unsweetened
orange juice or
apple juice
¼ cup oil
¼ cup honey
1 egg (optional)
1 teaspoon pure
vanilla extract

reduce water, orange juice or apple juice by 2 tablespoons.

Dried-Fruit Muffins

Makes 12.

Take your choice of dried fruit; raisins, dates, apricots, prunes and peaches all work fine.

1¾ cups sifted
amaranth flour
¼ cup sifted
arrowroot
2½ teaspoons baking
soda
1 teaspoon ground
cinnamon
½ teaspoon vitamin C
crystals
½ cup chopped nuts
¼ cup ground nuts
⅔ cup water
¼ cup oil
2 tablespoons honey
1 egg (optional)
1 teaspoon pure
vanilla extract
1 cup chopped dried
fruit

Sift the flour, arrowroot, baking soda, cinnamon and vitamin C crystals into a large bowl. Stir in the chopped nuts and ground nuts.

Whisk the water, oil, honey, egg and vanilla together in a small bowl. Pour into the flour bowl. Mix with a few swift strokes. Do not overmix. Gently fold in dried fruit.

Divide batter among 12 muffin cups. Bake at 375° for 18 to 20 minutes, or until center of muffin feels firm.

NOTE: You can replace the vitamin C crystals with 2 tablespoons lemon juice or vinegar; reduce the water by 2 tablespoons.

Spicy Pumpkin Muffins ⎯⎯⎯⎯⎯⎯⎯⎯⎯⎯⎯

Makes 12.

You'll never miss the eggs in this recipe.

1¾ cups sifted
    amaranth flour
¼ cup sifted
    arrowroot
2 teaspoons baking
    soda
1½ teaspoons ground
    cinnamon
½ teaspoon vitamin C
    crystals
½ teaspoon
    powdered ginger
¼ teaspoon grated
    nutmeg
¼ teaspoon ground
    cloves
½ cup raisins or
    chopped nuts
¼ cup ground nuts
1 cup pumpkin
    puree
¼ cup oil
¼ cup honey
⅓ cup water

Sift the flour, arrowroot, baking soda, cinnamon, vitamin C crystals, ginger, nutmeg and cloves into a large bowl. Stir in the raisins or chopped nuts and ground nuts.

Whisk the pumpkin, oil and honey together in a small bowl. Pour into the flour bowl. Mix with a few swift strokes. If needed, add a tablespoon or so of water. Do not overmix.

Divide batter among 12 muffin cups. Bake at 375° for 18 to 20 minutes, or until center of muffin feels firm.

NOTE: You can replace the vitamin C crystals with 2 tablespoons lemon juice or vinegar; reduce the pumpkin puree by 2 tablespoons.

Gingerbread Muffins ⎯⎯⎯⎯⎯⎯⎯⎯⎯⎯⎯

Makes 12.

1¾ cups sifted
    amaranth flour
¼ cup sifted
    arrowroot
2 teaspoons baking
    soda
¾ teaspoon
    powdered ginger
½ teaspoon ground
    allspice
    (optional)

Sift the flour, arrowroot, baking soda, ginger, allspice and vitamin C crystals into a large bowl. Stir in the chopped nuts and ground nuts.

Whisk the water, oil, honey, egg and vanilla together in a small bowl. Pour into the flour bowl. Mix with a few swift strokes. Do not overmix.

Divide batter among 12 muffin cups. Bake at 375° for 18 to 20 minutes, or until center of muffin feels firm.

½ teaspoon vitamin C
    crystals
½ cup chopped nuts
¼ cup ground nuts
¾ cup water
¼ cup oil
¼ cup honey
1 egg (optional)
1 teaspoon pure
    vanilla extract

NOTE: You can replace the vitamin C crystals with 2 tablespoons lemon juice or vinegar; reduce water by 2 tablespoons.

Fresh Blueberry Muffins

Makes 12.

1¾ cups sifted
    amaranth flour
¼ cup sifted
    arrowroot
2 teaspoons baking
    soda
½ teaspoon vitamin C
    crystals
½ cup chopped nuts
¼ cup ground nuts
½ teaspoon grated
    lemon rind
    (optional)
¾ cup water
¼ cup oil
¼ cup honey
1 egg (optional)
1 teaspoon pure
    vanilla extract
1 cup blueberries

Sift the flour, arrowroot, baking soda and vitamin C crystals into a large bowl. Stir in the chopped nuts, ground nuts and lemon rind.

Whisk the water, oil, honey, egg and vanilla together in a small bowl. Pour into the flour bowl. Mix with a few swift strokes. Do not overmix. Fold in the blueberries.

Divide batter among 12 muffin cups. Bake at 375° for 18 to 20 minutes, or until center of muffin feels firm.

NOTE: You can replace the vitamin C crystals with 2 tablespoons lemon juice or vinegar; reduce water by 2 tablespoons.

Pineapple-Pecan Muffins

Makes 12.

1¾ cups sifted amaranth flour
¼ cup sifted arrowroot
2½ teaspoons baking soda
½ teaspoon vitamin C crystals
½ cup chopped pecans
¼ cup ground pecans
8 ounces unsweetened crushed pineapple, packed in juice
¼ cup oil
¼ cup honey
1 egg (optional)
1 teaspoon pure vanilla extract

Sift the flour, arrowroot, baking soda and vitamin C crystals into a large bowl. Stir in the chopped pecans and ground pecans.

Place the pineapple in a strainer set over a bowl. Press lightly with the back of a spoon to extract excess juice. Set the pineapple aside. Measure the juice; add enough water to equal ⅔ cup.

Whisk the pineapple juice, oil, honey, egg and vanilla together in a small bowl. Pour into the flour bowl. Mix with a few swift strokes. Do not overmix. Gently fold in the pineapple.

Divide batter among 12 muffin cups. Bake at 375° for 18 to 20 minutes, or until center of muffin feels firm.

NOTE: You can replace the vitamin C crystals with 2 tablespoons lemon juice or vinegar; reduce the pineapple juice by 2 tablespoons.

Pumpkin Muffins

Makes 12.

These are light and fine textured, just like wheat muffins. If you can't eat eggs, opt for Spicy Pumpkin Muffins.

1 cup sifted oat flour
⅔ cup sifted brown rice flour
1½ teaspoons ground cinnamon
½ teaspoon baking soda
½ teaspoon cream of tartar
½ teaspoon grated nutmeg
¼ teaspoon powdered ginger
¼ teaspoon ground cloves

Sift the oat flour, rice flour, cinnamon, baking soda, cream of tartar, nutmeg, ginger and cloves into a large bowl.

In a medium bowl, beat the egg with electric beaters until light and foamy. Beat in the honey in a thin stream. Then beat in molasses and oil. Add pumpkin and mix well. Pour into the flour bowl, and stir quickly to blend. Fold in the pecans.

Oil 12 muffin cups or line them with cupcake papers. Divide the batter among the cups. Bake at 400° for 18 to 20 minutes.

Variation: Replace the pumpkin with mashed cooked butternut squash.

1 egg
¼ cup honey
2 tablespoons
    molasses
2 tablespoons oil
½ cup mashed
    cooked pumpkin
½ cup chopped
    pecans (optional)

Rhubarb Oat-and-Rice Muffins _____

Makes 12.

Oat and rice flours work well together, producing muffins that are tender and crumbly.

1⅓ cups oat flour
⅔ cup brown rice
    flour
2 teaspoons Corn-
    Free Baking
    Powder (see
    Index)
½ teaspoon baking
    soda
½ teaspoon ground
    allspice
1½ cups chopped
    rhubarb
½ cup water
¼ cup honey
3 tablespoons oil
1 egg

Sift the oat flour, rice flour, Corn-Free Baking Powder, baking soda and allspice into a large bowl.

Place the rhubarb and water in a saucepan. Bring to a boil, and cook until fruit is tender and has rendered its juices (about 15 minutes). Pour into a strainer set over a medium bowl. Reserve the rhubarb. Measure the juices. If necessary, add a bit of water to make them equal ¾ cup. Return juices to the bowl. Whisk in the honey, oil and egg.

Pour liquid mixture into the flour bowl. Stir briefly to combine. Do not overmix. Fold in reserved rhubarb and any accumulated juices.

Divide batter among 12 oiled muffin cups. Bake at 375° for 22 to 25 minutes.

Variations: Replace the allspice with 1 teaspoon ground cinnamon, ½ teaspoon grated nutmeg or ½ teaspoon ground cardamom.

To make Pineapple Muffins, replace the rhubarb with 8 ounces drained unsweetened crushed pineapple or 1½ cups diced pineapple. Use unsweetened pineapple juice in place of the rhubarb juices.

NOTE: Because the rhubarb season is so short, you may use frozen rhubarb in place of fresh. Simmer it briefly with the ½ cup water.

Yeast-Raised Rice-Flour Bread _____

Makes 2 loaves.

People who can eat yeast but not wheat will welcome this recipe. Slice the bread for toast or sandwiches.

2¼ cups warm water
4½ teaspoons dry yeast (see Appendix for a preservative-free brand)
¼ cup honey
4¼ cups brown rice flour
½ cup ground sunflower seeds
1 carrot, grated
4½ teaspoons guar gum (see Appendix)
1 teaspoon ground cinnamon
1 teaspoon wheat-free tamari sauce, dried herbs or grated lemon rind
⅓ cup oil
sesame seeds

Combine the water, yeast and honey in a cup. Set aside for 10 minutes, until the yeast is foamy.

Place the flour in a large bowl in a 200° oven for 10 to 15 minutes to warm it. Reserve 1 cup of the flour. To the remaining flour add the sunflower seeds, carrot, guar gum, cinnamon and tamari, dried herbs or lemon rind. Mix well.

Make a well in the center of the flour, and add the oil and the yeast mixture. Using electric beaters, beat at high speed for 3 minutes. Stop and scrape the sides of the bowl. Add the remaining flour. Beat at low speed 1 minute.

Scrape batter off beaters, and level the surface of the dough. Oil the top of the dough and the sides of the bowl above the dough.

Cover the bowl with a damp towel. Place in a draft-free place to rise. Allow to rise 1½ to 2½ hours, until doubled in bulk. Do not rush this step. Yeast should work slowly.

To knead dough, beat with electric beaters for 3 minutes.

Oil 2 8"-×-4" loaf pans. Scatter sesame seeds in bottoms, especially in corners. Divide the dough between the pans, pushing it into the corners with a spatula and smoothing the tops. Sprinkle with sesame seeds.

Allow to rise, uncovered, for 30 to 35 minutes, until dough just reaches the tops of the pans. Don't let it go higher or it may collapse.

Bake at 400° for 10 minutes. Place foil loosely over loaves, and bake 50 minutes more.

Variations: To make an Egg Bread, add 2 eggs to the flour along with the oil and yeast.

To make Yeast-Raised Rice-Flour Rolls, divide batter (either basic recipe or egg dough) among 24 oiled muffin cups with sesame seeds in the bottoms. Sprinkle tops with sesame seeds. Bake at 400° for 10 minutes, cover with foil, then bake another 6 to 8 minutes, until lightly brown.

To make Philadelphia Sticky Buns, add 1 teaspoon ground cinnamon to the dough. Then oil 24 muffin cups, and add 1 teaspoon honey to the bottom of each cup. Place chopped pecans or 2 to 3 pecan halves in each cup. (Or use raisins, currants or well-drained chopped unsweetened pineapple.) Place dough in the cups. Bake at 400° for 10 minutes, then cover with foil, and bake 6 to 8 minutes, until light brown.

NOTE: The secret to making yeast-raised gluten-free bread is the guar gum, a legume product that interacts with yeast. (See Appendix for purchasing source.) The distributor told me, "It'll even make sawdust rise." Even allowing for exaggeration, it's worth your while to seek out this helpful ingredient.

Banana Bread

Makes 1 loaf.

For breakfast or snacking, there's nothing like banana bread. People who are allergic to milk or wheat can enjoy this freely.

¼ cup nuts
1¾ cups sifted amaranth flour or sifted brown rice flour
½ cup arrowroot
2 teaspoons baking soda
½ cup chopped nuts
1½ cups very ripe mashed bananas
¼ cup oil
¼ cup honey
2 eggs
2 tablespoons lemon juice
1 teaspoon pure vanilla extract

Process the ¼ cup nuts in a blender until finely ground. Mix the nuts with the flour, arrowroot and baking soda in a large bowl. Stir in the chopped nuts.

In a separate bowl, mix together the bananas, oil, honey, eggs, lemon juice and vanilla. Then pour the liquid mixture into the flour bowl, and mix with a few swift strokes. Do not overmix.

Pour into a greased 9"-×-5" loaf pan or 2 7"-×-3" pans. Bake large loaf at 350° for 55 to 60 minutes, or small loaves for 45 minutes or until a cake tester inserted in the middle comes out clean. Let stand in the pan for 10 minutes, then turn the loaf out onto a wire rack to cool.

Steamed Savory Sandwich Loaf _____

Makes 2 or 3 loaves.

Quick breads don't have to be sweet and fruity. This loaf gets just a touch of sweetness from the applesauce and plenty of pizzazz from herb seasonings. You can slice it thinly for unbeatable sandwiches—it's great with roast meat, chicken, turkey, tuna or Tofu Salad.

2 cups sifted brown
    rice flour
⅔ cup amaranth flour
¼ cup Pizzazz
    Seasoning (see
    Index)
2 tablespoons kombu
    powder (optional)
1 teaspoon Corn-Free
    Baking Powder
    (see Index)
1 teaspoon baking
    soda
1 cup nuts
1 cup boiling
    unsweetened
    apple juice
1 cup Real
    Applesauce (see
    Index)
¼ cup oil
2 tablespoons water
½ teaspoon vitamin C
    crystals

In a large bowl, mix the rice flour, amaranth flour, Pizzazz Seasoning, kombu, Corn-Free Baking Powder and baking soda. Set aside.

Grind the nuts to a fine powder in a blender. Add the apple juice, and blend 20 seconds to mix well. Then add the Real Applesauce, oil, water and vitamin C crystals. Blend briefly to mix.

Pour the liquid mixture into the flour bowl. Stir briefly to moisten dry ingredients; do not overmix.

Generously oil either 2 1-pound coffee cans or 3 20-ounce fruit cans. Divide the batter among them. (Batter should not fill the cans more than two thirds full.) Cover each can with a square of wax paper or foil (shiny side down); tie wax paper on securely with a piece of string.

Place the cans on a wire rack in a Dutch oven or large stockpot. Add enough boiling water to the pot to come halfway up the sides of the cans. Cover the pot tightly, and steam the loaves over medium heat for 3 hours. Do not remove the cover during the cooking time.

Carefully remove the cans from the water. Place them in a 450° oven for 5 minutes. To unmold the breads, remove the wax paper or foil. Invert the cans on your kitchen counter, and slide the breads onto wire racks. (If the breads should stick, use a can opener to remove the bottom of each can. Push the bread out with the bottom of the can.)

To serve warm, cut the bread with a piece of thread. Slide it under the bread, then wrap it around the bread and pull the ends past each other until you have cut a perfect slice.

To serve cold, allow the loaves to cool on wire racks, then cut with a serrated knife, using a sawing motion.

Variations: Replace the amaranth flour with ⅔ cup finely ground toasted sunflower seeds or roasted peanuts.

Replace the Pizzazz Seasoning with 2 tablespoons dried dill weed, 2 teaspoons caraway seeds, 1 teaspoon ground fennel, 1 teaspoon ground cumin and ½ teaspoon dried thyme. For a Dill Loaf, use 2 tablespoons Pizzazz Seasoning plus 2 tablespoons dried dill weed.

Replace the nuts with 1 cup sunflower seeds or pumpkin seeds or some of each.

If you need to avoid apples, omit the apple juice and applesauce. Replace the juice by placing 2 tablespoons honey or maple syrup in a 1-cup measure; add water to fill. Bring to a boil, then proceed with recipe. Replace the applesauce with 1 cup mashed bananas, pumpkin puree, mashed cooked butternut squash or mashed cooked carrots, sweet potatoes or white potatoes.

Steamed Apricot Bread _____

Makes 1 loaf.

Steamed breads are firm, dense and moist without the addition of eggs to the batter. And they're just the thing for soup and salad luncheons.

¾ cup rolled oats
⅔ cup brown rice flour
¼ cup amaranth flour
1 teaspoon baking soda
½ cup almonds
¾ cup boiling water
⅓ cup molasses or honey
½ teaspoon pure almond extract
½ cup dried apricots

In a large bowl, combine the oats, rice flour, amaranth flour and baking soda.

Grind the almonds to a fine powder in a blender. Gradually add enough water to bring the level up to 1 cup. With the machine running, add the molasses or honey and almond extract. Add the apricots and process with a few on/off turns to chop them; do not puree.

Pour the liquid mixture into the flour bowl. Stir to mix. Turn out into an oiled 1-quart mold or 1-pound can. Cover with a square of wax paper or foil (shiny side down); tie wax paper securely with a piece of string.

Place the mold on a wire rack in a Dutch oven or large stockpot. Add enough boiling water to the pot to come halfway up the sides of the mold. Cover the pot tightly, and steam the bread over medium-low heat for 2 hours. Do not remove the cover during the cooking time.

Remove the mold from the pot. Cool the bread in the mold for 15 minutes, then turn out onto a wire rack to cool completely. For best results, slice with a serrated knife.

Variations: Replace the rice flour with ⅓ cup rice polish and ⅓ cup rice bran. You can also replace the amaranth flour with either ¼ cup soy flour, ¼ cup white buckwheat flour or ¼ cup ground sunflower seeds. (For directions on making white buckwheat flour, see Table 1, Cooking and Baking with Alternative Flours, in the section, Exploring New Ingredients.)

Steamed Apple-Raisin Bread _____

Makes 1 loaf.

A gluten-free, egg-free loaf. Dense and moist, it can be sliced without crumbling and goes brown-bagging very well.

1 cup brown rice flour
¼ cup ground
    sunflower seeds
    or amaranth flour
1 teaspoon baking
    soda
½ teaspoon ground
    cinnamon
½ cup walnuts
¾ cup boiling
    unsweetened
    apple juice
¼ cup honey or
    molasses
1 tablespoon lemon
    juice (optional)
½ cup dried apples
½ cup raisins

In a large bowl, combine the rice flour, sunflower seeds or amaranth flour, baking soda and cinnamon. Set aside.

Grind the walnuts to a fine powder in a blender. Add the juice, and blend 20 seconds. If the mixture doesn't reach the 1-cup mark, add a bit more apple juice. With the machine running on low, add the honey or molasses and lemon juice. Add the apples, and coarsely chop with a few on/off turns.

Pour the liquid mixture into the flour bowl. Stir briefly to mix. Stir in the raisins. Do not overmix. Turn into an oiled 1-quart mold or 1-pound can. Cover with a square of wax paper or foil (shiny side down); tie wax paper securely with a piece of string.

Place the mold on a wire rack in a Dutch oven or large stockpot. Add enough boiling water to the pot to come halfway up the sides of the mold. Cover the pot tightly, and steam the bread over medium-low heat for 2 hours. Do not remove the cover during the cooking time.

Remove the mold from the pot. Cool the bread in the mold for 15 minutes, then turn out onto a wire rack to cool completely. For best results, slice with a serrated knife.

Variation: For more fiber, replace the brown rice flour with ½ cup rice bran, ¼ cup rice polish and ¼ cup brown rice flour.

Grain-Free Boston Brown Bread _____

Makes 1 loaf.

A milk-free, egg-free and—yes—even grain-free version of a New England tradition. Very good, very moist.

1 cup plus 2 tablespoons amaranth flour
¼ cup arrowroot
1 teaspoon baking soda
½ teaspoon powdered ginger
½ cup currants
½ cup Brazil nuts
¾ cup boiling unsweetened fruit juice or water
¼ cup honey or molasses
1 tablespoon lemon juice or ¼ teaspoon vitamin C crystals

Generously oil a 1-quart mold or 1-pound coffee can. Fill a Dutch oven or stockpot with about 5 inches of water. Bring the water to a boil while you prepare the batter.

In a large bowl, combine the flour, arrowroot, baking soda and ginger. Stir in the currants.

In a blender, grind the nuts to a fine powder. Add the juice or water, and blend 20 seconds. If the ingredients in the blender don't reach the 1-cup mark, add a little more liquid. With the blender running on low, add the honey or molasses and lemon juice or vitamin C crystals.

Pour the liquid mixture into the flour bowl. Stir quickly to blend; do not overmix. Transfer to the prepared mold or can. Cover with a square of foil or wax paper; tie the wax paper securely with a piece of string.

Place the mold in the boiling water. (It should come halfway up the sides.) Cover the pot tightly, and steam for 2 hours over medium-low heat. Do not remove the cover during that time.

Remove the mold from the pot. Cool the bread in the mold for 15 minutes, then turn out onto a wire rack to cool completely. For best results, cut with a serrated knife with a gentle, sawing motion.

Variations: Substitute ground cinnamon or grated nutmeg for the ginger. Use pecans or walnuts instead of Brazil nuts. Replace the honey or molasses with ⅓ cup maple syrup. Instead of the currants, use dried unsweetened pineapple, apples, prunes or other dried fruit; use the corresponding juice as the liquid.

Quick Skillet Bread

Serves 2.

Resembling a large crepe, this is the easiest bread you'll ever make. There's no rolling, patting or cutting. And with so many flours to choose from (see Variations), you'll be able to eat it no matter what your allergies may be. Serve it warm with a hearty soup.

⅔ cup water
½ cup chick-pea flour
1 teaspoon wheat-free tamari sauce or kombu powder
2 teaspoons olive oil

Mix the water and flour in a bowl. The batter should be very thin. If it's not, add more water, 1 tablespoon at a time, until the desired consistency is reached. Stir in the tamari or kombu.

Heat a 12" non-stick sauté pan over medium-high heat until a drop of water will dance on the surface. Add 1 teaspoon oil, and swirl the pan to distribute it.

Stir the batter, and add all at once. Cover the pan, and cook for 2 minutes. Then dribble the remaining oil over the surface of the bread; use the back of a spoon to spread it around. Cook for 5 more minutes.

When the bread appears dry around the edges, loosen it with a spatula. Then flip it over, reduce the heat to medium-low, and cook another 5 minutes, uncovered. If you want the bread to be especially crisp, cook for an additional 5 minutes, flipping it over every minute or so.

Serve immediately, tearing into pieces.

Variations: Replace the chick-pea flour with either ½ cup oat flour, ½ cup white buckwheat flour, ½ cup amaranth flour (use medium heat instead of medium-high) or ⅓ cup brown rice flour. (For directions on making white buckwheat flour, see Table 1, Cooking and Baking with Alternative Flours, in the section, Exploring New Ingredients.)

NOTE: To serve 1, divide the recipe in half and cook the batter in a 10" sauté pan. To serve 4, make 2 separate breads. Keep the first one warm while the second is cooking.

Casserole Bread _____

Makes 1 bread.

Tender and crumbly like corn bread, but without the corn. A good source of protein, too. Spread with Old-Fashioned Fruit Butter, Pear Honey or other fruit spread for a double treat.

1¼ cups sifted brown
  rice flour
⅓ cup soy flour
1½ teaspoons baking
  soda
½ teaspoon dried
  marjoram
¼ teaspoon ground
  cumin
½ cup raisins
  (optional)
1 cup unsweetened
  apple juice or
  water
⅓ cup chopped
  onions
¼ cup soy oil
3 tablespoons lemon
  juice
2 tablespoons tahini
  or ground
  sesame seeds
2 tablespoons honey
  or molasses
1 tablespoon lecithin
  granules
1½ teaspoons wheat-
  free tamari sauce

In a large mixing bowl, combine the rice flour, soy flour, baking soda, marjoram, cumin and raisins.

In a blender or food processor, combine the apple juice or water, onions, oil, lemon juice, tahini or sesame seeds, honey or molasses, lecithin and tamari. Process for 30 seconds.

Pour the liquid mixture into the flour bowl. Stir to moisten dry ingredients, but don't overmix. Transfer to an oiled 8"- or 9"-square baking pan. Bake at 325° for 35 minutes, or until a cake tester inserted in the center comes out clean.

Allow to cool for 10 minutes before cutting into squares.

Buckwheat Tortillas

Makes 4 to 6.

These tortillas—and the four versions that follow—are tasty alternatives to traditional tortillas, which are made from corn or wheat flour. Tortillas are unleavened breads that contain a minimum of ingredients. But for all their simplicity, they have myriad uses. Wrap them around well-seasoned beans, salad fixings, chicken salad, roast turkey, guacamole, peanut butter spread—you get the idea. Another plus is that they freeze well, cooked or uncooked, so you can keep a supply on hand.

1 cup buckwheat flour
1 tablespoon Savory
    Seed Seasoning
    (see Index)
½ cup water

In a small bowl, mix the flour and Savory Seed Seasoning. Stir in the water, then evaluate the consistency. The dough should be soft but not wet—"earlobe" consistency—and mold easily into shapes. The dough will easily form a ball as you stir it. If necessary, add a bit more flour or water to achieve the proper consistency.

Pinch off balls of dough the size of golf balls. Roll them in additional flour to coat well. Knead each ball a bit as you pat or roll it into a flat circle that's about ⅛" thick and 5" or 6" across. Repeat with all dough.

Heat a heavy frying pan or griddle. Use no oil. Place each tortilla in the hot pan, and cook for a few minutes on each side. Tortillas should become lightly brown and start to appear dry. Cool on wire racks.

Store in the refrigerator up to 2 weeks, or freeze. Reheat in a toaster or warm oven.

Variations: If you're going to use the tortillas with a sweet filling, add ½ teaspoon ground cinnamon to the dough. Or try a pinch of grated nutmeg, powdered ginger, ground allspice or ground cloves.

Amaranth Tortillas _____

Makes 4 to 6.

1¼ cups amaranth
    flour
1 tablespoon Savory
    Seed Seasoning
    (see Index)
½ cup water

In a small bowl, mix the flour and Savory Seed Seasoning. Stir in the water, then evaluate the consistency. The dough should be soft but not wet, and mold easily into shapes. The dough will easily form a ball as you stir it. If necessary, add a bit more flour or water to achieve the proper consistency.

Pinch off balls of dough the size of golf balls. Roll them in additional flour to coat well. Knead each ball a bit as you pat or roll it into a flat circle that's about ⅛" thick and 5" or 6" across. Repeat with all dough.

Heat a heavy frying pan or griddle. Use no oil. Place each tortilla in the hot pan, and cook for a few minutes on each side. Tortillas should become lightly brown and start to appear dry. Cool on wire racks.

Store in the refrigerator up to 2 weeks, or freeze. Reheat in a toaster or warm oven.

Rice Tortillas _____

Makes 4 to 6.

1 cup brown rice flour
    or rice bran
1 tablespoon Savory
    Seed Seasoning
    (see Index)
½ cup water
2 teaspoons oil

In a small bowl, mix the flour or bran and Savory Seed Seasoning. Stir in the water and oil. Let stand for 5 to 10 minutes for liquid to be properly absorbed.

Pinch off balls of dough the size of golf balls. Roll them in additional rice flour to coat well. Knead briefly on a well-floured surface. Pat or roll each piece into a flat circle that's about ⅛" thick and 5" or 6" across. If the dough is too crumbly, add a bit more flour, knead briefly, and try again to form into a tortilla. It may be necessary to repeat that step a few times to get the proper consistency.

Heat a heavy frying pan or griddle. Use no oil. Place each tortilla in the hot pan, and cook a few minutes on each side. Tortillas should become lightly brown and start to appear dry. Rice tortillas will be nice and crisp, rather than soft. Cool on wire racks.

Store in the refrigerator up to 2 weeks, or freeze. Reheat in a toaster or warm oven.

Oat Tortillas

Makes 4 to 6.

1 cup oat flour
1 tablespoon Savory
    Seed Seasoning
    (see Index)
½ cup water

In a small bowl, mix the flour and Savory Seed Seasoning. Stir in the water, then evaluate the consistency. The dough should be soft but not wet, and mold easily into shapes. The dough will easily form a ball as you stir it. If necessary, add a bit more flour or water to achieve the proper consistency.

Pinch off balls of dough the size of golf balls. Roll them in additional flour to coat well. Knead each ball a bit as you pat or roll it into a flat circle that's about ⅛" thick and 5" or 6" across. Repeat with all dough.

Heat a heavy frying pan or griddle. Use no oil. Place each tortilla in the hot pan, and cook for a few minutes on each side. Tortillas should become lightly brown and start to appear dry. Cool on wire racks.

Store in the refrigerator up to 2 weeks, or freeze. Reheat in a toaster or warm oven.

Variations: Use 1 cup oat bran in place of the flour. Or use a combination of flour and oat bran. You can make your own oat flour by grinding 1 cup plus 2 tablespoons rolled oats in a blender until very fine.

Legume Tortillas

Makes 4 to 6.

1 cup chick-pea flour
2 tablespoons Savory
    Seed Seasoning
    (see Index)
½ cup water

In a small bowl, mix the flour and Savory Seed Seasoning. Stir in the water, then evaluate the consistency. The dough should be soft but not wet, and mold easily into shapes. The dough will easily form a ball as you stir it. If necessary, add a bit more flour or water to achieve the proper consistency.

Pinch off balls of dough the size of golf balls. Roll them in additional flour to coat well. Knead each ball a bit as you pat or roll it into a flat circle that's about ⅛″ thick and 5″ or 6″ across. Repeat with all dough.

Heat a heavy frying pan or griddle. Use no oil. Place each tortilla in the hot pan, and cook for a few minutes on each side. Tortillas should become lightly brown and start to appear dry. Cool on wire racks.

Store in the refrigerator up to 2 weeks, or freeze. Reheat in a toaster or warm oven.

Variations: Use soy flour, lima bean flour or a mixture of legume flours.

Fruited Flatbread

Makes 12.

This delicious, satisfying bread uses only two or three ingredients. To suit a Diversified Rotary Diet, spread it with Old-Fashioned Fruit Butter or serve with fresh or dried fruit.

1 cup white
    buckwheat flour
    (see Note)
½ cup mashed
    bananas
1½ teaspoons wheat-
    free tamari sauce
    (optional)

Place the flour in a medium bowl. Add the banana and tamari. Stir well to combine. If necessary, add water, 1 teaspoon at a time, to facilitate stirring. Divide dough in half, and form into balls.

Sprinkle a square of wax paper with additional flour. Roll one of the balls in the flour to completely coat. Then roll it into a circle about 10″ across. Cut into 6 wedges, and transfer to a hot ungreased griddle. Bake for 2 or 3 minutes on each side.

Repeat with remaining dough.

Variations: Use any other flour you desire. Brown rice, amaranth, oat, soy, chick-pea and lima bean are all good choices. You can also use a mixture of rice polish and rice bran.

Use any pureed fruit you want. Apricots, apples, pears, unsweetened pineapple, peaches, nectarines and stewed prunes or other dried fruit, stewed, work fine. Add a pinch of your favorite spice if you wish.

NOTE: For directions on making your own white buckwheat flour, see Table 1, Cooking and Baking with Alternative Flours, in the section, Exploring New Ingredients.

Stir 'n' Pour Flatbread

Serves 4.

This grain-free bread is coarse and chewy and goes great with soup or stew. Only ¼" thick and unleavened, it is a cross between crackers and bread.

1 egg
2 tablespoons water
½ cup cooked brown rice
½ cup oat flour
3 tablespoons amaranth flour
boiling water
¼ teaspoon wheat-free tamari sauce (optional)
sesame seeds (optional)

In a large bowl, beat the egg until thick and light. Stir in the water. Then add the rice, oat flour and amaranth flour. Add enough boiling water to make the batter the consistency of heavy cream. Stir in the tamari.

Pour into an oiled 8"-square pan, spreading batter to evenly cover the bottom. Sprinkle on sesame seeds.

Bake at 350° for 22 to 25 minutes. Serve warm, cut into squares.

Variations: Replace the amaranth flour with chick-pea flour, soy flour or ground toasted sunflower seeds. Replace the tamari with dried herbs, kombu powder, lemon juice or vitamin C crystals. You may also add Pizzazz Seasoning or other herbs.

NOTE: To reheat, warm bread in a toaster oven or dry frying pan for a few minutes.

Italian Crumbs

Makes ½ cup.

Use these crumbs instead of cheese on any Mediterranean-style casseroles.

½ cup Handy Crumbs
    (see recipe below)
1 tablespoon olive oil
½ teaspoon dried
    oregano
½ teaspoon dried basil
⅛ teaspoon onion
    powder
    pinch of garlic
    powder

In a frying pan, sauté Handy Crumbs in the oil for a few minutes. Stir in the oregano, basil, onion powder and garlic powder. Cook, stirring, for several more minutes, until seasonings are well distributed and crumbs are well coated with oil.

Handy Crumbs

Makes about 2¾ cups.

These crumbs are like an ace up the sleeve for spur-of-the-moment cooking. You can make them at your leisure, then store in the freezer for use on casseroles, puddings and meat loaves. Unless you will be using the crumbs on sweet dishes, omit the cinnamon from the Amaranth Pancakes recipe, and reduce the sweetener to 1½ teaspoons.

18 Amaranth Pancakes
    (see Index)

Allow the Amaranth Pancakes to cool on wire racks. Then place them in single layers on cookie sheets. Bake at 300° for about 15 to 25 minutes, until thoroughly dry. (Check by breaking the thickest pancake to see if center is dry.) If pancakes are not thoroughly dry after 25 minutes, turn off the oven and allow them to remain in it until dry.

Cool the pancakes thoroughly. Then break into pieces, and grind them into crumbs with a blender or food processor. (If using a blender, do about 1 cup of pieces at a time. If using a food processor, do half of the pancakes at a time.) Place crumbs in jars or cellophane bags, and store in the freezer.

Variation: You can also make crumbs by drying and grinding your choice of Tortillas.

NOTE: To use the crumbs as a casserole topping, briefly sauté the desired amount in a little oil. If you'd like, you can also add any seasonings that will complement the casserole.

Oat Scones

Makes 16.

Traditionally, scones were the backbone of Scottish and English tea parties. I like to serve them at informal brunches. These scones are flaky and taste great. They are even better the next day.

⅓ cup oil
2 tablespoons honey
2 tablespoons warm water
1 tablespoon lemon juice or ¼ teaspoon vitamin C crystals
1–2 cups oat flour
¼ cup brown rice flour
½ teaspoon baking soda (optional)
⅓ cup currants or raisins
⅓ cup rolled oats

In a 3-quart saucepan, combine the oil, honey, water and lemon juice or vitamin C crystals and warm slightly until the honey melts.

In a small bowl, mix ¾ cup oat flour with the rice flour and baking soda. Stir into the oil mixture. Stir in currants or raisins. Beat hard with a wooden spoon for 50 strokes.

Gradually add enough additional oat flour to make a dough that forms a ball and isn't sticky. Divide dough into 2 balls.

Scatter half of rolled oats on a board or countertop. Place 1 ball on top of them, and roll it to cover with the oats. Then flatten into a 6″ or 7″ circle about ⅜″ thick. Turn a few times to coat well with oats. Transfer to an ungreased cookie sheet scattered with more rolled oats. Cut dough into 8 wedges. Do not separate wedges.

Repeat with remaining dough and oats.

Bake at 325° for 25 minutes, or until light golden brown. Cool for 30 minutes on the baking sheet. Serve at room temperature.

Variations: For scones that are not at all sweet, omit the honey and replace with 4 teaspoons water. You can also replace the rice flour with an equal amount of oat flour.

NOTE: You can make oat flour by grinding oats in the blender. You'll need about 1¼ cups oats to make 1 cup oat flour.

Buckwheat Waldorf Stuffing _____

Makes 6 cups.

A grain-free stuffing that's great for poultry or wild fowl.

2 cups cooked
    buckwheat groats
1 unsprayed apple,
    chopped
⅔ cup chopped celery
⅔ cup raisins
½ cup chopped pecans
2 tablespoons lemon
    juice
½ teaspoon poultry
    seasoning
½ cup Homemade
    Mayo or Tofu
    Mayo (see Index)

In a large bowl, mix the groats, apple, celery, raisins, pecans, lemon juice and seasoning. Stir in Mayo, mixing lightly.

Variations: You can replace the Mayo with either 1 egg or ¼ cup oil. You can replace the lemon juice with ½ teaspoon vitamin C crystals and 2 tablespoons water.

Grain-Free Waldorf Stuffing _____

Makes about 4 cups.

Here's an even simpler stuffing to try.

1½ cups chopped
    unsprayed
    apples
1 cup chopped
    celery
¾ cup chopped
    walnuts
2 tablespoons lemon
    juice or ½
    teaspoon
    vitamin C
    crystals
¼ teaspoon poultry
    seasoning
    unsweetened
    apple juice
    (optional)

In a medium bowl, mix the apples, celery, walnuts, lemon juice or vitamin C crystals and poultry seasoning. Use to stuff a 5- or 6-pound chicken.

If you prefer to bake the stuffing separately, moisten ingredients with apple juice, and bake at 350° for 20 to 30 minutes in an oiled 1½-quart casserole dish.

Variation: Add 1 to 2 cups cooked brown rice. Moisten as desired with unsweetened apple juice.

Soups, Stews and Chowders

Soups, stews and chowders are much more than cold-weather comfort. They're a versatile way for allergic people to combine a few simple foods, especially for a Diversified Rotary Diet. Eating plain, steamed vegetables can easily grow tiresome. But those same vegetables, combined with a little meat or fish in seasoned stock, make a delightful soup. And stews are a reliable way to cook beans or game, foods that taste better and are easier to digest after long, slow cooking.

Creamy yet milk-free soups are easy to make with a blender or food processor. Try Potato Soup, Creamy Mushroom Soup, Asparagus Soup or Zucchini Bisque. Blending seems to bring out the best of the foods used. And blended soups have "body" otherwise achieved only by using milk, cream or wheat flour. You can thin or thicken cream-style soups by varying the amount of liquid used.

Whatever type of stock or soup you make, be sure to label it clearly, listing all ingredients. That's especially helpful if you will be freezing portions for later use. And labeling is essential if you are rotating ingredients such as chicken, meat or fish, or if different members of your family are allergic to different foods.

Stock

Makes 3 cups.

Stock is basic to any cook-from-scratch cuisine. But homemade stock is all the more essential to people with allergies, who can't always rely on canned or packaged soup mixes.

Reduced to its simplest terms, stock is the liquid in which something was cooked, imparting flavor. Thus when you boil beans or potatoes you are making bean or potato stock as a by-product, either one of which could also be used as vegetable stock. Meat, fish and fowl stocks, at their simplest, are made the same way, and include bones, fish heads and tails, and any of the fowl's giblets, necks, tails or wings.

While most "recipes" call for vegetables to be included—and indeed, they do improve the final flavor—you can vary the ingredients of any stock to fit your own needs, including a Diversified Rotary Diet. Thus, if you can't have those onions, carrots, celery and parsley, you revert to the original definition, and simmer the meat, fish or fowl in plain water. Long, slow simmering of the main ingredient will go a long way toward coaxing out the maximum flavor possible. The longer you cook the stock, the richer it will be. And your soups and sauces will be better than ever. Label the finished stock according to what you used to produce it.

2 quarts water
1 pound meaty
   bones and
   giblets
1 onion, quartered
   (optional)
1 carrot, sliced
   (optional)
1 garlic clove,
   halved
   (optional)
¼ cup celery or
   lovage leaves
4 parsley sprigs
1–2 bay leaves
1–2 teaspoons dried
   thyme
1 tablespoon kombu
   powder
   (optional)
¼ cup vinegar or
   lemon juice or 1
   teaspoon
   vitamin C
   crystals

Combine the water, bones and giblets, onions, carrots, garlic, celery or lovage, parsley, bay leaves, thyme, kombu and vinegar or lemon juice or vitamin C crystals in a Dutch oven or stockpot.

Simmer, partially covered, for up to 5 hours. Strain through a colander or sieve. Pour the strained stock into a clean pot, and boil for about 30 minutes to reduce to about 3 cups.

Either use at once, or pour into containers. Refrigerate for up to 5 days. For longer storage, freeze.

Variations: Replace thyme with any other herbs you like. You can also add a potato or small squash to the pot.

To make fish stock, use trimmings, bones and heads. Simmer for about 30 minutes. Then strain, and boil down as above.

NOTES: You may want to collect chicken, meat or fish bones in your freezer until you have enough to make stock. If you're in a hurry, buy inexpensive chicken wings or backs.

You can also make stock in an electric slow cooker. Simmer for up to 8 hours before straining and boiling down.

Asparagus Soup

Makes 1 quart.

A velvety green soup made primarily from members of the Lily family.

1 pound asparagus
  stalks, trimmed
2 medium leeks or 4
  large shallots
1 tablespoon olive
  oil
2–3 garlic cloves,
  minced
2 cups water or
  chicken Stock
  (see page 122)
1 teaspoon dried
  dill weed
  pinch of grated
  nutmeg

Slice off the tips of the asparagus stalks (about 2″), and reserve them. Cut the remaining stalks into 1″ pieces.

Slice the leeks in half lengthwise, and wash under cold running water to remove any sand. Slice into ¼″ pieces. (Or slice the shallots thinly.)

Sauté the leeks or shallots in the oil over medium heat until soft. Add the garlic. Cook, stirring, another minute. Add the water or Stock, dill and sliced asparagus stalks. Simmer for 10 to 12 minutes, until asparagus is tender.

Remove from the heat, and allow to cool 5 to 10 minutes. Puree, half at a time, in a blender. Or puree all at once in a food processor. Return mixture to the pan, add the reserved asparagus tips, and simmer for 3 to 5 minutes, or until tips are just barely tender. Add nutmeg. If soup is too thick, thin with additional water or Stock.

Variations: Replace the dill with ½ teaspoon of either dried savory, dried tarragon or dried thyme.

NOTE: You can avoid using oil by steam-stirring the leeks or shallots and garlic in 2 tablespoons water.

Creamy Mushroom Soup ──────────────

Makes 5 to 6 cups.

You'll never miss the milk in this soup. It tastes rich, smells delight-fully aromatic and has good body, even without any flour to thicken it.

½ cup raw cashews
3 cups boiling water or vegetable Stock (see page 122)
1 large Spanish onion, chopped
2 tablespoons olive oil
½ pound mushrooms, sliced
1 tablespoon Hungarian paprika
1½ teaspoons dried dill weed
up to ⅛ teaspoon cayenne pepper (to taste)
2 tablespoons dark miso
1 tablespoon lemon juice or ¼ teaspoon vitamin C crystals

Grind the cashews to a fine powder in a blender. Add 1 cup of the water or Stock, and blend 30 seconds. Add the remaining liquid.

Sauté the onions in the oil in a 3-quarter saucepan over medium heat. After 5 minutes, add the mushrooms. Cook until the vegetables are soft, about 10 minutes. Stir in the paprika, dill and cayenne.

Pour the cashew mixture into the pan. Simmer for 15 minutes. Just before serving, stir in the miso and lemon juice or vitamin C crystals.

NOTE: For a thicker soup, after you pour the cashew liquid into the saucepan, return about a cup of liquid and vegetables to the blender. Process until smooth. Return to pot and stir.

Potato Soup ──────────────────

Makes 2 quarts.

Here's a milk-free cream of potato soup.

2 cups chopped onions
2 tablespoons olive oil
4 cups rich chicken Stock or vegetable Stock (see page 122)
2 cups cubed potatoes

In a Dutch oven or stockpot, sauté the onions in the oil until tender. Add the Stock, potatoes, carrots, Pizzazz Seasoning, kombu, dill and hot pepper sauce. Bring to a boil, then reduce the heat, and simmer for 25 to 30 minutes, until vegetables are soft.

Transfer 1 cup of vegetables and broth to a blender. Process until smooth. Return to the pot. Add the parsley.

1 medium carrot,
    grated (optional)
1 tablespoon Pizzazz
    Seasoning (see
    Index)
1 tablespoon kombu
    powder (optional)
1 teaspoon dried dill
    weed (optional)
6 drops hot pepper
    sauce
¼ cup parsley leaves
    snipped chives
    (garnish)

Serve garnished with chives.

Variations: Use only 3 cups of Stock to cook the vegetables. Prepare a nut milk by blending ½ cup cashews with 1½ cups boiling water. Add 1 cup cooked vegetables, and puree well. Add to pot, and heat.

Add 1 teaspoon caraway seeds to the soup for a flavor surprise.

Simple Oriental Soup

Serves 4.

This is so simple that it will be ready in a flash—provided you've prepared the Stock ahead of time.

I'd forgotten how good simple broth and vegetables could be, until I saw this prepared by a "pro" at a dinner party featuring Chinese food. The cook had the clear broth simmering while he made the stir-fry, rice, fish course and poached pears for dessert. When everything else was ready, he dropped a few thinly sliced mushrooms and the white portions of the scallions into the broth. He served the soup just a minute or two later, in individual bowls. Utter simplicity—and ever so good!

To plan your own Oriental-style feast, serve with Cashew and Vegetable Stir-Fry, Tamari Basmati, broiled fish and Chinese Almond Cookies for dessert.

1 quart clear chicken
    Stock, strained
    (see page 122)
4 small mushrooms,
    thinly sliced
2 slender scallions,
    thinly sliced

Heat Stock in a medium saucepan. Separate white portion of scallions from green. Moments before serving, add mushrooms and white portions of scallions to stock. Simmer for a minute or two. Serve in individual bowls, garnished with a few scallion greens.

Variation: For a more substantial soup, add diced cooked chicken, cooked rice or cooked noodles to the Stock. Heat through, then add the mushrooms and scallions.

NOTE: If you prefer your scallions to be a little more cooked, simmer a few minutes longer.

Vegetable-Miso Soup _____

Makes 3 quarts.

A delicious Japanese-style soup. In Japan, they serve this for breakfast!

1½ cups sliced carrots
1½ cups sliced celery
1½ cups shredded cabbage
½ cup sliced onions
4 thin slices ginger root
1–2 garlic cloves, minced
2 tablespoons olive oil
8 cups water
¼ cup snipped dulse (optional; see Note)
2 tablespoons lemon juice or Oriental rice vinegar
1½ teaspoons wheat-free tamari sauce
1 teaspoon honey
⅛ teaspoon cayenne pepper
2 tablespoons light miso
2 scallions, chopped (garnish)
ground toasted sesame seeds (garnish)

In a Dutch oven or stockpot, sauté the carrots, celery, cabbage, onions, ginger and garlic in the oil for 10 minutes. Remove the ginger slices.

Add the water, dulse, lemon juice or rice vinegar, tamari, honey and cayenne. Cover the pot, and simmer for 10 minutes.

In a small bowl, mix the miso with a few tablespoons of hot soup until well blended. Add to the soup, stirring well.

Serve garnished with scallions and sesame seeds. (To reheat leftovers, use low heat and avoid boiling soup.)

Variations: For a Tofu-Vegetable Soup, use 6 to 8 ounces of tofu. Drain well, then cut into small cubes or julienne strips. Cook slowly in a little oil in a frying pan until browned and crisp on all sides. Add to the soup just before serving.

For Fish-Miso Chowder, add 8 ounces of cod, flounder, catfish or other mild fillets to the pot with the water. Just before serving, use a spoon to break the fish into bite-size pieces.

NOTE: Dulse is a sea vegetable that provides valuable minerals. Snip it with scissors before measuring. Then place it in a strainer and rinse well before using.

Thirty-Minute Bean Soup _____

Makes 1 quart.

This is a hearty, nourishing meal that can be put together from scratch when you need a hot lunch in a hurry. Vary the vegetables and seasonings to suit your diet.

½ cup chick-pea flour or ground-to-powder split

In a 3-quart saucepan, mix the flour and water. Place over medium heat, and add the turnips.

peas or lentils
(see Variations)
3 cups water
1–2 small turnips,
diced into ½"
cubes
1 cup chopped bok
choy stalks
½ cup chopped
onions
1 tablespoon oil
1 garlic clove,
minced
handful of bok
choy greens,
chopped
2 tablespoons tahini
or ground
sesame seeds
1 tablespoon kombu
powder or
Savory Seed
Seasoning (see
Index)
¼ teaspoon vitamin
C crystals
⅛ teaspoon ground
dried rosemary
⅛ teaspoon saffron
dash of hot
pepper sauce
(optional)

In a large frying pan, sauté the bok choy stalks and onions in the oil over low to medium heat for 10 minutes, until tender. Add the garlic, and sauté for 2 more minutes.

Transfer sautéed vegetables to the saucepan with the turnips. Add the bok choy greens, tahini or sesame seeds, kombu or Savory Seed Seasoning, vitamin C crystals, rosemary, saffron and hot pepper sauce. Cover the pan, and simmer for 15 minutes. The soup will be thick; if desired, thin with a bit of water.

Variations: Replace the bok choy stalks with chopped cabbage, and replace the bok choy greens with chopped spinach, chard leaves or turnip tops.

You can also replace the chick-pea flour with split peas or lentils that you have ground to a powder in the blender. Yellow split peas and red lentils make attractive, appetizing soups. (The secret to making this soup in 30 minutes is to have the split peas or lentils preground and waiting in the pantry.)

Quick Spinach Soup _____

Serves 4.

½ cup chopped
onions
1 tablespoon olive
oil
3 cups water or
chicken Stock
(see page 122)
8–10 ounces spinach,
chopped or
torn
1⅓ cups Mushroom
Brown Sauce
(see Index)
1 tablespoon
lemon juice
1 teaspoon wheat-
free tamari
sauce
¼ teaspoon grated
nutmeg

In a Dutch oven, sauté the onions in the oil until tender. Add the water or Stock, spinach, Mushroom Brown Sauce, lemon juice, tamari and nutmeg. Bring to a boil, then simmer a few minutes until spinach is wilted.

Minestrone _____

Serves 12.

This "big soup" is great for people with allergies because it offers a wide choice of ingredients that can be changed or deleted as desired.

2 cups chopped
onions
2 tablespoons olive
oil
2 cups sliced celery
2 cups sliced carrots
6–8 garlic cloves,
minced
2 teaspoons dried
oregano
2 teaspoons dried
basil (or 8
leaves, chopped
and added
during last 10
minutes of

In a Dutch oven or stockpot, sauté the onions in the oil for 5 minutes. Add the celery and carrots. Cook, stirring occasionally, for 10 minutes. Add the garlic, oregano, basil and chili powder or cayenne. Cook another 5 minutes.

Add the Stock or water, beans and tomato puree or tomatoes. Simmer gently for 30 minutes. Add the peppers, parsley, tamari, lemon juice or vinegar and honey. Simmer for 5 minutes.

To serve, put a spoonful of the rice or pastene in a bowl. Ladle soup over it. Top each serving with a generous sprinkling of sesame seeds.

NOTE: You can use your choice of beans. Try pintos, kidney beans, black beans, limas, Great

cooking)
1 teaspoon chili
    powder or ⅛
    teaspoon
    cayenne pepper
6 cups bean Stock
    or water (see
    page 122)
3 cups cooked
    beans (see Note)
2 cups thick tomato
    puree or 4 cups
    stewed tomatoes
⅔ cup chopped
    green peppers
½ cup chopped
    parsley
2 tablespoons
    wheat-free
    tamari sauce
1 tablespoon lemon
    juice or vinegar
1 teaspoon honey
2 cups cooked
    brown rice (or
    pastene
    macaroni,
    optional)
½ cup sesame seeds

Northerns, adzukis, chick-peas or soybeans. Use
one kind or mix them.

Fruit Soup ―――――――――――――――――――――――――――

Serves 6 to 12.

This fruit soup is perfect as a light summer lunch or a refreshing first course at dinner. For optimum flavor, choose a cantaloupe that smells sweet. Because cantaloupe, watermelon and honeydew are all members of the Gourd family, this recipe can be easily adapted for a Diversified Rotary Diet.

1 large cantaloupe
6 mint leaves
  (optional)
1 cup watermelon
  balls or cubes
1 cup honeydew balls
  or cubes
1 cup blueberries or
  sliced strawberries
  (optional)
1 cup diced peaches
  (optional)

Cut the cantaloupe in half, and remove the seeds. Scoop the flesh and any juice into a blender. Add the mint. Process until pureed. Set aside.

Combine the watermelon, honeydew, blueberries or strawberries and peaches in an attractive serving bowl. Pour the cantaloupe puree over them. Serve at once, or chill a few hours.

Lamb Stew ―――――――――――――――――――――――――――

Serves 4.

Thickened with vegetables only and ready in less than an hour!

1 pound extra-
  lean ground
  lamb
1 cup chopped
  onions
10–12 small new
  potatoes
5–6 carrots, cut into
  chunks
3–4 celery stalks,
  cut into 2-
  inch pieces
2–3 parsnips, cut
  into 2-inch
  pieces
1 teaspoon dried
  rosemary,
  crushed
water

Pat the lamb into a large flat square (about ½″ thick) on a piece of wax paper. "Dice" into small cubes. Brown the meat in a large pot. Drain off the fat. Add the onions, and cook 5 minutes.

Add the potatoes, carrots, celery, parsnips, rosemary and enough water to barely cover the vegetables. Cover and cook until the vegetables are tender. Transfer about 1½ cups of the stew to a blender. Process until smooth, then stir back into the pot. Simmer a few minutes more, to thicken.

Zucchini Bisque

Serves 4 to 6.

A creamy no-milk, no-wheat soup.

1 cup chopped
    onions
1 tablespoon olive
    oil
1–2 garlic cloves,
    minced
3 cups chicken
    Stock (see page
    122) or miso
    broth
1 large zucchini,
    shredded (about
    3 cups)
1 tablespoon
    minced basil or
    1 teaspoon
    dried basil
½ teaspoon grated
    nutmeg
    few gratings of
    black pepper
1 tablespoon lemon
    juice

Sauté the onions in the oil in a 2-quart saucepan until soft but not brown. Add garlic, and sauté 1 minute. Then add Stock or broth, zucchini, basil, nutmeg and pepper. Simmer for 15 minutes. Cool for 5 to 10 minutes.

Puree, half at a time, in a blender or food processor. Reheat. Stir in lemon juice, and serve.

Basic Beet Borscht

Makes 1 quart.

This is a good example of how vegetables from one family can be combined in a dish that suits a Diversified Rotary Diet. The basic recipe uses a meaty shin bone, but you can also use chicken or fish (see Variations).

2–3 small or 1 large
   beet
3 cups water or
   Stock (see page
   122)
1 meaty shin bone
1 cup chopped beet
   greens or
   spinach

Scrub the beets well. Place in a large pot with the water or Stock and bone. Cook until beets and meat are tender. Remove the bone, and chop the meat. Return meat to the pot.

Remove the beets from the pot, and slip off their skins. Either puree the beets in a blender of food processor, or shred them finely. Return to the pot.

Bring the soup back to boiling. Add the beet greens or spinach. Simmer for 5 minutes.

Variations: Replace the shin bone with either the wings, neck and back of a chicken or 4 ounces fillet of sole. Cook the sole for only 5 minutes; it will be colored slightly by the beet juices.

For a more complex borscht, add to the basic recipe ½ cup of chopped carrots, celery, celery root, parsnips, onions or leeks. Or add 1 cup shredded cabbage. Season with ½ teaspoon dried marjoram or fennel seeds, or 1 tablespoon lemon juice.

Top each serving with a dollop of Dairy-Free "Sour Cream" or Nutty Creme Topping in place of traditional sour cream.

Rabbit-Vegetable Stew

Serves 4 to 6.

You can buy frozen domestic rabbit in most supermarkets. Rabbit is all white meat, fine-grained, mild and low in fat. Preparing it is very much like working with chicken.

1 young frying rabbit
   (about 3 pounds)
2 cups sliced peeled
   sweet potatoes
2 celery stalks, cut
   into ¾" chunks
10 pearl onions or ½

Cut the rabbit into serving pieces. Arrange the rabbit and the sweet potatoes, celery, onions, peas, garlic and parsley in a small roasting pan. Sprinkle with lemon juice or vitamin C crystals, paprika and cayenne.

Mix the tapioca and water. Pour over the rabbit. Cover the pan, and bake at 350° for 1 to

cup chopped
onions
1½ cups peas
1 garlic clove,
minced
¼ cup chopped
parsley
2 tablespoons lemon
juice or ¼
teaspoon vitamin
C crystals
1½ teaspoons paprika
(optional)
⅛ teaspoon cayenne
pepper
⅓ cup quick-cooking
tapioca
2 cups water

1½ hours, until rabbit is tender. Stir every 15 minutes during baking time to distribute the seasonings and tapioca.

Variations: If you wish to avoid foods in the Nightshade family, omit paprika and cayenne. Replace with 2 bay leaves and 3 or 4 cloves.

For a 4- or 5-pound mature rabbit, use an electric slow cooker. Place onions and celery in bottom of pot. Cover with half the tapioca, then add the rabbit, sweet potatoes, peas, remaining tapioca, garlic and parsley. Sprinkle with lemon juice or vitamin C crystals and seasonings. Add 1⅓ cups water. Cover, and cook for 10 to 12 hours on low.

Marjorie Fisher's Venison Stew

Serves 4.

As president of the Chicago chapter of HEAL (Human Ecology Action League), Marjorie Fisher teaches classes in the Diversified Rotary Diet. She follows the diet herself, and this is one of her recipes. Since wild game is lean and muscular, it responds well to long, slow cooking.

2 pounds venison loin
roast, cubed
2 quarts spring water
4 carrots, sliced
6 celery or lovage
stalks, sliced

Place the cubed venison in a Dutch oven or other large pan. Add water to cover. Simmer for 4 to 5 hours, or until tender. Add the carrots and celery or lovage; simmer about 20 minutes, until tender.

Variations: Replace the carrots and celery or lovage with diced red beets and sliced beet tops. Serve with a spinach salad to keep the vegetables confined to one food family.

You can also use other game meat, such as elk, moose or beaver, instead of the venison.

Reprinted with permission from Marjorie Fisher, from Enjoy Nutritious Variety, *published by Nutrition for Optimal Health, Box 380, Winnetka, IL 60093.*

Chunky Lamb Stew _____

Serves 4.

This versatile stew can accommodate itself to any food allergies. You can easily omit the peppers and tomatoes for a Nightshade-free stew. For a Mint-free meal, omit the herbs given, and substitute Pizzazz Seasoning. This dish is nice served over potatoes, brown rice or sweet potatoes.

1 pound cubed
   lamb
1 large Spanish
   onion, chopped
1 large green
   pepper,
   chopped
2 carrots, sliced into
   1" chunks
2 celery stalks,
   sliced into 1"
   chunks
1–2 garlic cloves,
   minced
2 cups stewed
   tomatoes
   (optional)
2–4 cups water
1 teaspoon dried
   oregano
¼ cup arrowroot
   (optional)
½ cup water
   (optional)
2 tablespoons
   minced basil
2 tablespoons
   minced parsley
1 tablespoon lemon
   juice (optional)

Brown the lamb in a Dutch oven over moderate heat. Drain off all but about 1 tablespoon of fat. Add the onions, peppers, carrots, celery and garlic. Sauté for a few minutes.

Add the tomatoes and 2 cups water (or use 4 cups water if you omit the tomatoes). Stir in the oregano. Simmer for 1½ to 2 hours, until lamb is tender.

If you like a thickened sauce, combine the arrowroot with ½ cup water. Stir into the stew. Simmer 5 minutes.

Stir in the basil, parsley and lemon juice before serving.

Variation: For Lamb-Shank Stew, use 2 lamb shanks instead of cubed lamb. Have your butcher cut them into 2" pieces and trim off the fat.

Turkey-Pumpkin Stew _____

Serves 4.

Pumpkin is one of the least allergenic vegetables. This stew is a good way to utilize leftover holiday fowl.

1 pound cooked
    turkey
2 tablespoons oil
1 green pepper,
    cubed
1 red pepper, cubed
½ Spanish onion,
    sliced
1 cup pumpkin
    puree
4 cups turkey or
    chicken Stock
    (see page 122)
1 teaspoon honey
    pinch of cayenne
    pepper
    (optional)
3–4 cups peeled cubed
    pumpkin,
    uncooked
4 medium red
    potatoes, cubed
4 sage leaves,
    minced
    minced coriander
    leaves or
    parsley
    (garnish)

Cut the turkey into ¾" cubes. Sauté cubes in the oil in a Dutch oven until brown on most sides. Remove them to a bowl.

In the same pan, sauté the green peppers, red peppers and onions for 5 minutes, until crisp-tender. Add more oil, if needed.

Mix the pumpkin puree with the Stock, honey and cayenne. Add to the pot, and bring to a boil. Then add the cubed pumpkin and potatoes. Lower heat, and add the sage and turkey. Simmer for 30 to 40 minutes, until all vegetables are tender.

Serve in flat soup bowls, garnished with coriander or parsley.

Kidney-Bean Stew _____

Serves 6 to 8.

A tasty bean dish without tomatoes. You can vary the beans or herbs to suit your diet or taste buds.

2 cups chopped onions

3 tablespoons olive oil

8 garlic cloves, minced

7 cups Stock or water (see page 122)

1½ cups kidney beans, soaked overnight

1½ cups raw brown rice

2 tablespoons minced basil or 2 teaspoons dried basil

1 tablespoon Dijon-style mustard

1 teaspoon dried oregano

1½ cups chopped chard, spinach or beet greens

grated rind of 1 lemon (optional)

In a Dutch oven or stockpot, sauté the onions in the oil until soft, about 10 minutes. Add the garlic, and cook 2 minutes.

Add the Stock or water, and bring to a boil. Drain beans and discard the soak water. Add beans to stock. Stir in the rice, basil, mustard and oregano. Simmer for 1½ to 2 hours, until beans are as tender as you like them. Add the greens and lemon rind; simmer 10 minutes.

Catfish Chowder

Makes 2 quarts.

You might call this milk-free stew Manhattan-style fish chowder. If you don't have catfish, substitute any mild-flavored fillets.

1 cup diced onions
1 tablespoon olive oil
1 garlic clove, minced
2 cups crushed
    tomatoes
2 cups water
1 cup sliced celery
4 small potatoes,
    diced
2 carrots, sliced
1 medium zucchini,
    chopped
2 bay leaves
2 tablespoons wheat-
    free tamari sauce
1 teaspoon honey
¼ teaspoon fennel
    seeds
¼ teaspoon dried
    tarragon
  pinch of cayenne
    pepper
¾ pound catfish fillets

In a 3-quart saucepan, sauté the onions in the oil until soft. Add the garlic, and cook 1 minute. Add the tomatoes, water, celery, potatoes, carrots, zucchini, bay leaves, tamari, honey, fennel, tarragon and cayenne. Simmer 10 minutes.

Add the fish, and simmer 10 to 15 minutes, until fish flakes easily. Use a spoon to break fish into bite-size pieces.

Garbanzo Garden Stew ————————————————

Serves 4.

Best made in summer and early fall with garden-fresh vegetables. The secret to this dish is timing; the sauce develops a slow-cooked flavor that complements fresh vegetables simmered until just tender. Nice served over brown rice.

1 cup chopped onions
1 tablespoon oil
2 garlic cloves, minced
2½ pounds tomatoes, chopped
2 cups cooked chick-peas (also called garbanzo beans)
1–2 tablespoons wheat-free tamari sauce (optional)
2 tablespoons minced basil or 1 tablespoon dried basil, or more to taste
1½ teaspoons Pizzazz Seasoning (see Index)
1 cup thinly sliced carrots
2 cups zucchini chunks
1 cup thinly sliced celery
1 small red or green pepper, chopped
¼ cup minced parsley
up to ⅛ teaspoon cayenne pepper (optional)

In a large frying pan or Dutch oven, sauté the onions in the oil until soft. Add garlic, and stir 1 minute. Add the tomatoes, chick-peas, tamari, basil and Pizzazz Seasoning. Simmer, uncovered, for 25 minutes. Stir occasionally.

Add the carrots, and cook for 15 minutes. Add the zucchini and celery; cook for 5 minutes. When the vegetables are just crisp-tender, add the peppers, parsley and cayenne; simmer for 2 minutes.

Pasta

Not all pasta is Italian, and not all pasta contains wheat or eggs. That's welcome news to pasta lovers who are allergic to wheat or eggs.

Pasta sprang up spontaneously in various parts of the world, incorporating ingredients native to the Orient, the Middle East and other areas. As a result, we have pastas made of buckwheat, rice, sago, soybean, tapioca and many other grains and roots. You can find them in ethnic food stores. (Read labels. Some brands contain some wheat flour. Jerusalem artichoke pasta in particular may or may not have wheat flour.)

Versatility makes any type of pasta an allergic cook's delight. Even within Italy, each region has its own traditional types of pasta, and Italian cooks point out that almost any ingredient can be used in it, over it or with it. The recipes in this section reflect that versatility.

A note about cooking bean-thread noodles. As the many different brands may require different soaking times, begin testing the soaking noodles after three minutes to see if they're tender.

For other ways to work these pastas into your menu, see the Index for Mix-and-Match Stir-Fry. And for vegetable dishes that come across like pasta, see the recipes for Spaghetti Squash Italian, Vegetable "Pasta," Zucchini Lasagna and their variations at the end of this section.

Enjoy!

Grain-Free Pasta

Serves 2.

People who are allergic to wheat don't necessarily have to give up pasta. The two critical ingredients to making your own pasta are practice and patience. Once you get the feel of this dough, you'll enjoy the results.

1⅔ cups amaranth flour
⅓ cup arrowroot or tapioca-starch flour
2 eggs

Mix the amaranth flour and arrowroot or tapioca-starch flour in a small bowl. Measure out 1 cup of the flour, and set the rest aside.

In another small bowl, beat the eggs lightly with a fork. Gradually beat in the 1 cup flour until mixture forms a ball.

Use some of the remaining flour to flour a bread board or other work surface. Turn the dough out onto the flour, and pat and knead it for a minute. Then use a rolling pin to roll the dough very thinly into a large circle or rectangle.

Allow the dough to rest for 30 minutes. Then roll it up tightly from one end, like a jelly roll. Use a sharp knife to cut thick or thin noodles. Unroll the cut noodles. (If desired, cut them into shorter lengths.) Hang the strands over the edge of a bowl or pot until you're ready to use them. (If not using within 30 minutes, wrap well and store in the refrigerator.)

To cook, drop noodles into a large pot of boiling water. Cook until *al dente,* or just tender (anywhere from 3 to 8 minutes; test strands frequently to see if they're done). Drain, and serve at once.

Variations: Replace the amaranth-mixture flour with 2 cups white buckwheat flour. (For directions on making white buckwheat flour, see Table 1, Cooking and Baking with Alternative Flours, in the section, Exploring New Ingredients.)

To make lasagna noodles, roll dough into a rectangle that's about 24″ long and 12″ wide. Cut into 3″-×-12″ noodles. That's the perfect size for a 9″-×-13″ baking dish.

NOTE: If you will be baking the noodles after cooking, cook them until just pliable. Rinse with cold water and drain. That will assure that you don't overcook the noodles by the time your recipe is done.

Bean-Thread Pasta Salad ⎯⎯⎯⎯⎯⎯

Serves 6 to 8.

This makes a very light main course salad. Especially nice in hot weather.

2 ounces bean-thread noodles (see page 139)
3 cups boiling water
½ small cabbage, chopped
3 scallions, sliced
6–8 radishes, thinly sliced
2 cups water
¾ pound monkfish or other flavorful, white fish
½ cup Tofu Mayo (see Index) or other mayonnaise
3 tablespoons lime juice
grated lime rind
4–5 drops of hot pepper sauce or 1 tablespoon prepared horseradish

Place the noodles in a large bowl. Cover with the boiling water, and set aside for 10 minutes. Drain through a colander, then return to the bowl. Cut with 2 sharp knives or kitchen scissors. Toss with cabbage, scallions and radishes.

Bring the 2 cups water to a boil in a saucepan. Add the fish. Simmer 10 to 15 minutes, until cooked through at the thickest point. Drain. When cool enough to handle, remove the heavy membrane. Coarsely dice fish, and add to noodles.

In a small bowl, whisk together the Tofu Mayo or other mayonnaise, lime juice, rind and hot pepper sauce or horseradish. Pour over the salad. Toss to mix. Chill before serving.

Spaghetti Squash Italian _____

Serves 4 to 6.

I avoided spaghetti squash for years, mostly because I didn't know what to do with it. But now I realize it's a cinch to prepare. And it really is a perfect pasta substitute.

1 large spaghetti
squash (about 3½
pounds)
Italian Spaghetti
Sauce or Pesto Dip
(see Index)

Pierce the squash deeply in several spots with a knife or cooking fork so steam can escape as it cooks. Place in a jelly-roll pan or baking dish. Bake at 375° for 25 minutes. Turn over, and bake another 20 minutes, or until the skin yields to gentle pressure. Allow to cool for 10 to 15 minutes.

Cut the squash in half crosswise. Remove the seeds and strings from the center with a spoon. Take a fork, and gently separate the flesh into strands.

Transfer to serving plates, and top with Italian Spaghetti Sauce or Pesto Dip.

NOTE: A 3½-pound squash will yield 4 main-course servings or 6 side dishes. If you're cooking for 2, freeze the leftovers. Thaw them in a colander so excess water can drain easily.

Vegetable "Pasta" _____

Serves 1.

This recipe was born when it occurred to me that what I miss most about pasta is the flavor and aroma of tomato sauce. Zucchini and other vegetables make great stand-ins for pasta.

1 medium zucchini
⅔ cup Tomato Sauce
(see Index)

Shred the zucchini and steam briefly to cook through. Serve with heated Tomato Sauce.

Variations: Substitute 1 cup cooked spaghetti squash, 1 cup steamed finely shredded cabbage or 1 cup blanched mung bean sprouts for the zucchini.

Turkey Tetrazzini ——————————

Serves 4 to 6.

A simple casserole that's truly a delight for people who can't eat regular egg noodles.

¼ cup brown rice flour
¼ cup cool water
4 ounces bean-thread noodles (see page 139)
¼ pound mushrooms, sliced
1 tablespoon olive oil
½ cup Brazil nuts
3 cups turkey or chicken Stock, boiling (see Index)
1 tablespoon unsweetened white grape juice
1 tablespoon lemon juice
2 teaspoons kombu powder (optional)
2 teaspoons Pizzazz Seasoning (see Index)
5 drops hot pepper sauce (optional)
2 cups diced cooked turkey
¼ cup chopped parsley
¼ cup Italian Crumbs (see Index)

Combine brown rice flour and cool water and set aside to soak.

Place the bean thread noodles in a large pan or bowl. Pour boiling water over them to cover. Soak for 2 minutes, then drain promptly. Rinse in cold water, and set aside.

Sauté the mushrooms in the oil for several minutes. Set aside.

Place the nuts in a blender, and grind to a fine powder. Add the turkey or chicken Stock, and blend well. Add the flour mixture, grape juice, lemon juice, kombu, Pizzazz Seasoning and hot pepper sauce. Blend briefly.

Pour nut mixture into pan with mushrooms. Cook a few minutes to thicken sauce. Add the turkey, noodles and parsley, in that order. Turn into an oiled baking dish, and top with Italian Crumbs. Bake, covered, at 400° for 20 minutes. (If desired, remove cover for last 5 minutes.)

Zucchini Lasagna _____

Serves 4.

 This alternative to wheat-pasta lasagna is made without tomatoes, regular noodles or mozzarella. I've layered vegetables with sauce and ground lamb to achieve the same effect. The flavors meld nicely—which is the hallmark of a good lasagna.

3 medium zucchini
1 tablespoon olive oil
Tomato-Free
　Spaghetti Sauce
　(see Index)
⅛ teaspoon cayenne
　pepper (optional)
1 pound spinach
1 tablespoon lemon
　juice or ⅛
　teaspoon vitamin
　C crystals
1 teaspoon wheat-free
　tamari sauce or
　kombu powder
pinch of grated
　nutmeg
½ pound ground lamb
¼ cup Italian Crumbs
　(optional; see
　Index)

 Cut the zucchini lengthwise into ¼″ slabs. Coat each piece with oil. Set aside.

 Mix the Tomato-Free Spaghetti Sauce and cayenne. Set aside.

 Wash the spinach in plenty of cold water. Place in a large frying pan with just the water clinging to the leaves. Cook briefly to wilt. Drain, cool, squeeze out all moisture. Then chop finely, and mix with lemon juice or vitamin C crystals, tamari or kombu and nutmeg. Set aside.

 Sauté the lamb in a frying pan until all traces of pink disappear. Drain off fat, and set meat aside.

 Oil an 8″-square baking dish. Place a layer of zucchini in the dish. Cover with a thin layer of sauce. Then add half the spinach and half the lamb. Repeat layers. Top with zucchini and remaining sauce. Sprinkle with Italian Crumbs.

 Bake at 350° for 40 minutes, until top is brown and sauce is bubbly. Cut into large squares, and serve with a metal spatula.

Variations: Replace the zucchini with one of the following: ½ cooked spaghetti squash, 4 ounces cooked bean-thread noodles or 4 ounces cooked rice vermicelli; toss with the olive oil to coat.

 Replace the lamb with one of the following: 1 to 1½ cups cooked chick-peas, ½ pound sautéed ground pork, ½ to 1 cup diced cooked chicken or turkey, ½ pound halved Versatile Meatballs, ½ pound cubed or thinly sliced tofu, 2 to 4 ounces diced Soft Goat's-Milk Cheese or 2 ounces grated hard goat's-milk cheese.

 If desired, replace the tamari or kombu with additional lemon juice or vitamin C crystals, dried herbs or Savory Seed Seasoning.

NOTE: You can assemble the lasagna ahead and refrigerate until you're ready to bake it. Add 15 to 20 minutes to the baking time. To serve 8, double the recipe and bake in a 9"-×-13" baking dish.

Pesto Pasta

Serves 4.

A fragrant, colorful change from tomato-sauced pasta. Makes a great side dish with fish or fowl.

3¾ ounces bean-thread noodles (see page 139)
2 quarts boiling water
1 cup Pesto Dip (see Index)
pine nuts (garnish)

Place the noodles in a large bowl. Pour the water over them. Let stand for 3 minutes, or until tender. Drain well. Transfer to a serving bowl.

Using a knife and fork, cut across the noodles several times in each direction to coarsely chop them. Stir in the Pesto Dip. Sprinkle with pine nuts.

Variation: Use rice vermicelli, cooked as usual.

Pesto Salad

Serves 4.

A real treat on a hot summer day. And, like conventional pasta salads, it's so versatile.

1 cup Pesto Dip (see Index)
2 cups cold cooked rice vermicelli
12 cherry tomatoes, quartered (optional)
½ cup chopped Spanish onions

In a large bowl, gently fold the Pesto Dip into the vermicelli. Divide among 4 salad bowls or plates. Arrange tomato quarters around the outer edges of each salad. Top with onions. Serve immediately.

Variations: You can substitute cold cooked spaghetti squash or bean-thread noodles for the rice vermicelli.

NOTE: Because Pesto Dip discolors if it's allowed to stand exposed to the air, you should not mix the salad until you're ready to serve it.

Vegetables and Salads

With so many varieties to choose from, vegetables themselves aren't too much of a problem for people with food allergies. You simply may not be able to enjoy them creamed or topped with butter, Hollandaise or cheese sauce. Yet there are several tasty other options besides unadorned cooked vegetables.

First, eat more soups. I find them to be a most helpful medium for vegetables. To get started, browse through the section, Soups, Stews and Chowders. Second, eat more salads and use raw vegetables as snacks. My favorites are Spinach Salad and Jicama "Hot Stuff" Slaw. And third, stir-fry vegetables briefly in a little oil, as in the Cashew and Vegetable Stir-Fry.

When you do cook vegetables, steaming or baking conserves nutrients rather than boiling them away. (See the Timetable for Steaming Vegetables at the end of this section.) Steamed vegetables taste great with just a little mayonnaise or lemon juice. I've also found that a sprinkling of vitamin C crystals tastes much like lemon juice—a handy alternative if you avoid citrus.

To bake vegetables, put them in a casserole with a tight-fitting lid. If the vegetables aren't wet enough to steam as they bake, add 1 tablespoon of water. They average 45 to 75 minutes in a moderate oven, depending on size and variety. That works especially well for asparagus, broccoli, cauliflower, turnips, mixed carrots and celery. For more elaborate dishes, see the recipes for Company Cauliflower and other side dishes.

Mushroom Tarts

Serves 4 to 8.

These resemble English or Scottish pasties and can serve as appetizers, luncheon specials or fancy side dishes with dinner.

¾ cup amaranth flour
½ cup arrowroot
¼ cup ground nuts or seeds
½ teaspoon Pizzazz Seasoning (see Index)
½ teaspoon caraway seeds
3 tablespoons water
1 tablespoon oil
½ pound mushrooms, finely chopped
½ cup minced onions
2 tablespoons oil
1 teaspoon Pizzazz Seasoning
½ teaspoon dried dill weed
¼ cup Dairy-Free "Sour Cream" (see Index)
chopped red peppers (garnish)
minced parsley (garnish)
dill sprigs (garnish)
Dairy-Free "Sour Cream" (garnish)

To make the crust, mix the flour, arrowroot, nuts or seeds, ½ teaspoon Pizzazz Seasoning and caraway in a medium bowl.

In a cup stir together the water and 1 tablespoon oil. Pour over the flour mixture, and stir with a fork to blend. If necessary, add a bit more water to make a stiff dough.

Divide the dough into 8 pieces. Roll each piece into a ball, and place on a large cookie sheet. Using a jar lid, flatten each ball into a circle at least 3" across. With your fingers, form ½" high walls on each piece to contain filling. Bake at 400° for 15 minutes.

To make the filling, sauté the mushrooms and onions in 2 tablespoons oil in a frying pan over medium heat for 7 to 10 minutes, until mixture is dry. Do not burn. Remove from the heat, and stir in 1 teaspoon Pizzazz Seasoning and dill. Then stir in ¼ cup Dairy-Free "Sour Cream." Divide the filling among baked tart shells. Bake at 400° for 7 minutes.

Serve warm garnished with red peppers, parsley and dill sprigs over dollops of Dairy-Free "Sour Cream."

Bit O'Sweet Carrots

Serves 4.

Not "candied," but subtly sweet and delicious.

6 medium carrots, sliced into rounds
1–2 tablespoons maple syrup

Steam the carrots until tender, about 8 to 10 minutes. Transfer them to a serving dish, and drizzle with maple syrup to taste. Stir lightly. Serve hot.

Summer Salad Bowl ⎯⎯⎯⎯⎯⎯⎯⎯⎯⎯⎯⎯⎯⎯⎯

Salads are perfect for people with food allergies because they can be varied to suit anyone's needs. For a main course salad, choose from the following categories.

assorted fresh vegetables (choose several):

> spinach, torn into bite-size pieces
> romaine lettuce, torn into bite-size pieces
> cabbage, shredded
> carrots, sliced
> celery, sliced
> zucchini, sliced or diced
> cucumber, sliced or diced
> radishes, sliced
> scallions, chopped
> peppers, thinly sliced

source of protein (choose one):

> turkey, cooked and diced
> chicken, cooked and diced
> lamb, cooked and diced
> tuna, salmon or other fish, cooked and flaked
> hard-cooked eggs, sliced
> cooked beans or diced tofu, seasoned

Fresh-Tomato Salad Dressing (see Index)

Assemble all ingredients except dressing in individual salad bowls or 1 large salad bowl. Top with Fresh-Tomato Salad Dressing. Serve at once.

148

Spinach-Stuffed Mushrooms

Makes about 30.

An impressive change from routine cheese and crackers. Make these appetizers ahead of time, and chill them so that you can pop them into the oven at the last minute. Serve piping hot.

10 ounces spinach
½ cup chopped onions
4 garlic cloves, minced
4½ teaspoons olive oil
¾ teaspoon chili powder
1 pound mushroom caps (about 30)
¼ cup Tofu Mayo (see Index)
1 tablespoon lemon juice

Wash the spinach thoroughly. Steam it for 5 minutes, until just wilted. Allow to cool. Then place in a strainer, and press out excess moisture with a fork. Chop spinach finely.

Sauté the onions and garlic in the oil in a medium saucepan until the onions are soft. Stir in the spinach. Cook 5 to 7 minutes to blend ingredients. Stir in the chili powder. Set aside to cool slightly.

Brush the mushroom caps clean. Remove the stems, and reserve them for another use.

Stir the Tofu Mayo and lemon juice into the spinach mixture. Using a teaspoon or the large end of a melon-ball scoop, fill the mushrooms with the spinach. Arrange the filled caps on a small cookie sheet. Bake at 350° for 15 minutes. Or chill unbaked caps until needed, then bake them at 350° for 18 to 20 minutes.

Sicilian Salad

Serves 4 to 6.

This marinated salad is company fare at my table. It can be made a day ahead, so there's no last-minute hassle. And it's different enough that it sparks conversation.

12 ounces canned artichoke hearts
1 cup frozen peas, uncooked
12 medium mushrooms, thinly sliced
Basil Vinaigrette (see Index)
1 teaspoon dried oregano

Drain the artichoke hearts, and rinse well to remove salt. Cut into halves or quarters, depending upon their size. Place in a bowl with the peas and mushrooms. Drizzle with Basil Vinaigrette, and sprinkle on oregano. Toss well to coat all vegetables with dressing. Cover, and refrigerate for 2 hours or more. Flavors develop as the salad marinates.

Spinach Salad _____

A welcome change from sandwiches at lunchtime. Serve with Muffins.

fresh spinach
scallions, sliced
radishes, diced
mushrooms, sliced
hard-cooked eggs,
    sliced (optional)
chick-peas, cooked
    or canned
beets, cooked and
    sliced
sunflower seeds,
    toasted
Sesame-Lime
    Salad Dressing
    or other dressing
    (see Index)
sesame seeds
    (garnish)

Wash the spinach well in plenty of water. Dry well between cotton towels or in a salad spinner. Tear into bite-size pieces.

In a large bowl layer the spinach, scallions, radishes, mushrooms, eggs, chick-peas, beets and sunflower seeds.

Drizzle with Sesame-Lime Salad Dressing or other dressing. Sprinkle salad with sesame seeds.

Kidney-Bean Salad _____

Serves 6 to 8.

Dressed with either mayonnaise or oil and vinegar, this salad is a winner. Serve it with muffins or a dessert that contains nuts or seeds for a high-protein meal.

2 cups cooked kidney
    beans
½ cup sliced celery
½ cup chopped green
    peppers
½ cup sliced scallions
2 tablespoons
    chopped dill
    pickles or honey-
    sweetened pickle
    relish
dash of cayenne
    pepper
⅓ cup Homemade
    Mayo, Tofu Mayo
    or Nutty Mayo
    (see Index)

In a large bowl, toss together the beans, celery, peppers, scallions, pickles or relish and cayenne. Add the Mayo, and toss lightly to combine. Chill at least 2 hours before serving.

Variation: Replace the Mayo with 2 tablespoons oil, 2 tablespoons vinegar and, if desired, ½ teaspoon honey.

Three-Bean Salad

Serves 8 to 10.

A traditional sweet and sour favorite. By making this salad yourself, you avoid the corn syrup and sugar that are usually present in commercial products.

2 cups cooked green beans
1 cup cooked kidney beans
1 cup cooked chick-peas or wax beans
1 cup sliced celery
½ cup chopped green peppers
2 ounces pimientos, chopped
½ large, sweet Spanish onion, sliced
⅓ cup oil
⅓ cup vinegar
¼ cup honey
1 teaspoon wheat-free tamari sauce (optional)
1–2 garlic cloves
⅛ teaspoon cayenne pepper (optional)

Combine the green beans, kidney beans, chick-peas or wax beans, celery, peppers and pimientos in a large bowl. Separate onion slices into rings. Add to bowl.

In a blender process oil, vinegar, honey, tamari, garlic and cayenne until garlic is liquefied. Pour over the vegetables. Toss well. Refrigerate for several hours.

Variation: For a vinegar-free version, replace the vinegar with ⅓ cup water and 1 teaspoon or more of vitamin C crystals.

Hold-the-Lettuce Salad _____

Because lettuce is related to ragweed, many hay fever sufferers can't eat it. But it's easy to make a tasty tossed salad without lettuce. Choose as few or as many of these ingredients as you can eat freely. (You can even make this in a restaurant!)

celery
carrots
red or green
  peppers
scallions or onion
  rings
zucchini
tomatoes
radishes
kohlrabi
jicama
chick-peas
sunflower seeds
nuts, raw
mushrooms
avocado
beets, cooked
green beans,
  cooked
broccoli, raw or
  cooked
cauliflower, raw or
  cooked
  "C" Salad
  Dressing (see
  Index) or oil and
  vinegar

Chop vegetables to size you prefer. Toss together in individual bowls or large salad bowl. Drizzle with "C" Salad Dressing or oil and vinegar and toss to coat.

NOTE: For quick salads, chop enough vegetables to last 2 to 3 days. Add the dressing just before serving.

Tropical Fruit Salad _____

Serves 4.

Fruit makes delightful cold salads.

4 large romaine or leaf
  lettuce leaves
2 large bananas
1 tablespoon lemon
  juice (optional)
2 large or 3 medium
  oranges

Arrange the lettuce on 4 individual salad plates. Cut each banana in half both lengthwise and crosswise. Arrange 2 pieces on each plate (position them near the edges to resemble a pair of parentheses). Brush with lemon juice if you won't be serving the salad within 15 minutes.
  Peel the oranges and slice them thinly

Avocado-Grapefruit
  Dressing (see
  Index)
shredded
  unsweetened
  coconut (optional)
chopped macadamia
  nuts (optional)

crosswise. Divide among the plates, and arrange them between the bananas.

Drizzle with Avocado-Grapefruit Dressing, and sprinkle with coconut and macadamia nuts.

Variations: For a citrus-free salad, replace the oranges with 3 kiwis. Brush the bananas with pineapple juice, and use Nutty Mayo (see Index) in place of Avocado-Grapefruit Dressing.

For a more elaborate, luncheon-size salad, add other fruits, such as melon balls, berries, grapes, kiwi slices, peach slices, nectarine slices or apricot slices.

If desired, serve with amaranth-based Muffins (see Index) to bolster the protein content of the meal.

Cauliflower-Dill Salad

Serves 4 to 6.

A salad without lettuce, tomatoes or cucumbers.

1 small head
  cauliflower
1 cup fresh peas,
  lightly cooked, or
  frozen peas,
  thawed but not
  cooked
½ cup sliced scallions
½ cut Nutty Mayo (see
  Index)
2 teaspoons dried dill
  weed
2 teaspoons lemon
  juice
  hot pepper sauce
  (optional)

Separate the cauliflower into florets. Combine in a large bowl with the peas, scallions, Nutty Mayo, dill, lemon juice and pepper sauce to taste. Chill several hours or overnight.

NOTE: Although the peas add color and flavor, you may omit them if you cannot eat legumes.

Tangy-Sweet Slaw

Makes about 7 cups.

A refreshing change from traditional mayonnaise-based slaws. Serve with fish, chicken or other light meats.

1 small or ½ large
    head cabbage (1
    pound)
2 cups chopped
    unpeeled,
    unsprayed apples
1 cup unsweetened
    chopped or
    crushed
    pineapple
½ cup raisins
½ cup chopped onions
½ cup Homemade
    Mayo (see Index)
¼ cup Oriental rice
    vinegar or 2
    tablespoons apple
    cider vinegar
3 tablespoons
    unsweetened
    apple-juice
    concentrate
1 tablespoon lemon
    juice
½ teaspoon celery
    seeds (optional)
    chopped nuts or
    toasted sesame
    seeds (optional)

Core and shred or finely chop the cabbage. In a large bowl, combine the cabbage, apples, pineapple, raisins and onions. Toss well.

In a small bowl, whisk together the Homemade Mayo, vinegar, juice concentrate, lemon juice and celery seeds. Pour over salad, and mix well. If desired, allow to marinate an hour or more before serving. Sprinkle with nuts or sesame seeds before serving.

NOTE: If you're using a food processor to chop the cabbage, try this method. Cut cabbage into 1½″ cubes, and chop it with the metal blade, using on/off turns. It's quicker and easier this way than using the slicing disk.

Pickled Beets

Serves 4.

Many commercially pickled beets contain corn syrup. These don't.

¼ cup water
¼ cup honey
¼ cup Oriental rice
    vinegar
¼ teaspoon ground

Combine the water, honey, vinegar, cinnamon, cloves and allspice in a medium saucepan. Simmer for 2 minutes. Stir in the beets, and heat through. Serve hot or warm.

154

cinnamon
pinch of ground
cloves
pinch of ground
allspice (optional)
3 cups sliced cooked
beets

Variations: If you don't have rice vinegar, substitute 3 tablespoons of white or cider vinegar. Or use 3 tablespoons water and ¾ teaspoon vitamin C crystals or more to taste.

For Harvard-Style Beets, dissolve 1 tablespoon of arrowroot in ¼ cup of water. Add to the simmered liquid. Stir over heat for about 1 minute, until liquid thickens. Then add the beets and heat through.

Jicama "Hot Stuff" Slaw

Serves 4.

Jicama is an oft-neglected vegetable. Its brown exterior is normally tough and stringy, but its interior is tender, juicy and sweet. An average jicama measures 5" or 6" across. This recipe will use only part of one vegetable; slice the remainder to use as nibbles, either plain or with a dip.

2–3 cups shredded
jicama
1 carrot, shredded
6 radishes, thinly
sliced
½ large pepper,
diced
½ cup minced
parsley
3–4 scallions, thinly
sliced
½ cup Homemade
Mayo or Tofu
Mayo (see
Index)
1 tablespoon lemon
juice
1 teaspoon chili
powder, or
more to taste

In a large bowl, toss together the jicama, carrots, radishes, peppers, parsley and scallions.

In a small bowl, mix the Mayo, lemon juice and chili powder. Pour over the salad, and toss lightly to mix. Chill for 1 hour.

NOTE: This can be prepared quickly and easily with a food processor. Cut jicama, carrot and pepper into 1" cubes and combine with parsley in bowl and process with on/off turns, using the steel blade. Turn into mixing bowl and add sliced scallions and radishes, then the dressing.

Pineapple Gel Salad _____

Serves 9 to 12.

A wonderfully yummy, firm gel without sugar or artificial coloring.

20 ounces
    unsweetened
    crushed
    pineapple,
    packed in juice
4½ teaspoons
    unflavored
    gelatin
6 ounces
    unsweetened
    pineapple-juice
    concentrate
¾ cup water
¼ cup mayonnaise
2 tablespoons honey
    (optional)
3 tablespoons
    mayonnaise
    (optional)
2 tablespoons
    minced parsley
    (optional)

Drain the pineapple in a strainer. Reserve the juice.

Measure ¼ cup of reserved juice into a small saucepan. Sprinkle on the gelatin; allow to soften for 5 minutes. Stir in the juice concentrate, water and reserved pineapple juice. Bring to a boil, then reduce heat, and simmer for 5 minutes.

Remove the pan from the heat. Add mayonnaise and honey and whisk until smooth. Chill until slightly thick and syrupy. Either stir in the pineapple by hand or, for a lighter and fluffier gel, beat it in with an electric mixer.

Pour the mixture into a lightly oiled 8"-square baking dish or 6-cup gelatin mold. Chill until firm. Unmold, cut into serving pieces, and top each piece with a little mayonnaise and a sprinkling of parsley.

Variation: If you prefer a clear gel rather than a creamy one, or if you can't eat mayonnaise, omit the ¼ cup mayonnaise and substitute ¼ cup water. Or use Tofu Mayo (see Index).

Creamed Spinach _____

Serves 4.

A popular side dish made without milk or flour.

1 pound spinach
    hot water or Stock
    (see Index)
⅓ cup cashews or
    other nuts
1 tablespoon Dijon-
    style mustard
1 tablespoon
    arrowroot
¼ cup water
1 cup sliced onions
1–2 tablespoons olive
    oil

Wash the spinach in plenty of cold water. Drain slightly, then place wet leaves in a large frying pan or Dutch oven. Steam for 2 to 3 minutes, until spinach wilts. Transfer to a colander set over a bowl. Allow spinach to drain, but do not press out liquid or squeeze dry. Chop the spinach coarsely, and set aside.

Measure the liquid in the bowl. If you don't have ¾ cup, add enough hot water or Stock to make that much. Set aside.

Grind the nuts to a fine powder in the blender. Add the spinach liquid and the mustard. Blend well, until smooth.

Dissolve the arrowroot in ¼ cup water. Add to blender, and mix well.

In a large frying pan, sauté the onions in the oil until soft. Add the spinach; cook for 1 minute. Pour the sauce over the spinach mixture. Stir for 2 minutes over heat until thick.

Baked Onions

Serves 4.

Large sweet onions are much more than a condiment—they are vegetables in their own right. Baked onions are so easy to prepare that you can throw them into the oven and forget about them until they're done.

4 large Spanish onions

Make sure there are no soft spots on the onions. Brush off any loose dirt, but keep the skins intact. Place in a baking pan, and bake at 400° for 1 hour (or 350° for 1¼ hours).

To serve, remove the outer skins, and cut off the root ends.

Variations: To make Stuffed Baked Onions, bake the onions as above. Then carefully remove the centers, leaving a shell with a double-layered wall. Fill with Creamed Spinach or chopped asparagus tips that have been briefly steamed. Return to the oven for 10 minutes.

You can use the centers as the base for an Onion Sauce. Simply process until smooth in a blender, adding a little liquid if needed. Season with ¼ teaspoon dried thyme, and top vegetables, fish, fowl or meat.

NOTE: If they're available, you can use Walla Walla or Vidalia onions.

Cashew and Vegetable Stir-Fry _____

Serves 4.

This wonderful side dish is perfect with roasts, baked fish and roast fowl. Serve over brown rice.

2 tablespoons peanut oil
1 cup sliced mushrooms
1 cup sliced celery or Chinese cabbage
1 cup bean sprouts or snow peas
½ cup sliced scallions (¾" to 1" lengths)
½ cup thinly sliced jicama
½ cup cashew pieces
1 tablespoon wheat-free tamari sauce (optional)

Heat a wok or large frying pan over high heat. Add the oil and heat 30 seconds. Add the mushrooms and celery or Chinese cabbage; stir-fry for 2 minutes. Add the bean sprouts or snow peas, scallions, jicama and cashews. Stir-fry another 2 minutes. Add the tamari, and stir well to distribute.

Vegetable Stuffing _____

Serves 2.

Here's a grain-free stuffing which is also free of apples and nuts. Good with fowl or to stuff a squash.

1½ teaspoons tahini
1½ teaspoons sunflower oil
1 carrot, diced or shredded
1½ celery stalks, thinly sliced
1 small onion, minced
¼ cup minced parsley
2 tablespoons toasted sunflower seeds
¼ teaspoon poultry seasoning (optional)

In a large bowl, stir the tahini and oil together to mix well. Add the carrots, celery, onion, parsley, sunflower seeds and poultry seasoning. Toss well to combine.

Makes enough to stuff 2 chicken breasts or 2 Cornish hens.

NOTE: Double the recipe for a roasting chicken. Triple or quadruple it for a small turkey.

Saucy Dilled Carrots _____

Serves 4.

The sauce is thick—somewhat like a glaze—so these carrots can go onto a dinner plate without being "soupy."

¾ pound carrots, thinly sliced or julienne
⅓ cup unsweetened apple juice
1 teaspoon oil (optional)
2 teaspoons arrowroot
⅓ cup unsweetened apple juice
1 teaspoon dried dill weed

In a heavy saucepan with a tight-fitting lid, simmer the carrots and ⅓ cup apple juice until carrots are tender, about 12 to 15 minutes. If juice boils away, add a little water to prevent sticking. Add the oil.

In a cup, combine the arrowroot with ⅓ cup apple juice. Stir into the pan. Cook, stirring, for about 2 minutes, until the sauce is thick and clear. Stir in the dill.

Variations: To make Minted Carrots, omit the dill and substitute 1 tablespoon chopped mint. For a slightly sweet glaze, add 1 teaspoon honey to the cooked carrots before thickening.

Pizza-Style Eggplant _____

Serves 4 to 6.

Serve as an appetizer, side dish or evening snack. Top with grated goat's-milk cheese if you can eat it.

1 medium eggplant (about 1¼ pounds)
2 tablespoons olive oil
1 large Spanish onion, chopped
1 green pepper, chopped
2 cups chopped tomatoes or quartered cherry tomatoes
1 garlic clove, minced
1½ teaspoons Italian Seasoning (see Index)

Peel the eggplant (if you wish to) and cut into ½" slices. Brush both sides of each slice very lightly with oil. Arrange on a cookie sheet, and bake at 350° for 15 to 20 minutes, until tender.

Place remaining oil in a frying pan. Add onions, peppers, tomatoes, garlic and Italian Seasoning. Sauté until soft, about 15 minutes.

Place a heaping spoonful of vegetable sauce on each eggplant slice. (If desired, you can refrigerate eggplant at this point and bake later.) Bake at 350° for 10 minutes, or until heated through.

Company Cauliflower —————————————

Serves 3 to 6.

Good hot or cold. A tasty alternative to cauliflower with cheese sauce.

1 small head or ½
    large head
    cauliflower
2 scallions, sliced
2–4 tablespoons
    Homemade
    Mayo or Nutty
    Mayo (see
    Index)
  Savory Seed
    Seasoning
    (optional; see
    Index)

Cut the cauliflower into florets or bite-size pieces. Steam for 8 to 10 minutes, until tender. Transfer to a serving dish, and toss with scallions and enough Mayo to lightly coat. Sprinkle with Savory Seed Seasoning to taste.

Vegetable Potpourri —————————————

Serves 4.

A new format for carrots and celery.

2 cups sliced carrots
1½ cups sliced celery
1 cup chopped
    onions
½ cup water
1 tablespoon oil
¼ teaspoon dried
    thyme
1 tablespoon
    arrowroot
¼ cup water
1 tablespoon lemon
    juice or ¼
    teaspoon vitamin
    C crystals

Combine the carrots, celery, onions, ½ cup water, oil and thyme in a 2-quart saucepan. Bring to a boil, then reduce heat, and cook 12 to 15 minutes, until carrots are crisp-tender but not overcooked.

In a cup, stir the arrowroot into ¼ cup water. Add the lemon juice or vitamin C crystals. Stir this mixture into the vegetable pan. Cook, stirring constantly, for about 2 minutes, until sauce is thick and clear.

160

TABLE 5

Timetable for Steaming Vegetables

People who are on a very limited diet may need to eat vegetables plain and unadorned. To conserve flavor and nutrients, steam vegetables lightly in a stainless steel steamer or wire basket over boiling water, in a covered pot. (You can also use this chart to cook potatoes and other vegetables for salads and combination dishes.)

Vegetable	Steaming Time
Artichokes	
whole	12–15 minutes
Asparagus	
whole	10–15 minutes
2″ pieces	5–10 minutes
Beans, Snap	
whole	10–15 minutes
cut	7–12 minutes
Beans, Wax (Yellow)	
whole	10–15 minutes
cut	7–12 minutes
Beets	
whole	25–60 minutes (varies with size)
¼″ slices	10–15 minutes
Broccoli	
stalks	10–20 minutes
cut in pieces	5–15 minutes
Brussels Sprouts	
whole	10–15 minutes
Cabbage	
small head, whole (core removed)	15–25 minutes
thinly sliced	5–10 minutes
Carrots	
whole	20–30 minutes
¼″ slices	10–15 minutes
Cauliflower	
florets	10–15 minutes

SOURCE: Information compiled by the staff of the Rodale Test Kitchen.

continued

TABLE 5—*Continued*

Vegetable	Steaming Time
Celery	
whole stalk	15–20 minutes
2″ pieces	5–10 minutes
Chard, Swiss	
leaves	3–5 minutes
Corn	
on cob	7–10 minutes
cut	4–5 minutes
Dandelion Greens	
leaves	3–5 minutes
Endive	
leaves	4–8 minutes
Escarole	
leaves	4–8 minutes
Fennel	
whole bulb	7–10 minutes
½″–1″ slices	5–8 minutes
Green Pepper	
whole, core removed	6–10 minutes
¼″ slices	5–7 minutes
Kale	
leaves	4–8 minutes
Kohlrabi	
whole	15–20 minutes
¼″ slices	5–10 minutes
Leeks	
whole	7–10 minutes
½″ slices	5–10 minutes
Okra	
whole	15–20 minutes
sliced	5–7 minutes
Parsnips	
whole	10–15 minutes
¼″ slices	7–10 minutes
Pearl Onions	
whole	6–15 minutes
¼″ slices	3–6 minutes

Vegetable	Steaming Time
Peas	
shelled, green	5–8 minutes
Potatoes, Sweet	
whole	20–30 minutes
½" slices	5–7 minutes
Potatoes, White	
whole	15–25 minutes
½" slices	5–10 minutes
Scallions	
whole stalk	3–7 minutes
½" pieces	3–5 minutes
Snow Peas	
whole	3–5 minutes
Spinach	
leaves	3–5 minutes
Squash, Summer	
whole	10–15 minutes
cubed	5–10 minutes
Squash, Winter	
whole	20–30 minutes
cubed	7–10 minutes
Tomatoes	
whole (medium)	5–10 minutes
½" slices	3–5 minutes
Turnips	
whole (medium)	15–20 minutes
½" slices	5–7 minutes
Zucchini	
whole	10–15 minutes
cubed	5–10 minutes

Rice and Potato Side Dishes

Rice and potatoes are complex carbohydrates—starchy foods that digest slowly and help us feel satisfied after we've eaten. They also provide the fiber we need to stay healthy. If you don't have time to bake simple breads, rice and potatoes may be especially important to your diet and health.

Rice is a grain, although it's considered to be the least allergenic of the grains. The recipes here call for whole, unpolished rice. Rice Pilaf is a traditional rice dish that you can easily adapt to your taste and needs, and you can make it differently every time. You'll find some other new twists—like Tamari Basmati. Try Rice 'n' Yam Cartwheels with a roast or plain fish, too. To produce light and fluffy rice, do not stir the rice after the liquid has come to a boil. Stirring will make the grains stick together. (Rice flour is discussed in Table 1, Cooking and Baking with Alternative Flours, in the section, Exploring New Ingredients.)

Potatoes belong to the Nightshade family, along with tomatoes, peppers and eggplant. As a group, these foods are common allergens, but they are included anyway because many people do tolerate them well. Also, if you avoid potatoes for several months and then eat them again occasionally, you'll probably want a potato that's free of other potential allergens. So I've developed a handful of recipes that side-step traditional garnishes such as butter, sour cream and cheese. And for a totally new potato experience, try New Potatoes Vinaigrette.

164

Rice Pilaf

Serves 3 to 4.

A new twist on a menu basic: no mushrooms. For more efficient use of protein—especially if you're not using the optional meat—serve with lima beans, peas or green beans. Also nice with baked yellow squash, yams or sweet potatoes.

¼ cup chopped
    cashews
¼ cup sunflower
    seeds or sesame
    seeds
2 tablespoons oil
2 cups cooked
    brown rice
1 cup diced cooked
    meat or chicken
    (optional)
2–4 scallions, chopped
1–2 tablespoons water
    (optional)

Sauté the cashews and sunflower seeds or sesame seeds in the oil in a large non-stick sauté pan until lightly brown. Add the rice and meat or chicken. Stir gently just until rice is hot. Add the scallions and add the water, if needed to prevent sticking.

Rice 'n' Yam Cartwheels

Serves 4.

A great way to work in yams, a very nonallergenic food. This side dish is especially nice with chicken or turkey.

1 cup cooked brown
    rice or basmati
    rice (see
    Appendix)
1 cup mashed yams
    (about 1 medium)
2 tablespoons soya
    powder, ground
    peanuts or ground
    nuts
¼ teaspoon ground
    cinnamon
    pinch of grated
    nutmeg
2 tablespoons soya oil

In a medium bowl, combine rice and yams with the soya powder, peanuts or nuts, cinnamon and nutmeg with a fork. The mixture will seem dry.

Shape into 4 patties. Heat a large non-stick sauté pan, add the oil, and wait 30 seconds. Then add the patties, and sauté about 10 minutes on each side, until nicely brown. Serve hot.

NOTE: If you substitute sweet potatoes for yams, use the dark, orange variety.

Tamari Basmati _____

Serves 5.

Tired of brown rice? Basmati is a white whole-grain rice from India that has two distinct features: It cooks quickly, and it has a unique, delicate flavor. (See Appendix for purchasing sources, or look for basmati in health food and specialty stores.)

1 cup basmati rice
1¾ cups water
2 teaspoons wheat-
    free tamari sauce
    (optional)
1 scallion, minced
    (garnish)

Clean the basmati rice by washing it in several changes of cold water to remove dirt and loose hulls.

Combine the rice, water and tamari in a 2-quart saucepan. Bring to a boil, then reduce heat. Simmer, uncovered or with the lid ajar, for 12 to 15 minutes, or until rice is tender and all the water is absorbed.

Transfer to a serving dish, and sprinkle with scallions.

Tomato-Rice Casserole _____

Serves 4.

If you can eat tomatoes but not pasta, you'll like this option.

1 cup raw brown
    rice
1 cup Tomato Sauce
    (see Index)
1 cup water
1½ teaspoons wheat-
    free tamari sauce
¼ cup minced
    parsley (garnish)

Oil a 1½ quart casserole. Place the rice in the dish.

In a small bowl, combine the Tomato Sauce, water and tamari. Pour over the rice.

Cover the casserole, and bake at 350° for 1¼ hours. Sprinkle with parsley just before serving.

NOTE: Don't fill the casserole dish more than half full, to allow for expansion of the rice during cooking.

Festive Rice _____

Serves 4.

A fancy side dish made with foods from just two families! Great served with fish or fowl.

1 cup raw long-grain
    brown rice
⅓ cup raw wild rice

Mix the brown rice and wild rice in a 3-quart saucepan. Add the water, and bring to a boil. Then reduce the heat, cover the pan, and

3 cups water
⅓ cup coarsely
   chopped pecans
1 tablespoon walnut
   oil

simmer the rice for about 45 minutes, until all liquid has been absorbed. Let stand 5 to 10 minutes.

In a small frying pan, sauté the pecans in the oil until fragrant. Add to the rice, and toss lightly to mix. Serve immediately.

Mushroom-Rice Casserole

Serves 4.

A wonderful way to carry rice to a picnic or potluck supper. Just wrap the casserole in a terry towel or newspapers for insulation. It will stay warm for two hours.

2¾ cups Mushroom
   Brown Sauce
   (see Index)
½ cup water
½ tablespoon wheat-
   free tamari sauce
1 cup raw brown
   rice

Mix the Mushroom Brown Sauce, water and tamari.

Place the rice in an oiled 1½- to 2-quart casserole dish with a lid. Pour the sauce over the rice, and stir well. Cover casserole. Bake at 350° for 1¼ hours.

Variations: Add a can of tuna or diced cooked chicken, turkey or meat for a thrifty entree.

Place a layer of uncooked broccoli or peas in the casserole before adding the sauce.

NOTE: Don't fill the casserole dish more than one-third full, to allow for expansion of the rice during cooking.

Golden Mashed Potatoes

Serves 4.

There's no butter, eggs or milk, yet these potatoes are tasty and light as a feather.

6 large red potatoes
1 carrot, sliced
1 cup water
1 teaspoon wheat-free
   tamari sauce
1 tablespoon oil

Peel and quarter the potatoes. Place them in a heavy 2-quart saucepan that has a tight-fitting lid. Add the carrots, water and tamari. Cover, and simmer until the vegetables are quite soft.

Remove from the heat, but do not drain. Add the oil, and whip with electric beaters or a potato masher. If necessary, add a little more water to moisten.

Scalloped Potatoes

Serves 4 to 6.

You don't need milk to make fancy scalloped potatoes. These are a favorite at my house.

½ cup water
2 large Spanish onions, sliced
2 bay leaves
½ teaspoon dried thyme
pinch of garlic powder
few drops of hot pepper sauce
2 tablespoons olive oil
2¼ pounds red potatoes

Combine the water, onions, bay leaves, thyme, garlic powder and hot pepper sauce in a large frying pan. Cover and simmer for 20 minutes, until onions are soft. Remove the bay leaves.

Using a slotted spoon, transfer the onions to a blender. Liquefy, gradually adding enough cooking liquid to make a light sauce or medium-thin gravy. Blend in the oil.

If desired, peel the potatoes. Slice thinly into a large bowl. Pour the onion sauce over the potatoes, and stir to mix. Pour into an oiled 2-quart casserole or 9"-square baking dish. Cover, and bake at 400° for 1 hour.

NOTE: You can prepare the potatoes up to the point of baking, then refrigerate until later. Bake an additional 10 or 15 minutes. If you're baking something else at 350°, you can bake the potatoes for 1½ hours instead of 1 hour.

Eclectic Potato Salad

Serves 4 generously.

This is a cross between French and American versions of potato salad—with no mayonnaise.

1½ pounds small new potatoes (about a dozen)
¼ cup oil
¼ cup vinegar
½ teaspoon dried tarragon
½ teaspoon dry mustard
¼ teaspoon garlic powder
½ cup sliced celery
½ cup diced peppers

Scrub the potatoes well. Place in a large saucepan with cold water to cover. Bring to a boil, cover, then reduce heat, and cook until soft but not mushy. Drain and allow to cool until warm enough to handle. Slice into a large bowl.

In a small bowl, whisk together the oil, vinegar, tarragon, mustard and garlic powder. Pour over the warm potatoes, and toss gently to combine.

Add the celery, peppers, radishes and scallions. Toss gently. Chill for several hours for flavor to develop fully.

5–6 red radishes,
  sliced
4 scallions, sliced

Variation: For a more traditional potato salad, omit the oil and vinegar. Use ½ cup Homemade Mayo or Tofu Mayo to which you add the tarragon, mustard and garlic powder. Stir in a little warm water if the dressing is too thick to pour.

Potato Pancakes

Makes 10 to 12 pancakes.

Potato pancakes usually contain wheat flour, but these don't. Enjoy!

1 egg
1 tablespoon potato
  flour
2 teaspoons wheat-
  free tamari sauce
  (optional)
dash of cayenne
  pepper
1 small onion,
  minced
⅓ cup minced
  parsley
1¼ pounds baking
  potatoes, grated
  or finely
  shredded
2 tablespoons oil
  (optional)
Real Applesauce,
  warm (optional;
  see Index)

In a medium bowl, mix the egg, flour, tamari and cayenne with a fork. Stir in the onions, parsley and potatoes.

Heat the oil in a frying pan, or heat an ungreased non-stick griddle. Drop spoonfuls of batter onto the skillet; use the back of a spoon to flatten them to ½″ thick. Cook until browned on the bottom, then flip and brown the other side. Keep finished pancakes heated in a warm oven until all are cooked. Serve with Real Applesauce.

NOTE: With a food processor, use the shredding disk for quick and easy preparation.

New Potatoes Vinaigrette

Serves 4 to 6.

You don't have to dress potatoes in butter, sour cream or cheese sauce for them to taste good.

12 small new potatoes
Basil Vinaigrette
  (see Index)
minced parsley
  (garnish)

Scrub the potatoes, and place in a pan with cold water to cover. Boil for 15 minutes, or until tender. Drain. Immediately place the potatoes in a serving dish and quarter with a knife and fork. Drizzle with Basil Vinaigrette, and garnish with parsley. Serve at once.

Salad Dressings, Sauces and Condiments

An old ballad says, "Little things mean a lot. . . ." Even though people with allergies eat relatively plain food most of the time, we still need dressings, sauces or condiments to dress things up occasionally.

Simple salad dressings, such as the "C" Salad Dressing, are probably the best. And as with homemade dressing of any kind, the cook controls the choice of ingredients. Of the three versions of mayonnaise, I think Nutty Mayo is the most versatile, because you can choose the kind of nuts that agree with you.

In place of traditional cream sauces, you will find Susan Dart's Blender Sauce and Magic Mustard Sauce, both excellent over cooked vegetables and other plain food. And when fresh tomatoes are juicy and ripe, try the Tomato Sauce or Fresh 'n' Natural Tomato Sauce for a rare treat.

The fruit sauces were designed mostly with pancakes and waffles in mind, but may also top pudding or plain cake. Fruit-Solo Sauce and Tapioca-Fruit Sauce are my favorites.

Commercially available salt-free seasonings usually combine a little bit of a lot of things, involving too many food families for people on a Diversified Rotary Diet. So I formulated Pizzazz Seasoning and Italian Seasoning, each from a single food family. People who taste-tested those seasonings were very enthusiastic, and I think you'll like them, too. Savory Seed Seasoning represents a little bit of kitchen magic in that it tastes slightly salty, but is still quite low in sodium. For those who tolerate soy, this is a winner!

170

Basil Vinaigrette

Makes 1 cup.

A simple, additive-free homemade dressing that's very aromatic. Use fresh basil, if at all possible; it tastes heavenly. This vinaigrette goes well with salads and cooked vegetables, such as broccoli, cauliflower, beans, cabbage and spinach.

½ cup oil
¼ cup olive oil
¼ cup vinegar or lemon juice
6–8 large basil leaves, minced, or 1½ to 2 teaspoons dried basil
½ teaspoon dry mustard
1 garlic clove, minced

Place the oil, olive oil, vinegar or lemon juice, basil, mustard and garlic in a blender. Process for 1 minute. Store in a glass jar in the refrigerator.

Variations: Replace the basil with 1½ to 2 teaspoons dried oregano or tarragon.

"C" Salad Dressing

Makes about ½ cup.

This dressing gives you an oil-and-vinegar taste without any vinegar. Dress it up with your favorite herbs.

1 medium zucchini
¼ cup safflower oil
2 tablespoons olive oil
1 teaspoon Italian Seasoning (see page 185)
¼ teaspoon vitamin C crystals
1 teaspoon kombu powder (optional)
1 small garlic clove (optional)
minced herbs (optional)
pinch of Peppy (optional; see page 188)

For a green salad dressing, do not peel the zucchini; for a whiter dressing, peel it. Cut vegetable into 1" chunks. Place in a blender, and puree.

Add the safflower oil, olive oil, Italian seasoning, vitamin C crystals, kombu, garlic, herbs and Peppy. Blend 1 minute or until thick and creamy. Taste. If flavor isn't sharp enough, add a pinch more vitamin C crystals.

Serve immediately, or chill a few hours.

NOTE: For a dressing with lower fat content, you can omit the safflower oil without sacrificing flavor.

171

Homemade Mayo ────────────────────────

Makes about 2 cups.

Commercial mayonnaise may contain unspecified vegetable oil, spices, sweeteners and possibly the preservative EDTA. When you make your own, what you see is what you get. All ingredients should be at room temperature, so if you store your oil in the refrigerator, either allow it to come to room temperature or heat it ever so slightly in a saucepan. If making mayonnaise is new to you, use three egg yolks to insure success.

2–3 egg yolks
  2 tablespoons lemon juice
  1 tablespoon vinegar
  1 teaspoon Dijon-style mustard
  2 cups oil

Place the egg yolks, lemon juice, vinegar and mustard in a blender or food processor. Process about 30 seconds. With the machine running, add the oil in a *very* slow thin stream until the mayonnaise starts to thicken. Then pour the remaining oil in gradually.

Transfer to a glass jar and store in the refrigerator. Keeps for 3 weeks.

Tofu Mayo ────────────────────────

Makes 1½ cups.

A versatile, egg-free mayonnaise.

½ pound tofu
2½ tablespoons vinegar or lemon juice
  1 teaspoon Dijon-style mustard
¼ cup oil
  1 teaspoon honey
⅛ teaspoon sesame oil (optional)

Drain the tofu 20 to 30 minutes, pressing between cotton towels to extract as much excess moisture as possible. Crumble with a fork.

Place a quarter of the tofu in a blender with the vinegar or lemon juice and mustard. Blend until smooth, stopping to scrape the sides of the container as necessary.

Gradually add the remaining tofu, and blend well. With the machine running, gradually add the oil. Stop once or twice to scrape the sides of the container. Add honey and sesame oil; blend well.

Store Mayo in the refrigerator. Use within 1 week.

NOTES: Sesame oil is available in Oriental grocery stores.

If you're using a food processor, simply add all the ingredients to the bowl at once. Process until smooth, about 2 minutes, stopping once or twice to scrape the sides of the container.

Nutty Mayo _____

Makes about 1¼ cups.

Here's a versatile egg-free, soy-free spread for sandwiches, dips, vegetables and fish.

½ cup cashews or
    other nuts
¾ cup water
3 tablespoons
    vinegar or lemon
    juice
2 tablespoons oil
1 tablespoon
    arrowroot
1 tablespoon honey
1 tablespoon minced
    parsley
    (optional)
1 tablespoon
    snipped chives
    (optional)
1½ teaspoons Dijon-
    style mustard
    dash of cayenne
    pepper
    (optional)

Grind the nuts to a fine powder in a blender. Add the water, and blend 1 minute to make sure nuts are fully ground. Add vinegar or lemon juice, oil, arrowroot, honey, parsley, chives, mustard and cayenne. Blend until very smooth.

Pour into a saucepan, and cook a few minutes, until thick. Allow to cool, then transfer to a glass jar. Store in the refrigerator. Keeps well for 3 weeks.

Variation: You can replace the vinegar or lemon juice with 1 teaspoon vitamin C crystals.

Dairy-Free "Sour Cream" _____

Makes ½ cup.

This non-dairy "sour cream" has a smooth, creamy texture and an appropriately sharp tang. It's very useful in dips and toppings, on baked potatoes or other places where you'd use regular sour cream.

½ cup cashews or
    Brazil nuts
⅓ cup boiling water
2 tablespoons lemon
    juice
1 teaspoon honey
½ teaspoon grated
    lemon rind
¼ teaspoon wheat-free
    tamari sauce

Place the nuts in a blender, and grind to a fine powder. Add the water, and blend on high speed for 2 minutes, stopping once to scrape the bottom and sides of the container. Add the lemon juice, honey, lemon rind and tamari. Blend briefly to mix. Chill before serving.

173

Cucumber-Dill Sauce I ───────────────

Makes about 1½ cups.

Here is a mayonnaise-based sauce to top broiled fish or to bind fish salad. It's a classic with Poached Salmon.

1 cup Nutty Mayo (see page 173) or Homemade Mayo (see page 172)
1 medium cucumber, quartered, seeded and finely chopped
1½ teaspoons finely minced onion
1 tablespoon fresh dill or 1 teaspoon dried dill weed
1–2 tablespoons lemon juice, to taste

Combine ingredients in a small bowl and chill for about 30 minutes or more. Serve as a hot sauce or a mayonnaise substitute.

Avocado-Grapefruit Dressing ───────────

Makes about 1¼ cups.

A taste surprise to serve on fruit salads or greens, such as spinach. Wonderful with tuna. A great alternative to oil and vinegar.

1 ripe avocado
½ large grapefruit
1 tablespoon honey or unsweetened apple-juice concentrate

Cut the avocado in half. Remove the pit, and spoon the flesh into a blender. Cut the grapefruit into sections, removing all membranes. Add to the blender. Process for 15 to 20 seconds, until smooth.

Taste the mixture, and add enough honey or juice concentrate to balance the tang. Blend a few seconds, and taste again.

Use immediately, or store for 2 or 3 days in the refrigerator. (To maintain the green color, place oiled cellophane directly in contact with the dressing.)

Cucumber-Dill Sauce II _____

Makes about 1¼ cups.

Ground nuts make this sauce nearly as rich as sauces based on sour cream. To make the sauce as smooth as possible, don't skimp on the blending time. Like Cucumber-Dill Sauce I, this too is a natural accompaniment to cooked fish. It's also excellent as a topping for sliced tomatoes or as a dip for raw vegetables.

1 cup raw cashews
¾ cup boiling water
½ medium
    cucumber,
    quartered,
    seeded and
    finely chopped
2–4 tablespoons lemon
    juice
1 tablespoon finely
    minced onion
    or 1 finely
    sliced scallion
1 tablespoon fresh
    dill or 1
    teaspoon dried
    dill weed
6 drops of hot
    pepper sauce, or
    more to taste
    (optional)
snipped chives
    (optional)
pinch of garlic
    powder
    (optional)

Grind cashews in blender, about a third at a time, until they're a fine powder. Stop machine to scrape bottom of container, and blend again. Dump into a bowl and repeat until all are ground. Return all ground nuts to the blender and, with machine running, slowly add boiling water. Blend at highest speed for 2 or 3 full minutes. Scrape into a stainless steel bowl or other container and place in the freezer for 10 or 15 minutes.

Assemble remaining ingredients. When nut mixture is cool, add cucumber, lemon juice, onion or scallion, dill, hot pepper sauce, chives and garlic powder. Blend. Taste, and correct seasonings if necessary. Chill 20 minutes or more for flavors to blend.

Fresh-Tomato Salad Dressing _____

Makes about 1 cup.

A low-fat dressing without sugar or emulsifiers. Although this dressing will keep a few days in the refrigerator, it's best when used promptly.

1 cup Fresh 'n' Natural
    Tomato Sauce,
    chilled (see recipe
    below)
1 tablespoon olive oil
1 tablespoon Oriental
    rice vinegar
    minced basil or
    tarragon (garnish)

Mix the Fresh 'n' Natural Tomato Sauce, oil and vinegar in a small bowl. Taste, and add more oil or vinegar, if desired. Garnish with basil or tarragon.

Sesame-Lime Salad Dressing _____

Makes ⅔ cup.

This is my favorite dressing for spinach salads.

⅓ cup sunflower oil
3 tablespoons lime
    juice
2 tablespoons
    chopped onions
1 tablespoon honey
2 teaspoons sesame
    seeds
2 mint leaves
    (optional)

Place the oil, lime juice, onions, honey, sesame seeds and mint leaves in a blender. Process until smooth.

Fresh 'n' Natural Tomato Sauce _____

Makes about 2 cups.

A light tomato puree to serve over plain fish, pasta, marinated tofu, chicken, lamb, eggs, cooked rice or vegetables.

3 large tomatoes or 6
    Italian plum
    tomatoes
6 basil leaves
¼ cup chopped
    onions
1½ teaspoons olive oil

Dip the tomatoes into boiling water for 30 seconds. With a sharp knife, remove the stem end. The peels should slip off easily. Cut the tomatoes in half crosswise. Squeeze gently to remove seeds and excess juice. Chop tomatoes coarsely, and transfer to a blender or food processor. Process with the basil until pureed.

1 small garlic clove,
    minced
sliced olives
    (garnish)
snipped chives
    (garnish)

In a large frying pan, sauté the onions in the oil until soft; do not allow them to brown. Add the garlic, and sauté 1 minute more. Add the tomato puree, and heat through. Do not boil. Serve warm or cold, garnished with olives and chives.

Susan Dart's Blender Sauce

Makes 1⅛ cups.

I've adapted this white sauce from a recipe a friend developed. It works well with chicken, mushrooms, peas, pimientos, steamed celery and other foods that customarily take a cream sauce.

½ cup Zucchini Milk,
    Soy Milk or Nut
    Milk (see Index)
½ cup rich-flavored
    Stock (see Index)
2 tablespoons rolled
    oats
    pinch of curry
    powder

In a blender combine Zucchini Milk, Soy Milk or Nut Milk, Stock, oats and curry powder. Process until smooth. Transfer to a saucepan. Heat to boiling, and stir until thick.

NOTE: If using Zucchini Milk, double peel the zucchini to assure a whiter milk.

Tomato Sauce

Makes 2 cups.

A pared-down version of tomato sauce that's rich in flavor and robust.

½ cup minced onions
1 tablespoon olive
    oil
1 garlic clove,
    minced
1½ cups water
6 ounces tomato
    paste
1 tablespoon minced
    basil or 1
    teaspoon dried
    basil
1 teaspoon honey

In a medium saucepan, sauté the onions in the oil until soft. Add the garlic, and sauté 1 minute more. Add the water, tomato paste, basil and honey. Simmer 5 minutes. Serve warm.

Italian Spaghetti Sauce _____

Makes about 4 cups.

Enjoy this traditional favorite over spaghetti, rice vermicelli, Oriental bean-thread noodles, steamed spaghetti squash or steamed, shredded zucchini.

2 cups chopped onions
2 tablespoons olive oil
1 cup sliced celery
½ cup chopped peppers
3–4 garlic cloves, minced
¼ cup minced parsley
2 teaspoons dried oregano
1 teaspoon dried basil
3½ cups pureed tomatoes
6 ounces tomato paste
½ cup water
2 bay leaves
1 teaspoon honey
⅛ teaspoon cayenne pepper
¼ cup minced parsley

In a Dutch oven, sauté the onions in the oil for 5 minutes. Add the celery and peppers, and cook for 8 to 10 minutes, until soft. Add the garlic, ¼ cup parsley, oregano and basil. Cook 1 minute.

Add the tomatoes, tomato paste, water, bay leaves, honey and cayenne. Bring to a boil, then reduce the heat, and simmer for 1 to 3 hours, stirring occasionally to keep from scorching. If sauce becomes too thick for your taste, add a little water. Remove bay leaves. Stir in ¼ cup parsley just before serving.

Variations: Add any one of the following to the sauce, and heat through: ½–1 pound diced cooked chicken or turkey; ½ pound cubed tofu (fried, if desired); 1½ cups pureed beans; 1–2 cups diced cooked rabbit, venison or other game; ½–1 pound ground, lean lamb or pork, browned and drained.

Tomato-Free Spaghetti Sauce _____

Serves 4.

The oregano and basil lend real spaghetti-sauce flavor to this hearty pasta topping. Ideal for people who can't eat tomatoes.

1½ cups water
½ cup red lentils
1 cup chopped onions
2 tablespoons olive oil
½ pound

Place the 1½ cups water and lentils in a saucepan. Cover, and simmer for 15 minutes, or until tender.

In a large frying pan, sauté the onions in the oil until soft, about 10 minutes. Add the mushrooms, garlic, parsley or lovage, basil and oregano; sauté 3 minutes.

mushrooms,
sliced
1–2 garlic cloves,
minced
⅓ cup chopped
parsley leaves
or lovage leaves
1–2 tablespoons
minced basil or
1–2 teaspoons
dried basil
1 scant teaspoon
dried oregano,
or more to taste
2 cups water
3 tablespoons
arrowroot or 4
tablespoons
amaranth flour
1 tablespoon wheat-
free tamari
sauce or Savory
Seed
Seasoning
(optional; see
page 184)
Versatile
Meatballs
(optional; see
Index)

In a small bowl, whisk together 2 cups water and the arrowroot or amaranth flour. Add to the frying pan, and stir over medium heat until sauce thickens. Stir in tamari or Savory Seed Seasoning. Add lentils and as much of their cooking liquid as you desire. Add Versatile Meatballs, and heat through.

Variations: For a creamier sauce, use Nut Milk in place of the 2 cups water.

For a legume-free sauce, omit lentils and 1½ cups of water and use half as much basil and oregano.

Turkey Gravy

Makes 1 cup.

You can make such tasty gravy with rice flour that you'll never miss the wheat flour.

1 cup drippings from
Roast Turkey
Breast (see
Index)
1½ tablespoons brown
rice flour

Skim any fat from the drippings. Whisk together the drippings and flour in a small saucepan. Cook, stirring, until thickened. Reduce heat, and simmer for 10 minutes. If gravy thickens too much, thin it with a bit of stock or water.

NOTE: For 2 cups of gravy, add enough stock or water to the drippings to equal 2 cups. Use 2½ tablespoons brown rice flour.

Mushroom Brown Sauce _____

Makes about 2¾ cups.

This is especially good with vegetable entrees, such as Zesty Supper Loaf, that don't have meat drippings to make conventional gravy.

2½ cups Stock (see Index)
½ pound mushrooms, minced
2 tablespoons minced onions
3 tablespoons olive oil
3 tablespoons brown rice flour
1 teaspoon dark miso
1 teaspoon wheat-free tamari sauce

Bring the Stock to a boil in a small saucepan. Boil, uncovered, until Stock is reduced to 1½ cups. Set aside.

In a large frying pan, sauté the mushrooms and onions in 1 tablespoon oil until all the moisture the mushrooms have exuded evaporates, about 5 to 7 minutes. Transfer to a small bowl, and set aside.

Add the remaining 2 tablespoons oil to the pan. Warm over medium heat for 30 seconds. Then stir in the flour. Whisk together the oil and flour for 3 minutes to cook the flour. Then pour in the Stock. Whisk mixture until it is thick and bubbly. Then reduce heat to low.

Transfer 2 tablespoons of sauce to a small cup. Stir in the miso and tamari until smooth. Then whisk this mixture into the frying pan. Stir in the mushroom mixture, and heat briefly to rewarm it. (Do not allow sauce to boil.)

Serve immediately, or keep warm over hot water.

NOTE: To mince mushrooms in a food processor, use steel chopping blade with only a few on/off turns.

Magic Marinade and Stir-Fry Sauce _____

Makes 1 cup.

Use this pungent marinade for stir-fried chicken, meat, tofu and vegetables. It's totally free of the caramel coloring, monosodium glutamate and other additives you're apt to find in some commercial marinades. The recipe makes enough sauce to marinate half a pound of meat or vegetables.

½ cup water
2 tablespoons lemon juice
2 tablespoons unsweetened

Combine the water, lemon juice, grape juice or honey, tamari, ginger, cayenne and oil in a glass bowl or jar.

Variation: To use as a sauce, add 1 tablespoon

180

white grape juice
or 1 teaspoon
honey
1 tablespoon wheat-
free tamari sauce
⅛ teaspoon powdered
ginger
⅛ teaspoon cayenne
pepper
1 teaspoon Oriental
sesame oil

arrowroot to the marinade. Add to stir-fried dishes during the last 2 minutes of cooking. Stir to thicken sauce.

NOTE: To use the marinade, place it in a shallow bowl. Add food that has been cut into uniform pieces—cubes, julienne strips or slivers. Toss to coat pieces; marinate at room temperature for 30 minutes or in the refrigerator for up to 24 hours. Drain food before cooking. Reserve marinade, if desired, to use as a sauce (see Variation).

Peanut Sauce

Makes 1–1¼ cups.

An Indonesian-style accompaniment to rice dishes, such as pilafs, patties or croquettes.

2 cups water
½ cup chopped
onions
½ cup chopped
carrots
½ cup chopped
celery
1 tablespoon wheat-
free tamari
sauce (optional)
1 bay leaf (optional)
1 cup roasted
peanuts
1–2 tablespoons Dijon-
style mustard
natural peanut
butter (optional)

Simmer the water, onions, carrots, celery, tamari and bay leaf in a small saucepan for 20 minutes. Remove bay leaf.

Grind the peanuts to a fine powder in a blender or food processor. Add vegetable mixture and mustard to machine. Process until well blended. Stop and scrape the sides of the container as necessary. If sauce is not thick enough to suit you, blend in a bit of peanut butter.

NOTE: You can control whether the sauce will be smooth or chunky by how long you process the mixture.

Magic Mustard Sauce _____

Makes 1 cup.

What's the magic? This sauce is made and thickened in the blender. It's a natural to top members of the Mustard family, like cabbage, broccoli, cauliflower or brussels sprouts. And it's also excellent on fish, turkey and chicken.

⅓ cup cashews
2 tablespoons quick-cooking oats
1 cup boiling vegetable Stock (see Index)
1 tablespoon Dijon-style mustard
1 tablespoon lemon juice
1 teaspoon wheat-free tamari sauce (optional)

Grind the cashews and oats in a blender until they're a fine powder. Add enough boiling Stock to reach the 1-cup mark. Blend 30 seconds. Add the mustard, lemon juice and tamari. Blend again. Let stand in blender 2 or 3 minutes, to thicken. Serve warm.

Tender-Meat Marinade _____

Makes about 3 cups.

Papaya contains papain, an enzyme that can tenderize meat. And it's an alternative to commercial meat tenderizers for people who are allergic to monosodium glutamate. This marinade is especially useful with game and other lean meats.

Because papain works on exposed surfaces of meat, it will make small pieces more tender than it will whole roasts. The basic recipe below is suitable for stew meat. See the Variation for roasts and poultry.

1 papaya
Peppy (see page 188)
1½ cups water
1–2 tablespoons oil
½ teaspoon vitamin C crystals
½ teaspoon crushed dried rosemary

Cut the papaya in half and scoop out the seeds. Use them to make the Peppy seasoning.

Scoop the papaya flesh into a small bowl. Mash with a fork. Grind in a generous amount of Peppy plus the water, oil, vitamin C crystals and rosemary. Mix well.

To use, place cubed pieces of stew meat in a shallow dish. Cover with the marinade, and stir well to coat all surfaces. Allow to stand at least 1 hour before cooking. Drain the marinade, and use it as the base for stew gravy. Because of the marinade's tenderizing action, the meat may cook more quickly than usual.

Variation: Replace the rosemary with any other dried herb.

NOTE: To marinate roasts and poultry, reduce the water to ½ cup. The marinade will be the consistency of thick jam. Spread it on roasts, whole poultry or poultry pieces. Marinate poultry and small roasts for 1 hour. Marinate roasts that weigh more than 3 pounds for 2 hours. Roast the marinated poultry; cook the roasts with liquid in a covered pan.

Real Applesauce

Makes about 1½ quarts.

Delicious warm or cold, this dish makes a great topping for pancakes or waffles. I find that the best apples to use are McIntoshes, Jonathans, Rome Beauties and Yellow Delicious. Steer clear of Red Delicious; they tend not to be as flavorful. This applesauce freezes very well.

3 pounds unsprayed apples
6 ounces unsweetened apple-juice concentrate

Scrub the apples, then quarter and core them. Cut each piece into 4 chunks, and place in a large heavy-bottomed pan. Add the juice concentrate.

Bring to a boil over medium heat, then cover the pan, reduce the heat, and simmer until the apples are tender. Some varieties, like McIntoshes, will be soft in 15 minutes; others, like Jonathans, will require 40 minutes. If necessary, add a little water to the apples while cooking to prevent sticking. Stir often, and avoid cooking the apples until they're mushy.

Tapioca-Fruit Sauce

Makes 2½ cups.

This fruit sauce goes well with pancakes and waffles. It contains no arrowroot, so it's especially helpful if you're following a Diversified Rotary Diet.

¾ cup water
1 tablespoon quick-cooking tapioca
1½ cups blueberries or diced fruit
¼ cup honey

Combine the water and tapioca in a saucepan; soak for 5 minutes. Add the fruit, and bring the mixture to a boil over medium heat. Stir in the honey. Simmer for 5 minutes. Taste, and add a bit more honey, if needed. Serve warm.

Spicy Cranapple Sauce

Makes 1 quart.

A sugar-free sauce to garnish chicken, turkey and other holiday meals.

1 pound cranberries
1–1½ cups unsweetened apple-juice concentrate
½ teaspoon ground cinnamon
⅛ teaspoon ground cloves
1 tablespoon arrowroot
3 tablespoons water

Wash the cranberries carefully, and discard any imperfect fruit. Place the berries, 1 cup juice concentrate, cinnamon and cloves in a large saucepan. Bring to a boil, stirring occasionally. When bubbles first appear, reduce heat to low. Simmer for 10 minutes, or until most of the skins have popped.

Taste sauce. For a sweeter, juicier sauce, add remaining ½ cup juice concentrate. Increase spices, if desired. If sauce is too tangy, dilute with a little water.

Dissolve the arrowroot in the water. Stir into the hot berries. Cook, stirring, another 2 or 3 minutes until thick and clear. Serve warm or cold.

Fruit-Solo Sauce

Serves 1.

A one-ingredient topping that's especially helpful if you're limiting honey or maple syrup. The flavor of this topping depends entirely upon the sweetness of the fruit chosen, so try to pick fruits that are at the peak of ripeness. If the fruit you're using is a little tart, use this topping on a day that you can add honey or maple syrup.

1 piece fruit or 1 cup berries

Place the fruit or berries in the blender. For a chunky sauce, blend 20 seconds. For a smooth sauce, blend 1 or 2 minutes. Serve at once.

Variations: If you're using a peach, plum, nectarine or other fruit from the Plum family, add a few drops pure almond extract.

For a spicy fruit topping, add a pinch of your favorite spice.

Savory Seed Seasoning

Makes ½ cup.

Fill a large-hole saltshaker with this custom-mixed flavor enhancer. It contains only 43 milligrams of sodium per teaspoon, compared to 2,132 milligrams in a teaspoon of salt.

½ cup sesame seeds or sunflower seeds
1 tablespoon wheat-free tamari sauce
1 teaspoon dried basil
1 teaspoon dried oregano
¼ teaspoon onion powder (optional)
⅛ teaspoon garlic powder (optional)

In a blender, grind the sesame seeds or sunflower seeds to a coarse powder. Add the tamari, and blend a few seconds to mix. Scrape the mixture into a flat baking dish. Bake at 250° for about 30 minutes, or until it's dry and very fragrant.

Allow to cool. Then return mixture to dry blender, and process at high speed until it's reduced to a fine powder. Stop the machine, and scrape the bottom of the blender bowl. Add the basil, oregano, onion powder and garlic powder. Blend again to be sure all seeds are finely ground.

Variations: Substitute one or two of the following for the basil and oregano to create your own signature seasoning: 2 teaspoons Hungarian paprika, 1 or 2 teaspoons powdered kelp (unless you are allergic to iodine), 1 teaspoon dried tarragon, 1 teaspoon dried dill weed, 1 teaspoon dried savory, 1 teaspoon dried marjoram, ½ teaspoon crushed dried rosemary or ¼ teaspoon dried sage.

Italian Seasoning

Makes about ⅓ cup.

Shake this tasty blend of Mint-family foods over salads, dips, soups or stews. It's especially nice when you're using tomatoes. Feel free to omit any herbs that aren't to your liking.

2 tablespoons dried basil
1 tablespoon dried marjoram
1 tablespoon dried oregano
1½ teaspoons dried rosemary
1½ teaspoons dried savory
1½ teaspoons dried thyme
1 teaspoon dried sage

Combine the basil, marjoram, oregano, rosemary, savory, thyme and sage in a blender or spice mill. Process until finely ground. Store in a tightly capped spice jar.

Pizzazz Seasoning

Makes ½ to ¾ cup.

Eight interesting flavors from the Parsley family combine to make an ideal seasoning for steamed carrots, cooked celery, meatloaf, soups or stews.

1 small carrot
2 tablespoons dried
   dill weed
2 tablespoons dried
   parsley
1 tablespoon caraway
   seeds
1 tablespoon cumin
   seeds
1 tablespoon coriander
   seeds
1 tablespoon fennel
   seeds
1 tablespoon dried
   celery leaves

Peel the carrot. Leaving it whole, use a potato peeler to remove long, paper-thin slices (as for making carrot curls). Scatter the carrot strips on a cookie sheet, and bake at 200° for 1 hour, or until strips are very brittle and crumble easily.

Place the dehydrated carrots, dill, parsley, caraway, cumin, coriander, fennel and celery in a blender or spice mill. Process until finely ground. Pass through a coarse strainer. If many large pieces remain, return them to the blender or mill.

Store in a tightly capped spice jar.

Variation: You can substitute lovage leaves for the celery.

NOTE: To dry your own parsley, celery or lovage, wash and dry the leaves, then place them on a cookie sheet and bake as for the carrots.

Onion Seasoning

Makes ¼ cup.

Pack this in a small bottle or envelope to use as a handy substitute for fresh onions and garlic when camping and cooking.

2 tablespoons onion
   powder or onion
   flakes
4½ teaspoons freeze-
   dried chives
1½ teaspoons garlic
   powder

Place the onion powder or flakes, chives and garlic powder in a blender. Process for 30 seconds to pulverize. Store in a tightly sealed container.

Curry Powder _____

Makes about ½ cup.

Traditionally, curry is a potpourri of many skillfully blended flavors. Even so, this one is limited to only two or three food families, depending on whether or not you include cayenne.

1 tablespoon coriander seeds
1 tablespoon Pizzazz Seasoning (see opposite page)
4 teaspoons turmeric powder
1½ teaspoons powdered ginger
1½ teaspoons cardamom seeds
1½ teaspoons celery seeds
1½ teaspoons cumin seeds
¾ teaspoon cayenne pepper

Place the coriander, Pizzazz Seasoning, turmeric, ginger, cardamom, celery seeds, cumin and cayenne in a blender or spice mill. Grind finely. (Or grind with a mortar and pestle.) Store in a tightly capped jar.

NOTE: For a more interesting flavor, dry-roast the coriander seeds, cardamom seeds, celery seeds and cumin seeds in a heavy frying pan for a few minutes, shaking the pan often, until the seeds are crisp and fragrant.

Sea Seasoning _____

Makes ½ cup.

Kombu is a sea vegetable that is available in powdered form in health food stores and Oriental markets. Because it contains a fair amount of iodine, use kombu only if you are not allergic to that mineral. Use as you would salt and pepper, alone or with other seasonings.

¼ cup kombu powder
¼ cup Pizzazz Seasoning (see opposite page)

Mix kombu and Pizzazz Seasoning well. Store in a tightly capped jar.

Variations: Replace Pizzazz Seasoning with any dried herb or combination of herbs, Italian Seasoning or chili powder.

Peppy

Makes about ¼ cup.

Here's an innovative use for papaya seeds. If you're rotating foods, save this seasoning for times when you're serving fresh or dried papaya.

1 papaya

Cut the papaya in half, and scoop the seeds into a strainer. Reserve the flesh for another use.

Pick over the seeds to remove any bits of fruit that might be clinging to them. Wash the seeds under running water, and set aside to drain. Then spread the seeds in a single layer on a cookie sheet or jelly-roll pan. Bake at 200° for 1½ hours, or until seeds are brittle and look like peppercorns. (Test one by biting on it.)

Place the seeds in a peppermill. Use as you would dried peppercorns. An alternate method of using the papaya seeds is to grind them to a fine powder in a seed mill or blender.

Store in a tightly capped shaker jar.

Corn-Free Baking Powder

Makes 2 tablespoons.

Many brands of baking powder contain cornstarch; this one doesn't. For best results, always combine the dry and liquid ingredients separately, then combine quickly and pop batter into prepared pans and bake promptly.

2 teaspoons cream of
  tartar
2 teaspoons arrowroot
1 teaspoon baking
  soda

Sift together the cream of tartar, arrowroot and baking soda to mix well. Store in an airtight container.

NOTE: For best results, make only small batches and use within a reasonable amount of time. Be sure to use fresh baking soda. It's a good idea to buy only small boxes of baking soda and replace them several times a year. Old baking soda can always be used for cleaning and deodorizing kitchen work areas.

Egg Substitute

Makes about ¼ cup.

This mixture will bind patties, meat loaves, cookies and cakes as well as eggs do. But it will not leaven like eggs for soufflés or sponge cakes. This recipe makes enough to substitute for one egg; you can easily double or triple it.

⅓ cup water
1 tablespoon whole flaxseed

Place the water and flaxseed in a small saucepan. Bring to a boil, then reduce heat so mixture bubbles slowly. Cook for 5 minutes, or until mixture is the consistency of a raw egg white. Do not use too high a heat or mixture will become thick and gummy.

NOTE: Don't bother straining out the flaxseeds. They don't have much flavor and won't detract from whatever you're making.

Frozen Banana

Makes 1.

For best results, use very ripe bananas. Use in frozen shakes and frosty toppings.

1 banana

Peel the banana. Wrap tightly in foil, shiny side against the food, or cellophane. Freeze.

NOTE: You can make as many bananas as you choose. Wrap up to 3 in a package. For use in breads and cakes, allow to thaw just enough so you can mash the bananas. If they thaw completely, they're apt to turn to mush.

189

Meat, Poultry
and Game

Since beef sometimes triggers allergy, no beef recipes appear in this section. Instead, I've offered recipes for lamb, pork, rabbit and venison. If you can eat beef, you probably have other cookbooks with dozens of recipes telling you how to prepare it.

Though related to beef, lamb is considered to be relatively nonallergenic. Lamb appears in recipes for Cassoulet and Curry Surprise in this section, and in Lamb Stew and Chunky Lamb Stew in the Soups, Stews and Chowders section. Because Roast Lamb with Mint Sauce is an Easter favorite, that recipe appears in the Holiday Foods section.

Pork is also a good alternative to beef. While beef cattle breeders are trying to raise leaner cattle, beef steaks and roasts are still somewhat heavily marbled with fat. Hog farmers have had slightly more success breeding animals that are leaner than ever before. So pork, especially the tenderloin, is relatively low in fat. As an added benefit, pork is the highest nongrain source of thiamine, or vitamin B_1. Versatile Meatballs takes advantage of this alternative. Roast Pork appears in the Holiday Foods section.

Rabbit is now widely available—frozen rabbit in supermarkets and fresh rabbit at farmers' markets. Venison and other game can be ordered from suppliers listed in the Appendix. (See the Index for Rabbit-Vegetable Stew and Marjorie Fisher's Venison Stew and its variations for still other ways to prepare these less allergenic meats.)

I've also developed several chicken recipes that do away with conventional breading and other components that may be off-limits. The Roast Turkey Breast and Turkey Rollups are good all year 'round.

190

Recipes for duck, pheasant, quail and Cornish game hens are not included, although all are excellent choices that increase the variety of meat in the diet. I consider those birds treats and often order them in restaurants.

Moussaka Improvised

Serves 4.

Authentic Greek moussaka calls for tomato sauce. People who are allergic to tomatoes will enjoy the tomato-free version given here. And people who are allergic to beef will have yet another lamb dish to add to their repertoire.

1 medium eggplant
(about 1
pound)
1 tablespoon olive
oil
¼ teaspoon Italian
Seasoning (see
Index)
½–1 pound ground
lean lamb
1 cup chopped
onions
2 garlic cloves,
minced
1 tablespoon olive
oil
1 cup pumpkin
puree
1 cup water
¼ teaspoon Italian
Seasoning
¼ teaspoon dried
thyme
¼ teaspoon vitamin
C crystals
¼ cup Italian
Crumbs (see
Index)
2 tablespoons
grated goat's-
milk cheese
(optional)

Slice the eggplant lengthwise into ½" slabs. Place on a non-stick cookie sheet, and brush tops of slices with 1 tablespoon oil. Sprinkle with ¼ teaspoon Italian Seasoning. Bake at 400° for 12 to 15 minutes, or until just tender.

In a large frying pan, sauté the lamb, onions and garlic in 1 tablespoon oil until onions are soft and meat is no longer pink. Add the pumpkin, water, ¼ teaspoon Italian Seasoning, thyme and vitamin C crystals. Bring to a boil, stirring. Then remove from the heat.

Arrange half the eggplant slices in a single layer in a well-oiled 8"-square baking pan. Spread with half the meat mixture. Top with another layer of eggplant, then with remaining meat sauce. Sprinkle with Italian Crumbs and cheese.

Bake at 400° for 40 minutes (or at 350° for 50 minutes). Cut into squares to serve.

Variations: Replace the lamb with ground pork tenderloin or ground lean game. Or omit the pumpkin, water and herbs; replace with Tomato-Free Spaghetti Sauce.

If you can eat tomatoes, replace the pumpkin and water with 2 cups of your favorite tomato sauce.

NOTE: Some eggplants can be bitter, and it's often a guessing game which ones to buy. Some people, among them Julia Child, recommend selecting eggplants that have flat bottoms rather than dimpled ones. Opt for smaller rather than larger ones, using 2 small eggplants rather than 1 large one, if necessary.

191

Cassoulet

Serves 6.

This traditional bean stew originated among the peasants in southern France and went on to win fans all over the world. It's of special interest to people with allergies because it contains no tomatoes, potatoes, carrots, celery or parsley. This is a great way to use a leftover roast lamb shank bone. Don't hurry Cassoulet; slow cooking develops its special aromatic flavors.

1 meaty roasted lamb shank bone	Trim as much meat as possible from the bone. Remove any visible fat, dice the meat, and set it aside.
1 pound white beans (Great Northern, navy or lima), soaked overnight 6 cups water 1½ cups chopped onions 3–4 garlic cloves, minced ½ teaspoon dried thyme 4 cloves 1 bay leaf	Place the bone in a large pot. Drain the soaking beans, discarding the soak water, and place them in the pot. Add the water, onions, garlic, thyme, cloves and bay leaf. Bring to a boil, then reduce heat, and simmer, uncovered, until beans are tender, from 1½ to 2 hours.
1 pound additive-free pork sausage	Crumble the sausage into a large frying pan. Cook until light brown. Drain the sausage and discard the rendered fat. Set sausage aside. Add the reserved lamb meat to the frying pan, and sauté until light brown.
2 tablespoons lemon juice	When the beans are tender, remove the bone from the pan. Stir in the sausage, lamb meat and lemon juice. Transfer to an oiled 9″-×-13″ baking dish. Bean liquid should completely cover the beans; if it doesn't, add water.

Bake at 250° for 2 hours or more. Serve immediately, or cover the pan, reduce the heat to 150°, and hold in the oven up to 2 hours. Remove bay leaf and cloves before serving.

Variations: To make Cassoulet even more adaptable to food allergies, use goose, duck or wild game.

Cowboy Beans

Serves 4 to 6.

No tomatoes and no beef. But these beans are still red, saucy, "meaty" and tasty. Serve in flat soup bowls as you would chili, alone or over brown rice.

1 pound kidney
   beans, soaked
   overnight
½ pound additive-
   free pork
   sausage
1½ cups chopped
   onions
2–3 garlic cloves,
   minced
3 tablespoons
   minced basil or
   1 tablespoon
   dried basil
1 tablespoon wheat-
   free tamari
   sauce or kombu
   powder
1 tablespoon lemon
   juice or ¼
   teaspoon
   vitamin C
   crystals
1 teaspoon Italian
   Seasoning (see
   Index)

Drain the kidney beans and discard the soak water. Place in a large saucepan, cover with fresh water, and simmer for 2 hours.

Crumble the sausage into a large frying pan. Sauté until all pink is gone. Drain off all but 1 tablespoon of fat. Add the onions to the pan, and sauté until soft. Add the garlic, and cook for 1 minute.

Add the sausage mixture to the beans, and simmer until the beans are tender, about 1 to 1½ hours. Add the basil, tamari or kombu, lemon juice or vitamin C crystals and Italian Seasoning. Mash some of the beans with the back of a spoon to thicken the sauce a bit. Simmer for a few minutes.

Variation: Replace the Italian Seasoning with 1 tablespoon chili powder.

NOTE: Look for no-nitrite, additive-free sausage in the frozen foods department of grocery stores. Buy in bulk or remove any casings before using.

Oven-Fried Rabbit

Serves 4.

Here's a tender, juicy alternative to fried chicken. Use any flour you wish. See Table 1, Cooking and Baking with Alternative Flours, in the section, Exploring New Ingredients for notes on the browning characteristics of different flours.

1 young frying rabbit
   (about 3 pounds)
½ cup flour
   (arrowroot,
   amaranth,
   buckwheat, oat,
   potato or tapioca-
   starch)
   pinch of cayenne
   pepper (optional)
3 tablespoons oil
½ cup hot water

Cut the rabbit into serving pieces. Rinse under cold water. Shake off excess water, but do not pat dry.

Combine flour and cayenne in a pie plate or shallow dish. Dredge rabbit in flour to coat completely.

Heat oil in a large frying pan. Add rabbit, and brown over moderate heat. Transfer to a 9"-×-13" baking dish. Add the water. Cover the pan, and bake at 325° for 1 hour, or until tender.

Versatile Meatballs

Serves 5 or 6.

You can season these meatballs any way you like: Italian, Swedish, Mexican or "all-American" (a little of this and a little of that).

½ pound ground pork loin

½ pound additive-free pork sausage

⅔ cup water

¾ cup Handy Crumbs (see Index) or ground rice crackers

¼ cup powdered goat's milk (optional)

½ cup chopped onions

¼ cup minced parsley or lovage leaves

½ teaspoon ground black pepper or ⅛ teaspoon cayenne pepper

1 garlic clove, minced

2 teaspoons olive oil

In a large bowl mix the pork, sausage and water until well combined. Add the Handy Crumbs or ground crackers, powdered milk, onions, parsley or lovage, pepper or cayenne, garlic and oil. Mix well by hand or with electric beaters.

Form into whatever size meatballs you desire. This recipe will make either 50 cherry-size meatballs, 30 golf-ball-size ones or 8 to 10 lemon-size ones.

Place the meatballs on a rack set over a broiler pan or jelly-roll pan (that will allow fat to drain as meatballs cook). Bake at 400°. The cherry-size meatballs will take 20 minutes; the golf-ball-size ones 30 minutes; the lemon-size 40 minutes.

Variations: For Venison Meatballs, replace the ground pork and sausage with 1 pound ground venison.

To make Italian Meatballs, add 1 teaspoon dried oregano and 1½ teapoons dried basil to basic recipe. Serve with Tomato Sauce or Tomato-Free Spaghetti Sauce and your favorite pasta.

To make Swedish Meatballs, which are traditionally served in a creamy sauce, be sure to use the powdered goat's milk in the basic recipe. If you don't have any powdered goat's milk, replace both it and the ⅔ cup water with a Nut Creme. Make the cream by blending ½ cup raw cashews to a fine powder in a blender. Add enough boiling water to the blender to bring the liquid level up to ⅔ cup. Blend well to make a very thick liquid. Cool before adding to the meat mixture. Serve the meatballs in a creamy gravy made from more Nut Creme.

To make Mexican Meatballs, add ¼ teaspoon cayenne pepper to the basic recipe. If desired, also add finely chopped chili peppers. Serve with a spicy tomato sauce and rice or tortillas.

You can also make any of the preceding recipes into a Meatloaf. Mix meat as directed, then form into a meatloaf shape. Place on a rack that's been set over a pan, and bake at 400° for 1 hour.

NOTE: You can grind your own pork or venison with a meat grinder or food processor. Buy a loin cut, and divide into ½-pound pieces. Cut each portion into 1" cubes. Grind or place in a food processor, and grind with several on/off turns. When the meat has been ground to the proper consistency, it will tend to clump together in a ball.

Package and freeze whatever meat you will not be using immediately.

After you have ground the meat, you can mix the meatballs right in the processor. Add the water first, then the vegetables and seasonings. Add Handy Crumbs or ground crackers last. If your processor bowl is small, you might want to mix the meat in batches.

Quick Fresh Tomato Strata

Serves 2.

Wonderful for when fresh tomatoes are overrunning the garden. A good way to use leftover meat and other items.

1½ cups cold cooked brown rice
1 cup diced chicken, turkey or lamb
¾ cup Fresh 'n' Natural Tomato Sauce, chilled (see Index)
1 tablespoon minced basil
sliced olives (garnish)

On 2 individual plates or a serving platter, layer the rice then the chicken, turkey or lamb. Top with Fresh 'n' Natural Tomato Sauce and basil. Garnish with olives.

Variations: Replace the meat with flaked tuna, sliced hard-cooked eggs or diced marinated tofu.

195

Stuffed Zucchini

Serves 2.

A tasty entree that's ready in less than an hour. I especially like to use overgrown zucchini, which aren't good for a whole lot else. Allow about 6" of zucchini to serve two.

1 large zucchini (about 12 ounces)
½ pound additive-free pork sausage
⅓ cup chopped onions
½ cup shredded zucchini
1–2 garlic cloves, minced
1 bay leaf
¼ teaspoon dried thyme
dash of black pepper or cayenne pepper
½ cup Handy Crumbs (see Index) or ground rice crackers
¼ cup chopped parsley
⅓ cup chopped onions

Cut the zucchini in half lengthwise. Using a spoon or melon baller, scoop out the seeds to create a channel. Steam the zucchini shells for 5 minutes. Set aside, upside down, to drain.

Crumble the sausage into a frying pan. Add ⅓ cup onions, and sauté until sausage is no longer pink. Pour out excess fat. Add the shredded zucchini, garlic, bay leaf, thyme and black pepper or cayenne. Sauté over medium heat for 5 minutes. Remove the bay leaf. Remove from heat and add the Handy Crumbs or ground crackers and parsley.

Scatter the remaining ⅓ cup onions in the bottom of an oiled 8"-square baking dish. Place the zucchini shells on the onions, channel-side up. Spoon the stuffing mixture over them; it will be loose and heaped. Bake at 400° for 16 to 20 minutes, until brown.

NOTE: If you're using very large zucchini, remove the seeds before shredding. This recipe doubles easily.

Look for no-nitrite, additive-free sausage in the frozen foods department of grocery stores. Buy in bulk or remove any casings before using.

Polynesian Chicken

Serves 4.

A subtle sweet-and-sour dish, without sugar.

1½ cups raw brown rice
3 cups water
2 boneless chicken breasts (1¼–1½ pounds)

Combine the rice and water in a 2-quart saucepan with a tight-fitting lid. Bring to a boil, then lower the heat, and simmer until rice is tender (about 40 minutes).

Meanwhile, remove the skin and visible fat from the chicken. Cut breasts into halves. Brush

Basil Vinaigrette
(see Index) or
other oil and
vinegar dressing
8 ounces crushed
unsweetened
pineapple,
packed in juice
2 tablespoons
arrowroot
1 cup chicken Stock
(see Index)
2 tablespoons
wheat-free
tamari sauce
(optional)
1 tablespoon lemon
juice or ¼
teaspoon
vitamin C
crystals
¼ pound snow pea
pods
2 peppers
4 scallions
½ cup cashew pieces
1–2 tablespoons oil
2 tablespoons
shredded
unsweetened
coconut
(garnish)

both sides of each piece with the Basil Vinaigrette or dressing. Place pieces in a single layer in a glass baking dish. Bake at 400°, uncovered, for 15 minutes. When chicken is cooked through, keep it warm until remaining ingredients are ready.

Drain the pineapple, saving the juice. Set aside the pineapple. Combine the juice with the arrowroot, stirring until smooth. Add the Stock, tamari and lemon juice or vitamin C crystals. Set aside.

Remove stems and strings from snow pea pods; wash and pat dry. Dice peppers into ¾" pieces. Cut scallions into ¾" pieces.

In a dry skillet, toast the cashews until they just start to darken, about 5 to 7 minutes. Remove them to a small bowl. Add the oil, pea pods, peppers and scallions to the pan. Sauté over medium heat for 5 minutes, stirring them as they cook.

Stir the liquid ingredients, and add to the pan. Add the pineapple. Stir, and heat another minute, until sauce is thick and clear.

To serve, arrange portions of chicken and rice on each plate. Top with sauce and garnish with coconut.

Stir-Fried Jicama Chicken _____

Serves 4.

1 pound boneless
    chicken breasts
2–3 tablespoons
    peanut oil
3 large sweet
    potatoes, peeled
    and sliced
1 pound jicama,
    peeled and
    julienned

Remove the skin and all visible fat from the chicken. Cut flesh into 1" cubes.

Heat 2 tablespoons oil in a wok or large frying pan over medium-high heat. Add the chicken, and stir-fry until all traces of pink are gone, about 2 to 3 minutes.

Add the sweet potatoes. Stir-fry until crisp-tender, about 4 minutes. Add more oil, if needed.

Add the jicama. Stir-fry another minute or so.

Variation: Use another type of oil. Reduce heat to medium, and extend cooking times accordingly.

Slow-Cooked Chicken Dinner _____

Serves 4.

Chicken and gravy good enough to serve to company. And it's made without flour.

3 carrots, sliced
1 large onion, sliced
3 celery stalks,
    thickly sliced
½ cup chicken Stock
    (see Index) or
    water
¼ teaspoon dried
    basil
¼ teaspoon dried
    thyme
1 frying chicken
    (about 3 pounds)
2 tablespoons lemon
    juice or ½
    teaspoon vitamin
    C crystals
1 chicken liver
1½ teaspoons oil or 2
    tablespoons
    Stock
¼ cup rolled oats

Arrange two-thirds of the carrots, onions and celery in the bottom of an electric slow cooker. Add the Stock or water, and sprinkle with half the basil and thyme.

Cut the chicken into serving pieces. Remove the skin. Place the 2 breast halves in a single layer atop the vegetables. Sprinkle with 1 tablespoon lemon juice or ¼ teaspoon vitamin C crystals and a little basil and thyme. Add remaining chicken pieces and sprinkle with remaining lemon juice or vitamin C crystals, basil and thyme.

Cover pot tightly, and cook on low setting for 5 to 6 hours. Remove chicken and vegetables to a serving platter. Keep them warm in a low oven while you prepare gravy.

Pour cooking juices into a 2-cup measuring cup. If needed, add enough additional water or Stock to measure 2 cups. Reserve.

Either sauté the chicken liver in the oil for 10 minutes, or steam it in the Stock for 10 minutes. Remove from the pan, and chop finely. If

198

insides are still pink, return to pan and cook another minute.

To make giblet gravy, blend the oats to a fine powder in a blender. Add reserved Stock, and blend 20 seconds. Pour into sauté pan, add chopped liver, and bring to a boil. Stir as sauce thickens. Taste, and adjust seasoning, if needed. Pour into a gravy boat, and serve with the chicken.

Variations: Omit the rolled oats, and replace with 3 tablespoons oat flour. Whisk into reserved Stock, then proceed with making gravy. Or omit the oats altogether, and dissolve 2 tablespoons arrowroot in ¼ cup cold water. Whisk into 1¾ cups reserved hot stock, then proceed with gravy.

NOTE: You can cook the chicken for as long as 10 hours in the slow cooker. At that point, though, it will be so tender it will fall off the bones. Rest assured that it will be just as delicious, if not quite so elegant.

Morning-Glory Chicken

Serves 4.

Sweet potatoes and jicama both belong to the Morning-Glory family. Combine them with chicken for a simple dish that's perfect on a Diversified Rotary Diet.

1 frying chicken (about 3 pounds)
water
3 large sweet potatoes
1 pound jicama

Cut the chicken into serving pieces. Place in a large frying pan or Dutch oven. Add water to cover. Simmer, uncovered, for 20 minutes.

Peel the sweet potatoes, and cut into 1″ chunks. Add to the chicken, and cook 10 to 15 minutes, until just about tender.

Peel the jicama, and cut into julienne pieces (about ¼″ thick). Add to the chicken, and turn up the heat to a hard boil. Cook for 5 minutes, until jicama is just crisp-tender and liquid has reduced a bit.

Serve the broth with the chicken, or reserve for another use.

Variation: Replace the whole chicken with 4 boneless chicken breasts; remove the skin.

Chicken Cacciatore _____

Serves 4.

This popular entree is traditionally served over spaghetti but tastes just as good over spaghetti squash or rice vermicelli.

2 whole boneless chicken breasts (about 1¼ pounds)
1 cup chopped onions
2 tablespoons olive oil
½ cup chopped green peppers
½ cup chopped celery
1–2 garlic cloves, minced or pressed
3–4 cups Tomato Sauce (see Index)
1½ teaspoons dried oregano
1 teaspoon dried basil

Remove skin and visible fat from chicken. Cut meat into cubes or strips.

Sauté the onions in the oil until soft. Add the chicken, peppers, celery and garlic. Sauté until chicken is lightly browned. Add the Tomato Sauce, oregano and basil. Simmer until sauce is heated through.

Variation: You can use a cut-up fryer instead of chicken breasts. Sauté pieces until golden on both sides, then add Tomato Sauce, and simmer for 30 minutes, or until cooked through.

Chickburgers _____

Serves 4.

Serve with lettuce, tomato and Mayo on Amaranth Pancakes.

1 pound boneless chicken breasts
2 tablespoons tomato juice or wheat-free tamari sauce
¼ teaspoon poultry seasoning
1 tablespoon oil, optional

Remove the skin and any visible fat from the chicken. Cut breasts into 1″ to 2″ cubes. Place in the container of a food processor or blender with the tomato juice or tamari and poultry seasoning. Process about 30 seconds. Scrape the sides of the container, then process another 30 seconds, until mixture clumps together. (Mixture will be sticky.)

Turn the mixture out onto wax paper, and pat into 4 patties.

Preheat a non-stick frying pan or heat the oil in a large frying pan. Add the patties, and cook for 5 minutes on each side.

200

Variations: Substitute ¼ teaspoon dried tarragon, oregano or basil for the poultry seasoning.

NOTE: You can freeze the uncooked patties if you dust them well with any starch or flour before wrapping.

Creamed Chicken Livers

Serves 4.

Simple yet elegant. And you don't need flour to thicken the sauce. Serve over brown rice or baked potatoes.

2 large onions, sliced (about 1½ pounds)
1½ cups chicken Stock (see Index)
¼ teaspoon dried thyme
1 pound chicken livers
1 tablespoon oil
1 large green pepper, sliced (optional)
½ pound mushrooms, sliced (optional)
1 cup cherry tomatoes, halved (optional)

Simmer the onions and stock in a large covered frying pan or Dutch oven for 20 minutes, or until very soft. With a slotted spoon, transfer the onions to a blender or food processor, and liquefy them. Gradually add enough Stock to make the onions the consistency of a light sauce or medium-thin gravy. Add the thyme.

Using the same pan, sauté the chicken livers in the oil for 7 or 8 minutes, until lightly brown. Remove from the pan, and cut into bite-size pieces.

Sauté the peppers, mushrooms and tomatoes in the same pan. Return the livers to the pan, and cook just until the pink disappears. Don't overcook or they'll toughen.

Pour the onion sauce over the livers, and heat through.

Baked-Chicken Salad

Serves 4.

A wonderful buffet dish.

1 pound boneless
   chicken breasts
Basil Vinaigrette
   (see Index)
½ cup chopped dried
   apricots
½ cup sliced celery
½ cup chopped
   toasted almonds
⅓ cup Homemade
   Mayo or Tofu
   Mayo (see Index)
¼ teaspoon poultry
   seasoning
toasted sesame
   seeds (garnish)

Remove any visible fat from chicken. Brush both sides of breasts generously with Basil Vinaigrette. Place in a glass baking dish in a single layer, and allow to marinate in the refrigerator, covered, for 1 hour or overnight.

Place dish in the oven, and bake at 400° for 15 to 20 minutes, until chicken is cooked through. Allow to cool.

If the apricots are hard, soften them by simmering in a bit of water for a few minutes. Drain.

Dice the chicken. Combine in a large bowl with the apricots, celery, almonds, Homemade Mayo or Tofu Mayo and poultry seasoning. Taste, and add more poultry seasoning, if needed. Chill 1 hour or more. Garnish with sesame seeds.

Variations: Replace the apricots with 8 ounces drained crushed unsweetened pineapple or 1 cup seedless grapes. Use pecans or cashews in place of the almonds.

Turkey Rollups

Serves 4.

A wonderful way to use leftover turkey.

16–20 asparagus
   stalks,
   trimmed
4 large, thin
   slices cooked
   turkey breast
1 cup Magic
   Mustard
   Sauce (see
   Index)

Steam the asparagus stalks until just crisp-tender. Divide into 4 equal bundles. If turkey slices are large enough, wrap 1 around each bundle. (If necessary, secure with a toothpick). Place bundles in an 8"- or 9"-square baking dish. If the turkey slices are not large, place asparagus bundles directly in the baking dish; drape with the turkey.

Pour sauce over the bundles, and bake at 350° for 15 minutes. Remove toothpicks before serving.

Variations: Use about 32 whole green beans or 8 4" pieces of broccoli in place of the asparagus.

NOTE: You may be able to find nitrite-free baked turkey breast at your health food store, deli or supermarket. If slices are very thin, use 2 per bundle.

Roast Turkey Breast

There's no need to wait for Thanksgiving to enjoy turkey. And there's no need to cook a whole bird. Roast turkey breast is simple, classic and easy to dress up or down with trimmings.

1 turkey breast (allow ¼ pound per person)
1 tablespoon oil
Buckwheat Waldorf Stuffing or Grain-Free Waldorf Stuffing (see Index)

If you buy a frozen turkey breast, allow it to thaw in the refrigerator for 2 or 3 days.

Pat the turkey dry with cotton towels. Lightly coat the skin with the oil. Place, skin side up, on a wire rack in a 9″-×-13″ roasting pan. Bake at 325° according to the accompanying time-table; use the shorter time suggested.

For a stuffed breast, place the oiled breast, skin side down, on a washed 3-foot length of cheesecloth. Lightly pack the cavity with either Waldorf Stuffing. Bring the ends of the cheese-cloth up and fold them over the stuffing. If de-sired, tie kitchen string around the breast to hold the cheesecloth in place.

Turn the breast over and place it on a wire rack in a 9″-×-3″ roasting pan. Bake at 325° ac-cording to the accompanying timetable; use the longer time suggested.

To carve, let the turkey rest at room tem-perature for 10 minutes before slicing. For very thin slices perfect for sandwiches, chill turkey overnight before carving. Discard the skin as you carve.

Timetable

3–5 pounds—1½–2 hours
5–7 pounds—2–2½ hours
7–9 pounds—2½–3⅓ hours

NOTE: Some turkey breasts come equipped with a pop-up timer to indicate when the meat is done. Some work; some don't. Use the accom-panying timetable as a guide and check with a meat thermometer.

Curry Surprise —————————————————————————

Serves 4.

There are almost as many good curry recipes as there are cooks. That versatility makes curries perfect for people with allergies. You can curry leftover lamb, chicken, turkey, potatoes, yams, peas, beans or myriad other foods. My favorite combination is curried lamb over baked sweet potatoes. (When serving curries, be sure to serve something cool on the side—like chilled fruit.)

1½–2 cups cooked lamb, turkey, chicken, beans or mixed vegetables
½ cup chopped onions
2 tablespoons olive oil
1 tablespoon mild curry powder
2 tablespoons brown rice flour
2–3 garlic cloves, minced
2 cups vegetable or bean Stock (see Index)
¼ cup raisins
1 unsprayed apple, chopped
½ teaspoon powdered ginger
¼ teaspoon dried thyme
3 cloves
1 bay leaf
grated unsweetened coconut (garnish)

Dice the lamb, turkey, chicken or vegetables. Set aside.

In a 3-quart saucepan, sauté the onions in the oil until soft. Sprinkle on the curry powder, and stir over low heat for 3 minutes. Add the flour, and stir another 3 minutes. Add the garlic, and cook 1 minute. Add the Stock all at once, and cook until thick and smooth, stirring constantly.

Add the raisins, apples, ginger, thyme, cloves and bay leaf. Simmer for 10 to 15 minutes. Add the meat, beans or vegetables, and heat through. Remove the cloves and bay leaf before serving. Garnish with coconut.

Variations: For a grain-free curry, omit the rice flour. In its place, puree ½ cup cooked potatoes or sweet potatoes with the Stock in a blender until smooth. Add to the cooked onions after the garlic.

NOTE: Curry recipes are very flexible. You may prefer to add more curry powder and decrease the fruit. Or you may elect to omit a particular spice or fruit altogether. Experiment to suit yourself.

Venison Pepper Steak

Serves 4.

Whether you're allergic to beef or not, you'll love this version of the ever-popular pepper steak. Here, the secret to tender venison is thin slicing and quick cooking.

1 venison loin roast
　(1–1¼ pounds)
1 tablespoon oil
1 large Spanish
　onion, thinly
　sliced
2 large green
　peppers, thinly
　sliced
1 garlic clove,
　minced
1 tablespoon oil
¾ cup venison Stock
　(see Index) or
　water
1–2 tablespoons
　wheat-free
　tamari sauce
　(optional)
2–3 scallions, cut into
　½" pieces
1 tablespoon
　arrowroot
¼ cup water
3 cups hot cooked
　brown rice

Slice the venison very thinly across the grain.

Heat 1 tablespoon oil in a large frying pan over medium heat. Add the venison, and brown the pieces, stirring and turning, for 5 minutes. Remove to a plate.

Add the onions, peppers, garlic and 1 tablespoon oil to the pan. Cook on low heat until vegetables are soft, about 10 minutes. Return meat to the pan, and add the Stock or water, tamari to taste and scallions. Dissolve the arrowroot in the ¼ cup water, and add to pan. Cook, stirring, for 2 to 3 minutes, until thick.

Serve over brown rice.

Variation: If someone in the family eats wheat bread, serve them the pepper steak in pita pockets and reduce the amount of rice used.

Mix-and-Match Stir-Fry ——————————

Serves 4.

   Because the ingredients for stir-fried meals can be so varied and limitless, there's always lots you can eat—no matter what you're allergic to. My favorite stir-fries include a source of protein, a leafy vegetable, two or more crunchy vegetables and other delicious extras. Then I like to serve the whole thing atop bean-thread noodles or brown rice. Below is a sample stir-fry, followed by lots of tasty variations. Although stir-fries are quick cooking, they require a fair amount of advance preparation. If you're using a marinade, let the protein source marinate at least 30 minutes. Be sure all other ingredients are chopped and lined up next to the stove before you begin cooking. Because you'll be adding them to hot oil, try to have all vegetables patted as dry as possible. Naturally, you can vary all amounts to suit yourself.

¾ pound boneless
   turkey breast
Magic Marinade
   and Stir-Fry
   Sauce (see
   Index)
1 tablespoon
   arrowroot
2–3 tablespoons oil
½ cup cashews
¾ cup thinly sliced
   water chestnuts
¾ cup thinly sliced
   bok choy
½ cup thinly sliced
   nappa cabbage
2 cups hot cooked
   brown rice

   Cut the turkey into ½" cubes or slivers. Place in a bowl with the Magic Marinade and Stir-Fry Sauce. Mix well, cover, and let stand at room temperature 30 minutes. Drain through a strainer set over a bowl. The turkey is now ready for stir-frying. Add the arrowroot to the collected Marinade, and set aside.

   Heat a wok or frying pan for several minutes on high heat. (If using a wok on an electric range, make sure the collar is placed so the wider opening is facing up; that allows the wok to sit closer to the heat. If you're using a gas stove, place the collar with the wider opening down. Flat-bottomed woks can stand directly on the burner.)

   Pour 2 tablespoons oil into the wok or frying pan (if using a wok, dribble the oil down the sides rather than pouring it directly into the center). Swirl pan to distribute the oil.

   Add the turkey. Using a long-handled spatula, wooden spoon or Oriental scoop, stir-fry the turkey until it is cooked through, about 1 to 2 minutes. Remove to a plate, using a slotted spoon.

   Add the cashews, and stir-fry for 1 minute. Remove, and place with the turkey.

   If necessary, add more oil. Add the water chestnuts; stir-fry 2 minutes. Then add the bok choy. Stir-fry until heated through. Add the nappa cabbage, and stir-fry until heated through. This whole batch of vegetables should take no longer than 6 to 8 minutes to be done.

206

Return the turkey and cashews to the pan. Add the Marinade. Stir to reheat turkey and thicken Marinade; this should take only 1 minute.

Serve at once over the brown rice.

Variations: For a Chicken Stir-Fry, use cubed boneless chicken breasts; halved snow peas; sliced button, grass or cultivated mushrooms; shredded spinach; cashews; sliced bamboo shoots.

For a Fish Stir-Fry, try cubed firm-fleshed fish, such as halibut or monkfish (do not use delicate fillets like sole and flounder); scallops; sliced scallions; sliced red peppers; sliced nappa cabbage or bok choy; dried mushrooms that have been soaked for 30 minutes, then drained and sliced; pine nuts.

For a Pork Stir-Fry, use slivers of pork; julienne jicama; sliced scallions; sliced bok choy; julienne zucchini; diced red peppers; sliced water chestnuts; sliced lettuce.

For a Lamb Stir-Fry, try slivers of lean lamb; julienne (peeled) broccoli stalks, plus small florets; sliced scallions; sliced or diced carrots; tomatoes that have been peeled, seeded and chopped; sesame seeds.

Other ingredients for perfectly good stir-fries include: cubed or julienne pieces of drained and pressed tofu; whole or chopped shrimp; crab meat; crab claws; bean sprouts; julienne kohlrabi; sliced green beans; sliced or diced green peppers; small cauliflower florets; sliced celery; halved or quartered cherry tomatoes; whole or slivered almonds; sunflower seeds; peanuts.

If you must avoid tamari sauce, replace it in the Marinade with unsweetened pineapple juice. Or replace the entire Marinade with unsweetened pineapple juice.

NOTE: For quick meal preparation, prepare all ingredients ahead of time. Starting the morning, or even the evening, before, cut the protein ingredient, mix with the marinade, cover, and place in the refrigerator until needed. Cut all vegetables. Wrap each separately in cellophane bags or in kitchen towels placed in the crisper drawer of the refrigerator.

Stuffed Grape Leaves _____

Serves 4 to 6.

Grape leaves are a little-used resource that can add needed variety to the diet. Serve with broccoli or something else from the Mustard family.

18–24 grape leaves
    (see Note)
Rice Pilaf (see
    Index)
½ cup raisins
½ cup diced
    cooked lamb,
    turkey,
    chicken or
    fish (optional)
Magic Mustard
    Sauce (see
    Index)

Wash the grape leaves and pat them dry.

Prepare the Rice Pilaf, adding raisins and diced meat or fish.

Place about 2 tablespoons of rice mixture on each leaf. Fold in the sides, then roll up the leaf to enclose the filling. Place in a baking dish, with the flap underneath.

Pour the Magic Mustard Sauce over the bundles. Bake at 350° for 15 minutes.

NOTE: Pick grape leaves when they have reached 5″ or 6″ across. When the leaves become too large, they tend to toughen, so try to pick ones that are large enough to fill but not too old to be edible. With a little practice you'll be able to choose ones that are just right.

Fish

Fish has a lot going for it, in part because of what it doesn't have: artery-clogging saturated fat. That's why many people are eating more fish, whether they have allergies or not. This trend is reflected in both restaurants and supermarkets, where fresh or frozen fish is far more available now than it was a decade ago. Yet the best news of all, especially for people with food allergies, is that there are at least 33 different families of fish to choose from! (They're listed in Table 3, Food Families, in the section, Planning a Diversified Rotary Diet.) Try to seek out monkfish, catfish and other less-familiar fish when you shop, to diversify your diet.

Buy the freshest fish you can find. At a fish store, buy fish that has a mild and pleasant aroma. If fish sits around for a day or two, it deteriorates. An "off" odor is a dead giveaway that fresh fish is no longer "fresh." In that case, you're better off buying rock-hard packages of flash-frozen fish—preferably fish that was frozen the day it was caught, which is often stated on the label. (And never buy frozen food that's mushy.)

Thaw frozen fish in the refrigerator, then rinse in clear water and pat dry.

When cooking any kind of fish, simple preparation is usually best. You will find directions for baking and broiling fish and recipes for casseroles and other combination dishes. If in doubt about how to prepare a new type of fish, ask questions when you buy it.

Baked Fish Fillets _____

Serves 4.

Many people enjoy eating fish in restaurants but shy away from cooking it at home. If you follow these guidelines, you'll have a perfect catch every time.

First, use the freshest fish you can find. If fresh fish at the supermarket or seafood store does not look in peak condition and smell mildly pleasant, pass it by in favor of flash-frozen fish from the freezer case. Many packages even state that the fish was frozen the same day it was caught. (Look for brands that come from the waters around Greenland; it is considered one of the least contaminated areas for fishing.)

If using frozen fish, thaw it slowly in the refrigerator, then rinse in cold water, and pat dry. This recipe can be used for almost any type of fillets.

1½ pounds fish fillets
1 tablespoon oil or mayonnaise
4 lemon or lime wedges (garnish; optional)
Cucumber-Dill Sauce (optional; see Index)

Lay the fillets in a single layer in an oiled baking dish or on an oiled cookie sheet. Brush the tops lightly with oil or mayonnaise.

Bake at 400° for 10 to 20 minutes, depending upon the thickness of the fillets. (In general, allow 10 minutes for each inch of thickness.) Do not overcook the fish. It should be opaque at the thickest part and tender. Try to catch it just before it flakes easily with a fork.

Serve plain, with lemon or lime wedges or with Cucumber-Dill Sauce.

Broiled Fish _____

Serves 4.

This is probably the quickest and easiest entree you can make for dinner. Have all ingredients ready before you start cooking the fish.

1½ pounds fish fillets or steaks
1 tablespoon oil
4 lemon or lime wedges (garnish; optional)
3 tablespoons minced parsley (garnish)
dash of paprika (garnish)

Rinse the fish and pat dry. Oil the skin side, and place that side on a broiler rack. Brush the top side with oil. Add a little water to the bottom of the broiler pan to provide a bit of steam during cooking to help keep the fish moist.

Broil the fish 3″ to 4″ from the broiler element until they're opaque. (Allow 9 minutes for each inch of thickness. Most fillets measure ¾″ and will take 7 minutes.) Do not overcook the fish, and do not turn the fish unless it's more than 1 inch thick.

Serve garnished with lemon or lime wedges or a sprinkle of parsley and paprika, or all three.

Fish Fillets Florentine _____

Serves 4.

Truly a classic way to dress up fish if you can't have cheese sauce or butter.

20 ounces spinach
1 tablespoon olive oil
½ cup chopped
    onions
    grated nutmeg
1 pound flounder or
    sole fillets or
    other mild-tasting
    fish
1 teaspoon olive oil
2 tablespoons lemon
    juice
½ teaspoon dried dill
    weed
    paprika (garnish)

Wash the spinach well. Steam it for 3 minutes, or until wilted. Transfer to a strainer, and press with a fork to remove all moisture. Chop coarsely.

Place 1 tablespoon oil and onions in a frying pan. Sauté onions until barely soft. Add the spinach and a dusting of nutmeg. Stir.

Arrange the fish in a single layer over the spinach. Brush lightly with 1 teaspoon oil. Drizzle with lemon juice, and sprinkle with dill.

Cover the pan, and cook for 5 minutes or longer, until the fish is milky in color and flakes easily with a fork. Sprinkle with paprika.

NOTE: If you don't have fresh spinach, you can substitute 2 packages frozen spinach. Allow to thaw, then squeeze dry. Add to the pan after the onions have cooked.

Fish Amandine _____

Serves 4.

Use any mild-tasting fish in this recipe. I like trout, sole, scrod, snapper and catfish.

½ cup slivered or
    chopped
    almonds
1½ teaspoons almond
    oil
1½ pounds fish fillets
2 tablespoons lemon
    juice (optional)

Place the nuts and oil in a small saucepan. Sauté nuts until lightly browned. Set the saucepan aside.

Cook the fish in a non-stick frying pan until it's opaque and flakes easily with a fork.

Return the almonds to the heat. Add the lemon juice, and warm through. Pour over the fish.

Avocado Stuffed with Tuna _____

Serves 2.

Here's a dressy tuna salad that's free of celery, onions and egg mayonnaise. Makes a nice luncheon dish.

7 ounces water-packed tuna, drained
⅓ cup chopped walnuts
2 tablespoons olive oil, avocado oil or Tofu Mayo (see Index)
1 large avocado

Toss together the tuna and nuts in a small bowl. Add enough oil or Tofu Mayo to moisten lightly.

Cut the avocado in half lengthwise, and remove the pit. Fill the cavities with the tuna mixture, mounding the portions.

Poached Salmon _____

Serves 4.

Salmon breaks up the old chicken-beef-and-pork routine. And it's certainly an elegant change of pace. I like to serve poached salmon with Scalloped Potatoes and a tossed salad. Both those dishes can be prepared ahead so I can give all my attention to cooking the salmon.

1 quart water
½ cup sliced onions
1 carrot, sliced
½ cup celery leaves or lovage leaves
¼ cup parsley leaves
2 tablespoons lemon juice or ½ teaspoon vitamin C crystals
1 bay leaf
1½ pounds salmon fillets, preferably the tail pieces
Cucumber-Dill Sauce (optional; see Index)
lemon wedges (garnish; optional)

Make a court bouillon (poaching stock) by combining the water, onions, carrots, celery leaves or lovage leaves, parsley, lemon juice or vitamin C crystals and bay leaf in a large frying pan or Dutch oven. Simmer for 30 minutes.

Add the salmon to the pan. If the liquid doesn't cover the fillets, add a little extra boiling water. Watch the liquid for the first bubbles that indicate the stock has returned to a simmer. Reduce the heat so the liquid barely shimmers. Do not boil.

Cook for 8 or 9 minutes, or until the fish is cooked through and flakes easily with a fork. Remove from the liquid. Turn the fillets over and remove the skin, if present, with a fork. Cut fillets in half lengthwise, if desired, to make pieces that are roughly triangular in shape.

Serve topped with Cucumber-Dill Sauce or lemon wedges.

Creamy Cod Casserole _____

Serves 4.

This New England treat is usually made with cream and flour, but it's just as delicious without dairy and wheat products.

5–6 medium red potatoes
3 cups water
1 teaspoon dehydrated onion flakes
3 cloves
4 drops hot pepper sauce
1–2 bay leaves
1 pound cod fillets
1 large Spanish onion, sliced
2 tablespoons olive oil
¼ cup Brazil nuts
¼ cup Handy Crumbs or Italian Crumbs (optional; see Index)
snipped chives (garnish)

Scrub the potatoes well. Boil them whole in 1½ cups water until tender, about 15 minutes. Set aside to cool.

In another saucepan, combine remaining 1½ cups water with the onion flakes, cloves, pepper sauce and bay leaves. Bring to a boil, then reduce heat, and simmer for a few minutes. Add cod. Return to the barest simmer, then cover the pan, remove it from the heat, and let stand for 10 to 15 minutes.

In a large frying pan, sauté the onions in the oil for about 10 minutes, until soft. Set aside.

Place the nuts in a blender, and grind to a fine powder. Remove the fish to a plate, and strain the poaching liquid into the blender. Process briefly to combine. Take 1 potato, cut it into quarters, and add to the blender. Process for 2 minutes, until perfectly smooth. If the sauce measures less than 2 cups, add enough potato-cooking water to bring up the level.

Pour the sauce over the onions in the frying pan. Heat through.

Slice the remaining potatoes thinly. Place half of the slices in an oiled casserole. Add half the onions. Place the fish in a single layer over the onions. Top with the remaining potatoes, then the remaining onions and sauce. Sprinkle with the Handy Crumbs or Italian Crumbs.

Bake at 350° for 30 to 40 minutes, until brown and bubbly. Garnish with chives.

213

Salmon Salad _____

Serves 2.

A sandwich filling to help you diversify your diet and break out of the tuna-salad rut.

1 cup flaked
poached salmon
¼ cup Homemade
Mayo or Nutty
Mayo (see
Index)
¼ cup minced
parsley
1–2 tablespoons
minced onions
1–2 tablespoons
honey-
sweetened
pickle relish
(optional)
2 teaspoons lemon
juice
lettuce leaves or
spinach

In a large bowl, mix the salmon, Homemade Mayo or Nutty Mayo, parsley, onions, relish and lemon juice. Serve on lettuce leaves or spinach.

Asparagus-Sole Surprise _____

Serves 4.

A perfect marriage of subtle flavors. Serve with baked yams or sweet potatoes.

1¼ pounds sole fillets
or other mild-
flavored fish
1 teaspoon oil
24 thin asparagus
stalks, trimmed
(or 16–24 plump
stalks)
Magic Mustard
Sauce, warm
(see Index)
snipped chives
(garnish)

Pat the fish dry with cotton towels. Arrange in a single layer in a 9″-×-13″ baking dish. Brush lightly with the oil. Bake at 400° for 12 minutes.

Simmer the asparagus stalks in water in a covered frying pan for 10 to 12 minutes, until just tender. Arrange 6 stalks in the middle of each serving plate. Top with fish, then with warm Magic Mustard Sauce. Garnish with chives.

Hot Tuna Patties

Serves 4.

Serve as an entree with vegetables. Or place between slices of wheat-free bread as a burger.

1 cooked potato
¼ cup minced onions
¼ cup honey-sweetened pickle relish
2 tablespoons honey-sweetened ketchup
2 tablespoons Homemade Mayo or Tofu Mayo (see Index)
1 tablespoon minced parsley
7 ounces water-packed tuna, drained
potato starch (optional)
2 tablespoons peanut oil or other oil

Dice the potato. Place half the potato in a blender with the onions, relish, ketchup, Homemade Mayo or Tofu Mayo and parsley. Blend a few seconds, then start adding remaining potato. Blend until well chopped. Add tuna; blend 30 seconds. Stop machine to scrape sides as needed. If you need more liquid to operate the machine, add a tablespoon or so of water or tomato juice. Blend well, and turn into a bowl. If mixture is too wet to hold together properly, add a bit of potato starch.

Form mixture into 4 patties. Sauté in a large frying pan in the oil until brown and crusted on both sides.

NOTE: You can make this easily in a food processor. Just combine all ingredients except the oil in the machine, and process until well blended.

215

Vegetarian Main Dishes

It wouldn't hurt any of us to eat a meat-free meal once or twice a week. For one thing, it's a great way to reduce intake of animal fats and red meat. And if you or someone in your family is allergic to meat, poultry, or fish, vegetarian dishes give you a much wider choice of meals to prepare.

I've purposely avoided relying too heavily on soybeans and soy foods in this section, because of the growing number of people who are developing an allergy to that legume. Most of the recipes in this section offer a choice of beans, to meet individual needs and tastes. Savory Skillet Supper, Better Burgers and Vegetable Chili have all been enthusiastically received by vegetarian guests at my house, and the skillet supper has been a big hit at potluck suppers.

If you happen to be allergic to either grains or legumes, which are often combined to achieve maximum protein efficiency, you need a couple of alternatives. Zesty Supper Loaf, Grain-Free Stuffed Peppers and Egg Foo Yong do not include either grains or legumes.

216

Savory Skillet Supper

Serves 4.

So simple, fast and satisfying, you'll never miss the meat.

2⅓ cups water
1 cup raw brown rice
1 cup chopped onions
1 large celery stalk, sliced
2 medium carrots, thinly sliced
2 tablespoons olive oil
¼ cup chopped parsley
1 tablespoon wheat-free tamari sauce
2 teaspoons dried basil
1 teaspoon dried oregano
2 garlic cloves, minced
dash of cayenne pepper (optional)
2 cups cooked beans
2 tablespoons water
1 cup cherry tomatoes, halved or quartered
¼ cup chopped parsley

Bring the water and rice to a boil in a saucepan. Cover the pan, reduce the heat, and simmer for 40 minutes, or until rice is tender.

In a large frying pan, sauté the onions, celery and carrots in the oil until tender, about 12 to 15 minutes. Stir in ¼ cup parsley, tamari, basil, oregano, garlic and cayenne. Add the beans and water. Heat through.

On low heat, gently stir in the rice. Arrange tomatoes around the outer edges of the pan. Sprinkle with ¼ cup parsley. Cover and heat for 2 minutes.

Zesty Supper Loaf _____

Serves 6.

> *Cold slices make wonderful sandwiches.*

1 cup minced onions
1 cup minced celery
1 cup minced carrots
2 tablespoons olive
    oil
1 garlic clove, minced
1 cup finely chopped
    nuts
¾ cup rice bran or
    Handy Crumbs
    (see Index)
2 eggs or ½ cup Tofu
    Mayo (see Index)
¼ cup honey-
    sweetened
    ketchup
2 tablespoons wheat-
    free tamari sauce
½ teaspoon dried basil
½ teaspoon dried
    oregano
⅛ teaspoon cayenne
    pepper (optional)
    Tomato Sauce or
    Mushroom Brown
    Sauce (optional;
    see Index)

In a large frying pan, sauté the onions, celery and carrots in the oil until tender. Add the garlic, and cook another minute. Remove from the heat. Stir in the nuts and rice bran or Handy Crumbs. Set aside.

In a large bowl, beat together the eggs or Mayo, ketchup, tamari, basil, oregano and cayenne until well combined. Add the vegetable mixture, and mix well.

Grease a 7⅜"- × -3⅝" loaf pan with a mixture of oil and liquid lecithin (or oil the pan, line with wax paper, and oil the paper). Pat loaf mixture firmly into the pan. Bake at 350° for about 1 hour, until brown and set. Allow to stand at room temperature for 10 minutes before slicing.

Serve plain or with Tomato Sauce or Mushroom Brown Sauce.

Variations: You may replace the nuts with a mixture of chopped nuts and seeds. You may also replace the ketchup with a mixture of ¼ cup tomato paste and ¼ cup water.

Tostados Improvised _____

Serves 4.

The Rodale Test Kitchen staff served this at an open house party, and everyone raved about it! There's no corn, cheese or sour cream, yet it's very Mexican.

2 cups cooked brown
    rice or Tamari
    Basmati (see
    Index)
1 cup South-of-the-
    Border Sandwich

Place ½ cup of the rice on each of 4 heat-proof luncheon-size plates. Press into a round about ½" or less thick. Place the plates in a 300° oven for about 10 minutes to warm the rice.

Heat the South-of-the-Border Sandwich Spread in a non-stick frying pan. Spread ¼ cup

Spread (see Index)
1 cup Guacamole (see Index)
shredded lettuce
chopped onions
chopped or sliced black olives

of it on each plate of rice. Top each with ¼ cup of Guacamole. Top with lettuce, onions and olives.

Variations: Replace the rice with Amaranth Pancakes. Make the pancakes without cinnamon and maple syrup. Crisp them in a warm oven. Use about 4 per serving, and assemble as above.

You can replace the Sandwich Spread with chili-flavored beans that you've pureed with a little liquid in a blender and simmered in a pan until thick enough to spread (about 10 minutes).

Peanut Burgers

Makes 4 to 6 patties.

If you're allergic to beef—or eat it at four-day intervals only—you can feast on these "burgers."

1 cup roasted peanuts
½ cup diced celery
½ cup diced carrots
½ cup diced onions
½ cup chopped parsley
⅓ cup sunflower or sesame seeds
1 teaspoon ground cumin
1 teaspoon dried dill weed
½ teaspoon ground coriander
½ teaspoon ground fennel
1–2 tablespoons water (optional)

With a grinder or food processor, grind the peanuts, celery, carrots, onions, parsley and sunflower or sesame seeds into fine particles (but not into a powder or puree). Mix in the cumin, dill, coriander and fennel.

Turn the mixture into a bowl, and knead hard for 1 minute. If needed, add a little water to bind the ingredients. The mixture will be dry, though.

Lightly oil a cookie sheet. Drop the mixture into 4 large or 6 medium mounds. Flatten into round patties with the back of a spoon. Bake at 350° for 15 to 20 minutes, or until the burgers are golden and crisp to the touch.

Serve between Flatbread, with ketchup and mustard or alfalfa sprouts and Tomato Sauce.

Vegetarian Chili _____

Makes about 2½ quarts.

3 medium carrots, diced
3 celery stalks, diced
1 large green pepper, diced
1 large Spanish onion, diced
2 tablespoons olive oil
2–3 garlic cloves, minced
1½ pounds tomatoes, chopped
2 cups cooked kidney beans
12 ounces tomato paste
1 cup bean Stock (see Index) or water
2 tablespoons chili powder
2 tablespoons wheat-free tamari sauce (optional)
⅛ teaspoon ground cinnamon
chopped onions (garnish)
chopped olives (garnish)
toasted sesame seeds (garnish)
Guacamole (garnish; see Index)

In a Dutch oven or stockpot, sauté the carrots, celery, peppers and onions in the oil until soft, about 10 to 15 minutes. Add the garlic, and cook another minute.

Add the tomatoes, beans, tomato paste, Stock or water, chili powder, tamari and cinnamon. Simmer for 1 hour. If chili becomes too thick, thin with additional stock or water.

Serve garnished with onions, olives and sesame seeds. Top with Guacamole.

Mexican Supper

Serves 4.

A spicy entree that's free of corn but high in protein and fiber.

1 cup chopped
  onions
½ cup chopped
  celery
1–2 garlic cloves,
  minced
¼–½ teaspoon red
  pepper flakes
3 tablespoons oil
¾ cup buckwheat
  groats
1½ cups water
2 cups chopped or
  stewed
  tomatoes
2 cups cooked
  kidney or
  pinto beans or
  chick-peas
6 ounces tomato
  paste
1½ teaspoons chili
  powder
1 teaspoon honey
  or molasses
⅓ cup chopped
  peppers
⅓ cup minced
  parsley
chopped onions
  (optional)
chopped black
  olives
  (optional)
Guacamole
  (optional; see
  Index)

Combine the onions, celery, garlic, pepper flakes and 1 tablespoon oil in a large frying pan. Sauté for 5 minutes. Add the remaining oil and groats; cook, stirring, for 5 minutes.

Stir in the water, tomatoes, beans or chick-peas, tomato paste, chili powder and honey or molasses. Simmer for 30 minutes, covered, stirring occasionally. Stir in the peppers and parsley.

Serve with onions and olives sprinkled on top. Add a dollop of Guacamole.

Confetti Rice Salad _____

Serves 4.

A one-dish luncheon meal.

2 cups cooked brown
    rice
1 cup green peas,
    lightly cooked
4 scallions, chopped
1 celery stalk, thinly
    sliced
1 large carrot, diced
    or shredded
6 radishes, finely
    chopped
⅓ cup minced parsley
¼ cup toasted
    sunflower seeds
¼ cup oil
¼ cup lemon juice or
    vinegar
1 tablespoon wheat-
    free tamari sauce
    (optional)
1 tablespoon prepared
    horseradish
1 tablespoon minced
    tarragon or 1
    teaspoon dried
    tarragon
¼ teaspoon celery
    seeds

In a large bowl, toss together the rice, peas, scallions, celery, carrots, radishes, parsley and sunflower seeds.

In a small bowl, whisk together the oil, lemon juice or vinegar, tamari, horseradish, tarragon and celery seeds. Pour over the salad. Toss lightly to combine. Chill 1 hour or more.

Rice-Nut-Seed Croquettes _____

Serves 4.

High-protein patties for meatless dinners. Good with Peanut Sauce.

½ cup warm water
¼ cup soy grits
1 tablespoon honey
1 tablespoon wheat-
    free tamari sauce
    (optional)
1 tablespoon Dijon-

Combine the water, soy grits and honey in a small bowl. Set aside to soften for a few minutes. Stir in tamari and mustard.

In a large bowl, combine the rice, crumbs, walnuts, sunflower seeds, onion powder and garlic powder. Blend well. Stir in the soy-grits mixture.

222

style mustard
1¾ cups cooked
   brown rice
1 cup crumbs (see
   Note)
¾ cup chopped
   walnuts
½ cup ground
   sunflower seeds
2 teaspoons onion
   powder
½ teaspoon garlic
   powder

Form mixture into walnut-size balls, rolling them between your palms to make them firm. Bake at 350° for 25 to 30 minutes, until crispy and brown.

NOTE: Use pulverized brown rice crackers, Tortillas (see Index) or puffed brown-rice cereal.

Fancy Fried Rice

Serves 4.

This is a little more elaborate than the Fried Rice in the Breakfasts section. It's just the thing for brunch or lunch.

3 thin slices ginger
   root
2 tablespoons oil
10 mushrooms, thinly
   sliced
3 scallions, chopped
½ cup chopped
   peanuts
   (optional)
¼ cup sunflower
   seeds
2 tablespoons sesame
   seeds
3 cups cooked brown
   rice
2 eggs
2 tablespoons water
1 tablespoon wheat-
   free tamari sauce
1 teaspoon sesame oil
⅛ teaspoon cayenne
   pepper
¼ cup minced parsley
   (garnish)

In a large frying pan, sauté the ginger in the oil for 2 minutes. Discard ginger. Add the mushrooms, scallions, peanuts, sunflower seeds and sesame seeds. Sauté for 5 minutes. Add the rice, and cook 5 minutes more, stirring.

In a cup lightly beat the eggs, water, tamari, sesame oil and cayenne with a fork. Pour over the rice. Stir over heat for a few minutes until eggs are set. Serve garnished with parsley.

Variations: Add as many of the following as you want to the frying pan with the mushrooms and scallions: 1½ cups peas, 1 cup bean sprouts, 1 cup thinly sliced carrots, 1 cup thinly sliced celery and 1 chopped pepper.

223

Rice Cutlets

Serves 4.

If you're allergic to wheat bread, you can use these tasty cutlets in place of sandwiches.

1 egg or Egg
  Substitute (see
  Index)
1 tablespoon wheat-
  free tamari
  sauce (optional)
1 cup cooked brown
  rice
⅓ cup chopped
  green peppers
⅓ cup chopped
  onions
⅓ cup chopped
  celery
¼ cup soy flour
¼ cup rice bran
¼ cup oat bran
¼ cup chopped nuts
  or seeds
  pinch of cayenne
  pepper
  (optional)
1–2 tablespoons oil

Combine the egg or Egg Substitute and tamari in a large bowl. Whip lightly with a fork.

Add the rice, peppers, onions, celery, flour, rice bran, oat bran, nuts or seeds and cayenne. Stir well. Let stand a few minutes for liquid to be absorbed.

Shape into patties. Brown them on both sides in the oil in a medium-size skillet.

Better Burgers

Serves 6.

These are a great alternative to cold cuts in the lunch bag. Dress up these burgers with your favorite condiments.

½ cup minced
  onions
2 medium carrots,
  minced
2 celery stalks,
  minced
1–2 garlic cloves,
  minced
1 tablespoon olive
  oil
1 cup cooked beans,

In a large frying pan, sauté the onions, carrots, celery and garlic in the oil until soft, about 10 minutes.

In a large bowl, mix the beans, peanuts, sunflower seeds and sesame seeds. Add the cooked vegetables, and mix well.

In a cup, stir together the ketchup or tomato paste, tamari and cayenne. Add to the vegetable mixture, and stir well. If the mixture is too moist, stir in a little flour, 1 tablespoon at a time, until you can shape the mix into patties.

mashed
½ cup chopped
   peanuts
½ cup toasted
   sunflower seeds
¼ cup toasted
   sesame seeds
⅓ cup honey-
   sweetened
   ketchup or
   tomato paste
1 teaspoon wheat-
   free tamari
   sauce
⅛ teaspoon cayenne
   pepper
   (optional)
   amaranth flour,
   soy flour or rice
   flour
   Stir 'n' Pour
   Flatbread,
   Fruited
   Flatbread or
   Amaranth
   Pancakes (see
   Index)

Form into 6 patties. Cook in a non-stick frying pan until cooked through, or place on a lightly oiled cookie sheet, and bake at 350° for 18 to 20 minutes.

Serve in between 2 pieces of warm Flatbread or crisply toasted Amaranth Pancakes.

Grain-Free Stuffed Peppers

Serves 6.

For a brightly colored meal, use sweet red peppers, and serve with green beans or peas and baked yams.

6 medium green
   peppers
6 cups Buckwheat
   Waldorf Stuffing
   (see Index)
¼ cup minced parsley
   (garnish)
   paprika (garnish)

Cut the peppers in half lengthwise. Remove the seeds, stems and inner membranes. Drop the pepper halves into boiling water; blanch for 5 minutes. Rinse with cold water and drain.

Fill each pepper half with about ½ cup of Buckwheat Waldorf Stuffing, mounding it with a spoon or your fingers. Place in an oiled baking dish in one layer. Bake at 350° for 30 minutes, or until the apples and celery in the stuffing are tender.

Garnish with parsley and paprika.

Parmesan-Style Eggplant _____

Serves 6 to 8 (or 12 at a buffet).

This version of eggplant parmesan is free of cow's milk, eggs and wheat.

1 medium eggplant
(about 1 pound)
1 tablespoon olive
oil
2 cups cooked pinto
beans or chick-
peas
1 cup sliced or
diced onions
1 tablespoon olive
oil
½ pound
mushrooms,
sliced
2 garlic cloves,
minced
2–4 ounces Soft
Goat's-Milk
Cheese
(optional; see
Index)
3 medium zucchini
1 teaspoon dried
oregano
2 cups Tomato
Sauce (see
Index)
Handy Crumbs
(optional; see
Index)

Slice the eggplant lengthwise into ½" slabs. Brush both sides of all pieces with 1 tablespoon olive oil. Arrange on a cookie sheet. Bake at 400° for 15 minutes. Set aside.

Place pinto beans or chick-peas in a bowl or dish. Mash about half of them with a fork. Set aside.

In a large frying pan, sauté the onions in 1 tablespoon oil until soft. Add the mushrooms and garlic. Cook until the liquid that the mushrooms have released has evaporated. Set aside.

Crumble the cheese, and set aside.

Slice the zucchini lengthwise into ¼" slabs. Steam for 7 minutes, then drain on a cotton towel. Set aside.

To assemble, oil a 9"-×-13" baking dish. Arrange the eggplant slices in 1 layer in the bottom. Cover with the beans. Sprinkle beans with half the oregano. Then spread on the mushroom mixture, and top it with a layer of cheese. Sprinkle cheese with remaining oregano. Layer on the zucchini, then cover with Tomato Sauce and Handy Crumbs.

Bake at 350° for 45 minutes. Allow to stand for 10 minutes before cutting into squares and serving.

NOTE: You can assemble the casserole and refrigerate until ready to bake. Bake at 350° for 55 minutes.

If you omit the cheese, serve with a nut or seed dessert for added protein.

Egg Foo Yong

Serves 4.

Wonderful vegetable fritters, good any time of the day—for brunch, lunch or a light supper. For people who can eat eggs—even if only occasionally.

½ cup unsweetened apple-juice concentrate
½ cup water
1 tablespoon arrowroot
⅛ teaspoon powdered ginger
  dash of wheat-free tamari sauce (optional)
4 eggs
1 tablespoon wheat-free tamari sauce (optional)
½ cup grated carrots
½ cup finely shredded zucchini
½ cup bean sprouts
½ cup minced onions
½ cup chopped walnuts

To make ginger sauce, combine the juice concentrate, water, arrowroot, ginger and dash of tamari in a small saucepan. Stir to dissolve the arrowroot. Bring to a boil, stirring constantly. Sauce will become thick and clear. Keep sauce warm until eggs are ready.

In a medium bowl, mix eggs and 1 tablespoon tamari. Beat with an electric mixer for 2 minutes or with a whisk for 3 minutes. Stir in carrots, zucchini, sprouts, onions and walnuts.

Heat a non-stick griddle or frying pan. Drop about ¼ cup of batter onto griddle, and flatten with the back of a spoon or measuring cup. Cook over medium heat until bottoms are nicely brown. Turn and lightly brown other sides.

Serve with ginger sauce.

Variation: Use all one vegetable if you have a garden surplus.

NOTE: You can hold these pancakes briefly in a warming oven. If you need to hold them for an hour or more, as for a buffet, double the sauce recipe. Then place the pancakes in the sauce, and keep warm in a chafing dish or warming tray.

227

Goat's Milk and Cheese Dishes

Goat's milk and cow's milk are alike in some ways and different in others—different enough, in fact, that it is quite common for some people to be allergic to cow's milk yet thrive on goat's milk. Pediatricians have known that for some time, but somehow adults with allergies don't always realize that it applies to them, too. The fat globules in goat's milk are smaller than those in cow's milk, making it easier to digest. But like cow's milk, goat's milk does contain the milk sugar lactose, a potential problem for lactose-intolerant people. So whether you tolerate goat's milk or not will partially depend on what specific factor in milk bothers you. At any rate, goat's milk is a great find for those of us who can tolerate it.

Nutritionally, goat's milk stacks up very well next to cow's milk. Compared with cow's milk, 1 cup of goat's milk has 35 milligrams more calcium, 144 International Units more vitamin A, three times as much niacin, nearly four times as much manganese, 125 milligrams more potassium, 5 milligrams less cholesterol—and only 18 more calories.

Goat's milk does have somewhat less vitamin B_{12}, folic acid and zinc than cow's milk. All other nutrient values are approximately equal.

Search out a local source for fresh goat's milk. Although both canned and evaporated goat's milk are available, fresh goat's milk wins in a taste test, especially as a beverage. When buying goat's milk from a local supplier, you may have to supply your own containers. Collect a few large jars, wash well and scald them just

228

before going to get the milk. Most people I know prefer to drink, cook and bake with raw milk, as long as the goats are healthy and well cared for. If you want to make goat's-milk cheese, however, you should first pasteurize the milk by slowly bringing it to 161°F. (A candy thermometer is the only special equipment you will need.) Heating to that point destroys organisms that may cause an off-flavor and consistently gives high-quality results. It's best to pasteurize goat's milk as soon as it's purchased, but it can be done up to five days later. If you use very little milk or use it only occasionally, freeze small amounts and use within two months.

Goat's-Milk Onion Pie

Serves 4 to 6.

This one's designed for people who crave quiche but can't eat wheat or cow's milk. Take your pick of an Amaranth Pie Crust, a Rice-Flour Pie Crust or a Nut 'n' Seed Crunch Crust. Whichever you choose, omit the spices and honey; replace them with a little thyme, ¼ teaspoon dried dill weed and additional water.

1 large onion, sliced
1 cup water
1 cup chopped spinach (optional)
¼ cup powdered goat's milk
2 ounces Soft Goat's-Milk Cheese (see page 230)
½ teaspoon dried dill weed
¼ teaspoon dried thyme
¼ teaspoon grated nutmeg
2 eggs
1 9" Pie Crust, unbaked (see Index)

Place the onions and water in a small saucepan. Simmer for 20 minutes. Drain the water into a blender, and place the onions in a small bowl. Add the spinach to the onions; reserve.

With the blender running, gradually add the milk powder and Soft Goat's-Milk Cheese. Then add the dill, thyme and nutmeg. Allow to cool to lukewarm.

Add the eggs to blender, and process for 15 seconds.

Bake the crust for 5 minutes at 350°. Arrange the onions and spinach in the crust. Pour the cheese mixture over them. Bake at 350° for 35 to 40 minutes, or until a knife inserted in the center comes out clean.

Soft Goat's-Milk Cheese _____

Makes 1 pound.

This delicate, sweet cheese tastes much like ricotta. It's perfect for lasagna, casseroles or cheese spreads. Because this cheese isn't aged, it's a boon to people who are allergic to cheese mold—especially if you make the cheese with vitamin C crystals instead of vinegar.

For best results, you'll need a stainless steel or enamel pot and colander. Because the cheese mixture is high in acid, do not use an aluminum pot unless it is lined with a non-stick coating. You'll also need a kitchen thermometer that registers between 100° and 200°. There are special floating thermometers sold for cheesemaking as well as more standard candy thermometers to choose from. Make sure that all your equipment, including the jars your goat's milk is stored in, are impeccably clean, perhaps even scalded. If you buy your milk directly from someone who raises goats, take along scalded jars to carry the milk home in.

3 quarts whole goat's milk
6 tablespoons vinegar or ¾ teaspoon vitamin C crystals

Place the milk in a Dutch oven, and slowly bring it to 185° over medium heat. Stir often so milk doesn't scorch. Slowly stir in the vinegar or vitamin C crystals.

Turn off the heat, and allow the mixture to rest for 15 to 30 minutes. Keep an eye on the temperature. If it begins to dip, turn on the burner to the lowest heat. (If the temperature goes a little higher than 185°, you'll have a firmer and drier cheese. Under no circumstances, however, should you allow the mixture to boil.)

After 15 to 30 minutes, the mixture should have separated into curds and whey. If it has not, add another tablespoon or two of vinegar (or a bit more of the vitamin C crystals). Stir, and allow to rest again until clearly thickened.

Line a colander with about 1 yard of cheesecloth that you've folded into quarters. Place the colander in the sink, and pour boiling water through it to scald the cloth. Gently pour the milk mixture into the colander. Gather up the corners, and tie securely with string. Suspend the bag from the faucet above the colander. Allow to drain for 1 to 2 hours, until it reaches whatever consistency you prefer. Scrape the cheese off the cloth, and form it into a ball or flattened round. Wrap well, and chill at least 1 hour before eating.

NOTE: Goat's milk separates best when it is at least 3 days old. You're most likely to have trouble if the milk is first-day fresh.

You can make any quantity of cheese you desire. The general guide is to use 2 tablespoons vinegar or ¼ teaspoon vitamin C crystals for each quart of whole milk.

Adapted from Organic Gardening, *September, 1983.*

Onion Cheese Ball

Makes 1 ball.

Make this with goat's-milk cheese that is still soft enough to mix well. Then allow time for the flavors to ripen and the cheese to firm up. Serve with crackers or raw vegetables.

8 ounces Soft Goat's-
    Milk Cheese (see
    opposite page)
1 garlic clove, minced
1 tablespoon Savory
    Seed Seasoning or
    Onion Seasoning
    (see Index)
2 teaspoons grated
    onions
4 drops hot pepper
    sauce
    Hungarian paprika

In a medium bowl, mix the Soft Goat's-Milk Cheese, garlic, Savory Seed Seasoning or Onion Seasoning, onions and hot pepper sauce. Taste mixture. If needed, add more grated onions or hot pepper sauce.

Shape mixture into a ball. Wrap well, and chill for at least 1 day. Remove from the refrigerator 1 hour before serving. Roll in paprika to completely coat.

Refrigerate any leftovers. Cheese ball will keep for several days.

NOTE: An easy way to grate an onion is to take a sharp paring knife and firmly run it across the cut surface of a Spanish onion. Use the same motion you would if you were trying to hollow out a depression in the onion. Work directly over a bowl or measuring spoon to catch all the juice that's exuded.

Herbed Cheese Ball

Makes 1 ball.

8 ounces Soft Goat's-
    Milk Cheese (see
    page 230)
1 tablespoon Savory
    Seed Seasoning or
    Onion Seasoning
    (see Index)
1 tablespoon snipped
    chives
1 garlic clove, minced
2 teaspoons grated
    onions
½ teaspoon dried basil
½ teaspoon dried sage
¼ teaspoon dried
    tarragon
¼ teaspoon dried
    thyme
4 drops hot pepper
    sauce
    minced parsley

In a medium bowl, mix the Soft Goat's-Milk Cheese, Savory Seed Seasoning or Onion Seasoning, chives, garlic, onions, basil, sage, tarragon, thyme and hot pepper sauce. Taste, and adjust seasonings, if necessary.

Shape mixture into a ball. Wrap well, and chill for at least 1 day. Remove from refrigerator 1 hour before serving. Roll in parsley to completely coat. Firmly press parsley into ball to make sure it adheres.

Refrigerate any leftovers. Cheese ball will keep for several days.

Two-Tone Holiday Cheese Balls

Makes 2 balls.

Whether you're serving this for Christmas or the Fourth of July—or any time in between—your guests will exclaim over your creativity.

1 Onion Cheese Ball
    (see page 231)
1 Herbed Cheese Ball
    (see recipe above)

As suggested in the cheese-ball recipes, roll the onion mixture in paprika and the herb mixture in parsley. Carefully cut each ball in half, and form 2 new balls by pressing together contrasting halves.

Serve at room temperature. Store any leftovers in the refrigerator. They'll keep for several days.

Variation: For a red, white and blue theme, leave the Onion Cheese Ball white by eliminating the paprika step. Incorporate minced parsley into the Herbed Cheese Ball, then roll the ball in paprika. Cut and re-form balls as directed. Serve on a blue plate.

Rice-Flour Pizza with Goat's-Milk Cheese _____

Serves 4 to 6.

Pizza is one of the foods that people with allergies miss the most. This wheat-free version can satisfy everyone.

⅔ cup warm water
1½ teaspoons dry
  yeast
¼ teaspoon honey or
  maple syrup
1 cup brown rice
  flour
1 teaspoon guar gum
  (see Appendix)
1 cup Tomato Sauce
  (see Index)
chopped onions
chopped green
  peppers
sliced mushrooms
alfalfa sprouts
pinch of dried
  oregano or
  Italian Seasoning
  (see Index)
3 ounces firm goat's-
  milk cheese,
  shredded

To make the crust, combine the water, yeast and honey or maple syrup in a cup. Set aside for 10 minutes, until the yeast is foamy.

In a medium bowl, mix the flour and guar gum. Stir in the yeast mixture. Mix well. Turn the dough out onto a lightly floured board or work surface, and knead for about 10 minutes to form a smooth ball. Flour your hands as necessary to keep the dough from sticking, but try not to add much additional flour to the dough.

Place dough in an oiled bowl, and turn it to coat all surfaces. Cover and allow to rise in a warm, draft-free place until doubled in bulk, about 1 hour.

Punch down the dough, and place on an oiled cookie sheet. Roll into a 12″ circle with an oiled rolling pin. (If the pan has side walls, turn it over and oil the bottom for rolling and baking crust. Or roll crust on oiled wax paper and transfer to pan by wrapping gently around rolling pin and unrolling into pan.)

Turn up edges of crust slightly to fashion a lip around the dough. Bake at 425° for 5 minutes.

If your Tomato Sauce is not very thick, boil it down in a small saucepan. Spread sauce on crust. Then top with onions, peppers, mushrooms, sprouts, oregano or Italian Seasoning and cheese. Bake at 400° for 15 minutes.

Variations: If desired, use rice bran for half the rice flour.

To make a thick-crust, deep-dish pizza, double the crust recipe. Pat it into a 10″ frying pan. Do not prebake before adding toppings. Bake assembled pizza for 30 minutes.

For a yeast-free pizza, make a double batch of any Tortilla recipe (see Index). Roll dough into a large flatbread, shaping it to fit your pan. Use extra-thick sauce because there will be no sides on the crust to contain the sauce.

Goat's-Milk Yogurt _____

Makes about 1 quart.

To make this yogurt, you'll need powdered goat's milk and a non-dairy starter culture, both available at health food stores. I've had wonderful success using capsules of freeze-dried Lactobacillus acidophilus culture. These capsules also contain gelatin, pectin and magnesium stearate. They're formulated especially for milk-sensitive people and are sold under the brand name DoFus, manufactured by Miller Pharmacal, Inc. Look for them in the refrigerator case at your health food store, or order from their address given in the Appendix. Making yogurt can be a little tricky, but this thermos method usually gives very good results. Make sure all your equipment has been scalded with hot water first to remove any organisms that might compete with your starter culture.

3 cups hot water
1⅓ cups powdered
    goat's milk
1 DoFus capsule
    (100 million
    organisms) or 1
    tablespoon other
    freeze-dried
    Lactobacillus
    acidophilus

Scald a strainer, wire whisk, mixing bowl and 1-quart glass- or metal-lined, widemouthed thermos bottle with boiling water. (That also preheats the thermos so that it can more effectively incubate the yogurt.)

Place the water and powdered goat's milk in the bowl. Whisk until smooth. Test the temperature of the mixture with a thermometer; it should read between 100° and 110°. (Or dribble a bit of the liquid on your forearm; it should be comfortably warm.)

Break open the capsule, and sprinkle the powder on the milk mixture. (Or sprinkle the freeze-dried culture over the milk.) Whisk well. Pour through the strainer into the thermos bottle. Cap tightly. Allow to stand *undisturbed* for 5 to 8 hours. By that time, the yogurt should have firmed sufficiently and may have a thin layer of whey on top. Spoon the custardlike yogurt into a jar or bowl. Cover well, and refrigerate until needed.

NOTE: When testing your yogurt to see if it's ready, do not shake or jiggle the jar. If the yogurt is not done, you'll disturb the culture and it won't set properly.

You can also make yogurt with fresh goat's milk. Use about 4 cups. Heat to about 185° (to the stage when a skin forms on top), then cool to between 100° and 110°. Proceed with the recipe.

Maple-Pecan Goat's-Milk Ice Cream ────────────

Serves 4.

Make this ice cream with very fresh goat's milk, not more than three days old. The flavor will be outstanding—so it's a delicious way to enjoy goat's milk for the first time. And it's easy to make, too.

2 cups goat's milk
⅓ cup chopped
    pecans
1 tablespoon walnut
    oil
⅓ cup chilled maple
    syrup
1½ teaspoons pure
    vanilla extract

Pour the milk into an ice-cube tray or a 9″-×-5″ loaf pan. Freeze until solid.

In a small frying pan, sauté the pecans in the oil until lightly browned and fragrant. Transfer to a small bowl, and chill.

Remove the frozen milk from the tray or loaf pan. (You may have to place the container up to its rim in hot water for about 1 minute to loosen the frozen milk.) If you used a loaf pan, use a sharp knife to cut milk into cubes.

Chill a blender container by blending a few regular ice cubes and 3 cups water for 1 minute. Discard the water. Place the maple syrup, vanilla and 2 milk cubes in the container. Blend on high speed until pureed. Add remaining cubes, 2 or 3 at a time, until all are blended. Turn the mixture into a chilled bowl, and stir in the pecans.

If you like soft ice cream, serve at once in chilled bowls. Otherwise, place in the freezer for an hour or two.

Variations: Replace the maple syrup with 1 small chilled banana or ½ cup strawberries. With the machine running, add ¼ to ⅓ cup honey, then the frozen milk cubes. Add frozen fruit to suit yourself. Do not hesitate to mix fruits for wonderful combination ice creams. Peaches or nectarines with sautéed chopped almonds are heavenly.

235

Vanilla Goat's-Milk Ice Cream _____

Makes about 2 quarts.

This creamy dessert is made with fresh goat's milk and an electric ice-cream machine. Fresh goat's milk is a delight—it's mild, naturally homogenized and free of the strong flavor that characterizes canned and powdered milks. This recipe will fit a half-gallon ice-cream-making machine; if yours is larger, just multiply the ingredients accordingly. Naturally, it's most fun to make ice cream outdoors in the summer, but if you'll be working inside, you can set the machine in the kitchen sink for easier drainage and cleanup.

1½ cups goat's cream
⅔ cup honey
1 quart whole goat's milk
4½ teaspoons pure vanilla extract

Make sure the cream and milk are well chilled.

Pour the cream into your blender. With the machine running, slowly pour in the honey. Transfer the mixture to the canister of your ice-cream machine. Add the milk and vanilla; mix well. Insert the dasher, secure the lid, and proceed according to the directions included with your machine. (See Note for tips on the ice-to-salt ratio.)

When the ice cream has thickened properly, you have two choices. You can serve it immediately if you like soft ice cream. Or you can let it harden (or ripen) for a more conventional texture. To properly ripen the ice cream, first carefully pour most of the salt water from the outside container by opening the drain hole. Keep one hand firmly on top of the canister lid to prevent any salt water from getting into the ice cream. Then remove the dasher from the machine, cap the container and cork the lid tightly. Add more salt and ice to the outside container (1 cup salt to 3 pounds ice). Insulate the whole container with towels, blankets or newspapers. Allow to harden for up to 4 hours.

Variations: You can add chopped nuts or fruit to the ice cream after it has thickened but before you ripen it.

If you don't have fresh goat's cream, you may substitute a 12½-ounce can of evaporated goat's milk. If you have access to a quantity of goat's milk, you can skim off the cream yourself. But be aware that goat's milk doesn't separate as readily as cow's milk does. The fat globules are much smaller and remain evenly distributed longer. So you will need to allow the milk to stand undisturbed in the refrigerator for several days before carefully pouring off the cream.

If you prefer a sweeter ice cream, you can add up to ¾ cup honey instead of ⅔ cup.

To make Fudge Ripple Ice Cream, first make the vanilla ice cream above. After it has thickened properly but before you ripen it, add Carob-Peanut Fudge Topping as follows: Remove the dasher from the canister. That will leave a hole in the middle of the ice cream. Pour in ¾ cup of the chilled sauce. Use a rubber spatula to gently marble the sauce through the ice cream. Do not overmix, or you'll end up with carob ice cream (unless, of course, you want carob ice cream).

NOTE: The ice-to-salt ratio used when making ice cream has a great influence on the quality of the finished product. If there is too much salt, the ice cream will freeze too rapidly and have a coarse, crystalline texture. If there's too little salt, the mixture will stay very soft. I've found that I can produce smooth, velvety ice cream by using 1 cup rock salt to every 6 pounds of crushed ice (1¼ cups table salt to 6 pounds of ice cubes also works perfectly).

I find that homemade ice cream is at its best after 3 hours of ripening. If you need to hold it for more than 4 hours, repack the canister with ice and salt, or place the whole canister in your freezer. If there are any leftovers, use them within 3 days or the texture will become crystalline.

Strawberry Goat's-Milk Ice Cream _____

Makes about 1 quart.

This ice cream requires evaporated goat's milk, which is a convenient alternative to fresh. You will find, however, that the flavor will be somewhat stronger than if you used fresh goat's milk. You won't need an ice-cream machine to make this treat; your blender will work just fine.

12½ ounces evaporated goat's milk
½ cup water
1 small banana, chilled
⅓ cup honey or maple syrup
1 tablespoon lime juice or ¼ teaspoon vitamin C crystals
1½ teaspoons pure vanilla extract
1 cup frozen strawberries

Submerge the unopened can of milk in hot, but not boiling, water for 5 minutes. Shake can well, then open, and pour contents into an ice-cube tray. If there is enough room, add the ½ cup water to the tray. If there is not enough room, either freeze the water separately or determine how many of your regular ice cubes will equal ½ cup. Freeze until solid.

Slice the banana, and place in a blender. Process until liquefied. With the machine running, add the honey or maple syrup, lime juice or vitamin C crystals and vanilla.

Remove the frozen milk and water from the tray. (You may have to place the tray up to its rim in hot water for about 1 minute to loosen the cubes.)

Add 2 of the cubes to the blender, and process until liquefied. Add remaining cubes, 2 or 3 at a time, until all are liquefied. Add strawberries, and process until pureed. Taste, and if necessary, add a bit more sweetener.

If you like soft ice cream, serve at once in chilled bowls. Otherwise, transfer to a small bowl, and freeze for an hour or two.

Variation: Omit the banana; replace with ½ cup chilled strawberries.

238

Goat's-Milk Peanut-Butter Fudge ―――――――――

Makes about 1 pound.

This blond fudge is rich but nourishing.

1 cup natural peanut
    butter, room
    temperature
¼ cup honey
½ cup powdered
    goat's milk
½ cup chopped
    walnuts
¼ cup sunflower seeds
2 tablespoons raisins
    (optional)

In a medium bowl, blend the peanut butter and honey with a wooden spoon. Stir in the powdered milk. The mixture will be very thick, but do not add any liquids. Work in the walnuts and sunflower seeds; use your hands, if necessary.

Press the mixture into a 7"-×-11" baking dish or onto a dinner plate. Scatter raisins over top, and press in firmly. Chill, then cut into squares or bars.

Variation: Replace some of the honey with molasses.

Dips and Spreads

At party time, people with food allergies like to nibble just as much as anybody else. But what they don't like is to get sick. What's needed are party snacks other than sour cream dips, cheese and wheat crackers. The appetizers, dips and spreads given here can help you serve foods that hosts and guests alike can enjoy. Avocado is probably the least allergenic base upon which to build, and you will find recipes for both Guacamole and Pesto Dip, as well as bean, soy and mushroom dishes. These Dips and Spreads are almost interchangeable, because by controlling the amount of liquid used you can usually make a Spread into a Dip, and vice versa.

Of course, you need something to daub spreads on or dip. You'll find Crackers in the Snacks section and Tortillas in Breads. Raw vegetables also fill the bill—try to include more than one member of a food family, such as carrots and celery, or cauliflower, broccoli, radishes, thin slices of kohlrabi and sticks of raw turnip. And don't hesitate to use thin slices of jicama and other crisp vegetables described in Table 2, Unusual Fruits and Vegetables, in the section, Exploring New Ingredients.

Hummus Bean Spread

Makes 2½ to 3 cups.

This traditional Middle Eastern food has been adopted by American cooks and makes a tasty alternative to cheese spreads for people with milk allergy. It's customarily served with pita bread, but you can improvise with Crackers or Tortillas cut into wedges.

2 cups cooked chick-peas
¼ cup bean Stock (see Index)
¼ cup lemon juice or 1 teaspoon vitamin C crystals
2 tablespoons tahini
2 small garlic cloves
1 tablespoon wheat-free tamari sauce (optional)
olive oil
chopped scallions or minced parsley (garnish)

Place the chick-peas, Stock, lemon juice or vitamin C crystals, tahini, garlic and tamari in a blender or food processor. Process until smooth. Taste, and adjust seasonings; add more tahini, if desired. If hummus is too thick, thin with a bit of Stock or lemon juice.

Transfer to a serving bowl. Brush top with oil. Garnish with scallions or parsley. Chill for several hours. Before serving, allow to warm to room temperature.

South-of-the-Border Sandwich Spread

Makes about 2½ cups.

Best if made a few hours ahead to allow flavors to blend fully.

2 cups cooked pinto or kidney beans
¼ cup tomato paste or honey-sweetened ketchup
¼ cup minced parsley
¼ cup minced celery leaves
¼ cup chopped onions
1 tablespoon wheat-free tamari sauce (optional)
2 teaspoons chili powder
⅛ teaspoon cayenne pepper

Mash the beans with a fork. Stir in the tomato paste or ketchup, parsley, celery, onions, tamari, chili powder and cayenne. Taste, and adjust seasonings.

Variation: To use as a dip, process ingredients in a blender or food processor until smooth. Gradually add 2 to 4 tablespoons water or bean-cooking liquid until a dip consistency is reached.

241

Guacamole

Makes 1½ to 2 cups.

Most guacamole recipes call for sour cream. This one doesn't need it. Serve as a dip, a topping for Mexican casseroles or on salad.

2 large or 3 small ripe
    avocados
¼ cup chopped onions
¼ cup chopped green
    peppers
2 tablespoons lemon
    juice or ¼–½
    teaspoon vitamin
    C crystals
1 tablespoon water
½ teaspoon chili
    powder
1 small garlic clove,
    chopped
1 medium tomato,
    chopped

Cut the avocados in half, remove the pits, then scoop the flesh into a blender or food processor. Add the onions, peppers, lemon juice or vitamin C crystals, water, chili powder and garlic. Process until smooth.

Transfer to a small bowl, and stir in the tomato. Cover and chill. Use within 2 or 3 days. (To prevent darkening, coat top with a thin layer of oil.)

Variation: To make a Chunky Guacamole, mash the avocados with a fork. Finely chop the onions and pepper. Stir all ingredients together in a bowl.

NOTE: For a dip, serve with Savory Crackers or thin Oriental rice crackers and raw vegetables.

To make individual salads, marinate tomato slices in Basil Vinaigrette for 1 hour. Arrange tomatoes on lettuce leaves, then top with Guacamole.

For a topping, drop generous spoonfuls of Guacamole on individual servings of Vegetarian Chili, Tostados Improvised or Mexican Supper. Surround with shredded lettuce and diced tomatoes; top with sliced or chopped black olives.

Pesto Dip

Makes 1 cup.

This is for pesto fans who can't have cheese. Serve it with raw vegetables, rice crackers or Tortillas cut into wedges.

1 large ripe avocado
1 cup basil leaves
1 tablespoon lemon
    juice or ¼
    teaspoon vitamin
    C crystals
1 garlic clove, minced

Cut the avocado in half and remove the pit. Scoop out the flesh, and place in the bowl of a food processor. Add the basil, lemon juice or vitamin C crystals, garlic and pine nuts. Process for about 2 minutes, stopping several times to scrape the sides of the container. Transfer to a small bowl, and coat the surface with the oil.

242

or ⅛ teaspoon
garlic powder
powder
¼ cup pine nuts
½ teaspoon olive oil

Chill. Use within 24 hours. A few more pine nuts can be scattered on top when served.

NOTES: You can make the Pesto Dip in a blender, but you will need to stop and scrape the sides of the container quite often.

Pesto Dip will discolor if left exposed to the air, so if you don't plan to use it immediately, coat the surface with a film of oil.

Curried Tofu Dip

Makes 1¾ cups.

Make this dip a few hours or a day ahead. Serve as a dip for raw vegetables or as a sauce for cooked broccoli, cauliflower or green beans.

1 pound tofu
¼ cup oil
3 tablespoons lemon
    juice or ½ ¾
    teaspoon vitamin
    C crystals
2 tablespoons
    prepared
    horseradish
1½ teaspoons curry
    powder
½ teaspoon wheat-
    free tamari sauce
½ teaspoon
    powdered ginger
½ teaspoon
    Hungarian
    paprika
½ teaspoon ground
    cumin (optional)
1 large garlic clove
    or ½ teaspoon
    garlic powder
¼ cup minced
    parsley
2 scallions, minced

Drain the tofu. Roll in a cotton towel and press between 2 boards for 30 minutes. Then crumble tofu with a fork. Add it to a blender or food processor along with the oil, lemon juice or vitamin C crystals, horseradish, curry powder, tamari, ginger, paprika, cumin and garlic or garlic powder. Process until smooth, about 2 minutes. Stop and scrape the sides of the container as necessary.

Transfer to a bowl, and stir in parsley and scallions. Refrigerate a few hours.

243

Soy Pâté and Sandwich Spread _____

Makes approximately 1¾ cups.

A meatless party pâté that doubles as a change-of-pace sandwich filling.

1 cup cooked
    soybeans,
    pureed
¼ cup honey-
    sweetened
    ketchup
2 tablespoons
    chopped onions
1 tablespoon tahini
    or ground
    sesame seeds
1 tablespoon lemon
    juice or ¼
    teaspoon
    vitamin C
    crystals
1 tablespoon Dijon-
    style mustard
1 teaspoon wheat-
    free tamari
    sauce
¼ cup chopped
    walnuts
2–4 tablespoons
    chopped black
    olives
¼ cup minced
    parsley or 2
    tablespoons
    snipped chives
1–2 tablespoons finely
    chopped pickles
    or honey-
    sweetened
    pickle relish
2 tablespoons
    ground walnuts
    or sesame seeds

In a medium bowl, combine soybeans, ketchup, onions, tahini or sesame seeds, lemon juice or vitamin C crystals, mustard and tamari. Mix well. Stir in chopped walnuts, olives, parsley or chives and pickles or relish.

Turn the spread out onto a plate, and shape it into a loaf. Press the ground walnuts or sesame seeds into the surface. Chill. Serve with thin rice crackers as a pâté or with lettuce, sprouts and tomato slices as a sandwich filling.

244

Mushroom Pâté

Makes 2¼ cups.

Serve with freshly baked Caraway-Rice Crackers or Oat Crackers.

2 tablespoons
toasted sesame
seeds
½ pound mushrooms
¼ cup minced
parsley
2 tablespoons oil
1½ teaspoons wheat-
free tamari
sauce, kombu
powder or
Savory Seed
Seasoning (see
Index)
½ teaspoon onion
powder
¼ teaspoon garlic
powder
¼ teaspoon vitamin C
crystals
Hungarian paprika
(garnish;
optional)

Grind the seeds in a blender or nut grinder. Transfer to a large bowl.

Halve or quarter the mushrooms. Place half of them in a food processor. Process with several on/off turns to finely chop them; do not puree. Transfer them to the bowl with the seeds.

Place the remaining mushrooms in the food processor. Add the parsley, oil and tamari, kombu or Savory Seed Seasoning with the onion powder, garlic powder and vitamin C crystals. Process with several on/off turns until mushrooms are finely chopped but not pureed. Add to bowl with other mushrooms.

Use a fork to mix ingredients well. Transfer to a small decorative bowl and pat top into round dome shape. Garnish with paprika. Chill until serving time.

Variation: Replace the sesame seeds with sunflower seeds plus ½ teaspoon Oriental sesame oil. Grind the seeds as above. Add the oil to the food processor with the other oil.

NOTE: You can also make this pâté by finely chopping the mushrooms by hand and mixing all ingredients in a bowl.

Or you can use a blender, but be very careful not to process the mushrooms into a puree. Chop half the mushrooms by hand, and transfer to a bowl. Add the remaining mushrooms and seasoning ingredients to blender, and chop with several on/off turns.

245

Eggplant Appetizer

Makes 2½ cups.

Known as *baba ghannouj* in the Middle East. Mix it a few hours (or 1 day) in advance so flavors can meld. Serve with rice crackers or Tortillas cut into wedges.

1 medium eggplant
  (about 1¼
  pounds)
2–3 tablespoons lemon
  juice or ½–¾
  teaspoon
  vitamin C
  crystals
1–2 tablespoons tahini
1 tablespoon Savory
  Seed Seasoning
  (see Index)
1 tablespoon olive
  oil
1 garlic clove,
  minced
1 teaspoon honey
  (optional)
  snipped chives
  (garnish)

Pierce the eggplant in several places with a fork. Bake it (whole) at 350° for 45 minutes, or until tender when pierced with a fork. Cut in half and allow to cool.

Place 2 tablespoons lemon juice or ½ teaspoon vitamin C crystals, 1 tablespoon tahini, Savory Seed Seasoning, oil and garlic in a blender or food processor. Scoop out the flesh from the eggplant halves, and add it to the machine. Process until mixture is pureed.

Taste, and add more lemon juice or vitamin C crystals or tahini, if needed. If too tart, add the honey.

Spoon into a serving dish. Garnish with chives. Chill for several hours. Serve at room temperature.

Tofu Salad

Serves 4.

Much like egg salad, this is a nice luncheon dish, especially if served with Oriental rice crackers.

1 pound tofu
¼ cup chopped celery
4 scallions, minced
1 tablespoon oil
1 tablespoon wheat-
  free tamari sauce
2 teaspoons tahini
2 teaspoons lemon
  juice or a scant ¼
  teaspoon vitamin

Drain the tofu for 20 to 30 minutes, and press it between cotton towels to remove as much moisture as possible. Cut into small cubes, about ¼″ in size. Combine with celery and scallions in a mixing bowl.

In a small bowl, whisk together the oil, tamari, tahini, lemon juice or vitamin C crystals and honey. Pour over the tofu, and mix gently. Chill 1 hour or more before serving.

C crystals
1 teaspoon honey

Variation: For another citrus-free version, replace the lemon juice and honey with 2 tablespoons honey-sweetened pickle relish, available at health food stores.

Pineapple Preserves _____

Makes 2 cups.

Here's fresh fruit sweetened with juice concentrate. You can't get much simpler than that. Use as you would jam.

3 cups fresh pineapple
    chunks
6 ounces unsweetened
    pineapple-juice
    concentrate

Combine the pineapple and juice concentrate in a saucepan. Simmer over low heat for 1 hour.

Transfer to a food processor, and give it three short on/off turns. Do not puree; mixture will be chunky. Return to the saucepan, and simmer another 15 minutes, or until thick enough to suit you. Pour into a glass jar, and store in the refrigerator.

NOTE: If you don't have a food processor, you may use a blender. But be careful not to reduce the sauce to a puree. If you'd like, puree half of the mixture, and chop the rest by hand.

Pumpkin Butter

Makes 1 pint.

A fragrant, spicy topping for Pancakes, Flatbread or Muffins.

2 cups pumpkin
    puree
⅓ cup honey
¼ cup water
1 teaspoon ground
    cinnamon
½ teaspoon grated
    nutmeg
½ teaspoon powdered
    ginger
⅛ teaspoon ground
    cloves

Combine the pumpkin, honey, water, cinnamon, nutmeg, ginger and cloves in a saucepan. Either simmer for half an hour over very low heat or bake in a moderate oven, uncovered, for an hour or more. Stir often. When thick, pour into a sterilized pint jar. Cover and refrigerate. Use within 1 month.

NOTE: To make a large quantity, quadruple the recipe, and use the oven method. Use a Dutch oven and fill it no more than half full. When thick, spoon butter into 4 sterilized pint jars. Cover and refrigerate. Use within 1 month. Or pack into sterile jars and process in hot-water bath for 30 minutes and store at room temperature.

If you can't have any of the suggested spices, experiment with others. Pumpkin butter needs spices for seasoning.

Pear Honey

Makes 3 pints.

This excellent technique for preserving pears dates from colonial days. The short cooking time preserves the delicate flavor of fresh juicy pears much better than the standard fruit-butter recipes. I like to serve this puree the way my grandmother did—with hot biscuits to sop up the tasty juices.

15 juicy pears
½ cup water
½ cup honey

Peel, quarter and core the pears. Place 12 of the pears in a stainless-steel or enamel Dutch oven or 3-quart saucepan.

Coarsely chop the remaining 3 pears. Place them and the water in a blender. Process until pureed. Pour into the pan with the pear quarters.

Bring to a boil, then reduce the heat to a simmer. Stir in the honey. Cook until pears are tender, about 30 minutes.

Puree the cooked fruit in batches using a blender, food processor or food mill. The puree should be about the consistency of honey. If it is too thin, return it to the pan and boil it down a bit. If it is too thick, dilute with a little juice or water.

Pour into jars, and store in the refrigerator for up to 1 month. For longer storage, freeze the puree or pack it into sterile jars and process in a hot-water bath for 30 minutes and store at room temperature.

Simple-Simon Jam

Makes 2 cups.

This jam is so easy, and the variations are almost endless. See Variations for some especially good combinations. To serve as a pancake topping, just dilute with juice or water to the proper consistency and heat.

1 cup coarsely chopped dried fruit
1 cup unsweetened fruit juice, fruit puree or water

Combine the dried fruit with the fruit juice, puree or water in a saucepan. Boil for 5 minutes, then transfer to the blender. Blend briefly into a chunky sauce. Then return to saucepan and simmer another 5 minutes. Serve warm or cold. The mixture will firm up when chilled.

Variations: Use figs plus pineapple juice or blended crushed pineapple; raisins plus grape juice; dried apples plus apple juice and a few drops of lemon juice; dried peaches and peach puree; prunes plus prune juice; dried pineapple plus pineapple juice or strawberry puree; apricots plus apple juice, apricot puree or water; dates plus water and a few drops of lemon juice or a pinch of vitamin C crystals.

Peanut-Butter Spread

Makes 1¼ cups.

A great alternative to peanut butter and jelly. Spread on warm Flatbread or use in lunchbox sandwiches.

½ cup natural peanut butter
½ cup Real Applesauce (see Index)
sunflower seeds
¼ cup raisins

In a small bowl, blend the peanut butter and Applesauce with a fork. Stir in the sunflower seeds and raisins. Store in the refrigerator.

Old-Fashioned Fruit Butter

Makes about 1½ pints.

A less-allergenic alternative to jams and jellies. By making fruit butter yourself, you control the ingredients. It makes great gifts, too. Use any fruits you like, such as apples, pears, peaches or plums. Combine any members of the Plum family, or mix apples and pineapple, or try berries and apples or pineapple. The choices are endless.

12–14 cups chopped fruit
water, unsweetened juice or cider
¼ cup honey

Place the fruit in a large pot (don't fill it more than three-quarters full). Add enough water, juice or cider to just come up to the level of the fruit. Stir in honey. Bake at 275° to 300° until fruit is mushy. Do not let liquid boil.

Puree the fruit in a blender or food processor 2 cups at a time. Taste, and if necessary, add a bit more honey. Return to pot. Bake again, stirring every 30 minutes, until very thick. Test by dropping a spoonful onto a plate. It should remain in a mound and not give off any liquid.

Ladle into sterile canning jars. Seal tightly, place in a large pot, and add enough water to cover the lids by an inch. Boil for 30 minutes. Cool, label jars with ingredients, and store at room temperature.

Variation: To make Apple Butter, add 2 to 3 teaspoons ground cinnamon, ½ teaspoon ground cloves, ¼ teaspoon ground allspice and 2 to 4 tablespoons lemon juice to basic mixture.

NOTE: If you plan to use the fruit butter within a month, omit the hot-water bath. Refrigerate fruit butter as soon as it cools.

An alternate method of making fruit butter is to use a slow cooker. Place fruit and liquid in the pot. Let simmer for 2 hours. Puree the fruit, then return to the cooker. Cook, uncovered, for several hours, until thick. Stir occasionally.

Nut or Seed Butter

Makes 2 cups.

Nut or seed butter is the perfect answer for people who are allergic to peanuts. Choose any nut or seed that suits your diet. Toasted nuts and seeds taste mellower than raw and make richer-flavored spreads, but raw ones retain more nutrients. You decide.

2 cups nuts or seeds
2–4 tablespoons oil

In a blender or food processor, grind ½ cup of nuts or seeds at a time until of desired consistency. If you prefer a chunky butter, do not grind to a fine powder.

When all nuts or seeds are ground, place them back in the blender or food processor. With machine running, slowly add enough oil to produce a clumping action. Process on high until all nuts or seeds are moistened. Stop to scrape the sides of the container as necessary.

Store in the refrigerator.

Variation: Replace the oil with boiling water. Use only as much as absolutely necessary.

NOTE: You can toast your own nuts and seeds. Spread thinly on a cookie sheet or jelly-roll pan. Bake at 250°, stirring occasionally. Allow 20 to 25 minutes for sunflower seeds; 30 minutes for pecans or walnuts; 40 minutes for cashews, almonds or filberts.

Snacks

The great American pastime of snacking is not all bad. Some doctors now say that small amounts of food several times a day may be better for us than three square meals anyway—assuming that we select health-promoting foods and don't overeat.

There are so many possibilities for great snack foods—savory as well as sweet—that there is no reason for allergic people to feel deprived. To satisfy a sweet tooth, you will find Coconut-Date Confection, Stuffed Dates, and 12 kinds of cookies, among others. For an unusual treat, try the slightly sweet Fruit-Gel Cutouts.

Crunchy snacks include Fennel Pretzels, Chili Seeds, Savory Nut Mix and four kinds of Crackers.

You can serve some snacks, such as Almond-Rice Crispy Crunch, at breakfast. Wholesome snacks come in handy if you have children who turn up their noses at breakfast food—or skip breakfast out of lack of interest.

If you don't always have time to bake but need something to munch on, see the Appendix for names of companies that sell less allergenic snack foods.

Savory Crackers _____

Makes 3 to 4 dozen.

At last, crackers without wheat! Use for Dips and Spreads, or enjoy them plain.

¾ cup amaranth flour
½ cup arrowroot
¼ cup ground nuts, seeds or peanuts
½ teaspoon baking soda
1 teaspoon cream of tartar or ¼ teaspoon vitamin C crystals
½ teaspoon caraway seeds
¼ teaspoon onion powder
3 tablespoons oil
3 tablespoons water
4 teaspoons sesame seeds

In a large bowl, combine the flour, arrowroot, nuts, seeds or peanuts, baking soda, cream of tartar or vitamin C crystals, caraway seeds and onion powder.

Mix the oil and water in a cup. Add to the flour mixture. Stir briefly, until you can press the dough into a ball. If the dough is too dry and crumbly, add more water, 1 teaspoon at a time, until ball holds together nicely.

Scatter half of the sesame seeds directly on a cookie sheet. Divide the dough in half. Wrap half in wax paper and set aside. Roll the other half of the dough directly on the cookie sheet, onto the seeds. Roll until quite thin, ⅛″ to ¼″. Cut into 1½″ squares or triangles right on the cookie sheet and prick with a fork; do not remove crackers from sheet.

Bake at 350° for 12 to 15 minutes. Remove the crackers carefully from the sheet, and separate them. Place crackers on wire racks, then place the racks on cookie sheets. Return to oven for 5 to 7 minutes. Cool directly on the wire racks. Crackers will crisp as they cool.

Repeat with remaining sesame seeds and dough.

Store crackers in an airtight container. Handle carefully because crackers are very crisp.

Variations: Use one or more of the following in place of or in addition to the caraway seeds and onion powder: 1 teaspoon dried oregano, 1 teaspoon dried basil, ½ teaspoon dried tarragon, ½ teaspoon chili powder, ⅛ teaspoon garlic powder.

Sesame Wonders

Makes 2 to 3 dozen.

These tasty morsels are a lot like graham crackers. Eat them plain or spread with Old-Fashioned Fruit Butter.

½ cup amaranth flour
¼ cup chick-pea flour
¼ cup arrowroot
1 tablespoon sesame
   seeds
½ teaspoon baking
   soda
⅛ teaspoon vitamin C
   crystals
3 tablespoons water
2 tablespoons oil
   sesame seeds

In a large bowl, mix the amaranth flour, chick-pea flour, arrowroot, 1 tablespoon sesame seeds, baking soda and vitamin C crystals.

Mix the water and oil in a cup. Stir into the flour mixture with a fork until dough forms a ball. If necessary, add a bit more water.

Place dough on a lightly floured board, and pat into a rectangle.

Sprinkle sesame seeds on a cookie sheet. Transfer dough to the sheet, and sprinkle top with more sesame seeds. Roll into a thin rectangle or square on the cookie sheet. Cut into 1½″ to 2″ squares or triangles. Prick crackers all over with a fork.

Bake at 350° for 10 minutes, until crisp and lightly brown. Test a cracker in the middle of the sheet for crispness. If the outer ones are done, but the center ones aren't, remove the outer ones, and return others to the oven for 2 more minutes or so. Cool crackers on wire racks. Store in an airtight container, and use within 1 week.

Variations: Replace the chick-pea flour with soy powder or finely ground roasted peanuts.

Chili Seeds

Makes 2¼ cups.

If you love Mexican food, you'll savor this snack. It's great for parties, Halloween treats and trail food.

1 cup raw sunflower
   seeds
1 cup raw pumpkin
   seeds
¼ cup sesame seeds
1 tablespoon
   sunflower oil or
   light sesame oil
1 tablespoon chili

In a large bowl, mix the sunflower seeds, pumpkin seeds, sesame seeds, sunflower oil or sesame oil, chili powder, garlic powder and cayenne.

Spread out in a jelly-roll pan. Bake at 300° for 20 minutes, stirring every 5 minutes, until seeds are lightly brown and toasty. Cool, then store in an airtight container.

powder
⅛ teaspoon garlic
   powder
⅛ teaspoon cayenne
   pepper

Variations: Use ½ teaspoon Oriental sesame oil and 2½ teaspoons sunflower oil. For spicier seeds, add an additional ⅛ teaspoon cayenne pepper to the mix.

Caraway-Rice Crackers

Makes 3 to 5 dozen.

These crackers are delicate, thin and very crisp.

1 cup brown rice
   flour
¼ cup chick-pea flour
1½ teaspoons kombu
   powder
⅛ teaspoon vitamin C
   crystals
1 teaspoon caraway
   seeds
3 tablespoons oil
3 tablespoons warm
   water
1½ teaspoons honey or
   molasses
½ teaspoon baking
   soda

In a medium bowl, mix the rice flour, chick-pea flour, kombu and vitamin C crystals. Take ¼ cup of the mixture and transfer to a blender. Add the caraway seeds, and blend on high speed for 5 minutes. Return to the flour bowl, and mix well.

In a cup, mix the oil, water and honey or molasses. Stir in the baking soda.

Make a well in the flour, and pour in the liquid mixture. Stir with a fork, mixing until dough forms a ball. If necessary, add a bit more water.

Turn the dough out onto a lightly floured bread board or work surface. Pat dough with flour until it is no longer sticky. Transfer to a floured cookie sheet. Roll dough with a rolling pin into a very thin square or rectangle. Cut with a knife into 1½" to 2" squares, then cut each square in half to form triangles.

Bake at 350° for 12 to 15 minutes, until crisp and barely brown.

Variations: Replace the chick-pea flour with soy grits, soy powder, ground peanuts or amaranth flour. Replace the kombu with 1½ teaspoons wheat-free tamari sauce; add to the liquids.

Oat Crackers _____

Makes 16.

    This is my version of traditional Scottish flatbreads served at after-noon teas. They're light, delicate and quite simple to make. Good with soup or Simple-Simon Jam.

1 cup oat flour
2 tablespoons soy grits, amaranth flour or rolled oats
1 tablespoon kombu powder (optional)
⅛ teaspoon vitamin C crystals
2 tablespoons oil
4–5 tablespoons hot water
½ teaspoon baking soda
1 cup rolled oats

In a medium bowl, combine the oat flour, soy grits, amaranth flour or oats, kombu and vitamin C crystals. Make a well in the center, and pour in oil. Mix 4 tablespoons water and baking soda; pour into well with the oil. Stir with a fork until mixture holds together and forms a ball. If necessary, add a bit more water. Divide dough into 2 balls.

Scatter ½ cup rolled oats on a bread board or work surface. Scatter ¼ cup rolled oats on each of 2 cookie sheets.

Place 1 ball of dough on the work surface, and roll in the oats to cover it well. Transfer to 1 cookie sheet, and roll with a rolling pin into a thin circle about 10″ in diameter. Cut into 8 wedges. Separate the wedges slightly.

Repeat with remaining dough, using second cookie sheet.

Bake at 350° for 15 to 18 minutes, until crisp. Best served warm.

NOTE: Using soy grits or amaranth flour will increase the amount of protein in the crackers; using rolled oats will limit the number of food families involved.

Rice "Popcorn" Balls _____

Makes 6 to 12 balls.

    A fun-to-make snack for Halloween, birthday parties or snow days when the kids need something to do—and eat.

¼ cup honey
¼ cup molasses
6 cups crisp brown rice cereal (see Note)
½ cup roasted peanuts (optional)

Combine the honey and molasses in a 3-quart saucepan. Simmer over low heat for 10 minutes. Remove from the heat, and stir in cereal and peanuts. Stir well to coat cereal with sweeteners. Turn the mixture into a jelly-roll pan, spreading it evenly, and allow to cool a few minutes until you can handle it.

Shape into balls, pressing them firmly to hold mixture together. Place on wax paper or an oiled platter. Work quickly so you can form all the balls before the mixture hardens.

Wrap finished balls in cellophane or wax paper.

NOTE: Be sure to use a crisp, popped rice cereal, not a soft, puffed one. Crisp brown rice cereal is distributed by Erewhon (see Appendix) and is available in many health food stores.

Carrot Cookies

Makes about 30.

Delicious cookies, high in vitamin A.

¼ cup honey
3 tablespoons oil
3 tablespoons water or unsweetened juice
1 teaspoon pure vanilla extract
1 cup amaranth flour
⅓ cup arrowroot
1 teaspoon cream of tartar or ⅛ teaspoon vitamin C crystals
½ teaspoon baking soda
½ teaspoon ground cinnamon
¾ cup grated carrots
⅓ cup raisins

Combine the honey, oil and water or juice in a medium saucepan. Heat briefly to melt honey. Remove from heat, and stir in vanilla.

Sift together the flour, arrowroot, cream of tartar or vitamin C crystals, baking soda and cinnamon. Stir into liquid mixture. Stir in carrots and raisins.

Drop rounded teaspoonfuls of batter onto cookie sheets. Bake at 325° for 15 to 18 minutes, until cookies are lightly brown. Cool on wire racks. Store in paper bag. Use within a few days.

Fennel Pretzels _____

Makes 24.

Take these to Saturday afternoon football games or other sporting events. When freshly baked, they're crisp and crunchy. Within hours, they become more soft and chewy—which is how many Easterners like their pretzels anyway. (Allow ample time to make these—an evening or afternoon.)

¾ cup warm water
1 tablespoon dry yeast
1 tablespoon honey
½ cup white buckwheat flour (see Note)
2 tablespoons olive oil
1 tablespoon prepared horseradish
1½ teaspoons warm water
¼ teaspoon baking soda
¾ cup white buckwheat flour (see Note)
1 teaspoon guar gum (see Appendix)
1 tablespoon kombu powder (optional)
¾ teaspoon fennel seeds
¾ teaspoon anise seeds

In a large mixing bowl, combine ¾ cup water, yeast and honey. Let stand 10 to 15 minutes, until foamy. Stir in ½ cup flour. Beat hard with a wooden spoon or whisk for 2 to 3 minutes. Cover with a damp towel, and set in a draft-free place for a few hours or overnight. (Do not place near a pilot light or other warm place; yeast should work slowly.)

Later, stir down the batter. Mix the oil, horseradish, 1½ teaspoons water and baking soda in a cup. Add to the yeast mixture. Stir briefly.

In another bowl, mix the ¾ cup flour, guar gum, kombu, fennel and anise. Stir half of this mixture into the yeast mixture. Beat with electric beaters for 3 minutes, or beat by hand for 5 minutes. Add remaining flour mixture, and mix well.

Cover the bowl with a damp towel. Place in a warm, draft-free spot for 30 to 60 minutes. (Or leave at room temperature for 2 to 3 hours.)

Half fill a Dutch oven with water, and bring to a boil.

Punch down the dough, and divide it in half. Wrap 1 piece in a damp cotton towel to keep it from drying out, and set aside. Place the other piece of dough on a floured surface. Turn to coat all sides with flour. Divide into 12 pieces, then roll each piece into a thin pencil shape. Form each piece into a circle-shape pretzel, pressing the ends together firmly. Repeat until you have 12 pretzels.

Using a metal spatula, transfer 2 or 3 pretzels to the boiling water. When they rise to the surface, use the spatula to transfer them to a cotton towel to drain. Repeat until all 12 pretzels have gone through the water bath.

Arrange the pretzels on non-stick cookie sheets. Bake at 400° for 12 minutes. Flip them over, and bake another 5 to 7 minutes. Cool on wire racks or a dry cotton towel.

Repeat whole procedure with remaining ball of dough.

Store in an airtight tin. If desired, reheat briefly before serving to recrisp the pretzels.

Variations: If desired, form into traditional twist-pretzel shape. Or use this procedure for pretzel sticks: Divide dough into 4 pieces. Form each piece into a log about 8" long. Flatten with a rolling pin into a rectangle that's about 3" to 4" wide. Use a sharp knife to cut long strips about ⅜" wide. Drop 6 at a time into the boiling water.

You can replace the buckwheat flour with an equal amount of amaranth flour plus 2 tablespoons arrowroot. This dough will be a little more fragile than the buckwheat and is best shaped into circles or sticks.

NOTE: For directions on making white buckwheat flour, see Table 1, Cooking and Baking with Alternative Flours, in the section, Exploring New Ingredients.

Cookies on Parade ────────────────

Makes about 24.

A very basic cookie that is totally grain free.

¼ cup honey
3 tablespoons oil
3 tablespoons water or juice
1 teaspoon pure vanilla extract
1 cup amaranth flour
⅓ cup arrowroot
1 teaspoon cream of tartar or ⅛ teaspoon vitamin C crystals
½ teaspoon baking soda

Combine the honey, oil and water or juice in a medium saucepan. Heat briefly to melt honey. Remove from heat, and stir in vanilla.

Sift together the flour, arrowroot, cream of tartar or vitamin C crystals and baking soda. Stir into liquid mixture.

Drop rounded teaspoonfuls of batter onto cookie sheets. Bake at 325° for 15 to 18 minutes, until cookies are lightly brown. Cool on wire racks. Store in paper bag. Use within a few days.

Dream Cookies _____

Makes 20 to 24.

If you rotate your foods, you'll really find these simple, versatile cookies to be a dream. You can use any kind of nuts and sweetener you wish.

1 cup ground nuts
¼ cup maple syrup or honey
1 teaspoon pure vanilla extract (optional)
¼ teaspoon grated nutmeg (optional)

Mix the nuts with the maple syrup or honey, vanilla and nutmeg in a bowl or food processor.

Drop rounded half-teaspoonfuls of batter onto a cookie sheet lined with foil, shiny side up. Allow space between cookies for them to spread. Bake at 300° for 12 to 20 minutes, depending upon nuts and sweetener used. Watch carefully to prevent burning. Slip sheets of foil onto wire racks to allow cookies to cool completely. To remove, peel foil from cookies.

Variations: If using almonds, use pure almond extract. Use any spice or combination of spices you like.

For Lace Cookies, add ¼ cup water to the basic batter. Allow baked cookies to stand on the cookie sheet a minute or so before removing to wire racks to cool. Makes 24 to 36.

NOTE: If you're grinding the nuts in the food processor, add remaining ingredients to bowl after nuts are ground.

Date Doodles _____

Makes about 30.

Sweet treats that are free of wheat and eggs.

¼ cup honey
3 tablespoons oil
3 tablespoons water or unsweetened juice
1 teaspoon pure vanilla extract
½ teaspoon grated orange or lemon rind (optional)

Combine the honey, oil and water or juice in a medium saucepan. Heat briefly to melt honey. Remove from heat, and stir in vanilla and orange or lemon rind.

Sift together the flour, arrowroot, cream of tartar or vitamin C crystals, baking soda and cinnamon. Stir into liquid mixture. Stir in dates and nuts or seeds.

Drop rounded teaspoonfuls of batter onto cookie sheets. Bake at 325° for 15 to 18 minutes,

1 cup amaranth flour
⅓ cup arrowroot
1 teaspoon cream of
tartar or ⅛
teaspoon vitamin
C crystals
½ teaspoon baking
soda
½ teaspoon ground
cinnamon
½ cup chopped dates
⅓ cup chopped nuts
or 2 tablespoons
seeds

until cookies are lightly brown. Cool on wire racks. Store in paper bag. Use within a few days.

Savory Nut Mix

Makes 1 pound.

A perfect party nibble, golden brown and savory.

¼ cup wheat-free
tamari sauce
¼ cup water
pinch of cayenne
pepper
(optional)
1½ cups peanuts
1 cup almonds
¾ cup sunflower
seeds

Combine the tamari, water and cayenne in a large bowl. Add the peanuts, almonds and sunflower seeds. Toss to coat.

Turn mixture into a colander to drain off excess liquid. Then transfer the mixture to a cookie sheet or jelly-roll pan. Spread evenly. Bake at 325° for 20 to 25 minutes, stirring every 10 minutes, until nuts become brown and fragrant. Watch carefully after 20 minutes to make sure nuts don't burn. Cool, then store in a decorative tin until party time.

Spicy Ginger Gems

Makes about 24.

The wheat-free answer to ginger snaps.

¼ cup honey
3 tablespoons oil
3 tablespoons water or unsweetened juice
1 cup amaranth flour
⅓ cup arrowroot
1 teaspoon cream of tartar or ⅛ teaspoon vitamin C crystals
½ teaspoon powdered ginger
½ teaspoon ground cinnamon
½ teaspoon baking soda
¼ teaspoon ground allspice or ⅛ teaspoon ground cloves

Combine the honey, oil and water or juice in a medium saucepan. Heat briefly to melt honey. Remove from heat, and set aside.

Sift together the flour, arrowroot, cream of tartar or vitamin C crystals, ginger, cinnamon, baking soda and allspice or cloves. Stir into liquid mixture.

Drop rounded teaspoonfuls of batter onto cookie sheets. Bake at 325° for 15 to 18 minutes, until cookies are lightly brown. Cool on wire racks. Store in paper bag. Use within a few days.

Spicy Fruit Drops

Makes about 60.

Cookies that are moist, chewy and spicy. Follow the basic recipe, or customize it to your own taste with any of the variations below. If you can't use all the spices suggested, choose one.

1 cup chopped dates
1 cup raisins
1 cup boiling water
¼ cup unsweetened fruit juice (apple, grape, orange, pineapple or prune)
⅓ cup oil
2 tablespoons ground cinnamon

Place the dates and raisins in a 1-quart saucepan. Cover with water, then boil 1 minute. Set aside to cool to room temperature, then add the juice, oil, cinnamon, orange or lemon rind or vitamin C crystals, ginger and cloves. Stir for 1 minute.

In a large mixing bowl, combine the flour, arrowroot, baking soda, ground nuts and chopped nuts. Stir in the fruit mixture, and combine well. The dough will be stiff.

Drop rounded teaspoonfuls of dough onto

1 tablespoon grated
  orange or lemon
  rind or ¼
  teaspoon vitamin
  C crystals
½ teaspoon powdered
  ginger
¼ teaspoon ground
  cloves
1 cup amaranth flour
½ cup arrowroot
1 teaspoon baking
  soda
½ cup ground nuts
½ cup chopped nuts

ungreased cookie sheets. Bake at 350° for 13 to 15 minutes. Cool on wire racks.

Variations: Replace the dates and raisins with 1 cup chopped dried apricots and 1 cup chopped prunes. Or mix them up.
  Replace the amaranth flour and arrowroot with one of the following: 1 cup soy powder and ½ cup arrowroot; 1¼ cups brown rice flour; 1½ cups oat flour; ⅔ cup rice flour and ¾ cup oat flour.
  Replace the nuts with ½ cup whole sunflower seeds and ½ cup ground sunflower seeds.

NOTE: People on a Diversified Rotary Diet can coordinate the oil used with the nuts or seeds used. For example, use walnut oil with walnuts, sunflower oil with sunflower seeds, peanut oil with peanuts and so on.

Fudgies

Makes about 24.

Children love these cookies. And they never miss the chocolate.

¼ cup honey
3 tablespoons oil
3 tablespoons water
  or unsweetened
  juice
1 teaspoon pure
  vanilla extract
1 cup amaranth flour
⅓ cup carob powder
1 teaspoon cream of
  tartar or ⅛
  teaspoon vitamin
  C crystals
½ teaspoon baking
  soda
⅓ cup chopped nuts
  (optional)

Combine the honey, oil and water or juice in a medium saucepan. Heat briefly to melt honey. Remove from heat, and stir in vanilla.
  Sift together the flour, carob, cream of tartar or vitamin C crystals and baking soda. Stir into liquid mixture. Stir in the nuts.
  Drop rounded teaspoonfuls of batter onto cookie sheets. Bake at 325° for 15 to 18 minutes. Cool on wire racks. Store in paper bag. Use within a few days.

Variation: Omit nuts from batter. Press half a nut into the top of each cookie before baking.

Miracle Macaroons

Makes about 60.

Start these the night before you want to bake them.

3 cups rolled oats
1 cup date sugar
¾ cup oil
½ cup molasses
½ cup amaranth flour
2 eggs, lightly beaten
1⅛ teaspoons pure almond extract

Mix the oats and date sugar in a large bowl.

Combine the oil and molasses in a small saucepan. Heat gently, stirring, for 2 or 3 minutes. Pour over the oat mixture, and stir to mix. Cover, and let stand at room temperature for at least 6 hours (or overnight).

Mix in the flour, eggs and almond extract. Drop rounded teaspoonfuls of batter onto ungreased cookie sheets. Bake at 350° for 15 minutes, until cookies are nicely brown. Cookies will be crisp on the outside and soft inside. Store loosely covered or in a paper bag (if stored in an airtight container, they soften).

Variation: For a milder flavor, use half molasses and half honey.

Chinese Almond Cookies

Makes 50.

Delicate cakelike cookies that contain no wheat, butter, sugar or milk.

1½ cups sifted brown rice flour
¼ cup sifted arrowroot
1 teaspoon cream of tartar or ¼ teaspoon vitamin C crystals
½ teaspoon baking soda
1 egg
½ cup honey
½ cup oil
1 teaspoon pure almond extract
50 whole almonds

Sift the flour, arrowroot, cream of tartar or vitamin C crystals and baking soda into a medium bowl.

Beat the egg in a large bowl with an electric mixer for 1 minute. Beat in the honey in a thin stream. Beat in the oil the same way. Add the almond extract.

Add about half the flour mixture to the bowl, and beat in on low speed until thoroughly incorporated. Add the remaining flour, and mix in on low speed until well blended. Chill dough for 1 hour.

Drop rounded teaspoonfuls of the dough onto lightly oiled cookie sheets. Allow at least 1 inch between cookies for them to spread during baking. Press an almond into the center of each cookie.

Bake at 350° for 8 to 10 minutes, until golden. Let stand 1 or 2 minutes on the cookie sheets before removing cookies to wire racks to cool.

Peanutty Cookies

Makes 30 to 36.

Chewy cookies that taste great—without wheat flour, sugar or butter. Use either a food processor or a blender to grind your own "flour." (For details, see Table 1, Cooking and Baking with Alternative Flours, in the section, Exploring New Ingredients.)

1½ cups ground peanuts
⅔ cup arrowroot
½ cup natural peanut butter
½ cup honey
¼ cup peanut oil
1 egg
finely chopped peanuts

In a large bowl, combine the ground peanuts and arrowroot. Set aside.

In a food processor or blender, combine the peanut butter, honey, oil and egg. Process 30 seconds, stopping once to scrape the sides of the container. Pour into bowl with ground-peanuts mixture. Mix well. Chill 1 hour or overnight.

Pinch off walnut-size pieces of dough, and roll between your palms into balls. Roll in chopped peanuts to coat. Place about 2" apart on oiled cookie sheets. Press each ball lightly with a fork to flatten and emboss with a characteristic peanut-cookie pattern. Bake at 325° for 18 to 20 minutes, until lightly brown. Cool on wire racks. Store in airtight containers.

Variations: For egg-free cookies, replace the egg with a 1"-×-1"-×-2" piece of tofu that has been well drained.

To make Peanut Thumbprint Cookies, form dough into walnut-size pieces. Place on cookie sheets, and press with your thumb to flatten slightly and make an indentation in each. Spoon a bit of jam or fruit butter into depression before baking.

To make Cutout Cookies, divide chilled dough in half. Roll each piece into a ¼" thick rectangle on an arrowroot-sprinkled work surface. Cut into desired shapes with cookie cutters. If desired, decorate with raisins. Bake at 350° for 12 minutes.

Got-It-All Cookies

Makes 30 to 40.

Got what? Fiber, protein, complex carbohydrates, vitamins and minerals, plus good taste. These treats are a powerhouse of nutrients—anywhere, any time.

1¼ cups rolled oats
⅔ cup rice bran
½ cup raisins
⅓ cup soy flour or amaranth flour
¼ cup sesame seeds
1 tablespoon granular lecithin (optional)
1 teaspoon ground cinnamon
⅓ cup water
1 tablespoon whole flaxseed
½ cup honey
½ cup sunflower oil
2 teaspoons pure vanilla extract

Mix the oats, bran, raisins, flour, sesame seeds, lecithin and cinnamon in a large bowl. Set aside.

In a small saucepan, combine the water and flaxseed. Simmer for 5 minutes, or until thickened to the consistency of unbeaten egg whites. Remove from the heat, and stir in the honey, oil and vanilla.

Pour the liquid mixture into the oats bowl. Stir well to combine. Allow to stand a few minutes.

Drop by rounded teaspoonfuls onto ungreased cookie sheets. Bake at 350° for 10 to 12 minutes, until light brown. Cool on the sheets for 2 or 3 minutes before removing to wire racks. The cookies will crisp as they cool. Store in a paper bag, not in an airtight container.

NOTE: You can freeze these cookies. Their texture will become more chewy.

No-Bake Cookies

Makes 30.

Children will love to help roll these cookies.

6 ounces unsweetened pineapple-juice concentrate
2 tablespoons honey
2¾ cups crumbs (see Note)
1 cup ground nuts
½ cup date sugar
30 dates
finely grated unsweetened coconut

Boil the juice concentrate and honey in a 2-quart saucepan for 5 minutes. Remove from the heat. Stir in the crumbs, nuts and date sugar.

Wrap a rounded teaspoonful of the mixture around each date, shaping the cookie into an oval. Roll in coconut. Chill a few hours or overnight.

NOTE: Grind a batch of Amaranth Pancakes, Rice-Flour Pancakes, day-old Muffins or even cake in a blender or food processor to produce the needed crumbs.

Almond-Rice Crispy Crunch _____

Makes 12 to 16 pieces.

A nutritious snack for the after-school crowd. Great for breakfast, too. This recipe contains only three food families, making it a good choice for people on a Diversified Rotary Diet.

⅓ cup almond butter (see Nut or Seed Butter in the Index)

¼ cup honey or maple syrup

1 tablespoon almond oil

2 cups crisp brown rice cereal

¾ cup diced dried apricots, peaches or prunes (optional)

In a medium saucepan, combine the almond butter, honey or maple syrup and oil. Stir over low heat until blended. Remove from the heat. Stir in the cereal and fruit.

Press into an oiled 8"- or 9"-square baking pan with a wooden spoon. Chill, then cut into bars. Best eaten the first day, while crisp.

Variations: Replace the honey or maple syrup with rice syrup (see Appendix for purchasing source). That reduces the recipe to use of two food families.

For a less-expensive confection containing four food groups, use peanut butter, peanut oil and currants.

NOTE: Crisp brown rice cereal is distributed by Erewhon (see Appendix) and is available in many health food stores.

Carob Crispy Crunch _____

Makes 16 pieces.

Adapted from a recipe my mother made frequently when I was a child. This will delight kids of all ages.

3½ cups crisp brown rice cereal (see Note)

½ cup peanuts

½ cup honey

⅓ cup natural peanut butter

1½ teaspoons pure vanilla extract (optional)

⅓ cup carob powder

Combine the cereal and peanuts in a small bowl. Set aside.

In a 3-quart saucepan, combine the honey and peanut butter. Stir together over medium heat until the honey melts and the mixture is blended. Do not boil. Remove from the heat, and stir in the vanilla, then the carob.

Stir in the cereal-peanut mixture. Press firmly into an oiled 8"- or 9"-square pan. Chill for 1 hour before cutting into bars.

NOTE: Crisp brown rice cereal is distributed by Erewhon (see Appendix) and is available in many health food stores.

Seed-Butter Crispy Crunch _____

Makes 16 to 32 pieces.

Sunflower seeds and sesame seeds are less allergenic than peanuts and make great snack foods.

⅔ cup toasted
    sunflower seeds
2 tablespoons toasted
    sesame seeds
2 tablespoons
    sunflower oil
⅓ cup honey
3 cups crisp brown
    rice cereal

Grind the sunflower seeds and sesame seeds to a powder in a blender, working half a batch at a time. Return seeds to blender. With the machine running on low, add the oil, then slowly add the honey. Stop to scrape the sides of the container as necessary. Transfer mixture to a 3-quart saucepan.

Place the saucepan over low heat, and stir until mixture liquefies. Remove from heat, and stir in the cereal to coat well. Press into an 8"-square baking dish. Chill 1 hour or more. Cut into squares or bars.

Variation: Add ½ cup currants along with the cereal.

NOTES: To roast your own seeds, scatter them on a cookie sheet or jelly-roll pan, and roast at 275° for 20 to 40 minutes. Sesame seeds will roast faster than sunflower seeds, so bake them separately. Cool before storing.

Crisp brown rice cereal is distributed by Erewhon (see Appendix) and is available in many health food stores.

Buckwheat Ginger Cookies _____

Makes about 35.

Be sure to use unroasted groats to make these crunchy cookies.

¾ cup white
    buckwheat flour
    (see Note)
½ cup white
    buckwheat groats
½ teaspoon powdered
    ginger
¼ teaspoon vitamin C
    crystals
⅓ cup honey
2 tablespoons oil

Combine the flour, groats, ginger and vitamin C crystals in a bowl.

Heat the honey and oil in a 3-quart saucepan until honey liquefies. Remove from heat, and stir in flour mixture. Mixture will be the consistency of heavy batter. Stir in water.

Drop rounded half-teaspoonfuls of batter onto non-stick cookie sheets. Bake at 350° for 12 minutes, until brown and firm to the touch. Serve immediately.

2 tablespoons water

Variations: Use molasses for part of the honey, or replace both with maple syrup and omit ginger.

NOTES: Because these confections harden considerably as they cool, it's important to make them small (no larger than bing cherries) and to serve them fresh from the oven. For softer cookies, store in a tightly covered tin, with half an apple sliced in wedges and placed in a cup.

For directions on making white buckwheat flour, see Table 1, Cooking and Baking with Alternative Flours, in the section, Exploring New Ingredients.

Coconut-Date Confection

Makes ½ pound.

This sweet treat combines members of the Palm family. It's very festive for birthdays or holidays. For best flavor, prepare a day to a week ahead.

½ pound pitted dates
½ cup grated
    unsweetened
    coconut
grated unsweetened
    coconut

Grind the dates in a food processor or grinder. Add the ½ cup coconut, and mix well. Shape the mixture into small balls. Roll in additional coconut. Store in cookie tin until ready to serve.

Variation: Before rolling the balls in coconut, press half a nut into each. If desired, roll in ground nuts or a mixture of nuts and coconut.

Stuffed Dates

Makes 24.

A simple snack that children can make. To pack in lunchboxes, wrap two dates facing each other, to prevent the peanut butter from sticking to the wrapper.

24 large dates, pitted
½ cup natural peanut
    butter or other
    nut butter (see
    Nut or Seed
    Butter in the
    Index)
24 walnuts, pecans or
    almonds

With a sharp knife, slice open each date lengthwise along 1 side. Fill each with a teaspoonful of peanut butter or nut butter. Press a walnut, pecan or almond into the nut butter.

Variation: Use peanuts in place of the nuts. Use 3 per date.

269

Fruit-Gel Cutouts

Makes 1 9"- × -13" pan.

Colorful, sweet-tasting fun food that's free of sugar and artificial coloring. After the gelatin sets, the kids can cut out animals, stars and other playful shapes using cookie cutters. Kids especially like these because they can pick them up and eat them like cookies.

3 tablespoons unflavored gelatin
12 ounces unsweetened grape-juice concentrate
1½ cups boiling water

In a medium pan, soften the gelatin in the thawed juice concentrate. Add the water, and stir until the gelatin dissolves. (If necessary, place over heat a minute or two.)

Pour into a lightly oiled 9"- × -13" baking dish. Chill 1 hour or until firmly set. Cut into cubes or fancy shapes. Refrigerate leftovers in a covered container. (Finished gel can stand at room temperature up to 4 hours.)

Adapted from Finger Fruit Gel, in Cooking for the Health of It, *published by Nutrition for Optimal Health, Box 380, Winnetka, IL 60093.*

Ice Pops

Makes 3 or 4.

Parents of hyperactive children will appreciate these sugar-free, additive-free versions of a favorite summertime ice snack.

2 cups pureed watermelon, honeydew or cantaloupe
1 teaspoon lemon or lime juice (optional)

Mix the puree and lemon or lime juice. Pour into small, dispenser-size paper cups. Insert a wooden stick in each cup. Place cups in the freezer. Check in 30 minutes, and straighten the sticks if they've moved off center. Allow to freeze until solid. Best used within a few days. (For longer storage, remove pops from the cups and place in cellophane bags.)

NOTE: Wooden sticks are available at craft and hobby shops.

Beverages

When it comes to beverages, a little imagination goes a long way in avoiding milk, citrus juice and artificial juice drinks. Using nuts and fruits, you can improvise countless milk-free shakes. Or make Tea and Berry Punch for a party beverage without citrus fruit or soda pop. You can even make carbonated beverages out of ordinary tap or bottled water and fruit juice, using a Soda Syphon or other CO_2 dispenser. For cooking and baking, Nut Milk, Zucchini Milk and Pineapple Milk have proven to be very useful stand-ins for cow's milk.

The ingredients in beverages such as Nut Fruit Shake can be varied to use nuts or fruit of your choice, depending on what you can eat. I am particularly enthusiastic about discovering Zucchini Milk, which uses a prolific garden vegetable in a new and exciting way. It's a helpful option for people who are allergic to soy or nuts as well as milk.

When honeydew is in season, be sure to try my all-time personal favorite summertime beverage, Melon Cooler.

271

Soy Milk _____

Makes 6 to 7 cups.

This recipe was first developed at Cornell University and has since come into general use. The boiling-water method inactivates lipoxidase, an enzyme that would otherwise cause a bitter flavor, and gives this soy milk superior flavor.

1 cup dry soybeans
8 cups boiling water

Wash the beans, and soak in a large bowl of cold water for from 4 to 16 hours (refrigerate if beans will soak more than 6 hours). Drain.

Preheat a stainless-steel or glass blender by blending 2 cups boiling water for 1 minute. Discard. Place ¼ cup of beans and 1½ cups boiling water in the blender. Insulate the blender with a bath towel to keep temperature high. Blend beans for 2 to 3 minutes to grind well. Pour through a muslin bag (or through a strainer lined with several layers of washed cheesecloth) into a large bowl. Press bag or cheesecloth with the back of a spoon to extract all liquid.

Repeat 3 times with remaining beans and boiling water.

Measure the liquid, and make a note of the amount. Transfer to the top of a double boiler. Heat over boiling water for 30 minutes. Stir occasionally to prevent a skin from forming.

Measure the liquid, and add water to compensate for any milk lost through evaporation. Refrigerate immediately.

NOTE: For this recipe to work properly, the water must be at a rolling boil when added to the blender. For this reason, I strongly recommend that you use only a stainless-steel or glass blender, not a plastic one. Also, the preheating step is especially important for a glass blender to prevent cracking the container.

Fortified Soy Milk _____

Makes 6½ cups.

Served chilled, this is quite palatable for drinking.

6 cups Soy Milk (see
    opposite page)
¼ cup honey
2 tablespoons oil
1 tablespoon calcium
    carbonate powder
    (1,800 milligrams)
1 25- to 50-microgram
    vitamin B_{12} tablet,
    crushed
1 teaspoon pure
    vanilla extract
    (optional)

Combine the milk with the honey and oil. Mix well. Stir in the calcium carbonate, vitamin B_{12} and vanilla. Pour into a jar or bottle. Refrigerate until needed. Shake before using.

Variation: Replace 3 tablespoons of the honey with barley malt.

NOTE: Look for calcium carbonate in drugstores and health food stores.

Zucchini Milk _____

Makes about 1 quart.

When zucchini is made into a milk, its mild flavor disappears completely, leaving a versatile liquid that can be used in bread, cakes, pies and some cream soups. If you have enough freezer space, make the milk when zucchini is in season, and freeze in one-cup containers. If you desire a white milk, peel the zucchini thickly. Peeling the vegetable thinly will result in a pale-green milk.

2½ pounds firm
    zucchini

Peel the zucchini as desired. Cut vegetable into chunks. Place enough chunks in a blender to fill it about one-quarter full. Process until you have a liquid. Transfer to a saucepan.
    Repeat until all zucchini has been blended and placed in the saucepan. Heat to boiling to scald the milk. Cool, and store in the refrigerator. Use within 1 week. For longer storage, freeze.

Adapted from Organic Gardening, July, 1977.

Nut Milk _____

Makes about 1 cup.

Enjoy this "milk" as a beverage, cereal topping, cream sauce or cooking ingredient. You can achieve the desired richness and thickness by varying the proportions of nuts and water. Cashews, almonds, filberts and Brazil nuts all make wonderful nut milks.

¼–⅔ cup nuts
1 cup water
¼ teaspoon pure vanilla extract (optional)
1 teaspoon honey or maple syrup (optional)

Grind the nuts to a fine powder in a blender. Add the water, vanilla and honey or maple syrup. Blend until very smooth.

NOTE: You can easily double this recipe. If so, grind about ½ cup of nuts at a time. If you intend to use the nut milk for cooking cream sauces, soups, gravies or other savory dishes, omit the vanilla and sweetener. For a smoother consistency, strain.

Raw nuts contain live enzymes and more vitamin E than toasted nuts, while toasted nuts have a fuller, richer flavor.

Nut Fruit Shake _____

Serves 2.

A thick, refreshing, dairy-free shake for after-school snacking. It's also terrific over cereal.

1 cup Nut Milk (see recipe above)
2 cups chopped fruit (see Note)
1 tablespoon honey
1–2 teaspoons lemon juice (optional)

Place the Nut Milk in a blender. With the machine running, add the fruit, honey and lemon juice. Blend until smooth. Serve at once.

NOTE: Use your choice of fruit; strawberries, peaches, raspberries, blueberries, melon and bananas are all good. If you like, you can also use 1 cup of frozen fruit plus 1 cup fresh or stewed fruit to enjoy an out-of-season fruit. Since large chunks of frozen fruit won't pack down in the measuring cup, you might want to add a little extra to achieve the desired consistency.

No-Milk Shake

Serves 1 to 2.

Another delicious beverage for people who are allergic to both milk and soy. All of the following fruits make perfectly delectable shakes: berries, grapefruits, oranges, peaches, nectarines, stewed prunes, stewed apricots, apples, pears, cantaloupes and honeydews. So take your pick.

1 very ripe, large
   banana, sliced
1 cup chopped fruit
¼ cup water
2 teaspoons lemon
   juice or ⅛–¼
   teaspoons vitamin
   C crystals
   (optional)
honey (optional)

Place the banana, fruit, water and lemon juice or vitamin C crystals in a blender. Process until smooth, 30 seconds or more. Taste, and add honey or more lemon juice or vitamin C crystals, if needed. Dilute with a little more water, if desired. Serve in a tall glass with ice cubes.

Variation: To make a Minted Fruit Shake, add a few mint leaves to the blender with the other ingredients. Garnish with a mint sprig.

Pineapple Milk

Makes 1 quart.

Great on puffed rice, granola or other breakfast cereals.

1 ripe banana
2–3 cups unsweetened
   pineapple juice

Break the banana into chunks, and place in a blender. Add ½ cup juice, and puree until smooth. Add enough additional juice to bring the level up to 4 cups. Blend a few seconds until mixture is milky and frothy.

Variation: Replace the banana with 1 cup unsweetened pineapple chunks or 8 ounces crushed unsweetened pineapple. Blend with a little juice, then proceed with recipe. The resulting milk will be less opaque but will be limited to one food family.

NOTE: If you plan to store the Pineapple Milk for a few days, blend in ¼ teaspoon vitamin C crystals.

Fruit Fizz _____

Serves 1 to 2.

A carbonated juice drink without sugar or artificial ingredients.

¾ cup sparkling
   mineral water,
   chilled
¼ cup unsweetened
   grape-juice
   concentrate

Combine the mineral water and juice concentrate. Pour into tall ice-cube-filled glasses.

Variations: Try other juice concentrates, such as apple or pineapple. You can vary the amount of concentrate to suit your taste.

If you wish, use the Soda Syphon or other carbonated water dispenser to make sparkling water. (See Appendix for purchasing sources.)

Melon Cooler _____

Serves 2.

A cool, refreshing beverage that's thick and creamy like a milkshake but light as a feather and not too sweet.

4 cups ripe honeydew,
   cantaloupe or
   watermelon
   chunks, chilled
lime or lemon juice
   (optional)
mint sprigs (garnish)

Liquefy the melon chunks in the blender. Add lime or lemon juice to taste. Pour into 2 tall glasses, and garnish with mint sprig.

Variation: Make a Melon-Mint Cooler by adding 3 or 4 mint leaves to the blender with the melon.

Old-Fashioned Lemonade _____

Makes 1 quart.

Use the lightest, mildest honey you can find so its flavor won't dominate the lemonade.

¼ cup honey
¼ cup boiling water
3 cups water
½ cup lemon juice

Place the honey in a large Pyrex or stainless steel bowl. Pour the boiling water over it, and stir until honey is dissolved. Whisk in the water and lemon juice.

Serve in tall, ice-cube-filled glasses.

NOTE: If you'd like to add more honey to the finished lemonade, dissolve it in boiling water first. Otherwise, it's apt to congeal in the cold water.

Tea and Berry Punch ⎯⎯⎯⎯⎯⎯⎯⎯⎯⎯⎯⎯⎯

Makes 5 cups.

A pretty party punch that's based on foods of the Rose family. It's just as festive at a New Year's party as it is on the Fourth of July.

1⅔ cups boiling water
6 rosehip tea bags
⅓ cup honey
1 cup strawberries
¼ cup lemon juice
    sparkling mineral
    water
4 strawberries, thinly
    sliced (garnish)

Place the water in a Pyrex or stainless steel bowl. Add the tea bags, and allow them to steep for 10 minutes. Remove the bags, pressing out liquid from them. Stir in the honey. Refrigerate this concentrate until needed.

Just before serving, add the concentrate, strawberries and lemon juice to a blender. Blend on high speed for 1 minute. With the machine running at the lowest speed, add enough mineral water to fill the container completely.

Place sliced strawberries in a serving dish or small punch bowl. Add punch. Serve immediately.

NOTES: If you need to make larger amounts of punch, prepare individual batches of concentrate. Then blend each separately with berries, lemon juice and sparkling water as needed so the water won't lose its fizz.

If you wish, use the Soda Syphon or other carbonated water dispenser to make sparkling water. (See Appendix for purchasing sources.)

Nice Tea

Makes 2 quarts.

Cool, refreshing and free of caffeine. Ready to drink in 15 minutes.

⅓ cup loose herb tea
   (10–12 tea bags)
3 cups boiling water
3 cloves (optional)
3–4 tablespoons honey
1 lemon, thinly
   sliced
mint sprigs
   (garnish)

Place the tea in a teapot or Pyrex bowl. Add the water and cloves. Stir in the honey. Allow to steep for 5 minutes. Add the lemon, and steep 5 to 7 minutes more.

Place half a tray of ice cubes in a 2-quart glass pitcher. Fill the pitcher halfway with cold water. Strain the tea into the pitcher, pressing the residue with the back of a spoon to extract all the tea and lemon juice. Add enough cold water to fill the pitcher.

To serve, pour over ice cubes in tall glasses. Garnish with mint sprigs.

Variation: To make Mint Tea, omit the cloves, and substitute 6 to 8 mint leaves.

Real Soda Pop

This is one of the few recipes in the book that requires special equipment. But if your youngsters crave soda, you'll find that it's well worth the expense to be able to make your own natural, homemade carbonated beverages. What you'll need to convert tap water or bottled water into the carbonated water suitable for soda is a carbon-dioxide-powered water dispenser. (See the Appendix for manufacturer information.) Once you start using a carbonated water dispenser, you'll see how useful it is for birthdays, holidays and other party occasions.

There are two tricks to making sodas any time you want. One is to keep the syphon bottle filled with water and permanently stored in the refrigerator. The second is to have a ready supply of soda concentrates on hand. And that's certainly easy to do. You can make your sodas as plain or fancy as you desire. Possible combinations are virtually limitless. Probably the simplest way to make soda is to use unsweetened fruit-juice concentrates. Pick any flavor that suits you—apple, grape, orange, pineapple, grapefruit. Use it singly or in combinations. Try apple and grape together, or orange and pineapple. Maybe you'd like grapefruit enlivened with a squeeze of lime juice.

If you'd like a citrus soda, mix equal parts lemon juice and honey. Or try lime juice and honey. You can mix a batch of the concentrate and store it in the refrigerator for an instant cooler.

No matter what concentrate you use, the technique for mixing a soda is the same. Take a tall ice-tea glass (the kind that holds about 14 to 16 ounces), and add about ¼ cup of your chosen concentrate to it. Holding the glass at an angle, aim a stream of carbonated water down one side. If you're planning on adding ice cubes to your beverage, leave enough room for them. (If you have smaller glasses, use proportionately less concentrate. Experiment to see what quantities suit you best.)

Keep in mind that you'll have to change the cartridge every time you refill the syphon bottle. So if you're planning a party, make sure you have extra cartridges on hand.

Ginger Ale Concentrate

Serves about 7.

2 tablespoons minced ginger root
1 cup water
¾ cup honey

Place the ginger and water in a blender. Process until thoroughly pureed, about 1 minute. With the blender running, slowly pour in the honey. Mix well.

Strain into a jar. Refrigerate a few hours for flavors to meld. Use within 10 days.

To make soda, use about ¼ cup of concentrate for each 16-ounce glass. Add carbonated water and, if desired, ice cubes.

Strawberry Soda Concentrate

Serves 5 to 6.

1 cup whole strawberries
⅓ cup honey

Puree the strawberries in a blender until smooth. With the machine running, add the honey in a thin stream. Mix well.

Pour into a jar, and store in the refrigerator. Use within a few days.

To make soda, use about ¼ cup of concentrate for each 16-ounce glass. Add carbonated water and, if desired, ice cubes.

Cranberry Soda

Serves 1.

To make this soda, you'll need cranberry-juice concentrate. Do not buy the frozen kind, however, because that contains sugar. Look for a bottled unsweetened brand at health food stores.

3 tablespoons honey
2 tablespoons unsweetened cranberry-juice concentrate

Mix the honey and juice concentrate in a 16-ounce glass. Add carbonated water and, if desired, ice cubes.

Ice Cream Soda _____

Serves 1.

Here's a milk-free treat that can rival soda-fountain drinks.

1 scoop Peach-Almond
    Ice Cream or Soft
    Sherbet (see Index)
sparkling mineral
    water, chilled

Place the ice cream or sherbet in a tall glass. Add mineral water to fill.

NOTE: If you wish, use the Soda Syphon or other carbonated water dispenser to make sparkling water. (See Appendix for purchasing sources.)

Desserts and Dessert Toppings

Next to breads, desserts probably pose the most difficulty for people with allergies to commonly eaten foods. Commercial mixes and standard recipes invariably contain wheat, milk, eggs, sugar, corn syrup and other highly allergenic ingredients. So this section is the largest in the book, and will help you make pies, cakes and other treats that the whole family and all your friends can enjoy. Choices range from Two-Step Carrot Cake and Apricot-Rice Pudding to more elaborate Rice-Flour Cream Puffs and English Trifle—and everything in between. My favorite is Carob Fudge Cake, and it's easy enough to make often. For cookies and other lunch-box fare, see the Snacks section.

You'll be happy to learn that the pie crusts are simple and easy to press in place. They won't toughen with handling the way wheat flour crusts do. To familiarize yourself with the other characteristics of various ingredients in pie and cake recipes, read Table 1, Cooking and Baking with Alternative Flours, in the section, Exploring New Ingredients. Rice and oat flours, for example, are often used together or separately. You can make grain-free versions of many cakes from amaranth or buckwheat, often in combination with arrowroot or other starches.

Ground nuts are often incorporated as part of the flour to bolster the nutrient content. If you're allergic to the nuts specified, substitute another kind of nuts, or ground pumpkin or squash seeds. (When finely ground and used as a flour, nuts and seeds are easier to digest than when they're eaten whole.)

See also the Holiday Foods section for Nutty Pumpkin Pie, Tofu Pumpkin Pie, Steamed Cranberry Bread and other traditional holiday desserts, and the Goat's Milk and Cheese Dishes section for other ice cream recipes.

Carob Fudge Cake _____

Serves 9.

If you like chocolate cake and brownies, you'll love this cake and its brownie variation.

1 cup amaranth flour
½ cup arrowroot
¼ cup carob powder
1 teaspoon baking soda
⅔ cup warm water
⅓ cup oil
⅓ cup honey
1 tablespoon lemon juice or ¼ teaspoon vitamin C crystals
1 teaspoon pure vanilla extract
¼ cup chopped nuts (optional)

Sift the flour, arrowroot, carob and baking soda into a large bowl.

In a small bowl, whisk together the water, oil, honey, lemon juice or vitamin C crystals and vanilla until combined. Pour into the flour bowl, and mix quickly.

Pour batter into an oiled 8"- or 9"-square baking pan. Sprinkle nuts on top. Bake at 350° for 30 minutes, until some cracks appear on top and inside is still moist. Do not overbake. Serve warm or cold, cut into squares. Use within a day, or freeze for later.

Variations: Replace the amaranth flour with ¾ cup plus 2 tablespoons brown rice flour.

To make Carob Fudge Brownies, reduce the water to ¼ cup. The batter will be thick. Spread thinly in an oiled 7"-×-11" or 8"-×-12" baking pan. Bake at 350° for 20 to 25 minutes. Do not overbake; brownies should remain moist inside.

Two-Step Carrot Cake _____

Makes 1 loaf.

This festive dessert loaf is dense and moist like a fruitcake. Unlike most cakes, it doesn't contain eggs. I call it a two-step cake because you prepare the carrot mixture the night before and finish the cake in the morning.

1 cup packed grated carrots
1 cup raisins
½ cup shredded unsweetened coconut (optional)
1 teaspoon ground cinnamon
½ teaspoon grated nutmeg

Combine the carrots, raisins, coconut, cinnamon, nutmeg and cloves in a saucepan. Stir in the juice, honey and oil. Boil for 10 minutes. Refrigerate 6 hours or overnight.

Remove the carrot mixture from the refrigerator, and allow to reach room temperature. Stir in the walnuts or pecans and chopped pineapple.

Sift the flour and baking soda into a large bowl. Add the carrot mixture, and stir lightly to combine. Do not overmix.

¼ teaspoon ground
    cloves
1½ cups unsweetened
    pineapple juice
⅔ cup honey
¼ cup oil
½ cup chopped
    walnuts or
    pecans
3 dried,
    unsweetened,
    unsulfured
    pineapple rings,
    chopped
    (optional)
1¾ cups brown rice
    flour
2 teaspoons baking
    soda

Pour batter into a greased 7½"-×-11¾" loaf pan. Bake at 300° for 1 hour, or until a cake tester inserted in the center comes out clean. Cool in the pan for 10 minutes before removing from the pan.

Plum-Good Tea Cake

Serves 9.

Even if you don't drink coffee, you can have coffee cake. This is absolutely delicious—free of grains, milk and eggs, yet good enough to serve to company.

12 small or 8 to 10
    large purple
    plums
⅓ cup date sugar
1¼ cups sifted
    amaranth flour
¾ cup tapioca-starch
    flour
1 teaspoon baking
    soda
½ teaspoon ground
    cinnamon
    (optional)
    grated rind of 1
    lime (optional)
½ cup warm water or
    herb tea
⅓ cup honey
¼ cup oil
2 tablespoons lime
    juice or ¼
    teaspoon vitamin
    C crystals

Quarter and pit the plums. Place in an oiled 8"-square baking dish. Sprinkle with the date sugar.

In a medium bowl, combine the amaranth flour and tapioca-starch flour. Take 2 tablespoons of this mixture and sprinkle on the plums. Toss plums lightly to coat with date sugar and flour.

Mix remaining flour with baking soda, cinnamon and lime rind. Set aside.

In a small bowl, whisk together the water or herb tea and honey to dissolve the honey. Add the oil and lime juice or vitamin C crystals. Mix well. Pour into the flour mixture. Stir quickly to blend. Then pour over the fruit. Bake at 350° for 30 minutes, until lightly brown and top springs back when touched.

Variations: Replace plums with other chopped fruit. If desired, sprinkle nuts on batter before baking.

283

Pineapple-Prune Cake _____

Makes 1 cake.

    A moist, fruit-sweetened cake free of wheat, milk and sugar, this makes a festive, special-occasion cake.

1 cup chopped
    prunes
8 ounces crushed
    unsweetened
    pineapple,
    packed in juice
½ cup unsweetened
    pineapple-juice
    concentrate
½ cup raisins or
    currants
1 teaspoon ground
    cinnamon
¼ teaspoon ground
    cloves
¼ cup oil
1 tablespoon
    granular lecithin
    (optional)
2 eggs
1 teaspoon pure
    vanilla extract
1¼ cups sifted
    amaranth flour
½ cup arrowroot
1 teaspoon baking
    soda
¼ teaspoon vitamin C
    crystals
1 teaspoon Corn-Free
    Baking Powder
    (optional; see
    Index)
1 cup coarsely
    broken nuts
¼ cup unsweetened
    pineapple-juice
    concentrate
2 tablespoons water
2 tablespoons honey

In a 3-quart saucepan, mix the prunes, undrained pineapple and ½ cup juice concentrate. Add the raisins or currants, cinnamon and cloves. Bring to a boil, then simmer for 5 minutes. Remove from heat and stir in the oil and lecithin. Cool to lukewarm. Then stir in the eggs and vanilla. Beat for 2 minutes.

In a medium bowl, combine the flour, arrowroot, baking soda, vitamin C crystals and baking powder. Add flour mixture to saucepan, and stir to combine. Stir in the nuts.

Pour the batter into an oiled 8″-square baking pan. Bake at 350° for 30 minutes, or until cake springs back when touched lightly in the center.

While cake is still warm, prepare a glaze by simmering the ¼ cup juice concentrate with water and honey in a small saucepan until syrupy, about 5 minutes.

Prick the top of the cake at intervals with a fork. Pour the warm glaze over the warm cake. Spread to cover cake thinly. Allow cake to cool in pan before cutting.

Variation: Substitute 1¼ cups brown rice flour and ½ cup amaranth flour for the 1¼ cups amaranth flour and ½ cup arrowroot.

NOTE: If you are allergic to cinnamon or cloves, substitute other spices.

Rice-Flour Carrot Cake _____

Makes 1 cake.

Perfect for people who can have eggs but not wheat or milk. Have all ingredients at room temperature.

1¾ cups sifted brown
    rice flour
2 teaspoons baking
    soda
2 teaspoons ground
    cinnamon
½ teaspoon grated
    nutmeg
    (optional)
¼ teaspoon ground
    cloves (optional)
2 cups packed grated
    carrots
8 ounces crushed
    unsweetened
    pineapple,
    packed in juice
1 cup raisins
½ cup shredded
    unsweetened
    coconut
3 eggs
¾ cup honey
½ cup oil
½ cup chopped
    walnuts
    Whipped Creamy
    Topping (see
    page 307) or
    Maple-Nut
    Frosting (see
    page 304),
    optional

Sift the flour, baking soda, cinnamon, nutmeg and cloves into a bowl. Resift and set aside.

In a large bowl, combine the carrots, undrained pineapple, raisins and coconut. Set aside.

In a medium bowl, beat the eggs with an electric mixer until very light. Add the honey in a thin stream while beating. Beat until the mixture is very light and frothy. Add the oil in a thin stream while beating.

Pour the egg mixture into the carrot bowl. Stir gently to combine. Sift half of the flour mixture over the bowl. Gently fold in. Repeat with remaining flour. Fold in the walnuts.

Pour into a greased 7½"- × -11¾" baking pan or 2 8"- or 9"-round cake pans. Bake at 325° for 50 minutes (for the large pan) or 35 to 40 minutes (for the layers). Cool for 10 minutes in the pans, then turn out onto wire racks and cool completely.

Serve plain or with Whipped Creamy Topping or Maple-Nut Frosting.

Fruit-Fluff Pie

Serves 6 to 8.

A light, versatile dessert that contains no cream, sugar or egg whites. And it's easy to make.

1½ tablespoons unflavored gelatin
½ cup unsweetened apple juice
2 cups quartered strawberries
1 large, ripe banana, sliced (or 2 small ones)
¼ cup honey
1 tablespoon lemon juice or 1 tablespoon water and ¼ teaspoon vitamin C crystals
1 9″ Rice-Flour Pie Crust, baked (see page 289)
Whipped Creamy Topping (optional; see page 307)

In a small saucepan, sprinkle the gelatin over the apple juice; allow to soften for 5 minutes. Heat briefly to dissolve gelatin. Keep warm.

Place the strawberries, banana, honey and lemon juice or water and vitamin C crystals in a blender. Process until smooth. With the blender running on low speed, pour in the gelatin mixture. Mix well.

Pour into a mixing bowl, and refrigerate until mixture begins to set and forms mounds when dropped from a spoon. Whip with an electric mixer until light and fluffy. Spoon into the pie crust, and chill 1 hour before serving. Top with Whipped Creamy Topping.

Variations: For Fruit-Fluff Gel, omit the pie crust. Pour whipped fruit mixture into individual custard cups or a ring mold. Chill until firm. Unmold before serving.

For Fruit-Fluff Parfaits, alternate layers of whipped fruit mixture and Whipped Creamy Topping with whole or sliced strawberries in parfait glasses. Chill before serving.

NOTE: You can use frozen strawberries. Allow them to partially thaw in a bowl for 30 minutes, then add berries and juice to blender.

Double Apple Pie

Serves 6 to 8.

Even people without food allergies will love this version of America's most traditional dessert. Use baking apples that will hold their shape, such as Yellow Delicious, Greening and Jonathan. Do not use McIntosh, which will disintegrate.

1 9″ Rice-Flour Pie Crust, unbaked (see page 189)
½ recipe Amaranth (see page 293), Nut 'n' Seed

Bake the crust at 350° for 5 to 7 minutes. Set aside to cool. Make Streusel Crumbs.

In a large bowl, mix the apples, juice concentrate, tapioca and cinnamon, and let stand for 15 minutes. Taste the juice, and add a little honey if you need it.

286

(see page 292)
or Rice-Flour
(see page 293)
Streusel Crumbs
5–6 cups sliced
unsprayed
apples
6 ounces
unsweetened
apple-juice
concentrate
3 tablespoons quick-
cooking tapioca
1 teaspoon ground
cinnamon
(optional)
1–3 tablespoons honey
(optional)

Transfer the apple mixture to the crust. Bake at 350° for 15 minutes. Sprinkle on the Streusel Crumbs, pressing lightly. Return to the oven for another 20 minutes, until fruit is tender but not mushy.

Variations: Replace the crust with a Nut 'n' Seed Crunch Crust (see Index). If desired, add ¼ cup raisins or currants to apple mixture.

Strawberry Pie

Serves 6 to 8.

An all-time favorite in a wheat-free or grain-free crust.

1 tablespoon
unflavored gelatin
½ cup water
5 cups strawberries
2 tablespoons
arrowroot
½ cup honey
2 tablespoons lemon
juice or 2
tablespoons water
and ½ teaspoon
vitamin C crystals
1 9″ Rice-Flour Pie
Crust (see page
289) or Amaranth
Pie Crust (see
page 290), baked
Whipped Creamy
Topping (see page
307) or Nutty
Creme Topping
(see page 306),
optional

In a small saucepan, sprinkle the gelatin over the water. Allow to soften for 5 minutes. Heat briefly to dissolve gelatin; keep warm.

Puree about 1¼ cups of berries in the blender to make 1 cup of puree. Use more berries, if needed. Add arrowroot, and blend a few seconds.

Pour berry mixture into a 2-quart saucepan. Stir in the honey, and bring to a boil. Cook, stirring, for 30 seconds. Remove from the heat, and stir in the lemon juice or water and vitamin C crystals and gelatin.

Chill mixture in the saucepan until it is just thickened and forms mounds when dropped from a spoon.

Quarter or slice remaining strawberries. Fold into the gelatin mixture. Pour into the pie crust. Chill at least 2 hours before serving. Top with Whipped Creamy Topping or Nutty Creme Topping.

Variation: For a Molded Strawberry Dessert, omit the crust. Pour filling into a lightly oiled mold. Chill 2 hours or more. Unmold before serving.

Banana Chiffon Pie _____

Serves 6 to 8.

Fruit, nuts and air are the main ingredients in this light-as-a-feather dessert. It's naturally sweet yet not terribly rich.

2 very ripe bananas
1 9″ Pie Crust, baked
   (see Index)
   Lime Bavarian (see
    page 296) or Fruit-
    Fluff Pie filling
    (see page 286)

Slice the bananas into the pie crust. Pour Lime Bavarian or Fruit-Fluff Pie filling over them. Chill at least 1 hour.

Pear Streusel Pie _____

Serves 6 to 8.

Pears are one of nature's least allergenic fruits. They make great pies in fall and winter, when they're sweetest.

1 9″ Amaranth Pie
   Crust, unbaked
   (see page 290)
5 cups sliced, ripe
   pears
¼ cup quick-cooking
   tapioca
¼ cup honey
2 tablespoons lemon
   juice or ½
   teaspoon vitamin
   C crystals
2 tablespoons water
1 recipe Amaranth
   Streusel Crumbs
   (see page 293)

Bake the crust at 350° for 5 to 7 minutes. Set aside to cool.

In a large bowl, mix the pears, tapioca, honey, lemon juice or vitamin C crystals and water. If pears aren't particularly juicy, add 1 to 2 tablespoons water; if desired, add a bit more honey. Let stand for 15 minutes.

Place the pear mixture in the crust. Bake at 350° for 15 minutes. Sprinkle Streusel Crumbs on top, pressing lightly. Return to the oven for 15 to 20 minutes, until fruit is tender but not mushy.

Variations: Use a Rice-Flour Pie Crust and Streusel Crumbs or a Nut 'n' Seed Crunch Crust and Streusel Crumbs (see Index).

Peachy Blueberry Streusel Pie _____

Serves 6 to 8.

This foolproof seasonal pie is a favorite of mine.

1 9″ Amaranth Pie
   Crust, unbaked
   (see page 290)

Bake the crust and Streusel Crumbs at 400° for 12 to 15 minutes. Set aside to cool.

Place the peaches, water, arrowroot and

1 recipe Amaranth
    Streusel Crumbs
    (see page 293)
2 cups pureed
    peaches
⅓ cup water
2 tablespoons
    arrowroot
1 tablespoon
    unflavored
    gelatin
½ cup honey
¼ teaspoon pure
    almond extract
1½ cups blueberries

gelatin in a saucepan. Stir well to mix. Add the honey. Cook over medium heat, stirring constantly, until mixture reaches a boil. Cook at a full boil for 1 minute.

Chill the mixture until it is cool and very thick but not solidly set. Fold in the almond extract, then the blueberries.

Pour into prepared crust, and sprinkle with Streusel Crumbs. Chill for at least 2 hours before serving.

Variations: Use a Rice-Flour Pie Crust and Streusel Crumbs or a Nut 'n' Seed Crunch Crust and Streusel Crumbs (see Index).

NOTE: If you should allow the peach filling to gel until it's firm, let it soften at room temperature for 15 to 30 minutes. Then beat with an electric mixer for 30 seconds to achieve the desired half-set consistency. Fold in almond extract and berries, and chill.

Rice-Flour Pie Crust

Makes 1 crust.

A no-roll, press-in-place crust for your favorite filling. Fill it before or after baking.

⅓ cup whole almonds
¾ cup brown rice flour
¼ teaspoon ground
    cinnamon
    (optional)
  pinch of ground
    cloves (optional)
3 tablespoons water
2 tablespoons oil
2 tablespoons honey

Grind the almonds to a fine powder in a blender. Transfer them to a 9" pie plate. Add the flour, cinnamon and cloves. Mix well with a fork.

Combine the water, oil and honey in a small saucepan. Heat gently until honey liquefies. Pour into the pie plate. Stir with a fork until well blended. Let stand a few minutes for rice flour to absorb liquid.

Shape the crust by pressing mixture firmly into place with your fingers, covering bottom and sides of plate. Pat top edge of crust into a straight edge.

For an unfilled crust, bake empty shell at 350° for 18 minutes, or until lightly brown and marked with a few small cracks. Cool before filling.

For a filled crust, bake empty shell at 350° for 5 minutes. Then add desired filling, and finish baking as your recipe directs.

Amaranth Pie Crust

Makes 1 crust.

A versatile, grain-free crust.

¾ cup amaranth
    flour
½ cup arrowroot
¼ cup ground nuts,
    seeds or
    peanuts
½ teaspoon ground
    cinnamon
    (optional)
3 tablespoons oil
3–4 tablespoons water

In a large bowl, mix the flour, arrowroot, nuts, seeds or peanuts and cinnamon.

In a cup mix the oil and water. Blend into the flour with a fork. Stir until a ball can be formed. If dough is dry and crumbly, add more water, 1 teaspoon at a time, until dough sticks together.

Oil a 9″ pie plate. Either pat the dough directly into the plate, or roll it between 2 pieces of wax paper. Handle carefully; dough is fragile. You can mend any tears by patching with bits of extra dough. Prick crust all over with a fork.

For an unfilled crust, bake empty shell at 400° for 12 to 15 minutes, until lightly brown. Cool before filling.

For a filled crust, bake empty shell at 400° for 3 minutes. Then add desired filling, and finish baking as your recipe directs.

Nut 'n' Seed Crunch Crust

Makes 1 crust.

Excellent flavor, with crunch—a great alternative to graham cracker crust.

½ cup brown rice flour
½ cup ground nuts
¼ cup ground
    sunflower seeds
1 tablespoon
    arrowroot
½ teaspoon ground
    cinnamon
⅛ teaspoon ground
    cloves
2 tablespoons water
2 tablespoons oil
1 tablespoon honey

Combine the flour, nuts, sunflower seeds, arrowroot, cinnamon and cloves in a large bowl.

Combine the water, oil and honey in a small saucepan. Heat until honey liquefies. Pour over flour mixture, and stir with a fork until well combined.

Transfer the mixture to a 9″ pie plate. Shape the crust by pressing mixture firmly into place with your fingers, covering bottom and sides of plate. Pat top edge of crust into a straight edge.

For an unfilled crust, bake empty shell at 350° for 20 to 22 minutes, or until lightly brown. Cool before filling.

For a filled crust, bake empty shell at 350° for 10 minutes. Then add desired filling, and finish baking as your recipe directs.

Gingerbread _____

Serves 9.

A wheat-free, egg-free version of an all-time favorite.

1½ cups sifted brown
 rice flour
½ cup arrowroot
1 teaspoon baking
 soda
1 teaspoon ground
 cinnamon
¾ teaspoon
 powdered ginger
¼ teaspoon ground
 allspice
⅔ cup warm water
⅓ cup honey
¼ cup oil
2 tablespoons lemon
 juice
 Tofu Creme
 Topping
 (optional; see
 page 307)

Sift the flour, arrowroot, baking soda, cinnamon, ginger and allspice into a large bowl.

In a small bowl, whisk together the water, honey, oil and lemon juice. Pour into the flour bowl, and mix quickly.

Pour batter into an oiled 8"- or 9"-square baking dish. Bake at 350° for 30 minutes, until cracks appear in the top and the top springs back when lightly touched. Serve warm with Tofu Creme Topping.

Variation: For a citrus-free version, replace the lemon juice with ½ teaspoon vitamin C crystals and 2 tablespoons of water.

Rhubarb-Buckwheat Crumble _____

Serves 9.

A crumble is a fruit crisp made with honey. Rhubarb and buckwheat are a natural combination because they're members of the same family.

¼ cup oil
2 tablespoons honey
½ cup white
    buckwheat flour
    (see Note)
½ cup arrowroot
⅓ cup ground
    sunflower seeds
    or walnuts
1 teaspoon ground
    cinnamon
5 cups sliced rhubarb
¼ cup arrowroot
½ cup honey
⅓ cup water

Make the topping by heating the oil and 2 tablespoons honey in a saucepan until the honey has melted. Stir in the flour, ½ cup arrowroot, sunflower seeds or walnuts and cinnamon. The mixture should be dry and crumbly. Set aside.

Place the rhubarb in a 3-quart saucepan. Add ¼ cup arrowroot, and toss to coat. Stir in ½ cup honey and water. Cook over medium heat, stirring constantly, until mixture comes to a boil. Boil for 30 seconds. Pour into an oiled 8"- or 9"-square pan.

Crumble the topping with your fingers, and sprinkle it over the rhubarb. Bake at 350° for 35 to 40 minutes. Allow to cool for 30 minutes before serving.

Variation: Replace half of the rhubarb with 2 or 3 cups sliced strawberries.

NOTE: To make white buckwheat flour, see Table 1, Cooking and Baking with Alternative Flours, in the section, Exploring New Ingredients.

Nut 'n' Seed Streusel Crumbs _____

Another good way to top coffee cakes, fruit crisps and pies.

¾ cup brown rice
    flour
¾ cup ground nuts
6 tablespoons
    ground
    sunflower seeds
5 teaspoons
    arrowroot
½ teaspoon ground
    cinnamon
⅛ teaspoon ground
    cloves
1 tablespoon oil
1½ tablespoons honey

In a medium bowl, mix the flour, nuts, sunflower seeds, arrowroot, cinnamon and cloves. Drizzle with the oil and honey. Toss until evenly distributed.

NOTES: Tops 1 9"-×-13" or 2 8"- or 9"-square coffee cakes or fruit crisps, or 2 pies. Sprinkle the crumbs on top for the last 15 to 20 minutes of baking.

If you're making a pie that needs its filling baked, like a fruit pie, prebake only the empty crust for 5 minutes. Add the filling, and bake as your recipe directs. Sprinkle on unbaked streusel crumbs for the last 15 minutes.

Rice-Flour Streusel Crumbs —————————

Use these crumbs to top coffee cakes, fruit crisps or pies.

1 cup *plus* 2
   tablespoons
   brown rice flour
¾ cup ground
   almonds
¼ teaspoon ground
   cinnamon
⅛ teaspoon ground
   cloves
3 tablespoons oil
3 tablespoons honey

In a medium bowl, mix the flour, almonds, cinnamon and cloves. Drizzle with the oil and honey. Toss until evenly distributed.

NOTES: Tops 1 9"-×-13" or 2 8"- or 9"-square coffee cakes or fruit crisps, or 2 pies.
Sprinkle the crumbs on top for the last 15 to 20 minutes of baking. Unbaked crumbs may be frozen for later use.
If you're making a pie that needs its filling baked, like a fruit pie, prebake only the empty crust for 5 minutes. Add the filling, and bake as your recipe directs. Sprinkle on unbaked streusel crumbs for the last 15 minutes.

Amaranth Streusel Crumbs —————————

1 cup *plus* 2
   tablespoons
   amaranth flour
¾ cup arrowroot
⅓ cup ground nuts
½ teaspoon ground
   cinnamon
1–2 tablespoons honey
4 tablespoons oil

In a medium bowl, mix the flour, arrowroot, nuts and cinnamon. Drizzle with the honey and oil. Toss until evenly distributed.

NOTES: Tops 1 9"-×-13" or 2 8"- or 9"-square coffee cakes or fruit crisps, or 2 pies. Sprinkle the crumbs over pie filling or other dessert for the last 15 minutes of baking. Watch carefully to avoid overbrowning.
If you're making a pie that needs its filling baked, like a fruit pie, prebake only the empty crust for 5 minutes. Add the filling, and bake as your recipe directs. Sprinkle on unbaked streusel crumbs for the last 15 minutes.

293

Apple-Berry Tapioca Pudding _____

Serves 4 or 5.

A lovely, light way to end a meal. This pudding is just as good warm as chilled, so you can make and enjoy it on short notice.

1¼ cups unsweetened
    apple juice
1 cup pureed
    strawberries
¼ cup quick-cooking
    tapioca
1–2 tablespoons honey
    (optional)

Combine the juice, puree, tapioca and honey in a saucepan. Let stand for 5 to 10 minutes. Bring to a boil over medium heat, stirring often. When mixture reaches a full boil, remove from heat, and allow to cool for about 20 minutes. Stir well, and serve warm or chilled.

Variation: Omit the berries. Use 2¼ cups apple juice and, if desired, 2 tablespoons unsweetened apple-juice concentrate.

Pineapple Pudding _____

Serves 4 to 6.

A delicious pudding made without sugar or milk.

1 pound tofu
½ cup unsweetened
    pineapple-juice
    concentrate
3 tablespoons honey
2 tablespoons oil or
    walnut oil
16 ounces crushed
    unsweetened
    pineapple,
    packed in juice
⅓ cup walnut halves
    (garnish)

Drain the tofu for 20 to 30 minutes, pressing it between cotton towels to extract as much moisture as possible. Crumble with a fork.

Place the juice concentrate in a blender. Add about one-third of the tofu to the blender. Process until smooth. Gradually add the remaining tofu, and process until smooth. Stop to scrape the container as necessary.

With the machine running, slowly add the honey and oil. Blend well. Pour the mixture into a bowl.

Drain the pineapple well, and reserve the juice for another use.

Stir the pineapple into the tofu mixture. Chill for 1 hour or more. Spoon into individual serving dishes. Garnish each serving with walnut halves.

NOTE: As we've mentioned elsewhere, boiling pineapple juice for 2 minutes destroys the enzymes that may cause burning on the mouth or tongue.

Apricot-Rice Pudding

Serves 8.

A creamy, firm pudding that's free of milk and eggs. Apricots lend a unique sweet-and-tangy flavor. Serve leftovers for breakfast.

1 pound tofu
¾ cup dried apricots
　or 1 pound
　unsweetened
　apricots packed in
　fruit juice
½ cup water
⅓ cup honey
2 tablespoons oil
2 tablespoons lemon
　juice
½ teaspoon wheat-free
　tamari sauce
½ teaspoon pure
　almond extract
2 cups cooked short-
　grain brown rice
　grated nutmeg

Drain the tofu for 20 to 30 minutes, pressing between cotton towels to extract as much moisture as possible. Crumble with a fork.

Simmer dried apricots and water for 10 minutes; if water boils away, add a little more water. Drain, reserving 2 tablespoons of the liquid. If using canned apricots, drain and reserve 2 tablespoons juice.

Place the apricots, reserved liquid, honey, oil, lemon juice, tamari and almond extract in a blender. Process until smooth.

Add tofu a little at a time to the blender. Process until smooth, about 2 minutes.

Taste mixture. If necessary, add a little more lemon juice or honey.

Place rice in a greased 2-quart casserole. Pour apricot mixture over rice, and stir lightly. Dust with nutmeg.

Bake at 350° for about 40 minutes, until pudding is firm and has pulled away from the edges of the pan slightly. Serve warm or cold.

Fancy Parfaits

Serves 4.

½ recipe Apricot-Rice
　Pudding (see
　recipe above)
Frosty Fruit Sauce
　(see page 309)
½ cup chopped
　toasted almonds
　(optional)

Alternate layers of Apricot-Rice Pudding, Frosty Fruit Sauce and almonds in chilled parfait glasses. Serve immediately, or chill up to 8 hours.

Lime Bavarian

Serves 6 to 8.

This grand and elegant dessert is wonderfully easy. It's light and airy, yet free of eggs and cream. Best made with fresh, ripe honeydew, in season.

½ cup cashews
¾ cup boiling water
1 small honeydew
2 tablespoons
    unflavored gelatin
¼ cup honey
⅓ cup lime juice

Grind the cashews finely in a blender. Add the water, and blend at high speed for 2 minutes, until smooth. Pour into a stainless steel bowl, and place in freezer to quick-chill.

Cut the melon in half. Remove seeds. Cut flesh into chunks. Add a few chunks of melon to blender. Process until smooth. Continue to blend in a few chunks at a time until you have 3 cups of puree.

Pour ½ cup of melon puree into a small saucepan. Sprinkle gelatin over top. Allow gelatin to soften for 5 minutes. Heat briefly to dissolve gelatin. Stir in honey. Cool mixture to room temperature.

Add the lime juice to puree remaining in blender. With the machine running, pour in the chilled cashew mixture. Then pour in the gelatin mixture. Blend an additional 30 seconds.

Pour mixture into a lightly oiled 1-quart mold. Chill 8 hours or overnight. Unmold to serve.

Quick and Easy Banana Dessert

Serves 2.

2 large, ripe bananas
¼ cup chopped pecans
¼ cup maple syrup

Cut the bananas in half lengthwise. Then cut each piece in half crosswise. You will have 8 pieces in all.

Place in a non-stick frying pan with the pecans. Sauté over medium heat for 5 minutes, without turning, until the bananas are lightly browned on bottom and heated through. Drizzle with maple syrup, and heat 1 minute.

Poached Pear Melba _____

Serves 4.

This is fancier than plain fresh fruit, yet takes only minutes to prepare.

4 large pears
1½ cups unsweetened
　　pineapple juice
1 cup raspberries
2 tablespoons honey
　vitamin C crystals
　　(optional)

Halve, core and peel the pears. Place the pears and juice in a 3-quart saucepan, and simmer for 12 to 15 minutes, until tender but not mushy. With a slotted spoon, remove pears to a bowl. Cover and keep warm. Reserve juice for another use.

Place the raspberries in a blender, and puree. Strain them through a sieve, pressing to extract all juice from the seeds. Stir in honey to taste. If needed, add a pinch of vitamin C crystals.

To serve, place 2 pear halves on each dessert plate. Spoon sauce over them. Serve warm or cold.

Variation: For Poached Pears with Pineapple Sauce, omit the raspberries. After removing pears from the poaching liquid, boil down the liquid to about 1¼ cups. Stir in honey and vitamin C crystals to taste. Then stir in 1 tablespoon arrowroot that has been dissolved in 2 tablespoons cool juice or water. Combine with a whisk, then boil for 2 minutes. Serve warm or cold.

NOTE: To serve more than 4 people, cook pears in batches. If pears are very small, allow 3 halves per serving.

Fancy Fruit 'n' Nuts

Serves 4 to 6.

Patterned after that international favorite, Strawberries Romanoff, this dessert dispenses with the traditional cream—and you won't even miss it.

3 cups sliced
   strawberries
Nutty Creme
   Topping (see page
   306)
chopped nuts
   (optional)

Divide the fruit among chilled individual serving bowls. Top with Nutty Creme Topping and a sprinkling of nuts.

Variations: Replace the strawberries with either blueberries, raspberries, sliced peaches, sliced nectarines, sliced apricots or sliced bananas.

NOTE: You can limit this dessert to two food families—Plum plus a sweetener—by using peaches, nectarines or apricots as the fruit and almonds in the topping.

English Trifle

Serves 4.

Trifle is usually a concoction of ladyfingers soaked in rum with egg custard, fruit, jelly and whipped cream. This wonderful facsimile uses no wheat, cream or eggs but is just as delightful.

12 thin Amaranth
   Pancakes, about
   4½" across (see
   Index)
1 cup Apricot
   Topping (see
   page 308)
4 teaspoons
   unsweetened
   fruit-juice
   concentrate
¼ chopped toasted
   almonds
¾ cup Almond
   Dessert Sauce,
   chilled (optional;
   see page 308)

At least 6 hours ahead of serving time, arrange 4 Amaranth Pancakes next to each other on a large serving platter (or individually on dessert dishes). Spread each with about ¼" of Apricot Topping. Add a second pancake to each stack, and spread with more topping. Top with a third pancake. Cover the platter or plates with wax paper or cellophane, and chill for 6 hours or more.

At serving time, dribble a teaspoon of the juice concentrate over each stack of pancakes. Spread any remaining apricot topping over the stacks. Sprinkle with the almonds. For added flavor and richness, top with Almond Dessert Sauce.

NOTE: Whether or not you use the Almond Dessert Sauce depends upon your taste for sweets.

Molded Grape Gel

Makes 5 cups.

Dress this up or down for a light buffet dessert.

3 tablespoons unflavored gelatin
1 cup cool water
½ cup raw cashews
⅓ cup boiling water
12 ounces unsweetened grape-juice concentrate
1½ cups water
1 tablespoon lemon juice or ¼ teaspoon vitamin C crystals (optional)

Sprinkle the gelatin over 1 cup water in a small saucepan. Allow to soften for a few minutes, then heat briefly to dissolve gelatin. Set aside to cool to lukewarm.

Grind the cashews to a fine powder in a blender. Add the boiling water, and process 1 minute. Add the juice concentrate, and process on high speed for 2 minutes. Add 1½ cups water, and process briefly on low speed to mix. With machine running on low, add the gelatin mixture. Taste, and decide whether to add the lemon juice or vitamin C crystals for more tang.

Pour into individual glasses or a lightly oiled 5-cup mold. Chill until firm. If using the mold, unmold before serving.

Variations: To make Molded Pineapple Gel, replace the grape-juice concentrate with pineapple-juice concentrate. Boil it for 3 minutes, then set aside to cool before proceeding with recipe.

To make salad squares, allow completed gelatin mixture to chill until it just begins to thicken. Then fold in diced fruit or vegetables. Pour into an oiled 9"-×-13" baking pan. Chill until firm.

Rice-Flour Cream Puffs _____

Serves 4.

Free of both milk and wheat. Like all cream puffs, these take time to make. I suggest you prepare the puff shells, filling and topping ahead of time. Assemble just before serving so the puffs don't get soggy. For best results, keep the unfilled shells in an unheated oven until you're ready to use them.

½ cup water
3 tablespoons oil
½ cup brown rice flour
2 eggs
    Pineapple Pudding
      (see page 294),
      Whipped Creamy
      Topping (see page
      307) or Carob
      Frosting (see page
      304)
    Carob-Peanut Fudge
      Topping (see page
      306)

Bring the water and oil to a boil in a 2-quart saucepan. Reduce the heat to medium. Add the flour all at once. Stirring constantly, cook for 2 minutes. (The batter will form itself into a ball after about 30 seconds, but continue to cook for another 1½ to 2 minutes.)

Remove the pan from the heat. Allow to cool 5 minutes. Thoroughly beat in 1 egg with an electric mixer. When it is fully incorporated, beat in the second egg.

Lightly oil a large cookie sheet. Drop the batter from a large serving spoon into 4 equal mounds on the sheet, allowing space between them for the puffs to spread. Bake in a preheated 425° oven for 15 minutes. When puffs are lightly brown, reduce heat to 375° and bake 9 to 10 minutes longer. Puffs will be firm and crusty when done.

Remove them from oven. Using a sharp, serrated knife, slice the top third of each puff nearly all the way across. Scoop out soft, spongy interiors. Turn off the oven, and return the puffs to the oven. Prop the door open. Allow the puffs to stand in the oven, with lids propped open, for 15 minutes to dry and crisp the insides. Remove from the oven, and cool completely.

Fill with Pineapple Pudding, Whipped Creamy Topping or Carob Frosting. Top with Carob-Peanut Fudge Topping.

Variations: For a luncheon dish, fill the puffs with Baked Chicken Salad or Tofu Salad.

NOTES: You can use the basic recipe to make 18 appetizer-size puffs. Drop rounded teaspoonfuls of batter onto 2 cookie sheets to avoid crowding. Bake at 425° for about 20 minutes, or until puffs are golden and crisp. Slice tops as in basic recipe, and return puffs to turned-off oven for 5 minutes to further dry out.

You can double the basic recipe. Use 2 cookie sheets to avoid crowding puffs.

Unfilled shells can be frozen. Thaw and place in warm oven to crisp for 10 minutes, then cool and fill.

Peach-Almond Ice Cream

Serves 4 to 6.

A non-dairy ice cream that's also free of soy, and only involves two food families.

½ cup ground almonds
1 cup boiling water
½ cup honey
2 tablespoons almond oil (optional)
1 teaspoon pure vanilla extract (optional)
¼ teaspoon pure almond extract
4 ripe peaches, sliced

Place the almonds and water in a blender. Process for 1 minute. With the machine running, add the honey, oil, vanilla and almond extract. Transfer to a small stainless steel bowl, and place in the freezer to quick-chill.

Place the peaches in the blender, and process until well pureed. Pour the cooled almond mixture into the blender. Blend well.

Pour the mixture into a baking dish. Freeze until solid.

Cut the frozen mixture into 1" cubes. Transfer half of the cubes to the blender, and process until pureed to the consistency of soft ice cream. Repeat with remaining cubes. Serve at once in chilled dishes.

Banana-Fudge Sundaes

Serves 2.

This is a great stand-in for ice cream at birthday parties. And it's easy to make.

1 Frozen Banana (see Index)
Carob-Peanut Fudge Topping, chilled (see page 306)

Slice the banana thinly, and divide between 2 dessert dishes. Top each with a dollop of Carob-Peanut Fudge Topping. Serve at once.

Banana Sherbet

Serves 2.

Very easy, very simple—and very delicious.

2 large Frozen Bananas (see Index)
3 tablespoons water
1 tablespoon lemon juice or ¼ teaspoon vitamin C crystals

Slice the bananas into ¾" slices. Place a few slices in the blender with the water and lemon juice or vitamin C crystals. Puree well and gradually add remaining slices, stopping to scrape the sides of the container as necessary; this step may take 5 minutes in all. Serve in chilled dishes.

Soft Sherbet

Serves 4.

A refreshing, sugar-free sherbet for children and adults alike.

8 ounces crushed unsweetened pineapple, packed in juice
1½ cups frozen strawberries or bananas cut in 1" chunks
1–2 tablespoons honey or maple syrup

Place the pineapple and its juice in a stainless steel bowl. Place in the freezer for 1 hour, until super-chilled but not frozen. Transfer to a blender. Puree 30 seconds. With machine running, add frozen berries or banana chunks, 2 or 3 at a time. Continue until all fruit is pureed. Stop machine and scrape sides of container as necessary. Add honey or maple syrup to taste. Serve immediately in chilled dishes.

NOTE: To serve 8, make sherbet in 2 separate batches. Place first batch in the freezer while you make the second, but do not allow it to freeze solid.

Maple Frosting

Frosts 1 9″ layer cake or 1 9″-×-13″ cake.

You'll need to get a head start making this frosting because the buckwheat flour must soak for an hour or two. But don't finish the frosting until you're ready to use it, because it thickens too much to spread if allowed to stand.

½ cup water or
   unsweetened
   juice
3 tablespoons extra-
   fine white
   buckwheat flour
   (see Note)
2 tablespoons oil
½ cup maple sugar

Combine the water or juice with the flour in a medium saucepan. Set aside to soak for 1 to 2 hours. Then add the oil, and bring to a boil, stirring constantly. Reduce the heat, and allow mixture to bubble for a few minutes, until quite thick and smooth.

Remove from heat, cover and allow to stand for 10 minutes. Then beat in the maple sugar (make sure there are no lumps in the sugar). Beat hard for 1 minute. If you want frosting thicker or thinner, stir in more maple sugar or a little water or maple syrup. Use immediately.

NOTE: If your cake has apple or pineapple in it, use apple or pineapple juice. However, if you want a purer maple flavor, use only water.

To make extra-fine flour, grind ⅓ cup unroasted buckwheat groats in a blender for at least 5 minutes. Strain through a very fine strainer.

If you do not use the icing immediately and it becomes too thick to spread, heat over very low heat, and thin with a little water or maple syrup.

Carob Frosting

Frosts 1 9" layer cake or 1 9"-×-13" sheet cake.

This delicious frosting looks too sinfully rich to be good for you. But it's all "good stuff" and the perfect icing for a birthday cake.

½ pound tofu
2 tablespoons honey
2 tablespoons carob powder
4 teaspoons walnut oil or sunflower oil
4 teaspoons smooth natural peanut butter
1 teaspoon pure vanilla extract
¼ teaspoon wheat-free tamari sauce
1–2 tablespoons water (optional)

Drain the tofu for 20 to 30 minutes, and press it between cotton towels to extract as much moisture as possible. Steam for 5 minutes, then turn it out onto a towel to cool. Pat dry, then crumble with a fork.

Combine the tofu, honey, carob powder, walnut oil or sunflower oil, peanut butter, vanilla and tamari in a blender. Process until very smooth, stopping to scrape the sides of the container as needed. If necessary, add a little water to facilitate blending.

NOTE: For a super birthday cake, bake a double recipe of Carob Fudge Cake (in 2 layers). Frost with Carob Frosting, and pat chopped walnuts into top and sides.

To fill Rice-Flour Cream Puffs, double the frosting recipe.

Maple-Nut Frosting

Frosts an 8"- or 9"-square cake.

You can use this to decorate cakes.

½ pound firm tofu
¼ cup pecans or walnuts
1 tablespoon walnut oil or other oil
¼ cup maple syrup
extra pecans or walnuts, chopped (optional)

Drain the tofu for 20 to 30 minutes, and press it between cotton towels to extract as much moisture as possible. Cut the tofu into thirds lengthwise. Place in a steamer basket, and steam for 5 minutes. When cool enough to handle, pat dry, then press again with cotton towels to remove as much moisture as possible. Cut into 1" cubes.

Grind the nuts to a fine powder in a blender. Add the oil and process into a very smooth nut butter. Blend in the maple syrup.

Add half of the tofu to the blender, and process until smooth. With the machine running, add remaining tofu, one chunk at a time. Blend until very smooth. Stop and scrape sides of container as necessary. Chill at least 30 minutes before using. After frosting, press chopped nuts into frosting. Refrigerate frosted cake until ready to serve.

NOTE: For a super-smooth frosting that holds up on the cake, be sure to extract as much moisture as possible from the tofu before blending. To frost a layer cake, double the recipe.

Maple Creme Topping

Makes ¾ cup.

This goat's-milk topping is very rich and sweet, like sweetened whipped cream, so it's best reserved for holiday desserts.

¼ cup maple syrup
4 teaspoons ice water
½ cup powdered goat's milk
1 tablespoon lemon juice or ¼ teaspoon vitamin C crystals

In a deep bowl, combine the maple syrup and water. Beat with electric beaters to combine. Sprinkle on half the milk powder, and beat in on low speed. Gradually add remaining milk powder. When all milk powder has been incorporated, beat on high speed for 5 minutes. Add lemon juice or vitamin C crystals to taste. Chill.

Banana Topping

Serves 3.

This is a wonderful dairy-free topping for Banana-Buckwheat Breakfast Cake and other coffee-cake-type breads.

1 ripe banana
1 tablespoon maple syrup

Mash the banana and mix with maple syrup. Whip lightly with a fork until it's the consistency of heavy cream.

NOTE: If using Banana Topping on a buffet bread, multiply this recipe as needed and add ¼ teaspoon of vitamin C crystals, to prevent topping from darkening.

Carob-Peanut Fudge Topping _____

Makes about 2 cups.

This sauce is rich, so use it sparingly. Good on Rice-Flour Cream Puffs, plain cake or any of the Ice Creams (see Index).

1⅓ cups water
¼ cup natural peanut butter
½ cup honey
6 tablespoons sifted carob powder
1 tablespoon oil
2 teaspoons pure vanilla extract
1 drop liquid lecithin

Place the water and peanut butter in a blender. Blend a few seconds. With the machine running, add the honey. Blend for 3 to 5 minutes, or until very smooth.

Pour into a 2-quart saucepan. Boil, without stirring, for 5 minutes. Remove from the heat, then whisk in the carob, oil, vanilla and lecithin.

Serve hot or cold. Keeps well for up to 2 weeks in the refrigerator.

Nutty Creme Topping _____

Makes 1 cup.

This simple topping is free of both dairy and soy. Be sure to make it ahead of time so it can chill and thicken in the refrigerator. For an attractive salt-and-pepper effect, use nuts that have a brown coating, like Brazil nuts or unblanched almonds.

½ cup cashews, almonds or Brazil nuts
⅓ cup boiling water
2 tablespoons honey
½ teaspoon lemon juice or a pinch of vitamin C crystals, to taste (optional)

Grind the nuts to a fine powder in a blender. Add the water, honey and lemon juice or vitamin C crystals. Blend on high speed for 2 minutes. Pour into a bowl, and chill for 2 hours.

Variations: You can replace the honey and lemon juice or vitamin C crystals with either 2 tablespoons maple syrup plus a few drops pure almond extract or 2 tablespoons honey plus ¼ teaspoon pure vanilla extract.

Whipped Creamy Topping ──────────────

Makes 1¼ cups.

Make in advance and chill. Use as you would whipped cream.

8 ounces tofu
2 tablespoons
  chopped raw
  cashews
2 tablespoons
  safflower oil (or
  other mild oil)
2 tablespoons honey
2–4 tablespoons water
1 teaspoon pure
  vanilla extract

Drain the tofu for 20 to 30 minutes, pressing it between cotton towels to extract as much moisture as possible. Cut into 1″ cubes, and steam for 5 minutes. Place on a cotton towel to cool.

In a blender, grind the cashews to a fine powder. Add the oil, honey, 2 tablespoons water and vanilla. Blend well. Add tofu, a little at a time, until completely blended and creamy. If you desire a creamier consistency, blend in 1 to 2 tablespoons more water.

Store in the refrigerator. Keeps for 3 or 4 days.

Tofu Creme Topping ──────────────

Makes 1¼ cups.

A creamy accompaniment to Gingerbread and other snack breads, and less rich than Whipped Creamy Topping.

½ pound tofu
2 tablespoons
  cashews
2 tablespoons water
2 tablespoons honey
1 teaspoon pure
  vanilla extract
¼ teaspoon ground
  cinnamon
  (optional)

Drain the tofu for 20 to 30 minutes, pressing it between cotton towels to extract as much moisture as possible. Cut into 1″ cubes, and steam for 5 minutes. Drain, and cool on a cotton towel.

In a blender, grind the cashews to a fine powder. Add the water and honey; blend briefly. Add the tofu, vanilla and cinnamon. Blend until smooth. Refrigerate at least 2 hours.

307

Peachy Topping _____

Makes about 2½ cups.

Make this as smooth or chunky as you like. Serve over pancakes, waffles or desserts.

2 cups diced peaches
  (fresh or frozen)
6 ounces
  unsweetened
  apple-juice
  concentrate
½ cup water
2 tablespoons
  arrowroot
2 tablespoons lemon
  juice or ¼–½
  teaspoon vitamin
  C crystals

Place the peaches and juice concentrate in a saucepan. Bring to a boil, then lower heat, and simmer for 10 minutes. Cool slightly, then transfer to a blender or food processor. Process until it is whatever consistency you prefer. Return to saucepan.

Combine the water, arrowroot and lemon juice or vitamin C crystals. Add to the saucepan. Heat, stirring often, until mixture boils. Allow to boil for 2 minutes.

Serve warm. Leftovers will keep for a few weeks in the refrigerator.

Variation: For Blueberry Topping, use blueberries instead of peaches. Don't bother with blending step; add arrowroot mixture directly to saucepan.

Apricot Topping _____

Makes about 2 cups.

Great over pancakes in the morning or over dessert at night.

16 ounces apricot
  halves, packed in
  juice
2 tablespoons honey
1 tablespoon lemon
  juice or ¼
  teaspoon vitamin
  C crystals

Drain the apricots, and reserve the juice for another use. Puree the apricots in a blender for 10 to 15 seconds. Transfer to a small saucepan. Add the honey and lemon juice or vitamin C crystals. Boil for 5 minutes. Serve warm or cold.

Almond Dessert Sauce _____

Makes 1¼ cups.

Use this over any plain cake, pudding or fresh fruit as you would use cream.

⅓ cup blanched whole
  almonds

Place almonds and arrowroot in a blender and grind to a powder. Add the boiling water.

1 tablespoon
   arrowroot
1 cup boiling water
¼ cup honey
1 tablespoon almond
   oil
¼ teaspoon pure
   almond extract

Let stand 5 minutes. Then add the honey and oil; blend for 2 minutes.

Strain the mixture into a small saucepan. Cook over medium heat, stirring constantly, until mixture thickens and bubbles, about 2 or 3 minutes.

Remove from the heat, and add almond extract. Taste. If you want more almond flavoring, add a bit more extract.

Serve either warm or cold.

Frosty Fruit Sauce

Makes 2¼ cups.

Serve in place of ice cream atop your favorite cake. Try to serve this sauce while it's still thick and partially frozen, like a soft sherbet.

1 cup diced peaches,
   chilled
1½ cups sliced Frozen
   Banana (see
   Index)
2 teaspoons lemon
   juice or scant ¼
   teaspoon vitamin
   C crystals
1 teaspoon honey
   (optional)

Place the peaches in the blender. Process for 10 to 15 seconds, until pureed. Add the banana slices, a few at a time, until all are incorporated and mixture thickens into consistency of soft ice cream. Add the lemon juice or vitamin C crystals. Taste, and add either more lemon juice or vitamin C crystals or honey as needed.

Variations: Substitute strawberries, apricots, nectarines, cherries or blueberries for the peaches. You can even make a refreshing pineapple, orange or grapefruit sauce.

NOTE: You can also make this sauce using frozen peaches (or other fruit) and unfrozen bananas. Just remember that one fruit must be frozen, and one fruit must be a banana.

Pineapple Glaze

Makes about ¼ cup.

A quick glaze to jazz up plain cake.

¼ cup unsweetened
   pineapple-juice
   concentrate
2 tablespoons water
2 tablespoons honey

Combine juice concentrate, water and honey in a small saucepan. Simmer until syrupy, about 5 minutes. Use immediately to drizzle on warm cake.

309

Pineapple Cake Filling _____

Makes 1 cup.

A fruity, easy-to-make filling to sandwich between cake layers. Prepare this filling while the cake bakes, and allow it to cool to room temperature before spreading on the cake.

8 ounces crushed
   unsweetened
   pineapple,
   packed in juice
2 tablespoons
   arrowroot
1–2 tablespoons honey
   or maple syrup
⅛ teaspoon vitamin
   C crystals

Place the pineapple plus its juice, arrowroot, honey or maple syrup and vitamin C crystals in a blender. Process for 1 minute. Pour into a small saucepan. Cook over medium heat, stirring constantly, until thick and bubbly, about 3 minutes. Remove from the heat, and allow to cool at room temperature until needed.

NOTE: Using 1 tablespoon of sweetener will give a thinner filling that would work well with a Party Sponge Cake that's been sliced into horizontal layers. Using 2 tablespoons of sweetener yields a thicker filling that would be more appropriate for a Pineapple-Prune Cake (double the cake recipe for 2 layers). If you should need to thin the filling a bit, reheat on low heat, and stir in a few teaspoons of water.

Holiday Foods

"'Tis the season to be jolly. . . ." And anyone who has food allergies will feel jollier if holiday menus include foods they can eat freely, without risking a stomachache or other allergic reaction. Considering the emotional aspect of food at the holidays, that's especially important. Ask people about their holiday family traditions and they'll start to tell you about special meals that their parents and grandparents made.

You may cry, "But there's too much to do to make two versions of everything!" You're right. So the secret is to make delicious, satisfying "special" food that everyone can enjoy. That's what this section is all about. No one needs to know that the turkey gravy is thickened with rice, oat or amaranth flour as long as it tastes terrific. If everyone raves about the fruit cake, what difference does it make whether it's held together with wheat flour or oat flour?

Many of the dishes featured here are also big hits at birthday parties, bridal showers and other special events. For still other elegant party fare, see the sections, Meat, Poultry and Game; Salad Dressings, Sauces and Condiments; Desserts and Dessert Toppings; and Snacks.

Stuffed Squash

Serves 4 generously.

This makes a hearty meatless meal at Thanksgiving or for other festive occasions in fall and winter.

2 butternut or acorn
    squashes
1 cup water
½ cup chopped
    onions
1 unsprayed apple,
    chopped
2 tablespoons
    walnut oil or oil
¾ cup cooked chick-
    peas, soybeans
    or pinto beans
¼ cup bean Stock
    (see Index)
2 tablespoons lemon
    juice or vinegar
    or ½ teaspoon
    vitamin C
    crystals
1½ teaspoons wheat-
    free tamari
    sauce
1–2 teaspoons
    unsweetened
    apple-juice
    concentrate or
    maple syrup
¼ teaspoon ground
    cinnamon
½ cup chopped
    walnuts
¼ cup currants or
    chopped raisins
2 tablespoons
    sesame seeds

Split the squashes in half lengthwise. Scoop out the seeds. Place squash halves upside down in a baking dish with the water. Bake at 350° for 30 to 40 minutes, or until tender when pricked with a fork.

Sauté the onions and apples in the oil until apples are tender but not mushy. Set aside.

Place the chick-peas or beans, Stock, lemon juice or vinegar or vitamin C crystals, tamari, juice concentrate or maple syrup and cinnamon in a blender. Process until well mixed. Add to apple mixture in frying pan. Add nuts and currants or raisins. Mix well.

Divide stuffing mixture among squash cavities, piling each one high. Sprinkle with sesame seeds. Bake at 350° for 20 minutes.

Roast Lamb with Mint Sauce ———————————

Serves 8 to 10.

Lamb is most plentiful in the spring. That's part of the reason it's an Easter favorite. But lamb is a tasty alternative all year around for people who are allergic to beef, pork or other red meat.

5–7 pounds lamb shoulder or leg
Mint Sauce (see recipe below)

Remove the thin membrane covering the meat. Place the meat on a roasting rack, fat side up. Place the rack in a roasting pan. Roast, uncovered, at 325° for 20 to 30 minutes per pound. (Use 20 minutes for slightly rare meat; 160° on a meat thermometer. Use 30 minutes for well-done meat; 175° to 180°.) Allow roast to stand at least 10 minutes before carving. Serve with Mint Sauce.

NOTE: Half legs of lamb are commonly available for fewer servings.

Mint Sauce ———————————

Makes about 1¼ cups.

⅓ cup mint leaves
1 cup water
¼ cup honey
4 teaspoons arrowroot
2 tablespoons water
pinch of vitamin C crystals (optional)

Combine the mint and 1 cup water in a small saucepan. Simmer for 10 minutes. Strain liquid, then return to saucepan. Stir in honey.

In a cup, dissolve the arrowroot in 2 tablespoons water. Stir into the saucepan. Cook over medium heat, stirring, until slightly thick and bubbly. If you want a little tang, add vitamin C crystals. Serve warm.

Holiday Salad Mold ─────────────────

Serves 16.

A delicate pink salad for holiday buffets or potluck suppers. It's very colorful and flavorful—the whole crowd will love it.

3 cups cranberries
(12 ounces)
12 ounces
unsweetened
pineapple-juice
concentrate
½ cup water
20 ounces crushed
unsweetened
pineapple,
packed in juice
3 tablespoons
unflavored
gelatin
½ cup chopped
cashews
½ cup boiling water
½ cup Homemade
Mayo, Tofu
Mayo or Nutty
Mayo (see
Index)
1–2 tablespoons lemon
juice or ¼
teaspoon
vitamin C
crystals
½ cup water
1 tart unsprayed
apple, diced
1 cup halved
seedless grapes
½ cup chopped
pecans or
walnuts

Measure 2 cups of cranberries into a medium saucepan. Chop or grind the remaining cranberries, and set aside.

Add the juice concentrate and ½ cup water to the cranberries in the saucepan. Simmer for 10 minutes.

Drain the pineapple through a strainer set over a bowl, pressing to extract most of the liquid. Set the pineapple aside; measure the liquid. If there is not 1 cup of liquid, add some water. Sprinkle the gelatin over the liquid, and allow to soften for 5 minutes.

Stir the gelatin into the hot, cooked cranberries, and stir well to dissolve the gelatin. Set aside to cool.

In a blender, grind the cashews to a fine powder. Add the boiling water, and process for 2 minutes. Stop once or twice to scrape the sides of the container. Add the cooked cranberries, and process 1 minute. Add the Mayo and lemon juice or vitamin C crystals to taste. The blender will be getting full, so proceed carefully. With the machine on the lowest speed, add last ½ cup water.

Pour the mixture into a lightly oiled Bundt pan, 9"-×-13" baking dish or other large mold. Chill for about 20 minutes. When mixture has just begun to thicken, stir in the reserved cranberries, reserved pineapple, apples, grapes and pecans or walnuts. Allow to chill until firm, 2 hours or overnight.

If using a Bundt pan or decorative mold, unmold before serving.

Variations: Use 2 cups crushed fresh pineapple. Simmer in water for 10 minutes to deactivate the enzymes that would prevent the gelatin from gelling. Strain the cooked pineapple, and measure the liquid. Proceed as above.

You can replace the pecans and walnuts with pine nuts.

For a totally nut-free mold, omit cashews and chopped nuts. After the cranberry-gelatin mixture has cooled for 10 minutes, liquefy it in a blender. Increase Mayo to 1 cup, then proceed with recipe.

Roast Pork

Serves about 10.

Roast pork is a New Year's Day tradition, meant to insure good luck, good health and happiness in the year ahead. For people with food allergies, pork has additional allure as an alternative to beef and chicken. For people who are allergic to grain, pork is a rich alternative source of vitamin B_1.

1 pork leg or shoulder (about 5 pounds)

Insert a meat thermometer in the thickest part of the meat, making sure it isn't touching a bone. Place the roast on a rack set in a pan. Cook, uncovered, at 325° for 35 minutes per pound, until the thermometer registers 185°. Remove from oven, and allow to stand for 15 minutes before carving.

Sweet-Potato Casserole

Serves 10 to 12.

Make this side dish ahead of time to reduce the hassle of holiday meals. It travels well, too.

6 large sweet potatoes
20 ounces crushed unsweetened pineapple, packed in juice
2 tablespoons oil
2 tablespoons honey or molasses
⅓ cup chopped pecans (optional)

Scrub the sweet potatoes, and remove any bad spots. Bake on a cookie sheet at 350° for 1 hour, until tender. Allow to cool a few minutes, then remove the skins and slice the flesh into 1" pieces. Place in a large bowl.

Add the undrained pineapple, its juice, the oil and honey or molasses to the bowl. Beat with an electric mixer or a sturdy hand masher until well blended and fluffy. Taste, and add a bit more sweetener, if desired.

Turn into an oiled casserole or 9"-×-13" baking dish. Scatter pecans on top. (May be refrigerated at this point.)

Bake at 350° for about 45 minutes, or until casserole is bubbly and browning at the edges. (If covered tightly upon removal from the oven, this dish can be kept warm for quite a while.)

Nutty Pumpkin Pie

Serves 6 to 8.

A no-bake pumpkin pie that's free of eggs, soy and cream. Perfect for Thanksgiving!

½ cup Brazil nuts or cashews
1¼ cups boiling water
1⅓ cups pumpkin puree
½ cup honey
½ teaspoon ground cinnamon
¼ teaspoon grated nutmeg
¼ teaspoon powdered ginger
⅛ teaspoon ground cloves
3 tablespoons arrowroot
2 tablespoons water
1 Nut 'n' Seed Crunch Crust, baked (see Index)

In a blender, grind the nuts to a fine powder. Add the boiling water, and process for 2 minutes.

Add the pumpkin, honey, cinnamon, nutmeg, ginger and cloves. Blend well.

In a 3-quart saucepan, dissolve the arrowroot in the water. Stir in the pumpkin mixture. Bring to a boil, stirring often. Allow to boil for 3 minutes. Remove from heat, and cool until filling is lukewarm. Then pour into the pie shell. Chill a few hours before serving.

Variation: Replace half the honey with molasses.

NOTE: If desired, use Brazil nuts or cashews in the pie shell.

Tofu Pumpkin Pie

Serves 6 to 8.

A dairy-free, egg-free version of a favorite holiday dessert.

8 ounces tofu
1 9″ Rice-Flour Pie Crust, unbaked (see Index)
⅓ cup oil
2 tablespoons lemon juice or ½ teaspoon vitamin C crystals
1 tablespoon lecithin granules (optional)
1 teaspoon wheat-free tamari sauce

Drain the tofu for 20 to 30 minutes, pressing it between cotton towels to extract as much moisture as possible. Crumble with a fork.

Bake the pie crust at 400° for 5 minutes. Set aside.

In a blender or food processor, mix the oil, lemon juice or vitamin C crystals, lecithin and tamari.

Add half of tofu at a time to the machine; process until smooth. With the machine running, add the honey and molasses in a thin stream. Stop the machine to add the pumpkin, cinnamon, ginger and cloves. Process until smooth.

½ cup honey
2 tablespoons
   molasses
   (optional)
2 cups thick
   pumpkin puree
1¼ teaspoons ground
   cinnamon
½ teaspoon
   powdered ginger
¼ teaspoon ground
   cloves

Pour into the pie crust, and bake at 350° for 50 to 55 minutes. Pie is done when small cracks appear in the top. The filling will set more as the pie cools.

Variations: For an easy Pumpkin Pudding, omit the pie crust. Bake the filling in an oiled casserole or baking dish. Cool before serving.

If using a crust, replace the Rice-Flour Pie Crust with an Amaranth Pie Crust or Nut 'n' Seed Crunch Crust.

Pecan Pie

Serves 6 to 8.

Although free of eggs and corn syrup, this tastes as good as traditional pecan pie. And it's not as syrupy sweet as most other versions.

1 cup pecan halves
½ pound pitted dates
1 cup water
3 tablespoons
   molasses
1 tablespoon
   unflavored
   gelatin
1 cup water
1½ teaspoons pure
   vanilla extract
1 9″ Pie Crust, baked
   (see Index)

Scatter the pecans on a baking sheet. Bake at 200° for 25 minutes, until fragrant and toasted. Set aside.

Simmer the dates and 1 cup water in a medium saucepan for 5 minutes. Cool for 5 to 10 minutes, then transfer to a blender. Process until smooth. Add the molasses. Blend well. Return mixture to the saucepan, and keep warm.

In a small bowl, sprinkle the gelatin on 1 cup water. Allow to soften for 5 minutes, then add to the saucepan. Stir over low heat for 2 minutes to dissolve gelatin. Then cool for 10 minutes.

Stir in the vanilla. Then refrigerate mixture, in the saucepan, for 20 to 30 minutes, until thick and just starting to set. Pour into the Pie Crust. Arrange pecans on top, and press lightly. Chill for 2 hours before serving.

Variation: Omit the gelatin. Stir 4½ teaspoons arrowroot into the second cup of water. Add to date mixture in the saucepan. Bring to a boil, and allow to bubble for 3 minutes. Remove from heat and cool 10 minutes before adding vanilla. Chill for about 15 minutes, until cool to the touch. Pour into pie shell, and proceed with recipe.

Plum Pudding _____

Serves about 16.

This is one of the most traditional of all holiday desserts. (Any boiled or steamed pudding that contains fruit and spices is called a plum pudding, even if it doesn't have any plums.) If desired, serve with Almond Dessert Sauce.

2 cups unsweetened
    pineapple juice,
    apple juice or
    white-grape juice
½ pound dates,
    chopped
14 dried figs, chopped
⅔ cup honey or
    molasses, or
    some of each
⅓ cup oil
1 tablespoon grated
    lemon rind or ¼
    teaspoon vitamin
    C crystals
2¼ cups white
    buckwheat flour
    (see Note) or
    amaranth flour
¾ cup arrowroot or
    tapioca-starch
    flour
1½ teaspoons ground
    cinnamon
1 teaspoon baking
    soda
½ teaspoon grated
    nutmeg
½ teaspoon
    powdered ginger
¼ teaspoon ground
    cloves

Place the juice in a 3-quart saucepan. Add the dates and figs. Bring to a boil, then lower heat, and simmer for 5 minutes. Remove from the heat, and add the honey and/or molasses, oil and lemon rind or vitamin C crystals. Stir well. Set aside.

Sift together the buckwheat or amaranth flour, arrowroot or tapioca-starch flour, cinnamon, baking soda, nutmeg, ginger and cloves into a large bowl. Add the flour mixture to the fruit mixture. Stir well to thoroughly mix.

Bring a pot of water to a boil. Turn the flour-fruit mixture into an oiled 2-quart mold, or divide among 4 oiled 1-pound molds. Cover molds with wax paper or foil (shiny side down), and tie with string.

Place the molds in a Dutch oven or large stockpot. Add enough boiling water to the pot to come halfway up the sides of the molds. Cover the pot tightly, and steam the pudding over medium heat for 3 hours. Do not remove the cover during cooking time.

Carefully remove the molds from the water. Set aside to cool until you can handle the molds. Remove pudding from the molds. Either serve warm, or allow to cool completely, wrap and refrigerate until needed.

To reheat, wrap a slice or two in a cloth napkin and place in a steamer basket over hot water. Cover with a tight-fitting lid and steam until moist.

Variations: Use other fruits, such as chopped prunes, raisins and currants, to equal 3 cups. Replace the amaranth or buckwheat flour with 2 cups brown rice flour.

NOTES: The pudding will be grain-free if made without molasses.

For directions on making white buckwheat flour, see Table 1, Cooking and Baking with Alternative Flours, in the section, Exploring New Ingredients.

Gingerbread Men

Makes 10 to 15.

Old-fashioned gingerbread cookies are especially fun to make for Halloween, Thanksgiving and Christmas.

2 cups white
    buckwheat flour
    (see Note)
½ cup date sugar
1 teaspoon baking
    soda
1 teaspoon powdered
    ginger
¼ teaspoon vitamin C
    crystals
¼ cup safflower oil
¼ cup molasses
2 tablespoons water
    currants (garnish)
    dried papaya
    (garnish)

In a medium bowl, mix the flour, date sugar, baking soda, ginger and vitamin C crystals. Make a well in the middle.

In a cup mix the oil, molasses and water. Pour into the well in the flour. Stir to blend. If mixture is too crumbly to form into a ball, add a bit more water. Divide dough into 2 balls.

Roll out each ball between sheets of wax paper. Remove the top sheet, and cut the dough with cookie cutters. Use a wide metal spatula to carefully transfer the cookies to cookie sheets. Reroll trimmings until all are used.

Decorate the cookies by using currants for eyes and buttons. Shape thin strips of papaya into mouths, collars and belts.

Bake at 350° for 8 to 10 minutes, until cookies are firm and edges are just starting to brown.

NOTE: For directions on making white buckwheat flour, see Table 1, Cooking and Baking with Alternative Flours, in the section, Exploring New Ingredients.

Elegant and Easy Fruitcake _____

Makes 1 cake.

People with allergies to wheat and corn syrup can have their (fruit) cake and eat it, too. This version of the traditional holiday treat is so good that I served it at my son's wedding. Prepare the cake a few days ahead to allow flavors to "ripen."

¾ cup unsweetened apple juice
¼ cup unsweetened pineapple juice
1 cup chopped dates
¾ cup chopped dried papaya or dried apricots
½ cup raisins or currants
¾ cup sifted brown rice flour
¾ cup sifted oat flour
1 teaspoon baking soda
½ teaspoon ground cinnamon
¼ teaspoon grated nutmeg
2 large eggs at room temperature
½ cup oil
1 cup chopped pecans or walnuts or ½ cup of each
Pineapple Glaze (optional; see Index)

In a small saucepan, combine apple juice, pineapple juice, dates, papaya or apricots and raisins or currants. Bring to a boil, then turn off the heat, and cover the pan.

Into a large mixing bowl, resift the rice flour and oat flour with the baking soda, cinnamon and nutmeg.

In a small bowl, beat the eggs until well mixed. Slowly beat in the oil.

Alternately add the fruit mixture and the egg mixture to the flour. Stir until just mixed; do not overmix. Stir in the nuts. The batter will be very thick.

Transfer batter to an oiled 9"- × -5" loaf pan. Bake at 325° for 50 to 60 minutes, or until the cake is browned and fine cracks appear (or until a cake tester inserted in the center comes out clean).

Allow to cool in pan for 10 minutes. Then turn out onto a wire rack. If using Pineapple Glaze, prick the top of the warm cake in 8 or 10 places with a fork, then slowly drizzle with the glaze.

Cool completely. Wrap tightly in wax paper, cellophane or foil with the shiny side in (oil the portion of wrapping that will touch glaze to prevent sticking). Allow to ripen for a few days at room temperature.

Slice with a wet serrated knife. (For easiest slicing, freeze cake for 2 hours before slicing; allow slices to return to room temperature before serving.)

Variation: For a grain-free cake, replace the brown rice flour and the oat flour with 1 cup sifted amaranth flour plus ½ cup arrowroot.

NOTE: You can double this recipe and bake it in a Bundt pan.

Steamed Cranberry Bread _____

Makes 1 loaf.

What a festive holiday bread! And you can make it well in advance.

1½ cups cranberries
2 tablespoons honey
1½ cups oat flour
1½ cups brown rice flour
1 tablespoon Corn-Free Baking Powder (see Index)
½ teaspoon baking soda
½ teaspoon grated nutmeg (optional)
¾ cup chopped nuts
1 cup unsweetened pineapple juice or 1 cup water and ¼ teaspoon vitamin C crystals
½ cup oil
½ cup honey

Chop the cranberries in a food processor or food grinder. Place in a small bowl, and mix with 2 tablespoons honey. Set aside.

Sift the oat flour, rice flour, Corn-Free Baking Powder, baking soda and nutmeg into a medium bowl. Stir in the nuts. Set aside.

In a 3-quart saucepan, heat the juice or water and vitamin C crystals, oil and honey until the honey liquefies. The mixture should be barely lukewarm. Remove from the heat. Stir in the cranberries. Stir in the flour mixture, mixing just until all flour is moistened. Do not overmix.

Turn mixture into an oiled 2-quart mold. Cover with a piece of foil (shiny side down) or a double piece of wax paper. Tie securely with a piece of string. Place the mold on a rack in a Dutch oven or large stockpot. Add enough boiling water to the pot to come halfway up the sides of the mold. Cover the pot tightly, and steam over low heat for 4 hours. Do not remove the cover during cooking time.

Carefully remove the mold from the pan. Cool bread in its mold for 15 minutes. Then turn out onto a wire rack to cool completely.

Variations: For a grain-free version, replace the oat flour and brown rice flour with 3 cups white buckwheat flour or 2½ cups amaranth flour plus ½ cup of either arrowroot or tapioca starch flour. (For directions on making white buckwheat flour, see Table 1, Cooking and Baking with Alternative Flours, in the section, Exploring New Ingredients.)

To make Cranberry Muffins, beat 2 eggs until light and fluffy. Slowly beat in oil, then honey, in a thin stream. Add pineapple juice or water and vitamin C. Pour liquids over cranberry mixture, then stir in flour mixture to moisten. Spoon into 12 oiled or paper-lined muffin cups. Bake at 400° for 18 to 22 minutes, until brown. Best served warm. Leftovers freeze well.

321

Party Sponge Cake

Serves 10 to 12.

No one who tasted this cake could believe it doesn't contain wheat. It's as feather-light and airy as regular sponge cakes. Top it with a dessert sauce or fill and frost as directed below. Perfect for birthday parties, wedding showers and other special events.

¾ cup sifted maple sugar
1½ teaspoons grated lemon rind
¾ cup *plus* 2 tablespoons potato starch
¼ cup sifted maple sugar
1½ teaspoons Corn-Free Baking Powder (see Index)
6 egg yolks
¼ cup warm water
1 tablespoon lemon juice or 1 teaspoon pure vanilla extract
6 egg whites
½ teaspoon cream of tartar
Pineapple Cake Filling (optional; see Index)
Maple Frosting (optional; see Index)

In a small bowl, mix ¾ cup maple sugar and the lemon rind. Set aside.

Into a medium bowl, sift the potato starch, ¼ cup maple sugar and Corn-Free Baking Powder. Resift, then set aside.

In a small, deep bowl, beat the egg yolks with an electric mixer for 5 minutes, until light and thick. Transfer to a large bowl, and beat in the lemon-sugar mixture by rounded table-spoonfuls. Beat in the water and lemon juice or vanilla. The mixture should be very thick and fluffy. On low speed, beat in the flour mixture.

In another bowl, using absolutely *clean and dry* beaters, beat the egg whites on low speed until frothy. Beat in the cream of tartar. Beat on medium speed for 1 minute. Then increase speed to high, and beat until stiff, shiny peaks form, about 2 to 2½ minutes. *Do not* beat until whites become dry.

Using a rubber spatula, gently fold the whites into the yolk mixture. Mix just until all trace of whites disappears, otherwise you might deflate the whites and impair their ability to raise the batter.

Pour into a clean, dry angel-food pan with removable bottom. Bake at 350° for 35 to 40 minutes, until top is a deep golden brown with a crack and cake springs back when lightly touched. Remove from oven, and invert pan on a wire rack. Allow to cool for 1½ to 2 hours in the pan. Then run a thin knife around the sides of the cake to loosen it. Press firmly on the bottom of the pan to remove it from the pan. To completely free the cake from the pan, run the knife around the bottom, then around the inside edges next to the tube.

Gently invert the cake onto a serving plate. Brush all loose crumbs from top and sides. Using a serrated knife, gently cut cake in half horizontally. Fill with Pineapple Cake Filling. Reassemble cake, then frost top with Maple Frosting (if desired, frost sides, too). Chill until about 30 minutes before serving.

Variation: Replace the potato starch with sifted white buckwheat flour. (For directions on making white buckwheat flour, see Table 1, Cooking and Baking with Alternative Flours, in the section, Exploring New Ingredients.)

NOTES: If you have a food processor, you can use it to grate the lemon rind and mix it with the maple sugar. First, process all your maple sugar in the food processor to remove any lumps and reduce it to a fine powder. That takes the place of sifting it. Measure out 1 cup, and store the rest in an airtight container. Set aside the ¼ cup of maple sugar that you'll sift with the flour. Place the rest back in the processor bowl. Add about 10 2" strips of lemon peel that you've removed with a potato peeler from scrubbed, organically grown lemons. Process for 1 to 2 minutes until finely ground.

    Eggs separate most easily when they're cold. Make sure that there are no specks of yolk in with the whites, because they'll prevent the whites from being beaten into stiff peaks. Allow the separated yolks and whites to stand 15 to 20 minutes, covered, to warm to room temperature before beating.

    Do not substitute a Bundt cake pan for the tube pan. You need to be able to remove the cake from the pan with a knife.

Hidden Treasures

Makes about 40.

There's no cooking involved in these easy-to-make treats, but they're elegant enough to present as a hostess gift or to serve at holiday dinners or birthday parties. And they're easy enough to make that the kids can help.

1 cup natural peanut
    butter, room
    temperature
½ cup honey
½ cup carob powder
    raisins or toasted
    almonds
    shredded
    unsweetened
    coconut or toasted
    sesame seeds

In a medium bowl, cream together the peanut butter and honey with a fork until well mixed. Gradually mix in the carob. The mixture will be quite stiff and rather dry. Test the consistency by pinching a bit of dough between your fingers. It should mold well and hold its shape. If not, add a tiny bit of water.

Place the raisins or almonds and coconut or sesame seeds in individual bowls.

To make the treasures, take a small cluster of raisins (about 4 to 6) or 1 almond. Shape about a teaspoonful of dough mixture around them, covering the center completely. Roll in either coconut or sesame seeds. Repeat until all dough is used. Refrigerate for 1 hour before serving. Store in the refrigerator.

Variations: Replace the peanut butter with almond butter or cashew butter.

Carob–Peanut Butter Fudge

Makes about 32 pieces.

This is a rich confection, so cut it into small squares. Most other fudge recipes use milk powder.

1 cup natural peanut
    butter
¼ cup honey
¼ cup carob powder
¼ cup ground peanuts
¼ cup chopped
    peanuts
2 tablespoons toasted
    sesame seeds
    (optional)
    raisins (optional)

In a medium bowl, stir together the peanut butter and honey with a wooden spoon. Stir in the carob, ground peanuts, chopped peanuts and sesame seeds. The mixture will be very thick and heavy, but don't add any liquid.

Press into an 8″-×-4″ loaf pan. If desired, press raisins into the top. Chill. Cut into 1″ squares.

Variations: Omit the ground peanuts. Replace them with ¼ to ½ cup grated unsweetened coconut. If desired, sprinkle top of fudge with coconut in addition to or instead of the raisins.

Spiced Fruit Compote

Makes about 6 cups.

While this is a festive treat to make during the holidays, it's also convenient when you don't have time to bake a cake or pie for dessert. If you want to serve this as a side dish, omit the honey.

1 cup prunes
1 cup dried apricots or peaches
1 cup quartered dried figs
1 cup raisins
2 cinnamon sticks
¼ teaspoon ground cloves
1–2 tablespoons lemon juice or ¼ teaspoon vitamin C crystals (optional)
1–2 tablespoons honey (optional)

Place the prunes, apricots or peaches, figs, raisins, cinnamon and cloves in a 3-quart saucepan. Add enough water to just cover the fruit. Bring to a boil, then lower the heat, and simmer for 15 minutes. If needed, add water to keep fruit covered. Cool slightly, then add lemon juice or vitamin C crystals and honey to taste. Serve warm or cold.

Store in the refrigerator. Keeps up to 1 month.

Cranberry Mulled Cider

Serves 32.

Rosy-colored and fragrant, this holiday punch is pleasingly tart yet slightly sweet.

1 gallon apple cider
3 cups cranberries (12 ounces)
6 ounces unsweetened apple-juice concentrate
12 cloves
4 cinnamon sticks
3 small unsprayed apples studded with cloves (garnish)

In a Dutch oven, combine the cider, cranberries, juice concentrate, cloves and cinnamon. Bring to a boil, then lower the heat, and simmer for 30 minutes. Cool for 10 minutes. Strain into a punch bowl. Let cool a few minutes, then garnish with the apples.

Mulled Cranberry Punch

Serves 32.

An apple-free alternative to cider.

3 quarts unsweetened pineapple juice
1 quart water
4 cups cranberries (1 pound)
½ cup honey
12 cloves
4 cinnamon sticks
8 ounces unsweetened pineapple rings, packed in juice (garnish)

In a Dutch oven, combine the juice, water, cranberries, honey, cloves and cinnamon. Bring to a boil, then lower the heat, and simmer for 30 minutes. Cool for 10 minutes, then strain into a punch bowl. Garnish with drained pineapple rings.

Picnic, Camping and Outdoor Foods

Do you have a Boy Scout or Girl Scout in your family? Or a hiker? Does your family enjoy camping? With a few adaptions, you can stick to an allergy diet in the great outdoors just as you do at home.

One of the things that we can learn from the prepackaged foods on the market is the convenience of using pre-mixed food. Sunny Camp Cakes and Mung-Bean Chowder are two examples of mixes that you can easily make yourself and are perfect for outdoor meals. But you can adapt several recipes throughout this book for campsite cooking. For example, practice making Tortillas (a Bread recipe) at home until you are comfortable with the process. It's simple to do and a natural for primitive conditions. Marjorie Fisher's Venison Stew and Rabbit-Vegetable Stew (from the Soups, Stews and Chowder section) can be adapted to other meats and cooked over the campfire. Or make the Catfish Chowder from that section. You can also bake fish, wrapped in foil, over the coals at the campsite or on the patio grill at home. (See the Index for recipes for Baked Fish Fillets and Broiled Fish.)

When you think about it, campsite cooking is no more complicated than at-home cooking. In fact, it's easier, since dishes are usually simple one-pot mixtures of just a few foods.

327

No-Bake Granola _____

Serves 8.

This is a nice breakfast food for campers to carry. Because it doesn't need honey or oil, this recipe is less sweet and rich than traditional granolas, but it still captures that characteristic flavor and crunch. I like to use the less-common nuts like Brazil nuts, filberts, macadamias and pine nuts.

2 cups quick-cooking
    oats
½ cup sunflower seeds
1 cup chopped nuts
½ cup grated
    unsweetened
    coconut
½ cup chopped dried
    unsweetened
    pineapple
½ cup chopped dried
    papaya
    Pineapple Milk (see
    Index) or herb tea

Place 1 cup of the oats and the sunflower seeds in a blender or food processor. Grind finely. Transfer to a large bowl. Add the remaining oats, nuts, coconut, pineapple and papaya. Toss to combine. Store in the refrigerator.

Serve moistened with Pineapple Milk or herb tea.

Variations: Replace the pineapple and papaya with your choice of dried apricots, dried peaches, dried apples, prunes, raisins or currants.

People on a Diversified Rotary Diet can choose either sunflower seeds or nuts—but not both—to limit the number of food families involved.

NOTE: To prepare the granola at the campsite: Omit the grinding step to produce a granola that's coarser but delightfully chewy. To serve, moisten with fruit juice or herb tea, and allow to soak for 5 minutes.

Trail Mix _____

Makes 5 cups.

Don't reserve this just for backpacking. It's a wonderful snack any time. You can vary the ingredients to suit your personal tastes. Use either raw or toasted nuts, as you choose.

1½ cups raisins
1 cup peanuts
½ cup almonds
½ cup walnuts or
    pecans
½ cup sunflower
    seeds
½ cup pumpkin

Combine the raisins, peanuts, almonds, walnuts or pecans, sunflower seeds, pumpkin seeds and cashews in a large bowl. Store in glass jars in the refrigerator.

Variations: Replace half of the raisins with quartered dried apricots. You could replace any of the nuts with Brazil nuts, macadamia nuts,

seeds
½ cup cashews

filberts or pine nuts. You can vary the seeds, too, but note that very small ones, like sesame, can be difficult to eat with your fingers.

NOTE: If you're on a Diversified Rotary Diet, you might want to make smaller quantities of Trail Mix using fewer food families.

Carrot Survival Sticks

Makes 8.

These are not a cookie or a casual snack food. They're designed so that just a few of them supply all the nutrients needed for a single meal. My guess is that they are adequate in all of the essential nutrients except vitamin D. And if you're out hiking or swimming, you're getting your quota of that vitamin from the sun. Make them at home and carry them with you—they're amazingly satisfying.

2 cups grated
    carrots
⅔ cup rolled oats
⅓ cup amaranth
    flour
⅓ cup oat bran
⅓ cup ground
    sunflower seeds
2 tablespoons
    sesame seeds
    (optional)
¼ teaspoon anise
    seeds
¼ teaspoon vitamin
    C crystals
3 tablespoons oil
2 tablespoons honey
    or molasses
1–2 tablespoons water
    (optional)

If the carrots aren't grated to the texture of coarse meal, place ½ cup at a time on a cutting board, and chop with a knife. Place in a large bowl, and add the oats, flour, bran, sunflower seeds, sesame seeds, anise and vitamin C crystals.

Heat the oil and honey or molasses in a small saucepan until the sweetener liquefies. Stir into the carrot mixture. If mixture is too dry to hold its shape, add a bit of water.

Shape ¼ cup of the mixture at a time into a small log, a little shorter and fatter than a hot dog. Place the logs on a non-stick baking sheet. Bake at 350° for 20 minutes. Turn the logs over, and bake another 20 to 25 minutes.

Cool on wire racks. Store in an airtight container. Sticks will keep for a few days at room temperature, for 2 weeks in the refrigerator and for a few months in the freezer.

Variations: Replace the amaranth flour with soy powder, ground peanuts, ground nuts, ground seeds or buckwheat flour. Replace the oat bran with rice flour, rice polish or rice bran. Replace the anise seeds with ¼ to ½ teaspoon dried herbs of your choice.

NOTE: To chop carrots with a food processor, use a steel blade, not a grating disk.

Fig Fudge ─────────────────────────────

Makes ¾ pound.

Dried fruits and seeds are concentrated sources of nutrients and energy, making them perfect trail food. Make this fudge at home a day or so before your outing. It keeps well and packs easily.

¼ cup toasted
    sunflower
    seeds
1 cup chopped
    dates
8–10 large figs,
    chopped
¼ teaspoon vitamin
    C crystals
2 tablespoons
    toasted
    sunflower
    seeds
    (optional)

Place the ¼ cup sunflower seeds in a food processor, and process briefly. Add the dates, figs and vitamin C crystals. Process until well chopped and mixture forms a ball atop the metal blade. Press mixture into a loaf pan or mess kit. Press additional sunflower seeds into top. Chill until needed.

Variation: Form the fudge into a log shape. Roll it in ½ cup or more seeds, pressing the seeds into the fudge.

NOTE: You can also make this fudge by grinding the fruit and seeds through a food grinder. Sprinkle on the vitamin C crystals, and work them in by hand.

Rice-and-Lentil Camp Supper ─────────────

Serves 2 to 3.

Made in one pot, this is a less-expensive, homemade version of dehydrated meals sold in many camp-supply stores. Very nutritious, too.

1 cup raw brown
    rice
½ cup lentils
2 tablespoons
    dehydrated
    onion flakes
1 tablespoon kombu
    powder or
    Savory Seed
    Seasoning (see
    Index)
1 bay leaf
½ teaspoon ground
    cinnamon
½ teaspoon

Combine the rice and lentils in a small container.

Combine the onion flakes, kombu or Savory Seed Seasoning, bay leaf, cinnamon, ginger, cardamom, garlic powder, cloves and cayenne in another small container.

Label the packages and tape together. Make a notation to use 3½ cups water and 3 tablespoons oil to cook.

To make, place the rice and lentils in a large pot or other container. Add 3½ cups water, cover, and allow to soak all day.

At dinnertime, heat the oil in a large frying pan or pot. Add the contents of the seasoning packet. Stir for a few minutes, then add the

powdered
ginger
½ teaspoon ground
cardamom
¼ teaspoon garlic
powder
2–3 cloves
pinch of cayenne
pepper
(optional)
3½ cups water
3 tablespoons oil

soaking rice and lentils and their liquid. Bring to a boil, and cook for about 25 minutes.

Variations: Replace the cinnamon, ginger and cardamom with 2 to 3 teaspoons Curry Powder (see Index). Replace the kombu or Savory Seed Seasoning with 1 teaspoon dried lemon rind or 1 to 3 teaspoons wheat-free tamari.

NOTE: An alternate method of cooking this dish is to heat the oil in a large frying pan. Stir in the seasonings, and sauté for a few minutes. Then add the unsoaked rice and lentils, plus 3½ cups water. Cook over low heat for 50 to 60 minutes.

Mung-Bean Chowder

Serves 4.

Pack this at home, and take it on camp outings for a quickly prepared, satisfying on-site soup.

½ cup mung beans
½ cup rolled oats,
rice grits or raw
basmati rice (see
Appendix)
¼ cup toasted sesame
seeds
1½ teaspoons
dehydrated
onion flakes
1 tablespoon Pizzazz
Seasoning (see
Index)
1 tablespoon kombu
powder or
Savory Seed
Seasoning (see
Index)
¼ teaspoon garlic
powder
3½ cups water

Combine the mung beans with the oats or rice grits or basmati rice, sesame seeds, onion flakes, Pizzazz Seasoning, kombu or Savory Seed Seasoning and garlic powder in a container. Label, and make a note to add 3½ cups water to cook.

To cook, mix the dry ingredients with the water. Bring to a boil, and cook for about 30 minutes, stirring occasionally.

Variations: Replace the Pizzazz Seasoning with 1 teaspoon parsley flakes, ½ teaspoon ground cumin, ½ teaspoon dried dill weed, ½ teaspoon ground fennel, ¼ teaspoon ground caraway seeds and ¼ teaspoon ground celery seeds. Replace the kombu or Savory Seed Seasoning with 1 teaspoon dried lemon rind or 1 to 3 teaspoons wheat-free tamari.

You can also add bits of meat or a small fish to the chowder.

Door County Fish Boil _____

Serves 4.

The culinary specialty of Door County, Wisconsin, is the fish boil, and it's a real treat. Tourists seek out public dinners and make reservations a week ahead. Locals cook up big pots of the fragrant stock over back-yard grills and fireplaces. The festivities may even begin at dawn with the fishing party going after the day's catch. Recipes vary widely, with everyone having an opinion on which seasonings are best and whether or not to add onions and potatoes to the pot. I favor putting the vegetables in the pot to simplify preparation. Although an authentic fish boil is served with melted butter, the simple dill sauce given here makes an excellent substitute. This recipe serves four, but you can easily multiply it for a crowd. Serve with coleslaw and a do-ahead dessert for a simply memorable meal.

1½ quarts water
1 small onion, quartered
½ cup celery leaves or celery stalks cut into 1" chunks
1 tablespoon vinegar or lemon juice
1 bay leaf
1 teaspoon dried tarragon or dried dill weed
¼ teaspoon crushed fennel seeds
12 small new potatoes
6 carrots
1¼–1¾ pounds whitefish fillets (see Variations)

In a Dutch oven or stockpot, combine the water, onion, celery, vinegar or lemon juice, bay leaf, tarragon or dill and fennel. The pot should not be more than half full. Bring to a rolling boil, then lower the heat, and simmer for 30 minutes or more.

Place serving platter and plates in a warming oven, or near the fire if outdoors.

Scrub the potatoes, but do not peel them; add to the pot. Cut the carrots into thick sticks about 3" long; add to the pot. Cook at a rolling boil for 15 minutes.

Divide the fish into 4 portions. Wrap 2 portions in a square of well-washed cheesecloth. Repeat with remaining 2 portions. Add to the pot. When the stock returns to a boil, lower the heat, and simmer the fish gently for 10 minutes.

Remove the fish and vegetables to the warm platter, and keep them warm while you prepare the sauce.

Bring the cooking liquid to a full boil, and cook for 2 minutes to reduce it to 2 cups. Strain 2 cups of the liquid into a measuring cup.

In a blender, grind the oats, dill and paprika to a fine powder. Add the oil and strained liquid. Process for 30 seconds. Transfer to a small

2 tablespoons
 rolled oats
4½ teaspoons
 dried dill
 weed
1 tablespoon
 Hungarian
 paprika
2 tablespoons oil
 lemon wedges
 (garnish)

saucepan. Bring to a boil, stirring constantly. When the sauce has thickened, taste it and adjust the seasonings as you desire.

Either pour the sauce over individual servings of fish and vegetables or place it in a gravy boat and pass it separately. Garnish servings with lemon wedges.

Variations: If you don't have small new potatoes, use 4 large red potatoes, and cut them into quarters.

For a more authentic fish boil, use about a 2-pound whole, cleaned whitefish. When using whole fish, allow 15 minutes for it to cook.

You can replace the whitefish fillets with 2 pounds of monkfish.

NOTE: If you will be serving a large crowd, you may elect to prepare the sauce ahead. I like to cook a smaller version of the fish boil a week ahead of time so I can use the stock to make as much sauce as I'll need for the party. Then I can prepare the sauce and freeze it until I need it. It's a simple matter to reheat the sauce while the fish cooks. And it insures that the piping-hot fish and vegetables will be served promptly to hungry guests.

Sunny Camp Cakes ————————————————

Serves 2.

These pancakes are specifically designed for campers. Mix the dry ingredients at home, then add the liquids when you're ready to cook. Double or triple the recipe for multiple servings. Serve with maple syrup or fruit butter.

½ cup brown rice flour
¼ cup rice bran
¼ cup rice polish
¼ cup ground
    sunflower seeds
1 teaspoon Corn-Free
    Baking Powder
    (see Index)
¾ cup *plus* 2
    tablespoons water
2 tablespoons
    sunflower oil
1 tablespoon maple
    syrup or Old-
    Fashioned Fruit
    Butter (optional)

Combine the flour, rice bran, rice polish, sunflower seeds and Corn-Free Baking Powder. Wrap well, and label.

To make, mix the water, oil and maple syrup or Old-Fashioned Fruit Butter in a medium bowl. Add the flour mixture, and stir to mix well.

Drop tablespoonfuls of batter onto a hot griddle or frying pan. Cook for 3 minutes or more, until bubbly on top and brown on the bottom. Turn and cook another 3 minutes or more.

Variation: Replace the sunflower seeds with ¼ cup powdered goat's milk for browner, more flavorful pancakes.

Bar-B-Q Chicken ————————————————

Serves 4.

Because this chicken is cooked indoors and then carried out to the picnic table to serve, it's a good alternative for people who are allergic to the fumes from gas or charcoal cookers.

Commercial barbecue sauces may contain sodium benzoate, cornstarch, corn syrup, hickory smoke flavor, caramel color and unspecified spices and flavorings. If any of those ingredients are a problem for you, try this recipe.

1 frying chicken
    (about 3 pounds)
¼ cup honey-
    sweetened
    ketchup
2 tablespoons lemon
    juice
2 tablespoons honey
1 teaspoon Dijon-style
    mustard

Cut the chicken into serving pieces. Remove the skin from all pieces except the wings. Arrange in a single layer in a glass baking dish.

In a small saucepan, combine the ketchup, lemon juice, honey and mustard. Simmer for 5 minutes. Brush the sauce on the chicken. Sprinkle with sesame seeds.

Bake at 400° for 35 to 45 minutes, until chicken is tender.

sesame seeds

NOTE: You can double or triple the recipe to serve a crowd. You can also use boned chicken breasts. Allow 1 individual breast per person, and bake for 30 minutes.

Bar-B-Q Baked Beans

Serves 6.

Commercially prepared baked beans can be a problem for people with allergies because they often contain sugar and corn syrup, plus ambiguous ingredients such as modified food starch and "natural flavoring." Slowly baking these beans contributes to their wonderful flavor and aroma.

1 cup chopped onions
⅔ cup chopped celery
⅔ cup chopped green peppers or chili peppers
2 tablespoons olive oil
2 garlic cloves, minced
6 ounces tomato paste
2 cups water or bean Stock (see Index)
¼ cup molasses or honey
¼ cup vinegar
2 tablespoons wheat-free tamari sauce (optional)
2 tablespoons tahini or ground sesame seeds
2 tablespoons Dijon-style mustard
dash of hot pepper sauce or ⅛ teaspoon cayenne pepper
4 cups cooked navy or Great Northern beans (1⅓ cups dry) (discard soak water)

In a large frying pan or 3-quart saucepan, sauté the onions, celery and peppers in the oil until soft. Add the garlic, and cook another 2 minutes. Stir in the tomato paste, water or bean Stock, molasses or honey, vinegar, tamari, tahini or sesame seeds, mustard and pepper sauce or cayenne. Simmer for 10 minutes.

Stir the beans in. Transfer to an oiled 2-quart casserole. Bake uncovered at 300° for 2½ hours.

NOTE: For picnics and back-yard barbecues, you can keep the casserole warm for 2 hours by wrapping it in a bath towel.

335

Appendix

Directory of Foods, Kitchen Aids and Information Services

Compiled with the assistance of Pamela Boyer

A number of distributors sell foods specially made for people with food allergies. And some of the recipes in this book call for ingredients that you may not find in supermarkets or in all health food stores. To further help you cope with food allergies, we've compiled a guide to foods, kitchen aids and allergy-information services. This directory is by no means an all-inclusive list of sources nor does it constitute endorsement of any product or service by the author or publisher. However, we feel that the information will help you make the most of this cookbook. (Please contact mail-order sources for order forms, catalogs or other up-to-date ordering information. Call retail companies for locations of stores in your area that sell their brands.)

Source	Product or Service	Ordering Information
Air Filters and Purifiers		
Air Cleaners for Allergy Problems 9550 Deering #310 Houston, TX 77036 (713) 995-6110	Medisphere Air Purifier/Ionizer	Mail Order

338

Source	Product or Service	Ordering Information
Air Techniques, Inc. 1717 Whitehead Rd. Baltimore, MD 21207 (301) 944-6037	Cleanaire furnace and room-size HEPA filters	Retail through hospital and surgical suppliers
Bio-Tech Systems P.O. Box 25380 Chicago, IL 60625 (800) 621-5545 (312) 465-8020	Cleanaire HEPA room air filters, Space Gard furnace filters, Bio-Tech Dust Guard furnace filters	Mail Order
E. L. Foust Co. Box 105 Elmhurst, IL 60126 (312) 834-4952	Foust all-steel activated-carbon room, auto and desk air filters; Dustron furnace filter	Mail Order
High Country Air Systems 4324 Sunbelt Dr. Dallas, TX 75248 (214) 386 9615	High Country Air Filter	Retail, Mail Order
Research Products Corp. 1015 E. Washington Ave. P.O. Box 1467 Madison, WI 53701 (800) 356-9652 (608) 257-8801	Space Gard room and furnace air filters, E Z Kleen commercial air filters; kitchen exhaust filters	Retail through hospital and surgical suppliers
Vitaire Corp. 81–13 Broadway Elmhurst, NY 11373 (212) 335-8589	Vitaire HEPA room air filter	Retail through hospital and surgical suppliers

Allergy Identification

Source	Product or Service	Ordering Information
Health Enterprises, Inc. 15 Spruce St. North Attleboro, MA 02760 (617) 695-0727	Identification bracelets and necklaces listing allergies or other medical problems; medical-alert cards for wallets; medical-alert information kit for the home	Retail

Source	Product or Service	Ordering Information

Allergy Identification—continued

Source	Product or Service	Ordering Information
Medic Alert Foundation International P.O. Box 1009 Turlock, CA 95380 (209) 668-3333	Identification bracelets and necklaces listing allergies or other medical problems; 24-hour emergency answering service; wallet identification	Mail Order

Associations

Source	Product or Service	Ordering Information
Allergy Research Group 2470 Estand Way Pleasant Hill, CA 94523 (415) 685-1228	Provides information and a physician-referral service	
American Allergy Association P.O. Box 7273 Menlo Park, CA 94026 (415) 322-1663	Organization of patients and others interested in problems created by allergies; provides allergy information	
American Celiac Society 45 Gifford Ave. Jersey City, NJ 07304 (201) 432-1207	Provides information	
Asthma and Allergy Foundation of America 1302 18th St. NW Suite 303 Washington, DC 20036 (202) 293-2950	Provides information and educational materials to the public; maintains a library and speakers bureau	
Feingold Association of the United States Drawer AG Holtsville, NY 11742 (516) 543-4658	Provides information on food allergies	

Source	Product or Service	Ordering Information
Gluten Intolerance Group P.O. Box 23053 Seattle, WA 98102 (206) 854-9606	Provides information on gluten intolerance; offers various services for children, including counseling	
Human Ecology Action League (HEAL) 505 N. Lake Shore Dr., Suite 6506 Chicago, IL 60611 (312) 836-0422	Provides a directory of physicians practicing clinical ecology; publishes *The Human Ecologist*	
Society for Clinical Ecology P.O. Box 16106 Denver, CO 80216	Write for referrals to clinical ecologists (environmentally oriented allergists and other physicians)	

Baked Goods

Source	Product or Service	Ordering Information
Barbara's Bakery, Inc. 15 Commercial Blvd. Novato, CA 94947 (415) 883-3393	Cookies and snacks (no chemical additives or preservatives); ingredient listing available on request	Retail
Ener-G Foods, Inc. P.O. Box 24723 6901 Fox Ave. S Seattle, WA 98124 (206) 767-6660	Baked gluten-free rice bread, baked gluten-free brown-rice bread (made without wheat, eggs, sugar or lactose)	Retail, Mail Order
Pride O' the Farm Southern Food Products Co., Inc. 5353 Downey Rd. Vernon, CA 90058	Cookies, granolas, others (preservative free; some made without milk)	Retail
Wuest Dietary Baked Foods, Inc. P.O. Box 283 Roslyn, NY 11578 (516) 484-3322	Gluten-free bread, other breads free of chemical additives and preservatives	Retail

341

Source	Product or Service	Ordering Information

Cleaning Products

Allergen-Proof Encasings, Inc. 1450 E. 363rd St. Eastlake, OH 44094 (800) 321-1096 (216) 946-6700	APE mold remover and mold preventative	Mail Order
Amway Corp. 7575 E. Fulton Rd. Ada, MI 49355 (616) 676-7134	L.O.C. (Liquid Organic Cleaner)	Home Demonstration
Ar-Ex Products Co. 1036 W. Van Buren St. Chicago, IL 60607 (312) 226-5241	Safe-Suds liquid detergent, hand lotion	Retail
Arm & Hammer Division Church & Dwight Co., Inc. 20 Kingsbridge Rd. Piscataway, NJ 08854 (201) 885-1220	Baking soda and oven cleaner, Super Washing Soda (household cleaner)	Retail
Bio-Pur/Divison of Bio-Basic 2049 N. 7th St. Philadelphia, PA 19122 (215) 236-3771	Bio-Pure All-Purpose Cleaner	Mail Order
Bio-Tech Systems P.O. Box 25380 Chicago, IL 60625 (800) 621-5545 (312) 465-8020	REP-60 mold-preventative spray	Mail Order
Caswell-Massey Co. Catalogue Division 111 Eighth Ave. New York, NY 10011	Castile soap (nondetergent), naturally fragranced soaps	Mail Order (catalog available)
Clorox Co. P.O. Box 24305 Oakland, CA 94623	Clorox 2 (nonchlorine bleach)	Retail

Source	Product or Service	Ordering Information
Faultless Starch/ Bon Ami Co. 1025 W. 8th St. Kansas City, MO 64101 (816) 842-1230	Bon Ami nonchlorinated cleaning soap and cleaning powder without perfumes, dyes or ammonia; glass cleaners without ammonia	Retail
Janice Corp. 12 Eton Dr. P.O. Box 1292 West Caldwell, NJ 07007 (201) 226-7753	Chef's Soap, unscented, free of detergents and chemicals; wrapped in pure cellophane	Mail Order (catalog available), Phone
I. Rokeach & Sons, Inc. 560 Sylvan Ave. Englewood Cliffs, NJ 07632 (201) 568-7550	Rokeach kitchen soap made from coconut oil	Retail

Condiments

Source	Product or Service	Ordering Information
American Spoon Foods, Inc. 1015 E. Mitchell Petoskey, MI 49770 (616) 347-9030	Fruit preserves, dried morel mushrooms, seasonings, spices (free of artificial preservatives)	Retail, Mail Order (catalog available)
Chico-San, Inc. 1264 Humboldt Ave. P.O. Box 1004 Chico, CA 95927 (916) 891-6271	Condiments and herb teas (no chemical additives or preservatives)	Retail
Eden Foods 701 Clinton-Tecumseh Hwy. Clinton, MI 49236 (313) 973-9400	Additive-free tamari	Retail
Norganic Foods Co. 163 E. Liberty Ave. Anaheim, CA 92801 (714) 870-1820	Dressings, butters, preserves, juices, dried fruit, herb teas (no chemical additives or preservatives)	Retail

343

Source	Product or Service	Ordering Information

Condiments—*continued*

Source	Product or Service	Ordering Information
Polynesian Brand 　Soy Sauce Allied Old English, Inc. Port Reading, NJ 07064	Wheat-free, corn-free soy sauce	Retail
Poiret Division, Life-Tone 　International, Inc. P.O. Box 1717 Boca Raton, FL 33432 (305) 391-1611	Poiret Pear and Apple Spread (free of sweeteners, preservatives and artificial colors)	Retail
San-J Division National Sales 　Consultants 640 S. 45th St. Boulder, CO 80303 (303) 499-3394	San-J Tamari; wheat-free (no artificial chemicals or preservatives)	Retail
Sorrell Ridge Farm 100 Markley St. Port Reading, NJ 07064 (201) 636-2060	Conserves and fruit toppings (preservative free)	Retail
Spring Tree Corporation P.O. Box 1160 Brattleboro, VT 05301 (802) 254-8784	Spring Tree maple syrup and carob powder (no artificial preservatives or additives)	Retail, Mail Order
Sunburst Farms 20 S. Kellog Ave. Goleta, CA 93017 (805) 964-8681	Sunburst Farms Unketchup (free of preservatives and additives)	Retail
Vermont Country 　Maple, Inc. Box 53 Jericho Center, VT 05465 (802) 864-7519	Pure Maple Syrup Granules (preservative free)	Retail
Westbrae Natural Foods 4240 Hollis St. Emeryville, CA 94608 (415) 658-7518	Westbrae Wheat-Free Natural Tamari	Retail

Source	Product or Service	Ordering Information

Dairy Substitutes

Source	Product or Service	Ordering Information
Loma Linda Foods 11503 Pierce St. Riverside, CA 92515 (714) 687-7800	Soyagen milk substitute, also available with carob flavoring	Retail, Mail Order
Miller Pharmacal P.O. Box 279 W. Chicago, IL 60185 (312) 231-3632 (800) 323-2935	DoFus Non-Dairy Yogurt Cultures	Retail, Mail Order, Phone
Worthington Foods, Inc. 900 Proprietors Rd. Worthington, OH 43085 (614) 885-9511	Soyamel dairy substitutes (no lactose, chemicals, preservatives or additives)	Retail, Mail Order

Food Storage and Equipment

Source	Product or Service	Ordering Information
Amana Corporation Amana, IA 52204	Corning Top Stove	Retail
The Chef's Catalog Co. 3915 Commercial Ave. Northbrook, IL 60062 (800) 331-1750 (312) 480-9400	Soda Syphon and CO_2 cartridges; stainless steel bakeware and cookware	Mail Order (catalog available), Phone
Erlander's Natural Products P.O. Box 106 Altadena, CA 91001 (213) 797-7004	Cellophane	Mail Order
Janice Corp. 12 Eton Dr. P.O. Box 1292 West Caldwell, NJ 07007 (201) 226-7753	Cellophane bags, 100% cotton potholders and other untreated, all-cotton products	Mail Order (catalog available), Phone

Source	Product or Service	Ordering Information

Food Storage and Equipment—*continued* _____

The Keeper % Sharper Image P.O. Box 26823 San Francisco, CA 94126-6823 (800) 344-4444	The Keeper Food Storage Unit; keeps food chilled (to 40°) or hot (to 150°)	Mail Order
Kool Mate % Udo Corporation 282 Main St. Salem, NH 03079	Kool Mate travel cooler; maintains temperatures from 34°–180°	Retail, Mail Order

Foods—General _____

Diet House 1826 N. Second St. Highland Park, IL 60035 (312) 433-4766	Extensive product line, including basmati rice, guar gum	Retail, Mail Order (ships by UPS)
Elam's 2625 Gardner Rd. Broadview, IL 60153 (312) 865-1612	Elam's grains, mixes, flours, cereals, peanut butter (additive free)	Retail, Mail Order
El Molino Mills P.O. Box 2250 345 N. Baldwin Park Blvd. City of Industry, CA 91746 (213) 962-7167	El Molino grains, seeds, legumes, flours, cereals; carob drinks and snacks	Retail
Ener-G Foods, Inc. P.O. Box 24723 6901 Fox Ave. S. Seattle, WA 98124 (206) 767-6660	Extensive product line including egg substitutes, wheat-free and gluten-free Rice Mix and Potato Mix, wheat-free Barley Mix and Oat Mix	Retail, Mail Order

Source	Product or Service	Ordering Information
Erewhon, Inc. 236 Washington St. Brookline, MA 02146 (800) 222-8028	Erewhon and Aztec cereals, nut butters, snacks, legumes, nuts, cheeses, grains, seeds, oil, flour, pastas, teas, condiments (free of preservatives and additives)	Retail, Mail Order (catalog available), Phone 10:00 A.M. to 9:00 P.M. Boston time
Featherweight Products Sandoz Nutrition Corp. P.O. Box 40, 405 E. Shawmut Ave. La Grange, IL 60525 (312) 352-6900	Featherweight cereal-free baking powder, grainless mix, corn flour, tapioca-starch flour; many corn-free, wheat-free, soy-free, egg-free products (check the labels or contact the company)	Retail, Mail Order
Fruitful Yield 4950 W. Oakton Skokie, IL 60077 (312) 679-8975	Guar gum	Mail Order
Hain Pure Food Co. P.O. Box 54841 Terminal Annex Los Angeles, CA 90054 (213) 538-9922	·Hain vegetable oils, safflower oil margarine, dressings, vegetable juices, fruit concentrates, nut butters, soup mixes, dessert mixes, condiments, vinegar, snacks, dips (preservative free and additive free)	Retail
Jaffe Bros. 28560 Lilac Rd. P.O. Box 636 Valley Center, CA 92082 (619) 749-1133	Organic dried fruits, oils, nuts, seeds, natural confections, grains, legumes, pastas, carob (preservative free and additive free)	Mail Order

347

Source	Product or Service	Ordering Information
Foods—General—*continued*		
Lifestream Natural Foods Ltd. 12411 Vulcan Way Richmond, BC V6V 1J7 (604) 278-7571	Baked goods, bread, kosher products (preservative free and additive free)	Retail
Mrs. Woods Farms J. Wood Products Co. Box 62 Suamico, WI 54173 (414) 434-3173	Pickles, sauerkraut, unsweetened cranberry juice, preserves, vegetables; packed in glass, use well water, free of all pesticides, organically grown (no artificial flavors, colors or preservatives)	Retail
Natural and Kosher Foods, Inc. 14110 S. Broadway Los Angeles, CA 90061 (213) 204-5966	Variety of foods (preservative free and additive free)	Retail
Olde Fashioned Foods, Inc. 123 N. 18th Street Fort Smith, AR 72901 (501) 782-6183	Fruits and vegetables (in season), honey, flours, cheeses, meat, poultry, herb teas	Mail Order
Shiloh Farms P.O. Box 97 Sulphur Springs, AR 72768 (501) 298-3297	Shiloh Farms mixes, nuts, flours, legumes, meat, cereals, carob plus a variety of other products; will pack order in paper bags on request for those allergic to plastic	Retail, Mail Order
Universal Foods Corp. 433 E. Michigan St. Milwaukee, WI 53201 (414) 271-6755	Red Star Yeast (preservative free)	Retail

348

Source	Product or Service	Ordering Information
Walnut Acres Penns Creek, PA 17862 (717) 837-0601	Extensive stock—from soups to nuts and most things in between (additive-free and organically grown products)	Mail Order

Fruits, Nuts and Seeds

Ahler's Organic Date and Grapefruit Garden P.O. Box 726 Mecca, CA 92254 (619) 396-2337	Grapefruit from January to July; dates available year 'round (organically grown, preservative free)	Mail Order (price list available)
American Spoon Foods, Inc. 1015 E. Mitchell Petoskey, MI 49770 (616) 347-9030	Hickory nuts, fruit preserves, dried mushrooms, dried tart red cherries (no chemical additives or preservatives)	Retail, Mail Order (catalog available)
K. B. Hall Ranch 11999 Ojai S.P. Rd. Ojai, CA 93023 (805) 646-4512	Dried apricots and walnuts (preservative free)	Mail Order
Heinke's 5365 Clark Rd. Paradise, CA 95969-6399 (916) 877-4847	Fresh fruit juices without sweeteners; Brazil nuts, filberts, cashews	Retail
International Protein Industries, Inc. P.O. Box 871 Smithtown, NY 11787	Protein-Aide (chemical-free hulled sesame seeds)	Retail

Source	Product or Service	Ordering Information

Fruits, Nuts and Seeds—*continued* _____

Source	Product or Service	Ordering Information
Jaffe Bros. 28560 Lilac Rd. P.O. Box 636 Valley Center, CA 92082 (619) 749-1133	Jaybee dried unsulfured fruits (pineapple, apples, apricots, figs, peaches, pears, papaya, raisins, dates); nuts (almonds, filberts, cashews, walnuts, pecans); oils; seeds; some fresh fruit	Mail Order
Lee Anderson's Covaldo Date Co. P.O. Box 908 Coachella, CA 92236 (619) 398-3441	Dates, pecans, Brazil nuts, citrus fruits (will ship order in paper bags rather than in plastic upon request)	Mail Order
Nelson's Organic Fruit 2823 Summit St. Fort Pierce, FL 33480	Organically grown oranges and grapefruit	Mail Order
Quiet Meadow Farm, Inc. 8 Quiet Meadow Lane Mapleton, UT 84663 (801) 489-9056	Fresh organically grown cherries and peaches shipped by air the same day they're picked (customer pays air freight)	Mail Order, Phone ("fruit reservations" available for seasonal fruit)
Sid Alpers Sales Co. P.O. Box 242 Oradell, NJ 07649 (201) 265-3695	Granolas and dried fruits (preservative free)	Retail (Eastern seaboard only)
Timber Crest Farms 4791 Dry Creek Rd. Healdsburg, CA 95448 (707) 433-8251	Sonoma and Timber Crest Farms dried fruit (preservative free, unsulfured; some organically grown)	Retail, Mail Order

Source	Product or Service	Ordering Information

Goat's Milk Products

California Goat Dairymen's Association Turlock, CA 95381	Miracle Brand Goat's Milk (powdered and evaporated)	Retail (write for a source)
Jackson-Mitchell Pharmaceuticals, Inc. Box 5425 Santa Barbara, CA 93108 (805) 962-9171	Meyenberg goat's milk (powdered and evaporated)	Retail

Grains and Grain Products

Arrowhead Mills, Inc. P.O. Box 866 Hereford, TX 79045 (806) 364-0730	Arrowhead Mills whole grains, beans, seeds, nuts, oils, flours, snacks	Retail
Barry's Natural Food Store 1729 W. Golf Rd. Mt. Prospect, IL 60056 (312) 439-0455	Amaranth flour, basmati rice, rice polish, rice syrup, nuts, seeds, oils	Mail Order, Phone
Beechnut Nutrition Corp. P.O. Box 127 Ft. Washington, PA 19034	Beechnut Rice Cereal and Barley Cereal (gluten free; no chemical preservatives, additives or coloring); Nutrition Hotline for product information: (800) 523-6633; in PA (800) 492-2384; in NY (212) 226-0750	Retail
Bon Appetit, Hard-to-Find Foods P.O. Box 775 Culver City, CA 90230	Basmati rice	Mail Order

Source	Product or Service	Ordering Information

Grains and Grain Products—*continued* _____

Chico-San, Inc. 1264 Humboldt Ave. P.O. Box 1004 Chico, CA 95927 (916) 891-6271	Chico-San, Spiral and Feather River grains, seeds, beans (additive free)	Retail
Con-Agra, Inc. 1 Central Park Plaza Omaha, NE 68102 (402) 978-4000	Rye cereal	Retail
Eden Foods 701 Clinton-Tecumseh Hwy. Clinton, MI 49236 (313) 973-9400	100% Buckwheat Noodles (additive free; no wheat flour)	Retail
Ener-G Foods, Inc. P.O. Box 24723 6901 Fox Ave. S Seattle, WA 98124 (206) 767-6660	Extensive product line, including wheat-free and gluten-free Rice Mix, wheat-free Barley Mix and Oat Mix	Retail, Mail Order
Erewhon, Inc. 236 Washington St. Brookline, MA 02146 (800) 222-8028	Crispy Brown Rice Cereal (gluten free, no preservatives or additives); kosher foods	Retail, Mail Order (catalog available), Phone 10:00 A.M. to 4:00 P.M. Boston time
Select Origins, Inc. Box N Southampton, NY 11968 (516) 288-1382	Basmati rice, seasonings	Mail Order
Sultan's Delight 409 Forest Ave. Staten Island, NY 10301	Basmati rice, other grains	Mail Order (catalog and price list available)
Walnut Acres Penns Creek, PA 17862 (717) 837-0601	Rices and grain flours (preservative free)	Mail Order

352

Source	Product or Service	Ordering Information

Grain Substitutes

DeBoles Nutritional Foods, Inc. 2120 Jericho Tpk. Garden City Park, NY 11040 (516) 742-1825	American Jerusalem artichoke pasta and baked goods	Retail
Featherweight Products Sandoz Nutrition Corp. P.O. Box 40, 405 E. Shawmut Ave. La Grange, IL 60525 (312) 352-6900	Featherweight Grainless Mix (baking mix)	Retail, Mail Order
Illinois Amaranth Co. P.O. Box 464E Mundelein, IL 60060	Amaranth flour	Mail Order
Walnut Acres Penns Creek, PA 17862 (717) 837-0601	Amaranth and amaranth flour	Mail Order

Guar Gum

See Foods—General: Diet House, Fruitful Yield

Legumes

Autumn Harvest Natural Foods 1029 Davis St. Evanston, IL 60201 (312) 475-1121	Fresh organically grown produce, flours, sea vegetables	Mail Order, Phone (ships via UPS)
Fearn Soya Foods % Richards Foods Corp. 4520 James Pl. Melrose Park, IL 60160 (312) 345-2335	Fearn beans, carob products, cereals, flours, grains, mixes, seeds, soy products (additive free)	Retail, Mail Order
Dynasty % JFC International S. San Francisco, CA 94080	Dynasty Saifun Bean Threads (additive free)	Retail

Source	Product or Service	Ordering Information

Legumes—*continued*

Loma Linda Foods 11503 Pierce St. Riverside, CA 92515 (714) 687-7800	Gravy mixes, soybeans, meat substitutes (all products are milk free; some have no wheat, corn, yeast or eggs); further product information on request	Retail, Mail Order

Meat, Fish and Game

Czimer Foods, Inc. Rte. 7, Box 285 Lockport, IL 60441 (312) 460-2210 (312) 460-3503	Full selection of game birds and meats; seafood (packed and shipped in dry ice)	Mail Order
D'Angelo Bros. Products, Inc. 909 S. Ninth St. Philadelphia, PA 19147 (215) 923-5637	Wild game (shipped in insulated coolers, next-day delivery; contact the company for further details)	Mail Order
Lobel's 1096 Madison Ave. New York, NY 10028 (212) 737-1372	Full selection of wild game (packed and shipped in dry ice or ice packs)	Mail Order
Long Island Beef Co. 565 West St. New York, NY 10014 (212) 243-1120	Venison, Scottish hare, game birds (packed and shipped in dry ice)	Mail Order
Ottomanelli Bros. 1549 York Ave. New York, NY 10028 (212) 772-7900	Wild game (chill-packed immediately after cutting; shipped air freight, refrigerated)	Mail Order
Teel Mountain Farm Standardsville, VA 22973 (804) 985-7746	Organically raised beef and veal	Mail Order

Source	Product or Service	Ordering Information
Wally Sea Products Corp. 400 C St. Boston, MA 02210 (617) 357-5010	Acadian frozen fish and seafood (preservative free)	Retail

Nutritional Supplements

Amway Corp. 7575 E. Fulton Rd. Ada, MI 49355 (616) 676-7134	Nutrilite supplements (no artificial colors or preservatives)	Home demonstration
Bronson Pharmaceuticals 4526 Rinetti Lane La Canada, CA 91011 (213) 790-2646	Complete listing of supplements free of sugar, starch, wheat, soy, yeast, corn, artificial colors, flavors and preservatives; contact for specific ingredient information	Mail Order
J. R. Carlson Laboratories, Inc. 15 College Dr. Arlington Heights, IL 60004 (312) 255-1600	Supplements (no artificial colors or preservatives), including vitamin C crystals, soy-derived vitamin E, and vitamin A from carrot oil	Retail, Mail Order,
Freeda Vitamins 36 East 41st St. New York, NY 10017 (212) 685-4980	Starch-free and sugar-free all-vegetarian supplements; no additives; yeast-free selenium; lactose-free acidophilus (approved by the Feingold Association and the Hypoglycemia Association; kosher), vitamin C crystals available	Retail, Mail Order

Source	Product or Service	Ordering Information
Nutritional Supplements—*continued*		
KAL Nutritional Supplements 8357 Canoga Ave. P.O. Box 1067 Canoga Park, CA 91304 (213) 998-9966	KAL supplements (no sugar, wax, preservatives, starch, wheat, wheat starch, coloring, flavoring or soy protein); contact company for complete ingredient listings	Retail
Kennedy's Natural Foods 1051 W. Broad St. Falls Church, VA 22046 (703) 533-8484	Supplements with no artificial colors, sugar or cornstarch	Mail Order
Klaire Laboratories, Inc. P.O. Box 618 Carlsbad, CA 92008 (714) 438-1083	Vital Life supplements (no sugar, starches or additives)	Mail Order
Maxson Laboratories, Inc. 4769 Coldstream Dr. Atlanta, GA 30360	Hypoallergenic supplements, some derived from sago palm	Mail Order
Nutri-Cology, Inc. 2470 Estand Way Pleasant Hill, CA 94523	Supplements formulated for people with allergies; no preservatives, additives or colors; contact the company for complete ingredient listing	Mail Order
Plus Products 2681 Kelvin Ave. Irvine, CA 92714 (800) 854-3323 (714) 556-8600	Plus supplements (no preservatives, artificial colors or artificial flavors)	Retail

Source	Product or Service	Ordering Information
Schiff Bio Food Products Moonachie Ave. Moonachie, NJ 07074 (201) 933-2282	Schiff supplements (no chemical additives, synthetics, preservatives or artificial dyes, colors or flavors; rice-based B vitamins without yeast, corn, wheat, liver, gluten or milk)	Retail
Shiloh Farms P.O. Box 97 Sulphur Springs, AR 72768 (501) 298-3297	Shiloh Farms supplements (no dyes or sugar)	Retail, Mail Order
Wm. T. Thompson Co. 23529 S. Figeroa St. Carson, CA 90745 (213) 830-5550	Thompson supplements (no artificial colors, preservatives or sugar)	Retail
Tru-Vita Corp. 4324 Sunbelt Dr. Dallas, TX 75248 (214) 248-7620	Vitamin formulas contain no preservatives, coating coloring, dairy products, wheat, soy, yeast, corn, sugar or chlorine	Mail Order
Twin Laboratories, Inc. 174 E. Industry Ct. Deer Park, NY 11729	Hypoallergenic supplements, including vitamin C derived from sago palm	Mail Order
Walnut Acres, Inc. Penns Creek, PA 17862 (717) 837-0601	Walnut Acres supplements (no sugar, salt, coal-tar dyes, artificial colors, artificial flavors or preservatives); also sells a vegetarian vitamin and mineral tablet	Mail Order

Source	Product or Service	Ordering Information

Nutritional Supplements—*continued*

Willner Chemists, Inc. 330 Lexington Ave. New York, NY 10157 (212) 685-2538	Supplements with no sugar, starch, artificial colors or artificial flavors	Mail Order

Snacks

Barbara's Bakery, Inc. 15 Commercial Blvd. Novato, CA 94947 (415) 833-3393	Snacks, baked goods (preservative and additive free); ingredient listing available upon request	Retail
El Molino Mills P.O. Box 2250 345 N. Baldwin Park Blvd. City of Industry, CA 91746 (213) 962-7167	El Molino Allergy Cookies; ingredient listing available upon request	Retail
Farm Foods, Inc. Summertown, TN 38483	Ice Bean (soy-based ices containing no dairy products)	Retail
International Protein Industries, Inc. P.O. Box 871P Smithtown, NY 11787 (516) 231-7940	Protein-Aide sesame-seed snacks, tahini and peanut butter (preservative free)	Retail, Mail Order
Soken Trading, Inc. 591 Redwood Hwy. Suite 2125 Mill Valley, CA 94941	Vegetable Chips (an alternative to corn chips), brown rice crackers (preservative free)	Retail

Source	Product or Service	Ordering Information

Water Purifiers

Ametek, Inc. Plymouth Products Division 502 Indiana Ave. Sheboygan, WI 53081	Ametek in-line cartridge water filter	Retail
Astro-Pure, Inc. 4900 N.W. 15th St. Margate, FL 33063	Astro-Pure under-the-counter water filter	Retail
Brunswick Technetics Filterite Consumer Products 5 West Aylesbury Rd. Timonium, MD 21093	Filterite CF-10 in-line cartridge home water filters	Retail
Chief Equipment Corp. P.O. Box 4538 Denver, CO 80204 (303) 825-8169	Health-Flo countertop and under-the-counter water filters	Retail
Everpure, Inc. 660 N. Blackhawk Dr. Westmont, IL 60559 (312) 654-4000	Everpure home water-filtration systems	Retail
Filtercold Corp., Inc. 2810 S. 24th St. Phoenix, AZ 85034	Filter Flask pour-through water-filtration units	Retail
General Ecology, Inc. 151 Sheree Blvd. Lionville, PA 19353	Seagull IV under-the-counter water filters	Retail
Neo-Life 25000 Industrial Blvd. Hayward, CA 94545	Water Dome countertop water-filter units	Retail
Norelco North American Phillips Corp. Consumer Products Div. High Ridge Park Stamford, CT 06904	Clean Water Machine water-filtration appliance	Retail

359

Source	Product or Service	Ordering Information
Water Purifiers—*continued*		
Pollenex Associated Mills, Inc. 111 N. Canal St. Chicago, IL 60606	Pure Water 99 end-of-faucet water filter	Retail
Pure Water, Inc. 3725 Touzalin Ave. P.O. Box 83226 Lincoln, NE 68501 (402) 467-2577	Clean Water Machine, Aqua Clean, Midi Still, Aqua Fountain and Aqua Still D portable home and office water distillers	Retail
Puro Corporation of America 56–45 58th St. Maspeth, NY 11378 (212) 326-7000	Puro activated-carbon water filters	Retail

Index to Recipes
for a Diversified Rotary Diet

The following reference aid is a short-cut for people planning a Diversified Rotary Diet. Most of the recipes listed here include foods from three food families only, especially if optional ingredients are omitted, and a few involve four food families.

When choosing ingredients, remember to coordinate any nuts or seeds in a recipe with any oil used, so that together they involve one food family only: sunflower oil with sunflower seeds, almond oil with almonds, and so forth. Reserve olive oil for recipes that call for neither nuts nor seeds.

Select vitamin C crystals in place of lemon juice or vinegar whenever it's an option. Vitamin C and baking soda are basic compounds, unrelated to any food, and need not be counted as foods. (That's true for salt, too, although you won't find it listed as an ingredient.)

Those simple steps will enable you to use dozens of additional recipes that would otherwise have too many ingredients to be eligible for a Diversified Rotary Diet.

Index

Page numbers set in bold indicate tables and charts.